Philander Priestley Claxton

Crusader for Public Education

By

CHARLES LEE LEWIS

KNOXVILLE

The University of Tennessee Press

1948

TYPOGRAPHY, PRINTING, AND BINDING IN THE U. S. A. BY
KINGSPORT PRESS, INC., KINGSPORT, TENNESSEE

TO THE MEMORY OF MY TEACHER

William Newton Billingsley

Preface

THIS biography could not have been written without the cordial co-operation of Dr. Claxton himself, who permitted the author to use his great collection of private papers and allowed himself to be questioned freely during numerous conferences, and patiently answered long lists of questions sent him by mail. He also read the manuscript of the biography and corrected errors of fact. But he made no suggestions as to changing the author's interpretations of the facts. Mrs. Claxton was also of great assistance. For many years before her marriage she was Librarian of the Nashville Carnegie Library. Being a trained and experienced librarian, she has classified her husband's papers after a plan which rendered the author's research much easier than it would have been without this aid. She also supplied much interesting background material from her own recollection of events in Claxton's life. Other members of the family gave cheerful assistance, particularly the oldest daughter, Mrs. Claire (Claxton) Mayo, who furnished many revealing facts concerning her father when he was a comparatively young man.

It is not practicable to mention by name the hundreds of persons, former students and associates of Claxton, who supplied information on request by letter. Without their help it would have been impossible to portray the human traits of Claxton's complex personality.

The author is also grateful to the personnel of the many libraries from which he gathered material—particularly the Library and the Archives of the Office of Education of the Department of the Interior in Washington, the Library of Congress, the Library of Johns Hopkins University, the Library of the United States Naval Academy, the Library of The University of Tennessee, the Tennessee State Library, the Library of George Peabody College for Teachers, and the Library of the College for Women of the University of North Carolina at Greensboro. Many other libraries cheerfully answered minor inquiries.

Though the author has known Dr. Claxton for over forty years, having been his student in the Department of Education of The University of Tennessee and one of his "office boys" during one session of the Summer School of the South, it has been only during the last four or five years that he has become his veritable Boswell. It has indeed been an inspiring experience to become so intimately associated with a man of such wide knowledge and profound wisdom, of such true culture and Christ-like character—a real gentleman. The author sincerely hopes that, in this biography, he has been able to do his subject justice—to portray Claxton at least approximately as he really is and to record with clarity his extraordinary contributions to the development of public school education in the United States.

Annapolis, Maryland
September 17, 1947   C. L. L.

Contents

Philander Priestley Claxton

Bedford County Boy

◇◇◇

B Y SEPTEMBER, 1862, most of the state of Tennessee had been
lost to the Confederacy. After the capture of Fort Henry on
the Tennessee River and Fort Donelson on the Cumberland,
Nashville had to be evacuated. With the capital of the state in the
hands of a Union army, Andrew Johnson, a former governor of
Tennessee who had opposed secession, was made military governor
of the state. Grass and weeds already covered the graves of the
thousands who had died in the great battle of Shiloh in an un-
successful attempt to drive the Federal army out of West Tennessee. In September, however, a part of General Buell's army was
hurrying through Bedford County from Alabama to aid in the defense of Nashville from attack by a Confederate army commanded
by General Bragg that had set out from Chattanooga and Knoxville
on an ambitious Kentucky campaign.

On the 28th day of this month of conflicting hopes and fears, of
confusion and disintegration, there was born in a one room log
cabin in Bedford County, Tennessee, a boy who was destined to
do more to repair the ravages of this war in the South than probably any other man. He was to become the Horace Mann of the
South, and as a leader in the development of public schools was
to make possible a New South. His parents named him Philander
Priestley Claxton.[1]

"Some of my earliest and most vivid recollections," Claxton declared [2] when an old man, "are of this war and of the things grow-

ing out of conditions produced by it, . . . a half dozen Federal soldiers in our cabin home early in the morning waiting for breakfast to be prepared by my mother, the return of an uncle from the army, the general disorder and desolation of the section of the country over which armies had swept and over which soldiers from disintegrated armies had wandered in retreat. I do not remember, except by hearsay, the death of my sister caused by contagious disease brought by soldiers. I always regarded this as an actual casualty of the war. For these reasons I have from my earliest recollections had a horror and a hatred of war, which have been confirmed by observation and reason in later years."

Claxton was of English, Welsh, Dutch, and German ancestry. His great-grandfather James Claxton [3] came with his son, also named James, from North Carolina into Tennessee early in the nineteenth century. By 1817 they had moved into Bedford County and were settled on a farm about eight or ten miles from Shelbyville on the old Nashville road. Young James enlisted in General Jackson's army at Fayetteville and participated in the expedition against the Creek Indians. On his return he married Elizabeth Rathler, by whom he had eight sons and four daughters, Philander Claxton's father being named Joshua Calvin. About 1850 James Claxton moved to Missouri with all his family, except the oldest daughter Elizabeth (Mrs. Steve Saunders) and her brother Joshua Calvin. There considerable wealth was accumulated in land and stock. According to tradition, Steve Saunders and his family went with the Claxtons to Missouri but remained only one day. Returning to Tennessee, he became a large landholder, always eager to buy what was "adjining" his farm. The religion of his large family of sons and daughters was work. The Missouri Claxtons increased and multiplied; when Calvin visited them about 1875 he saw forty-two first cousins, nephews, and nieces. They then lived in the vicinity of Springfield and Hartsville, and later spread through Missouri, Oklahoma, and Texas. [3]

About four years after his father and most of the family went to Missouri, Calvin Claxton married Ann Elizabeth Jones in Bedford County. Her father, a physician, had come to Tennessee from North Georgia. Her mother's name was Sykes, which is Dutch. She had unusual initiative and independence, and after her husband's death and her children's marriages she lived alone but quite happily in the family home. Claxton's mother had an unusually good mind but only such education as could then be acquired in a country school and later by her own efforts. His father, a man of strong native ability, had only three months of schooling. They were well educated, however, in the practical school of experience —a school with a varied and extensive curriculum at that time in Bedford County.

After his marriage Calvin Claxton purchased one hundred acres of woodland twelve miles southwest of Shelbyville in the Shearin and Smith Bend of the Duck River. He bought more land from time to time until he eventually owned one hundred eighty-five acres. It was all virgin land and had to be cleared for cultivation. Like most of the Claxtons, Calvin was to be a farmer; the family coat of arms indicates that the ancestors in England were also farmers. The land was densely forested with white oak, poplar, ash, hickory, cedar, and many other kinds of trees. "There were more varieties of trees and kinds of soil on our farm," remarked Claxton [2] reminiscently, "than are to be found in the whole state of Kansas." The land was cleared for the plow with fire and those indispensable tools of the American pioneer, the axe and the grubbing hoe.

Some of the timber was used to build the log cabin, the barn, and other farm buildings, and also to construct the typical rail fences once so commonly seen in Tennessee. Some was cut in proper lengths for winter firewood; but so bountiful was the supply of timber and so small was the need for it that great piles of logs had to be burned to get them out of the way. This usually called for the assistance of neighbors in what was known as "logrollings."

The Claxton cabin, in which Philander Priestley, the fourth child and the oldest son, was born, was built of unhewn ash logs. The cracks between them were filled with sticks and daubed with clay. The lower part of the chimney, including the fireplace, was constructed of stone; the rest was made of daubed sticks. Iron nails being scarce, the boards for the roof were held in place by logs laid crossways and supported by large stones. Most of the furniture was homemade and primitive. There was a little loft "upstairs" reached by a ladder. When young Claxton was four years old, the first part of a second house was built and the old cabin was torn down so that the logs could be used in burning lime for the chimney and pillars of the new house.

This was a well built house with hewn cedar logs as sleepers and sills. All wallboarding, flooring, and ceiling were of poplar. When completed, the house had two long rooms, with a front porch extending their combined length, and a third room used as dining room and kitchen.

The Claxton farm land was somewhat rolling. In the summer, the house was secluded, but in the winter when the leaves had fallen, one neighbor's house could be seen. On this farm young Claxton was "raised," as Tennesseans used to say. "My boyish theory was," declared [4] Claxton, "that Bedford County was in the middle of Tennessee, Tennessee in the middle of the United States, the United States in the middle of the world. This was definitely proven when I climbed a tree on my father's farm and saw clearly that the sky came down to the ground at the same distance in every direction. And it is literally true. On the surface of a sphere any point is central."

From the time Claxton could handle a hoe or pile brush he worked with his father on the farm when the land was being cleared. Having unusual physical strength, he began plowing in the spring before he was eight years old. "The most fun I ever had was plowing the land," he wrote.[5] The chief crops which he helped to produce were of corn, wheat, oats, clover, grasses for pasture and hay, and cotton enough for clothing and the taxes. There were two apple orchards, and peach trees grew in practically all the corners of the worm rail fences. Horses, mules, cattle, sheep, hogs, chickens, and geese were raised. It was subsistence farming with surplus enough to pay for things that had to be bought. Very seldom was any food purchased except salt and sugar. The mother and her daughters made the clothing for the family from the home grown cotton which they carded and spun, and from the wool of their own sheep. Beds and pillows were made from the feathers of their geese. Bedcovers, table cloths, carpets were all homemade. The father mended the shoes on rainy days. The family never spent more than $400 a year for food, clothing, and other household and farm necessities.

The nearest village for trading was Poplin's Cross Roads, two and a half miles distant from the farm. This had two country stores, a cotton gin, a blacksmith shop, and two or three residences. One of these stores sold whiskey as openly as it did molasses or sugar, and on Saturday afternoons there was a great deal of drinking. The Claxtons also traded at the village of Unionville (popularly known as "Dolittle"), four miles from the farm. They took their wheat and corn two miles to Wilhoite's Mill (later Hall's Mill) on Duck River to be ground into flour and meal respectively. To purchase more important articles they traveled the twelve miles to Shelbyville, an all day journey.

Interspersed with farm labor were many country sports, but young Claxton did not enjoy them much. He went fishing occasionally; but if the fish did not bite within half an hour or so, he went home. "I had no time to waste on fish that did not bite," he remarked [6] with a twinkle in his blue eyes. He did not hunt much either, though his father kept hounds, and fox hunting was popular in the community while he was a boy. He sometimes went hunting at night for o'possums and coons with the boys of the neighborhood.

"Philie" Claxton, as he was nicknamed, started to school when he was four years old at Shearin Schoolhouse, a mile and a half from his home. He already knew his ABC's, could "read pictures," and could count accurately up to one hundred. His mother, a strong believer in the value of education, had taught him this much. In spite of her many household duties, she found time during the war to teach in her home not only her own children but also those of the neighbors. Otherwise they would have received no schooling at that time. Several years after the war, when a school (semi-public and semi-subscription) was opened in that district, her husband Calvin became a member of the school board, and throughout his life continued to be deeply interested in the education of young people.

When "Philie" started to school, his father promised him a pair of red-topped, brass-toed boots when he could spell up to the word "baker." This was the first word on a page of words of two syllables in Webster's *American Spelling Book* (the famous "Blue Back Speller"). He won the boots the first week, and when the school term closed after three months he had reached page 114 in the

[7]

famous spelling book, having learned to spell "on the book" 6800 words from one to eight syllables in length. For example, to spell "on the book" one must say: m-u-l, mul; t-i, ti, multi; p-l-i, pli, multipli; c-a, ca, multiplica; t-i-o-n, tion, multiplication. In this way the children learned that a word was composed of syllables and the syllables of letters with sound values. The only book used by the teacher, Mr. Tucker, for all the lessons during the first two years was Webster's *Spelling Book*.

This schoolhouse had only one room, about 18 by 20 feet. It was built of heavy boards placed on end "depot style," between which were cracks one could see through. There were no glass windows but only holes in the wall. There was no ceiling, and the floor was not nailed down. The seats were made of split logs, fastened to blocks of wood with wooden pegs. There were no backs to them, and the scholars could sit facing front or back or even sit astride.

Tucker was a good teacher whom the pupils liked, but the next, a Mr. Stewart, was a poor teacher who was disliked by the children. "Philie" quit school two weeks before the end of the term. There were about fifty pupils, whose ages ranged up to twenty-one or over.

In the "Blue Back Speller" the scholars learned not only how to spell and pronounce words but also how to read. After each group of words, there were sentences, illustrating their use or defining them. From these they learned a great deal about all sorts of things; for example, "Nero was a wicked tyrant at Rome," "The President is elected once every four years," and "The fixed stars are at immense distances from us; they are so distant that we cannot measure the number of miles." To this last sentence might be traced Claxton's later extraordinary knowledge of astronomy. There was to be found also moral and religious instruction in such sentences as: "Do not attempt to deceive God; nor to mock him with solemn words, whilst your heart is set to do evil" and "The drunkard's course is progressive; he begins by drinking a little, and shortens his life by drinking to excess." In the back of the book were fables with illustrations, each teaching a moral truth; among these were the story of old dog Tray and another entitled "The Cat and the Rat."

At the age of six Claxton attended a better three months school, two and a half miles from his home, taught at the Thompson's Ford Lutheran Church by its minister, Mr. Anthony. This frame building had pews with the seats so high that the feet of the small children dangled far above the floor. The high backs afforded excellent screens for the mischievous pupils. The country folk thought the teacher was too progressive because he taught the children to read from McGuffey's *First Reader* and tried to teach them to sing.

Then young Claxton went to school for three years at a schoolhouse called "Yaller Cat," named after a tall yellow Negro who had lived in the cabin. It was situated about a mile from his home practically in the forest. It was built of cedar logs, between which were large spaces. One of these was large enough for a child to crawl through, and "Philie" and others liked to use it as an exit, though they had to crawl over the writing table to get to it. This was a large poplar board two or three inches thick and two feet wide, which rested on pegs at a slant that gave it the appearance of a writing desk. When the weather became cold, the teacher and the school boys "chinked and daubed" the cracks with clay. There was only one door and only one window, without glass, which could be closed by board shutters. The large stone fireplace was seven or eight feet wide. In cold weather, oak, hickory, and ash logs with cedar kindling made a blazing fire. In the hot coals and embers the pupils roasted sweet potatoes, a welcome addition to a cold lunch of bread, meat, and sorghum molasses brought in baskets.

The teacher, Claxton's Uncle Bailey Jones, was considered the best in the county. He knew Latin, Greek, and mathematics, which he had learned at the Academy in Unionville. He also knew how to play marbles, cat, bull pen, and other games with the boys. The term of school was five months. On the last day, the boys barred the door and window, and would not let the teacher in until he promised to treat. He was usually prepared with a supply of candy and apples, or he sent two boys to the nearby store to buy some. This was the general custom.

In this school, there were other books than Webster's *Blue Back Speller*. When Claxton was eight, he was also studying McGuffey's *Fifth Reader*, Smith's *English Grammar*, and Davies' *Elementary*

Arithmetic. There was little attempt at graded classification of students. During the first week "Philie" learned the preliminary definitions in his arithmetic book, and did the problems in addition and subtraction. On Friday he and Mollie Simmons were assigned the multiplication table up to twelve times twelve. On Monday he was prepared to recite it through correctly, but poor Mollie could not. The teacher discovered that she could not count to one hundred. Claxton then went his way alone, and made good progress in arithmetic as well as in the other subjects.

Discipline was strict. The "hickory stick" was used freely by the teacher. "Philie" never got a "licking" in school, for he knew this would be followed by another one when he got home. Some things for which pupils would now be punished were not considered wrong then; for example, reading and talking aloud. "No attempt was made," Claxton wrote,[7] "in any of these schools to maintain silence. All children studied aloud and talked aloud among themselves on any question of interest to them, from the shape of the earth and the double rule of three to marbles, fox hunting, and neighborhood gossip. The school was considered the best that made the most noise. No such thing as assigning children to separate seats and expecting them to occupy them continuously had ever been heard of. They selected their own seats and moved from one to another at their own sweet will. If two happened to desire the same seat at the same time, they settled the matter after their own way, by generous, altruistic rivalry, by bargain, or by main strength. Seldom did they burden their teacher by calling on him for a decision. If one or more children wanted to leave the room, they did so and returned at their pleasure." This behavior may have been carried over from the ante bellum schools in which the children often chanted their lessons in unison. A noteworthy example was "singing geography," which could be heard, according to Matthew Fontaine Maury,[8] a mile from the school.

All the schools which Claxton attended had unusually odd names. After three years at "Yaller Cat," he went to Shanghai near Poplin's Cross Roads. This was three miles from home; so he stayed with his grandmother Jones from Monday through Friday, her house being only a half-mile from the school. The schoolhouse was an abandoned log Methodist church. Tom Sykes, an uncle of

Claxton's mother, was the teacher but he was not a very good one.

After a year or so, the district school committee, through the influence of one of the members, decided to hold the school for two months at Shanghai and then two months at a place two miles distant, near the influential member's home. The children called the latter schoolhouse "Corner of Nowhere." It was an abandoned, dilapidated log cabin, about 16 by 20 feet, with the door off its hinges and only seats for forty of the sixty-three children. The "ciphering boys" sat outdoors on logs, stumps, and stones while studying their arithmetic and other lessons, and went inside only to recite. Sixty-three pupils, whose ages ranged from four to twenty-one and whose lessons ranged from ABC's to Latin and Greek, were not considered too many for one teacher to instruct.

In all these schools, a popular diversion was a spelling bee. The students stood in a ring round the room, and when one spelled a word that had been misspelled he moved toward the head of the line above the one or more who had misspelled the word. It was a high honor to be at the head of the line at the close of the spelling contest.

On Friday afternoons the older pupils read original compositions or declaimed selections from famous orations. The younger children recited poems. One of Claxton's recitations, which he still remembered when past eighty, was as follows:

"Of all the planets in the sky
    The brightest is the sun.
Lest your patience I should try,
    Ladies and gentlemen, I am done."

Other selections in his repertoire were "Twinkle, Twinkle, Little Star," "Mary Had a Little Lamb," and poems with a moral, such as,

"The lark is up to meet the sun;
    The bee is on the wing;
The ant its labor has begun;
    The woods with music ring.

Shall ants and birds and bees be wise,
    Whilst I my moments waste?
Oh, let me with the morning rise
    And to my duties haste."

Another poem which Claxton recalled, when he was an old man, began with these lines:

> "How big was Alexander, pa,
>   That people called him great?
> Was he like old Goliah tall,
>   His spear a hundred weight?
>
> Was he so large that he could stand
>   Like some tall steeple high;
> And, while his feet were on the ground,
>   His hands could touch the sky?"

The country schools which Claxton attended were typical of the South at that time. The entirely inadequate system of free schools in Tennessee had been swept away by the war and by the confusion and partisan politics incident to the early period of reconstruction. Taxable property had been cut in half; 275,000 slaves had been set free. Railroads had been largely destroyed and turnpikes were worn out. It was not an opportune time, the politicians thought, to appropriate money for public education.

Though recognition of education had been given in the new state constitution of 1834, public support of free education was then almost negligible. There was much prejudice against such schools, which became synonymous in the minds of many with the "pauper schools," established in the early history of the state. The wealthy slave owners sent their children to private schools or employed tutors for them, as they were opposed to having them associate with the children of "poor whites." Naturally, they resisted being taxed to supply education for such people; and being the larger taxpayers, they presented an insurmountable barrier to tax-supported free schools which they did not wish to patronize. It was therefore altogether remarkable that some definite progress was made in public schools after 1854. This was a clear indication of the growing political influence of the non-slaveholding, middle class citizens of Tennessee.

The legislation in 1854 first stipulated that a part of the poll tax and a portion of the property tax were to be used to support the common schools. Hitherto the schools had been forced to depend on the meager returns from the school lands, yielding only $100,000 annually for the education of 250,000 children. As a consequence, in 1850 one fourth of the whites over twenty were illiterate. But by 1859, provision had been made for a 75 cents per capita school tax.[9]

It should be added, in justice to Tennessee, that in 1830 there was no general recognition in the United States of the obligation of the government to educate the children at public expense. Indeed, it was the period between 1830 and 1860, which, as Carl Russell Fish writes,[10] "saw the acceptance of the fundamental principles of the American public school system by the nation and . . . [laid] the actual foundations."

In 1867 a measure re-establishing the common school system was enacted in Tennessee, but lack of finances, lack of co-operation, and outright opposition by many influential citizens made practically impossible the inauguration of such a system. Two years later the legislation was all repealed, and it was not until 1873 that the influence of the more farseeing citizens became strong enough to cause the passage of an educational law, which is sometimes referred to as the "parent act" of the public school system now existing in the state of Tennessee.[11]

When Claxton was about thirteen years old, his father who was then a member of the district school committee gave an acre of land on his farm for the location of a new schoolhouse. But the committee decided to consolidate three or four schools and build a two-story schoolhouse about two miles from the Claxton farm. By contributions of money, lumber, and labor the citizens of the district built the best schoolhouse in that part of the county, the first one constructed for school use in the district. It was called the Turrentine Academy. Similar schools, though private, had been established in Bedford County long before the war. Salem Academy at Bellbuckle dated back to 1820, and Dixon Academy was founded at Shelbyville, the county seat, the same year.[12]

There was a large room on each floor, and two teachers. A young woman had charge of the primary classes, and a Cumberland Presbyterian preacher, named White, taught the other students. A ten months' session was made possible by supplementing the small public fund with voluntary subscriptions. Claxton considered White a very good teacher, and recalled that he had a book on teaching by Page, which was the first of its kind he had ever seen.

"I liked this teacher very much," he declared,[13] "and from him I probably got my first incentive to become a teacher."

The last chapter of Page's *Theory and Practice of Teaching* [14] begins with the following quotation from Horace Greeley: "Far above the conqueror of kingdoms, the destroyer of hosts by the sword and the bayonet, is he whose tearless victories redden no river and whiten no plain, but who leads the understanding a willing captive, and builds his empire, not of the wrenched and bleeding fragments of subjugated nations but on the realms of intellect which he has discovered and planted, and peopled with beneficent activity and enduring joy."

After two years White was replaced by a Methodist preacher, not a very good teacher whom the students disliked. He in turn was followed by a graduate of Peabody Normal School. He dressed well and had good manners but lacked teaching ability. Claxton and some of the other students thought they knew more than he did. These teachers were paid $50 per month, then considered a large salary.

During his three and one-half years at the Turrentine Academy Claxton completed Davies' *Elementary Algebra*, Davies' *Bourdon*, a French algrebra, and Davies' *Legendre*, a French geometry, both translated by Professor Davies of West Point and used as textbooks there. In those days it was not the custom to skip problems; he did all of them in those books. In mathematics, he also gained some knowledge of surveying and navigation. He memorized all the questions and answers, lesson by lesson, in Pineo's *English Grammar* as well as most of the illustrations of principles in Quackenbos's *Rhetoric*. He had one and one-half years in Latin and one-half in Greek. He devoured J. Dorman Steele's famous series, *Fourteen Weeks*, in Zoology, Physiology, Physics, Chemistry, and Astronomy. Each of the books was supposed to be finished in fourteen weeks. According to Claxton,[15] "Steele was consciously or unconsciously a Herbartian and had the power to write most interestingly, using the common observations and expressions of boys and girls."

At this school, Claxton studied what he wished and when he chose. He advanced as fast as he was able. He studied at night and on Sundays. Also on the way to school through the fields and woodlands, he studied as he walked, learning to carry in mind somewhat long and complicated algebraic equations and visualizing geometric figures. Other lessons were learned in this way; consequently he had much full time at school during which he listened to the recitations of the other classes. When he was sixteen he was asked to teach some classes in arithmetic, grammar, and spelling. He received no money for this, but his father's subscription of $25 to the school was canceled.

The school day was from 7:30 in the morning to 4:30 in the afternoon. But the day on the farm was longer, from earliest daylight until after dark; and there was always work for Claxton to do on Saturdays and when he got home from school on other days. Though his father frequently needed his help on the farm, he kept him out of school for this reason only one week. This was displeasing to his mother and on the following Sunday he overheard his father saying to her, "I will never do it again." [16] He remembered missing only one day on account of illness. When he did not feel well some mornings, his father would wisely say, "Run on to school. You'll feel better by the time you get there." [16]

There were many churches in the community—a Protestant Methodist at Ray's Chapel, a Northern Methodist near Poplin's Cross Roads, a Lutheran at Thompson's Ford, and a Southern Methodist (named Pleasant Valley), in which the Claxton family held membership. "Philie" was much impressed by the sermons of a Lutheran preacher known as Uncle Billy Jenkins, who frequently warned his congregation that a war with the Roman Catholics was probable. Two Methodist preachers, George Cooke and Mike Thompson, were frequent visitors in the Claxton home and influenced "Philie" most. Cooke was a farmer and, being also a stone mason, he built the chimneys of the Claxton house. He worked hard on week days and preached on Sundays without pay. Claxton regarded him one of the best preachers he ever heard. "Philie" joined the Southern Methodist Church (was "converted") at a protracted meeting at Zion's Hill, when he was twelve years old. It was generally agreed among the preachers, who visited his home and talked about the "ways of salvation," that a child was reasonably safe for salvation in case of death before that age; but after reaching twelve conversion was necessary. Living in a rural community in the days of camp meetings and revivals, young Claxton went to the "mourners' bench and professed."

The season for camp meetings was from four to six weeks in the autumn. They were held to turn the sinners from their evil ways. Drunkenness was the most prevalent evil, as whiskey could be bought for fifty cents a gallon. Dancing, even the Virginia Reel, was considered a sin by the Southern Methodists. There were many instances of members' being turned out of the church for playing the fiddle. Card games also were prohibited. A camp meeting, according to the best religious psychology of that day, should begin on Saturday. The following Sunday morning a sermon with a general appeal was delivered, and that evening the Methodists would accept a sermon on hell fire and damnation. In that church, conversion was not an easy process, to be completed merely by shaking the preacher's hand. After the protracted meeting, one was looked upon as being either on the road to heaven or on the broad way to hell. Salvation could be obtained only during the revival weeks; afterwards "the harvest was past."

When Claxton was seventeen, he was superintendent of two rural church Sunday schools. That at the Pleasant Valley Methodist Episcopal Church, South, met on Sunday mornings and that of the Thompson's Ford Lutheran Church on Sunday afternoons. Both were well attended and in the early autumn a Sunday school festival was held at Pleasant Valley. The children marched, and Judge Calwell, one of the most prominent men in the county, gave an address. Throughout his life Claxton continued to give much of his time, study, and effort to Sunday school work, endeavoring to destroy the significance of the old conundrum: "When is a school not a school? (Answer) When it is a Sunday school."

The books Claxton read were chiefly serious ones. The family Bible in large print with many illustrations he read frequently for its stories, the beauty of its language, and its high moral teaching. Others were Frost's *History of the World*, Weems' biographies of Washington and Francis Marion, a biography of Daniel Webster, which inspired him to become an orator, and the *Royal Path of Life*, a book of inspiring essays. David Crockett's *Autobiography* and some novels constituted his lighter reading.

Claxton's parents had strong convictions. His mother belonged to that heroic band of pioneer women who made America great and respected. His father, when the war broke out, had found himself in a serious dilemma. He belonged to the Whig political party, and owning no slaves, was opposed to slavery and secession. But he joined neither side. Long after the war, Claxton asked him why he took no part in the war. He replied, "I could not make up my mind to fight against my country's flag or against my neighbors." The sentiment in the community was about equally divided. Claxton's mother had two brothers, one in the Confederate army and the other on the Federal side. Indeed, Bedford County furnished almost as many soldiers for the Northern armies as for those of the South.[17] This brought the war into many homes in its most tragic aspect, dividing families in a way which was comparatively unknown in the North and in the "deep" South.

The early life of Claxton in Bedford County was restricted and narrow in many ways, but living on a farm always develops self-reliance and an aptitude in many trades and skills, and affords a growing boy a wide knowledge of the fundamental things in life and character. Edward J. Bok has written [18] that the "two keywords to success are thrift and thoroughness." These were certainly practiced by the Claxtons. Until Philander was fifteen years old, he never wore any clothing that was not entirely made by his mother and his sisters in the home, except his shoes and hats which were bought in the country stores. The Claxtons were accordingly self-sufficient and independent. They made their own living, expecting nothing from anybody else except the respect and friendship of their neighbors. "We did not know," Claxton declared,[19] "that any persons were better than others, unless they were better in character."

❧ II ❧

University of Tennessee Student

◇◇

WHEN PHILANDER CLAXTON was about seventeen years old, his parents one evening were sitting before the wood fire. "Philie wants to go to college," remarked the father; "but I don't see how we can get that much money now." They sat for awhile, quietly thinking. Then the mother, unwilling to recognize that obstacles to so worthy an ambition were insurmountable, replied, "But Philie must go to college!" Eventually it was arranged for him to borrow the necessary money from two neighbors on notes endorsed by his father, whose honesty and integrity were highly regarded.

On entering The University of Tennessee, young Claxton had $37.50 which he had earned by hauling lumber. During his senior year he was paid ten dollars a month for five months for turning the gas on and off at the gas house for the lights, and for ringing the college bell. This had to be rung at six in the morning and at ten in the evening, and hourly for classes during the day. To perform this service he had to climb to the second story of Old College and pull the rope attached to the bell in the tower. A state agriculture scholarship released him from paying tuition fees. Students holding such scholarships were supposed to do some manual work. Claxton remembered only spading about a dozen shovels full of dirt on a road being graded on the campus. When he graduated, he owed about $600, but he was relieved of $125 of this. His father gave him this sum in lieu of a horse which fathers were accustomed then to give their sons when they were "set free" at the age of twenty-one. Claxton, then lacking four months of being twenty, had early "become of age." All the borrowed money was repaid two years after graduation.[1] It was the best possible financial investment.

Claxton entered The University of Tennessee in January, 1880. He had never been more than twenty miles from home and his first ride on a railway was experienced in his journey to Knoxville. At that time the University had a preparatory school of three years, and his preparation for college had been so irregular that he was placed in the middle of the second preparatory year in Greek, the middle of the third preparatory year in Latin, the freshman class of the college in English, the sophomore class in mathematics and physics, and the junior class in biology. After three weeks, he was promoted to freshman Latin. The following summer at home he "made up" all preparatory requirements in Greek and the next year began college work in that language. In brief, by taking thirty-two hours of work instead of the usual sixteen a year, he graduated, after two and a half years, in June, 1882, second in his class. Besides fulfilling the requirements for the A.B. degree he had taken more sciences, languages, and mathematics than were required, and had covered in one year each the two years of both German and French, only one of which was required for the degree. It was indeed an amazing accomplishment.

The year previous to Claxton's becoming a student at The University of Tennessee was a momentous one in its history. It was at commencement in 1879 that the inaugural ceremonies of the new "University of Tennessee" were celebrated.[2] It thus superseded the University of East Tennessee, which had evolved from Blount College in 1807.[3] The latter had been founded in Knoxville in 1794, two years before Tennessee was admitted into the Union. It was Claxton's good fortune to enter The University of Tennessee at the time when it broadened its horizon and took definite steps toward becoming a great state university.

The President of the University, while Claxton was a student there, was The Reverend Thomas William Humes, S.T.D., an Episcopal minister who had been President of East Tennessee University since 1865. During the war he had been a bitter Union man, and it is reported that one Sunday while he was praying in the Episcopal Church of which he was rector in Knoxville he was shot by a Secessionist. As a result he became lame and had to walk with a stick. He was a slender, gray-haired man of pious appearance and speech, and the University students somewhat irreverently nick-named him "Limping Jesus." [4]

The members of the faculty [5] at that time were Eben Alexander, B.A., Professor of Ancient Languages and Literature; Edward S. Joynes, M.A., LL.D., Professor of Modern and English Languages and Literature; James Dinwiddie, M.A., Professor of Pure Mathematics; Samuel H. Lockett, M.A., Professor of Applied Mathematics and Mechanical Philosophy; William G. Brown, B.S., Professor of Chemistry and Mineralogy; Hunter Nicholson, Professor of Natural History and Geology; John M. McBryde, Professor of Agriculture, Horticulture, and Botany; Samuel B. Crawford, M.A., Commandant of Cadets and Instructor in Mathematics and Military Science; William Gibbs McAdoo, M.A., Librarian and Instructor in English and History; Thomas Oakley Deaderick, M.A., Instructor in Ancient Languages; William Everett Moses, Assistant in Analytical Chemistry; Gustav Robert Knabe, Instructor in Vocal and Instrumental Music; and Robert James Cummings, Farm Superintendent.

Claxton, in two years and a half, took four years of Latin, three years of Greek, four years of mathematics, two years each of German and French, one year of Spanish, and courses in chemistry, physics, astronomy, physiology, botany, zoology, biology, geology, history, English, logic, and Christian ethics. Accordingly, he met most of the faculty in the class room. He was particularly influenced by Lockett, Joynes, and Alexander, and most of all by the latter. Eben Alexander, a graduate of Yale, was a great scholar and a real gentleman. He dressed well, wearing a high hat and carrying a cane. From The University of Tennessee he later went as Professor of Greek to the University of North Carolina. There Claxton once noticed that some one had chalked on his office door, "Eben is a gentleman." [6] Later still Cleveland appointed him minister to Greece and other Balkan States. He spent money freely, and after his return from Athens, Claxton asked him how much money he had saved. "That is interesting," he replied;[6] "I sent Mrs. Alexander home three months ahead and saved enough to pay my own traveling expenses."

Dr. Edward S. Joynes was also an excellent scholar and a good teacher. He was the author of German and French grammars and the editor of some German readers. He wore a Prince Albert coat with a white cravat and carried a gold headed walking stick which he liked to twirl as he walked. Later he went to the University of South Carolina as professor of modern languages. At that time, stress was laid on the reading of foreign languages; no facility in the writing or speaking of them was acquired or expected. In English the emphasis was placed on language with illustrative selections; there were then no courses in English or American literature.

Colonel Samuel H. Lockett, a West Point graduate, had attained that rank in the Confederate army. After the war he had served in the army of the Khedive of Egypt and then, being an engineer, he had helped construct the pedestal of the Statue of Liberty. He eventually left the University and built railroads in South America. He was well liked by the students, his several young daughters probably contributing to his popularity.

Claxton also highly regarded Colonel Samuel B. Crawford, ever-smiling commandant of cadets, a graduate of The University of Tennessee. He was a Sunday school teacher in the Church Street Methodist Church, which Claxton attended. During his first year at the University, Philander became fourth sergeant in "B" Company in the battalion of cadets and the second year he was promoted to 2nd Lieutenant in "D" Company. According to the University records,[7] his uniform was as follows: "Single-breasted blouse of navy blue flannel, made in strict conformity with an approved pattern, with United States staff brass buttons, and with no ornaments other than those prescribed for distinguishing the different cadet officers. Pantaloons of cadet grey cloth with black stripe one inch wide down outer seam. Cadet cap of navy blue cloth ornamented with wreath and the letters U. T. Cadet officers of the grade of Captain and Lieutenant shall wear a double-breasted blouse." This complete uniform cost from $20 to $23. No photograph of Claxton in cadet uniform is extant, but he must have appeared to advantage in military dress. He had then about reached his full height of five feet ten and a half inches, and weighed only

136 pounds. His hair was black, but his complexion was fair and his eyes blue; his features were well moulded and pleasingly proportioned as was his whole physique.

Some of his other professors Claxton considered scholarly men but not exceptionally good teachers. Dr. Humes, who taught Christian ethics, logic, and history, he thought inefficient both as president and as teacher. None of the professors were paid more than $1800 a year. Instruction in all subjects was carried on in what is now called the textbook method. Lessons were assigned and the students recited them. The laboratories were very poorly equipped, and the sciences were not as well taught as the languages. The library contained only about 4000 books.

The examinations were always written and, as they were designed to require the student to make an analysis of the subject, they were six to eight hours in length. Cheating, known as "skinning," became so prevalent that in 1882 students were required to make a statement in writing, before beginning the examination, that they would not misstate the facts when they signed the pledge at the close of the examination. This pledge that they had not given or received undue help in the examination had been in effect for some years. Sometimes a teacher carelessly wrote the questions on the blackboard the day before an examination, and desperate students climbed over the transom to get a preview of the coming event.

Two faculty members were required to be in a class room during an examination. One day Colonel Lockett and his assistant discovered a tall athletic young man cheating in a mathematics examination. He was ordered to leave the room, but he refused and began to argue the case. Lockett collared him and ejected him by main strength. He afterwards became a successful lawyer and business-man in Texas and a member of the Legislature of that state.

Alexander used a more psychological method against cheating. With no assistant in the room, he directed the attention of his students to a few questions and directions on the blackboard which would require an hour or two for answering. Then in a calm manner he added,[8] "Young gentlemen, you know you must take an examination. I do not know why. If, after having taught you three or four years, I do not know how much Greek you know, I probably could not find out this morning. You probably don't know much. You have had a mighty poor teacher. You know you must sign a pledge that you have not had any undue assistance. You must be the judge of that. On my desk here are some good grammars, dictionaries, and translations, and some interlinears. If I can answer any question for you, I shall be glad to do so." After awhile he said,[8] "If you get through the examination before I return, put your papers on my desk and place this paper weight on them so they won't blow off." Then he took his hat and cane and left, probably for town. One student who had come fully prepared with greased papers and other aids rose and said,[8] "A man who would cheat in Eben Alexander's class would steal fodder from a blind sheep. Goodbye, boys, I'll see some of you here next year." Another who had to pass in order to graduate that year proceeded to cheat as he had planned, signed the pledge, and placed his paper with the others on the desk. It was necessary to secure a mark of 50 to pass. Alexander gave him 49.5 but did not accuse him of cheating. When the man argued, pleaded, and tried to bluff him into raising his grade, the Professor's only reply was,[8] "Mr. ——, I think I have given you all your paper is worth." The student did not graduate, but afterwards he became a lawyer of good reputation.

The number of students at the University during Claxton's first year was only 141 plus 92 in the preparatory school.[9] The second year the total increased to 169 plus only 46 in the preparatory school.[10] A large proportion of the students were country boys like Claxton. He roomed a year and a half in the building afterwards called Humes Hall, situated on the side of the hill toward the city; and the rest of the time in "D" Building, the most westward of a group of three buildings crowning the top of the hill. The central building, afterwards known as Old College, contained the chapel, the library, and some class rooms. Seven main buildings comprised the physical equipment of the University. There was no general heating system or water system. The rooms were heated by coal grates, and water was supplied from cisterns.

One of Claxton's roommates, Bill Sayres of Texas, had the habit of proclaiming on Monday morning as soon as he got out of bed, "Day after tomorrow is Wednesday; week half gone and nothing done yet." [11] He was a hard-working student, who was accustomed to sitting up late studying the night before an examination. Claxton usually went to bed early with the belief that, if he did not already know the subject, he could not learn it properly in one night.

Being a college which was partially supported by the Morrill Act of 1862, the University was required to teach military tactics. By six o'clock all the students had to be up and report at reveille in front of their respective dormitory. After getting their rooms in order, they marched to breakfast. This was followed by chapel, at which there was compulsory attendance. Military drill came in the afternoon after the routine of recitations. But the students all marched to classes and to meals in military formation in the approved West Point manner. Discipline was strict and severe. Demerits were imposed for infractions of the regulations; and if a student received 100 demerits in one month, he might be dismissed.

One of the first disciplinary incidents Claxton remembered, after his becoming a student, took place at the battalion dress parade on a Friday afternoon. The Officer of the Day read a special order to the effect that Lieutenant —— was deprived of his official rank, discharged, and expelled from the battalion and from the college for "profanity, gambling, drunkenness, and corrupting the morals" of the other cadets. The lieutenant, standing tall and erect, turned on his heels, went into a room in "C" Building (known later as East College), and throwing his sword on the table, exclaimed,[11] "I'll be damned if I don't go to Vanderbilt and study for the ministry." He did that very thing, and later became a very influential minister in the Methodist church and a successful college president. Another student who used to receive 75 or 80 demerits the first week or two each month afterwards held a high office in one of our greatest universities and in the United States government. It is difficult to predict the future of a young man from his conduct at college.

Claxton himself had two clashes with the college authorities. After entering the University, he "made up" two or three chapters in the textbook on analytical geometry, but was given no examination on that part of the book. This was discovered by the faculty near the end of his senior year and he was informed that he was required to take the examination. He replied that, since that time,

he had finished two and a half years of analytical geometry, calculus, and the philosophy of mathematics (more than was required
for the A.B. degree), and had passed all the examinations. Arguing
that if those early chapters had any value he had properly made use
of them, he definitely refused to take the examination and added
that, if such were required, he would not graduate. He heard no
more about the matter, and had reason to believe that his courage
won the respect of the faculty, particularly that of Professor Alexander.

The other clash had to do with the Philomathesian Literary Society, of which Claxton was President during his senior year. He
was also a member of its debating team. It was customary for this
society to have an annual debate in Staub's Opera House before a
large audience of city folk. A debater had, on a previous occasion,
made objectional remarks and the faculty had then required all
speeches to be submitted in writing for their approval. Two days
before the debate in which Claxton was to participate, all the debaters were detained after chapel services and informed by President Humes that all speeches must be limited to fifteen minutes.
Upon being asked the length of his speech, Claxton replied,[11]
"Twenty minutes." "But, Mr. Claxton, you will not be permitted
to speak longer than fifteen minutes." "Too late now to rewrite my
speech. I shall speak twenty minutes," Claxton answered. "You
will be called down," said Dr. Humes. "Our society is chartered by
the state just as the University is," replied Claxton, "and if we are
interfered with, policemen will be present to protect us." The
faculty then met and informed the debaters that the average length
of the speeches must not be longer than fifteen minutes. Clearly,
this could not be determined until all had spoken, and nothing
further was heard of the matter. These two incidents are related
somewhat in detail, because they well illustrate one of Claxton's
fundamental characteristics—he has always acted fearlessly with
the courage of his convictions.

The two literary societies then comprised the most important
extracurricular activity on the campus. They had been organized in
1836. Upon the banner of the Philomathesian Society were these
words: "Be just and fear not. Let all the ends thou aim'st at be thy
Country's, thy God's, and Truth's." Its motto was "Nulla vestigia

retrorsum" (No steps backward). Each society met monthly in its own room, which contained a small library of well selected books. The regular programs consisted of orations, declamations, readings of essays, and debates. Sometimes a member of the faculty gave an address. A magazine was also issued by each society. The *Chi Delta Crescent* was hand written; but the *Philo Star* was printed, beginning with the issue of January, 1882.[12] Claxton was its chief editor the remainder of that year. From 300 to 400 copies were printed for each monthly issue.

The editorials and unsigned articles were written by Claxton. Some of these show a remarkable maturity of mind for a young man under twenty. In "Character of the Progress of Today"[13] he dwells on the importance of selecting a profession while young when one's "inclinations and temperament are being formed." For the January issue, he wrote "The New Year,"[14] in which reference was made to the appearance during the preceding year of a comet that had caused terror among the ignorant, and to "the black and hideous crime" which had robbed the nation of President Garfield. "We bid farewell to the Old Year," he writes, "as it rolls back with the great multitude of years that have passed into oblivion. We hail with delight, with burning hopes and high expectations the New Year, as it comes in from the great and yet unknown future." In "Small Words"[15] he ridicules the debater who refers to the proposition as the "momentous question now presented to your intelligent and august body for consideration, expostulation, deliberation, elucidation, and decision," and the sophomore who speaks of rain as "a slight condensation of the aqueous vapor in the superior regions of the atmosphere whence it has been transported by evaporation and a precipitation of the same on the terrestrial surface of this mundane sphere." Then, he illustrates his main idea by quoting from Pope, Bishop Hall, Byron, Milton, Scott, Tennyson, and Dr. Addison Alexander. The quotation from the latter begins,

> *"Think not that strength lies in the big round words,*
> *Or that the brief and plain must needs be weak."*

Claxton's early inclination to make full use of that which was immediately at hand is illustrated in "The Beauties of College

Hill," [16] in which there is the following excellent description of Knoxville and the river: "As I write, I look from my window and see the sparkling waves upon the surface of the Tennessee, as it rolls its majestic waters westward, bathing the southern foot of College Hill. Just beyond the narrow level tract which forms the immediate bank on the opposite side rises a number of rounded shrub-covered hills. On the sides of one of these once thundered the dread voice of battle, and from its summit the swift winged messengers of death took their flight, breathing hot their sulphurous breath. But these thunders have passed away, and this hill is now as peaceful and quiet as the far famed Mount of Olives, to which it has been compared by an Oriental traveller."

He even wrote some verse, called "The Student's Soliloquy," a parody on the soliloquy of Hamlet. It began,

> "To study or not to study, that is the question:
> Whether 'tis nobler to lay my books aside
> And trust to good fortune on my examinations,
> Or to take up my books and by studying
> Make my passing sure."

After weighing the evils which may follow lack of study, the soliloquy ends with these lines:

> "These examinations do greatly oppress us all;
> And thus the happy hours of pleasure
> Are siclied o'er by thoughts of Chemistry and Calculus,
> And when we would think on 'love and noble subjects,'
> German, French, Latin, Greek, yea Spanish turn
> Our thoughts awry; while Geology and snakes
> Disturb our dreams; and Astronomy and Botany
> Rob the heavens and nature of their natural beauty."

"The rude jostlings of man against man in the struggle for bread or wealth," he wrote in "Practical People and Practical Education," [17] "grows ruder as civilization advances and population increases. The man who should apply the tactics of Alexander to the armies of the 19th century, and use the raw hide buckler as a defense against needleguns and rifled cannon would reason no better than he who attempts to apply the methods of fifty years ago to the practice of today."

In an article on "Biography" [18] he shows rare discrimination in his approval of Johnson's *Lives of the Poets*, Boswell's *Johnson*, Moore's *Life of Byron*, and Lockhart's *Scott*. "Biographies of great, but especially of good, men," he writes, "are most instructive and useful as helps and incentives to others, giving valuable examples, teaching high living, high thinking, and energetic action for their own and the world's good. In conclusion, they show that great men of science, literature, and art, the fashioners of great thoughts and lords of the great heart, have belonged to no exclusive class. They have come alike from colleges, workshops, farmhouses—from the hovels of the poor men and the mansions of the rich, exhibiting in language not to be misunderstood what is in the power of each one to accomplish for himself, even of the humblest rank, working out an honorable competency and a solid reputation."

A reportorial article, "Class Tree Planting," [19] gives a full account of the formal ceremony incident to the planting of a tree by Claxton's class on April 14th. The battalion was drawn up in hollow square at the spot, a prayer was offered, the class sang a poem written for the occasion, and Colonel Lockett delivered an oration. This was followed by a song by the Class of 1883 and the benediction by President Humes. This class tree, now a great spreading yellow poplar (tulip), still stands on the University campus. Colonel Lockett's address on the meaning of the class motto, "Architects of Our Own Fortune," was printed in full. Claxton likewise preserved two of Lockett's addresses to the Philomathesian Society on "How to Study" and "What Should Be Taught in Our Common Schools?" It is not unlikely that the practical ideas on educational methods contained in these addresses found lodgement in young Claxton's mind; and germinating there, later influenced him in deciding to devote his life to teaching and to the reformation of the common schools.

It would, indeed, be difficult to exaggerate the beneficial influence of those literary societies on the students of the University. Fraternities, which were introduced during Claxton's last year, eventually supplanted them, and student publications and debating teams later carried on some of their functions.

College sports were then limited, military drill being the chief form of exercise. One game which was played was town ball, a kind of combination of English cricket and the later game of baseball. A rubber ball was thrown to the batter, who stood at the home base. When a batted ball was caught, he was "out" and one of the "fielders" took his place.

Occasionally there were dances at the University, particularly during commencement. But as there were no co-eds on the "Hill" then, the social life was considerably handicapped. The wealthier students attended dances in Knoxville, but as Claxton did not have money to spend in this way and besides was a member of a church which frowned on such frivolities, he did not participate in that form of entertainment. He served one year as secretary of the newly organized YMCA. As he recalls, the students then were not more religiously inclined than in later years. They probably drank more, and were more independent and had less respect for members of the faculty. But, on the whole, they did a lot of hard studying, probably more than their sons and grandsons did.

All the commencement ceremonies incident to the graduation of Claxton's class of 1882 were held in Staub's Opera House on Gay Street.[20] The Baccalaureate Sermon was delivered on Sunday evening, June 4, by the Reverend J. Llewellyn Evans, D.D., of Cincinnati on the text, "And Jesus himself began to be about 30 years of age." The following evening Colonel W. A. Henderson of Knoxville addressed the students and guests on "The New Temple of the South," and the literary societies awarded diplomas to their respective members of the graduating class. The next evening J. W. Caldwell, Esquire, of Knoxville, spoke to the Alumni Association on "Lessons from the Life of a Great Man" [Emerson].

On Wednesday morning, the faculty and graduating class marched in procession to the Opera House. No caps and gowns were worn. According to Claxton,[21] that kind of "garbage" was not worn in those days. At nine o'clock, the exercises commenced. President Humes read his address in Latin, and the diplomas were handed to the graduates. Degrees were conferred on sixteen[22] young men. Six, among whom was Claxton, received the A.B. degree; eight, the B.S.; and three, the B.C.E. [Bachelor of Civil Engineering]. Among the latter was Joseph Edward Lopez, who also received the B.S. Claxton was awarded a "Certificate of Distinction" in Astronomy and a "Certificate of Proficiency with Distinction" in Modern Languages and English and in Ancient Languages. At commencement the previous year he had been given a "School Certificate of Proficiency with Distinction" in Mathematics.

Thus Claxton reached one of the important milestones on the high road to success. He had arrived at this milestone by rapid, long strides nearly four months before he was twenty years old. And young as he was, when he returned home to his parents who had been unable to be present at his graduation, he was quite uncertain as to the direction his high road to fame and fortune would lead him.

⋐ III ⋑

North Carolina School Teacher

◇◇

INFLUENCED BY his success as a debater, Claxton had decided before graduation from The University of Tennessee to study law,
and he returned home with the expectation of entering Vanderbilt
University the following January to prepare himself for this profession. But he had been at home less than three months when on an
important Saturday morning late in August a letter which changed
his whole life was handed to him at the Poplin's Cross Roads Post
Office.[1]

The letter was from Knoxville and bore the signature of E. P.
Moses,[2] then entirely unknown to Claxton. Moses, who was spending his vacation with relatives in Knoxville, wrote that Claxton had
been recommended to him by Professor Eben Alexander for a position as teacher in the graded school of Goldsboro, North Carolina,
of which he was superintendent. Goldsboro was described as a
pleasant country town and a cheap place in which to live. The proposed salary was $50 a month for ten months. "If you are inter-
ested," he concluded, "meet me in Knoxville on the second Sunday
from the date of this letter."

Claxton returned home, looked up Goldsboro, of which he had
never heard, on the map, and asked his parents for advice. His
mother, who had sorely missed her son during the past two years,
thought that Goldsboro was too far from home, and advised him
not to accept the offer. His father said, "You must now make decisions for yourself";[3] so Claxton, who was already in debt for his

education at the University, decided to postpone the study of law and wrote to Moses that he accepted his offer and would meet him in Knoxville, as requested.

Borrowing from his father some money for necessary expenses, Claxton went to Knoxville and, meeting Moses at the appointed time, traveled with him to Goldsboro by rail, a tedious journey then by way of Warm Springs, Asheville, Salisbury, and Greensboro. "All the way from Knoxville to Goldsboro," wrote [3] Claxton, "on the train, in the hotel and on the grounds of Warm Springs, on the streets of Salisbury, Greensboro, and elsewhere, Moses talked school: methods of teaching, history of education, need for the education of all the people of North Carolina, state loyalty, and the possibility of valuable work for education in the state. He told me what he had recently heard of teachers' institutes, about the modern method of teaching reading, about the new plan of organized public schools with several levels in grades as they had recently been organized in New England towns. On this trip I heard more than I had ever heard or read before about education, the need and means of improving schools, and so forth."

Arriving at Goldsboro hot and dusty in the late afternoon, they met Edwin A. Alderman, a recent graduate of the University of North Carolina, who had accepted a similar position at the same salary Moses had offered Claxton. After spending the night at the Gregory House with Moses, Claxton and Alderman arranged for room and board with a Mrs. Speight, for $15 a month. Together they occupied a large corner room with four windows affording pleasant views of the large yard with its many oak trees. The room was comfortably furnished, and in winter heated by an open fireplace. There was an abundance of excellently cooked Southern food, and the atmosphere of the place was that of a cultured home.

Moses soon took his new teachers to see the school building on the opposite side of the town. A four-story building of thirteen rooms, it had originally been a girls' college, and was taken over by the Board of Education for the graded school which Moses had organized the year before. There were four rooms on each of the four floors except the fourth, where two rooms and a hall had been thrown together to make an assembly place and gymnasium. Both the building and its grounds were well adapted to use as a public school.

The Goldsboro graded school was one of the first [4] to be organized under the Dortch Act, which became a state law in 1881. It permitted white people of an incorporated town or city to tax themselves and their property for free schools for white children, and also Negroes to provide similar schools for their children in the same way. In some communities much opposition developed among church leaders who thought such schools would undermine the influence of private schools which were directly or indirectly under the control of various religious denominations. There was also strong opposition among many of the well-to-do citizens who considered it a tax on "thrifty men to pay for the education of the children of other people." [5] It was different in Goldsboro, where Moses had the support of the leading families. Among the progressive citizens were Julius A. Bonitz and Joe Robinson, editors of the two local papers, Ed Borden, a banker named Howell, the Deweys, the Carnegies, and Colonel L. W. Humphrey, who was a prominent, wealthy Republican. [6] Goldsboro, which was about 75 miles southeast of Chapel Hill, then had a population between three and four thousand. According to Alderman, [7] it was "a small, sincere, dignified, progressive community, not given to over-praise or over-blame, but level-headed, equable, just, and wonderfully kind." It was "almost as well adapted," he thought, [7] "to train the young citizen as Chapel Hill had been to train the young scholar."

Moses, a graduate of the University of East Tennessee and a former teacher in the Knoxville schools, had received his elementary education in New Hampshire, where his father sent his family during the war to reside with their grandparents. From childhood he had thus been familiar with the organization of graded schools, and took, like a duck to water, to the superintendency of such a school in Goldsboro. He had Claxton and Alderman and the other teachers, all of whom were women, to meet him at the school, where he lectured to them on the right methods of organizing a graded school and the best methods of teaching. When the school opened a week later, all were afire with his enthusiasm, indoctrinated with his ideas, and prepared to act harmoniously in the performance of their duties.

[33]

In one year the school had already made a reputation for itself throughout the State. Scores of teachers visited it to study the new methods. Superintendent D. B. Johnson from Newbern was in Alderman's room the first morning of the new term to observe how he taught history, English, and Latin in the sixth, seventh, eighth, and ninth grades. Favorably impressed, he asked Alderman how long he had been teaching. With his keen sense of humor, he replied, on consulting his watch, "An hour and fifteen minutes, sir." [8] Claxton taught mathematics, geography, and the other subjects in the four upper grades. His room also had many visitors. One good old lady from Wilmington spent practically a whole week observing his teaching. As this was his first week as a teacher, he wondered what she learned about this difficult art. Many people from Goldsboro came to visit the school and brought their out-of-town visitors as they might have to the zoo or the art gallery, had there been such in town. One day Claxton looked over his room and counted sixteen guests. The school was really the talk of the town and its show place.

Proud of his handiwork, Moses lost no opportunity of exhibiting the children at work and at play. When a prominent visitor was present, the bell might ring at any time for a class or even the whole school to march to the large hall and give an exhibition of calisthenics. Moses conducted these exercises either free hand or with wands, dumbbells, and Indian clubs. He also drilled the children to march in and out of the building and the classrooms to the beat of drums or the music of a piano. It was a thrilling sight to see them march by classes in order of height four times a day in and out of the building. Many Goldsboro people would stop on the street or come onto the grounds to see such an unusual sight.

Claxton and Alderman studied hard, usually sitting up until eleven or twelve at night, getting ready for the next day's work and discussing general plans for the term or the entire year. Inexperienced, they had to guard against the temptation of giving assignments that were too long. Even so, toward the end of the first quarter they found they had covered nearly half of the year's work. Alderman suggested that they slow down or they would soon be out of a job. They accordingly did more reviewing and found that the students' acquirement of knowledge became more definite. Another principle of teaching which Claxton learned was the value of first hand observation and experience, and he frequently took groups of children on Saturdays on tramps through the fields and forests to study plants, trees, and geographical features.

Moses held frequent teachers' meetings, in which Claxton took an active part by reading papers and entering freely into the discussions. Moses, well-informed, was always interesting and inspiring, and sometimes brilliant. His criticism was keen but always kind. He did not confine himself to theorizing in teachers' meetings, but spent most of his time during school hours in the classrooms, demonstrating his principles and methods in actual teaching. He could teach quite well all the subjects in all the grades. He could take over a recitation in Caesar without even referring to the book. He was a dynamo of energy, and all who came into contact with him, whether students or teachers, were energized and stimulated mentally as they would have been physically when subjected to an electric current. Dr. Mayo, editor of the New England Journal of Education, made an extensive tour, visiting schools from Boston to California, North and South; and after finishing his study, said that Moses was the best superintendent of schools he had seen.[8]

"From Moses and Alderman," wrote [9] Claxton, "I got much of the inspiration which finally led me to become a teacher." "Moses was naturally aggressive," Claxton declared [9] somewhat critically, "and sometimes a bit erratic in his thinking, willing to try anything new that looked good; a bit socialistic. Had read about Pestalozzi and would like to imitate him. Active and energetic, wholly devoted to his work and therefore very inspiring."

Alderman, like Claxton, had planned to study law, and they agreed to read law together as soon as they became sufficiently familiar with their school work. This, however, never materialized. Alderman came in one evening and said, "Claxton, I have been nosing around, and I find only one lawyer in Goldsboro is making as much as $1000 a year. He is Senator Dortch. I believe we can do that well teaching school." Dortch had given his name to the then recent school enactment. Of him, Josephus Daniels relates [10] that at a Primitive Baptist meeting at Wilson, North Carolina, the preacher said of the Senator, who was in the audience, "I see Colonel Bill Dortch here to-day. He is the brainiest lawyer in North Carolina, but he haint got no more religion than my old mule." There were other brainy lawyers in Goldsboro; such as, Charles B. Aycock and Frank Daniels, brother of Josephus. If such young men could not earn more than $1000, while Moses' salary as superintendent was then $1200, the profession of teaching was worthy of serious consideration.

The role of being one of the leaders in a new movement appealed strongly to both Alderman and Claxton. It was evident that education in North Carolina was in great need of improvement not only in the common schools but also in the institutions of higher learning. After finishing the ninth grade, students could enter the state university or any other college in North Carolina. "In fact," Claxton declared,[11] "they might enter some of these colleges from the seventh grade, graduate, and return home before their classmates in the Goldsboro Graded School finished the ninth grade. This was true for some years not only of this school but of other graded schools, so low was the standard of the colleges." And so it came about that one profession lost two probable legal lights of the first magnitude, and another gained two of its greatest leaders.

"I remember Mr. Claxton," wrote one [12] of his pupils sixty years afterwards, "as a young man rather tall, fair, thin, clean-shaven, gentle, polite to his pupils. His dress—simple, conservative. His voice and breathing showed serious catarrhal trouble. His pupils were fond of him. As a teacher he had the ability of making them think and get more from a lesson than merely memorizing the text. . . . I can say but one thing against Mr. Claxton. His pupils considered it a stigma for they could not understand why a teacher had never learned to write. His handwriting was the most illegible I have ever seen. It took hard work on the part of his pupils to decipher his notes, written on the blackboard." His mind has always raced ahead so fast that he has been unable to form his letters properly.

In the early summer of 1883, Claxton was elected, without his application for the position, superintendent of the graded school at Kinston, North Carolina, at a salary of $1000 a year. A part of the summer preceding his going to Kinston he spent at the summer school of the University of North Carolina. There he made the acquaintance of President Kemp P. Battle; George T. Winston, professor of Latin, later president of the University, and later still president of the University of Texas; Dr. Graves, the brilliant professor of Mathematics, whose sister later married Alderman; Dr. Toy, professor of Modern Languages; and other professors and former students of the University. He also met John C. Scarborough, State Superintendent of Schools. His associations there gave him a very favorable impression of the leading educators of North Carolina. He was charmed with the atmosphere of the University, which he found more to his liking than that of The University of Tennessee. The halls of the two literary societies particularly appealed to him. Their walls were covered with portraits of former members who had become famous. They had libraries even better than that of the University. These societies then were also responsible for the discipline of students, all of whom belonged to one or the other, and had the power even to dismiss a student from college.

After returning home for a visit, he went to the Louisville Exposition. Among the interesting and instructive exhibits in agriculture, industry, and art, he remembered particularly two rather incongruous objects: a painting, "The Helping Hand," which ever afterwards had a strong appeal to him, and a cucumber, still green, from Sumner County, Tennessee, weighing ninety-six pounds. He returned home by way of Mammoth Cave, where he spent a day in most profitable sightseeing, and then made his first visit to Nashville, stopping at the Maxwell House, known as the best hotel in the South. On Sunday he went to services at the then famous McKendree Methodist Church. "I think I slept through part of the sermon," Claxton recalled.[13]

His experiences and observations during that summer gave him interesting material for illustrating his talks to the children in the Kinston school when he began his work there as superintendent. The school was to be organized under the provisions of the Dortch Act, the citizens having voted a tax for this purpose. In this town of about 1800 inhabitants, the center of an agricultural community, there had been no adequate schools for many years. Illiteracy

[37]

among the Negroes and "poor whites" was very high. There was an average of more than one saloon to every one hundred inhabitants.

The school board was composed of the best men in town. The chairman was Dr. Pollock, a physician, who was the originator and dispenser of a patent medicine called "Seven Golden Seals." He was very egotistical and pompous and inclined to be self-assertive, though he was a kindly man of integrity and ability. Claxton roomed and boarded at his home. The other members were mainly merchants in the town. The teachers, who had already been employed, Claxton found to be women of great native ability and culture with some teaching experience and a willingness to learn and to work. Especially good teachers were Cynthia Tull and Amelie Hardee, a niece of General Hardee of the Confederate Army.

The school was housed in an old rambling residence to which a one-story wing had been added. With the help of some boys and one hired man Claxton put up some necessary partitions for organizing the school in seven grades. He held preliminary teachers' meetings for instructing them in the methods of teaching he had learned from Moses, which were new to them. The school opened in August, 1883. Claxton was then not yet twenty-one years old. All went to work enthusiastically. Besides superintending the school, Claxton also taught arithmetic, algebra, geography, and gymnastics and coached plays.

One evening at the end of the second or third week, Dr. Pollock came to his room and, standing in the doorway, proclaimed,[13] "Mr. Claxton, I have come to ask an explanation of what you are doing at the school. People ask me and members of the board. We are unable to answer them." His manner implied that he thought the methods all wrong. "Dr. Pollock," Claxton replied, "you elected me to this position without my request or knowledge. I suppose you must have thought I was capable of doing the work. I am doing the best I know. I can only do what I think to be right and best. When your board believes I am not suited for the position, my resignation is in your hands. I shall be glad to have any suggestions from you or any member of the board; but while I stay, I can act only on my knowledge and convictions. With this understanding, will you come in and have a seat?" Abandoning his haughty manner, he came in and they talked the matter over quietly and satisfactorily. That was the only unpleasantness Claxton had with the board, which afterwards supported him loyally.

Claxton, in looking back on this experience, thought that it taught him lessons valuable in after life, that "responsibility and authority must be coterminous"; that "the world stands aside for one who knows where he is going"; and that, "for success, one must think only of his work and not of his personal interests." [13]

The discipline in the school was difficult in the beginning. Many of the pupils were very old for their grade and became unruly. Claxton found that his military training at The University of Tennessee was very helpful. He found it necessary to "thrash" one boy as old as, and larger than, he. He took the punishment and profited by it, but Claxton soon found it unwise to depend very much on corporal punishment. He confirmed, what he already knew, that the first principle of good school discipline is to keep the students busy, and that the second is to assume that children will obey rational requests and conduct themselves orderly. The discipline improved after the dismissal of the weak principal before the year was half gone. He was replaced by George Grimsley, who had been educated at the excellent Bingham School and at Peabody Normal School. His scholarship, good character, and military training made him a valuable assistant. Later he became superintendent of the Greensboro schools and afterwards president of successful life insurance companies in North Carolina.

One of Claxton's teachers at Kinston recently said [14] of him, "He was dignified but very 'folksy.' He was considerate of everyone, most efficient, and the grandest superintendent. He was humorous, and nothing too fine can be said about him."

Claxton was asked to remain at Kinston a second year to conduct a semi-private school at a salary of $1200. This was to be organized to take the place of the public graded school because early in 1884 the state Supreme Court had declared the Dortch Law unconstitutional. The schools organized under this act thus found themselves without support or legal authority. Funds for their continuance had to be raised by private subscription until people could be persuaded to vote for taxes on all property and polls to support schools for all children, irrespective of color.

The offer was not accepted by Claxton. As Kinston was only twenty-four miles by rail from Goldsboro, he had frequently gone there during week-ends to see Moses, Alderman, and other friends. On one of these visits Alderman and he had agreed to go to Johns Hopkins University the following year. Though Alderman changed his mind and remained at Goldsboro, Claxton, having received a graduate scholarship which paid his college fees at Hopkins, adhered to his plan. But before leaving North Carolina, he lectured for four weeks on education in a Peabody Summer Institute for Teachers at Wilson, North Carolina. It was there that he first met Dr. J. L. M. Curry, Secretary of the Peabody Fund, and heard him lecture one morning on the need for, and possibilities of, popular education in the South—education for all the people at the cost of all the people. This marked the beginning of the great influence Curry was to have on Claxton during the next eighteen years, through his speeches which were characterized by prophetic vision and persuasive eloquence.

At the close of the summer institute, Claxton went to Blowing Rock for several weeks, chiefly because his fiancée, Varina Moore, and her sister Annie were there. The climate was ideal. For recreation the young people did much walking in the mountains. One party climbed Grandfather Mountain and spent the night on its top. They slept on beds of spruce boughs. "Most of the party did," Claxton recalled; [13] "Joe Holmes and I spent most of the night cutting wood and keeping the fire going. Next morning, all the country below was covered with oceans of clouds, a mountain peak here and there rising above them like an island. Well worth climbing and spending the night to see."

This was Claxton's first experience with mountains, and he was so charmed with Blowing Rock that he conceived the idea of building a hotel and establishing a summer school there. At that time there was no hotel and summer visitors stayed in farm houses, room and board costing fifty cents a day. On the way to his home in Tennessee, he stopped in Chattanooga to see his college friend, Nick Van Dyke, who had just returned from a fishing trip on the

Watauga River. He readily became interested in the idea of building a hotel, agreeing to become a partner if a third party could be found who knew the country and owned land on which to build. After visiting his family, Claxton returned to Blowing Rock and found the third party, George Finley, a tall man about thirty-five with a red beard like that of the god Thor. He owned twelve acres of land, on which was a big spring, the source of the Yadkin River. It was an ideal location. So the three formed a partnership. Claxton drew up the plans for a hotel of fifty rooms, wrote the specifications, and made the contract for pine lumber to be sawed at a nearby sawmill at nine dollars a thousand. He then left for Baltimore and Johns Hopkins University.

❦ IV ❧

Johns Hopkins Graduate Student

◇◇

W HEN CLAXTON entered Johns Hopkins University in September, 1884, he was not in the best of health. For the past four years he had been studying and working too hard with an average of only five hours of sleep at night. The climate at Kinston had been very bad. There were many malaria-bearing mosquitoes, and he became ill of the disease, having one very hard chill but fortunately only one. Just before leaving Blowing Rock, he had gotten caught in a heavy rain and had taken a severe cold. This had further diminished his physical strength, and he was not in proper condition for the rigorous program of intensive study which he soon laid out for himself.

Johns Hopkins University was then only five years old, having been opened by President Daniel C. Gilman in 1879 as the first real university in the United States. Mr. Johns Hopkins, a merchant in Baltimore, had bequeathed to it as an endowment a large part of his fortune, nearly seven million dollars to be divided equally between the university proper and the medical school and hospital.[1] The first building to be occupied, which constituted the nucleus of the academic group, was located at the corner of Howard and Little Ross Streets. Adjacent to it on the west was the geological laboratory, which contained the first general lecture hall of the university. Next to this, on Little Ross Street, was the chemical laboratory, which was opened in 1883. At the southeast corner of Eutaw and Little Ross was the biological building, a brick structure

[42]

in architectural harmony with the chemical laboratory.[2] The buildings in use when Claxton was at the University were the Administration Building, Hopkins Hall, and the Chemistry and Biological Laboratories.[3] Many classes met in rented rooms in dwelling houses. A German visitor referred to the university buildings as a group of workshops.

Claxton went to Hopkins with the intention of studying hydroelectrical engineering. Henry A. Rowland, the famous professor of physics, was then a member of the Hopkins faculty. "By his own admission," declared[4] Claxton, "he was the best physicist in America." As a matter of fact, he did then rank among the great physicists of the world. But G. Stanley Hall, the most widely known professor of education of his day, was also a member of the Hopkins faculty. Claxton's two years of teaching had gotten into his blood. The inspiration and enthusiasm of E. P. Moses had left deep impressions. He had also been greatly inspired by Dr. J. L. M. Curry whom he had heard lecture, a few months before, at a teachers' institute at Wilson, North Carolina. As he walked the streets of Baltimore at night for a week or two trying to make up his mind whether to continue his studies in engineering, the influence of Moses and Curry and "a certain streak of altruistic enthusiasm"[4] caused him finally to resist the "tempting vision of harnessing Niagara Falls"[4] and to decide to devote all his life and energies to the improvement of education in the Southern States—"a decision which I still think was wise,"[4] he concluded late in life.

Claxton took for his "principal subject"[5] (major, as now called) not Psychology and Pedagogics but the Teutonic Languages. The first half year he studied Lessing's *Minna von Barhelm* and Goethe's *Prosa* with Dr. George Hempl and Selected Readings in German Literature with Hempl and Dr. Henry Wood. He also studied Anglo-Saxon with Dr. Wright and Early English with Dr. Egge. The second half-year he read Goethe's *Faust* and Lessing's *Prosa* with Hempl, continued the Readings in German Literature, Goethe's *Prosa*, Early English, and Anglo-Saxon, and added Oral Practice in the German Language under direction of Dr. Wood. For minor subjects he took Dr. J. Franklin Jameson's course on the English Constitution the first semester and his American Constitutional Law the second semester, and Dr. Herbert B. Adams' full year course on International Law.[5] Besides these he had courses in Education with Dr. G. Stanley Hall, Spanish with Todd, Physics with Perkins, and Economics with Dr. Richard T. Ely.[6] It was a staggering load for a young student to attempt to carry. Somewhat like Bacon, the ambitious young Claxton was taking all knowledge for his province.

His best teachers, according to Claxton, were Hall, Jameson, and Todd. "Jameson," he wrote,[7] "was clear, deliberate, accurate. Lectured slowly enough to permit full note taking." According to Ray Stannard Baker,[8] Jameson was "tall, thin, scholarly looking, a fellow in the University, who was to become one of the most distinguished of American research historians." One of the features of the University then was the Historical Seminar. "Professors, fellows, and students," writes Baker,[9] "were all brought together in the room in the old biological building devoted to the famous Bluntschli Library (Bluntschli was professor of international law at the University of Heidelberg, and upon his death German citizens of Baltimore purchased his valuable library and presented it to Johns Hopkins University). . . . There were small tables all about for the use of students, and immediate access to the crowded volumes on the shelves. A motto from Freeman, painted in large letters at one end of the room, peculiarly defined his own sense of the relationship of his favorite studies: History Is Past Politics and Politics Present History." All about the room were pictures and busts of famous statesmen and historians. A special honor was rendered Professor Bluntschli in the course in international law by using his *Allgemeines Staatsrecht*, which the students read in the original German.[10]

Claxton considered his course under G. Stanley Hall to have been "most inspiring and informational" and thought young Todd was "one of the best teachers" he had ever known. He was apparently not particularly impressed by the diminutive Dr. Ely, then just beginning a long career as a moulder of economic thought in the United States; but was much interested in his subject. Nor was he very favorably impressed with Dr. Adams who introduced the monographic study of history into American universities. Ely and Adams brought from Germany the "look and see" method of keeping close to reality.[11]

The total number of students at Hopkins was 274, of whom 163 were doing graduate work.[12] Most of the latter had scholarships or fellowships. Claxton's scholarship was worth $250 per year. There was no campus and there were no dormitories for the students. Claxton roomed and boarded with a German family at 4 McCulloh Street. Among the dozen or more students rooming there were two very interesting Japanese. Sato, son of the Mayor of Tokyo, afterwards occupied a prominent position, possibly the presidency of the University of Tokyo. Ota, later known as Dr. Nitobe, was the author of *Bushido*, a member of the secretariat of the League of Nations, and a member of the Japanese Senate. At number 8 on the same street roomed Woodrow Wilson, then a graduate student in history, economics, and law.[13] According to Ray Stannard Baker,[14] this was "a neighborhood of dignified old brick houses with blinds, and little steps that let one quickly into the thoroughfare—houses now worn and shabby, given over to Negro tenants."

Though Claxton studied harder than he should have, he by no means lived the life of a recluse. He visited the Walters Art Gallery and for the first time saw a large collection of paintings and other art objects. He went to the theater frequently, and saw *Hamlet* played by a company of noted artists. At the Academy of Music he also saw plays, and heard Henry Ward Beecher lecture and Mark Twain read. Beecher's subject was "The Rise of the Common People." With powerful physique and excellent voice he was very impressive. Sixty years afterwards, Claxton remembered that he said that he had pious friends who talked about what God was thinking as if they had just been talking with Him on a street corner. Another remark he recalled was that Beecher said he had several years before predicted that there would be no more war, and since that time there had been three very destructive ones.

Mark Twain, then in his prime, was applauded and encored. After an encore, he paced back onto the stage and remarked, "I see by the billboards that I am to read a story here to-morrow night, if you can call it reading when you say it without the book and don't lose your place. Let me practice on you now." Then he told the story of the man with the golden arm—evidently new to most of the audience as it was to Claxton. There was intense attention, and when he closed with "Where is my golden arm? You have got it," [15] there was a universal shriek and several screams. Claxton was especially interested in observing dignified professors and other solemn people laughing hilariously.

He attended the churches quite regularly. At the Presbyterian Church, which seemed to him to be a very tall steeple with a church attached, he attended a series of lectures by the minister on the history of the church. At one lecture he arrived just in time to hear the preacher say, "Adam was a Presbyterian, Noah was a Presbyterian, Abraham was a Presbyterian, David was a Presbyterian, Isaiah was a Presbyterian, and, with all due reverence do I say it, Jesus Christ was a Presbyterian." His Presbyterian audience assented.

He was present at some of the sessions of the Centennial Conference of the Methodist Church. The senior bishop preached the Conference sermon to a crowded house with standing room only. Claxton stood two hours listening. Finally the bishop began to skip over some of the pages, and from over the house there came a shout, "Read it; read it." So he continued to read. His sermon dealt with the relation and conflict of science and religion. Claxton recalled only this: [15] "I hear the brethren complaining of the dangers of science and modern learning. We Methodists are largely responsible. We started it a hundred years ago. If you are not able and willing to take the consequences, get out." The church he attended most frequently was a Methodist Church, whose pastor later became Bishop Wilson and in whose choir was a very beautiful young woman, a "second object of distant worship." [15]

What the young lady might have thought of Claxton, even if she were aware of his adoration, is problematical. At that time, he had his handsome face covered with a full beard. This was then the style. Woodrow Wilson appears in a picture of a Hopkins musical club, wearing sideburns.

Claxton was a member of the Shakespeare Club, of which Dr. Remsen, famous professor of chemistry, was the leader, and heard some of the twenty lectures on Shakespeare which were delivered, from January 23 to March 11, 1885, by Professor Hiram Corson of Cornell. Other special lecturers whom he heard were Simon Newcomb, the American astronomer, and Sir William Thomson (Lord Kelvin), mathematician and physicist.

On Commemoration Day, February 23, an honorary degree was given to Greely, the famous Arctic explorer. The degree of Doctor of Philosophy was conferred on four candidates. President Gilman delivered the annual address on "The Benefits Which Society Derives from Universities." "Gilman was an excellent man," Claxton declared,[15] "with fine ideas of what a university should be. He knew that teachers make schools and make them in their own image and likeness. Members of his faculty were chosen with great care."

Excessive study caused Claxton to have a nervous break in March which forced him to leave Hopkins. "Probably the most important result of my year at Hopkins," Claxton considered,[15] "was learning something of what real scholarship means—the difference between exact comprehensive knowledge and the rather jejune work at The University of Tennessee. Possibly this was Hopkins' greatest contribution to America at that time."

From Baltimore Claxton went first to Blowing Rock to see what progress had been made in the hotel project, work on which he had been directing by letter during the winter. He got off the train at Roanoke for breakfast and then let the train leave without him, partly that he might spend some time observing the city public schools. During the day he saw the new hotel in Roanoke, which gave him an idea for improving his hotel. While waiting for the next train, he sat down on the railroad track and sketched a new plan. His original plan provided for fifty rooms with two stories and a long sloping roof. All the framing, weather boarding, ceiling, and flooring had been cut accordingly. The revised plan added twenty-five rooms and two second-story porches, twelve feet wide, extending the full length of the building. When he arrived at Blowing Rock, much to his surprise, all the larger framing fitted this new plan perfectly, and no lumber, already cut, had to be discarded. The cost of construction was only $500 more, as doors and windows had to be added. "A skilled architect," Claxton thought,[15] "probably could not have done it."

One morning while talking to the workmen, he fell to the floor unconscious. Soon recovering, he rode next day a gray mule twenty-seven miles through the untracked snow to Cranberry, and boarded a train for Chattanooga. There he conferred with his partner, Nick Van Dyke, and learned that he had lost heavily on an unwise investment in cotton and was unable to meet his part of the payment which was then due. He had only $500 left, which he offered to Claxton to release him from the contract, but Claxton refused to take the money. After a short visit with his family, he returned to Blowing Rock, where he and Finley found another partner, a farmer and trader named Newt Corpening, to take Van Dyke's place.

Claxton spent all spring in directing the completion of the hotel. A ram was installed in the spring to force water through pipes to the hotel. The rates of the Watauga Hotel, as it was named, were advertised at $1.50 a day for room and board. It was open and ready for guests on July 1, and Claxton then went to Snow Hill, North Carolina, to hold a two weeks' institute for teachers. The hotel did not fill up the first week, and Finley and Corpening thought it advisable to reduce the rates to one dollar a day, though no change was made in the advertisements. This was ill advised, for as Claxton returned from Snow Hill forty-five guests went up the mountain with him. The hotel soon became overcrowded; some had to sleep on the porches and in the halls.

All summer Claxton was busy looking after the hotel. For exercise he climbed mountains. This outdoor life was good for him, as he still "had the feeling of a jelly fish, all nerves," [15] and it was several years before he completely recovered from the nervous disorder.

The hotel remained crowded until the middle of September, when it closed for the season. There had been 750 guests from a large number of states North and South. Among these were prominent people, the Woodrows of South Carolina, the Battles and Senator Ransom and family of North Carolina. The food was excellent and plentiful. Beef then cost only four cents a pound, milk ten cents a gallon, and butter twelve cents a pound. Potatoes, apples, berries, beans, etc., cost fifty cents a bushel. After the hotel closed, Claxton and Tom Ransom, son of the Senator, stayed on at the hotel, living chiefly on the surplus food. He and his partners made that summer ten per cent on the cost of the hotel and its furnishings. "This experience was well worthwhile," Claxton concluded. [15]

V

Student of German Schools

◇◇

HAVING DECIDED to get married and go to Europe to study the German school system, Claxton sold his interest in the Watauga Hotel to his partners for what he had invested in it, about $1500. Early in December, 1885, he was married to Varina Staunton Moore, the daughter of Dr. William Moore and Emily Webb Moore. Claxton first met Varina while she was visiting her younger sister Annie, who taught in the Goldsboro schools while he was there. He became better acquainted with her during the following summer in a "campus course" during the summer school at the University of North Carolina. Her mother, of Newbern, was considered the most beautiful woman in North Carolina in her day. For awhile she was the principal of the Goldsboro Academy for Women, where her two daughters were afterwards educated. She died when they were small children, and Miss Corinne Dortch, daughter of the Senator, became practically their mother. Their father married again—a rather unhappy marriage, to which several children were born. Sometime before Claxton first went to Goldsboro, Dr. William Moore had died. Varina and Annie lived with their Aunt Nellie Moore, widow of an uncle, in Goldsboro and with Dr. Duncan Moore, another uncle, in Wilson. Annie taught in Goldsboro, and Varina in a school in Selma, of which the principal was Henry Louis Smith, afterwards president, in turn, of Davidson College and Washington and Lee University.[1]

The Moores were descended from Roger Moore who led a disastrous rebellion in Ireland in 1643 and had to flee to Flanders. His grandson, James Moore, was sent to Barbados as an endentured slave, where he was released by adherents of the Stuarts. He there eventually married the daughter of Sir John Yeamans, whose father had been hanged at Bristol because of his loyalty to King Charles I. Some years later James Moore came to Carolina, and his family intermarried with the Quince family, successful and wealthy shipowners. There were traditions in the family of Moore estates and a Quince inheritance in England which might be recoverable, but all these reports proved to be mirages.[2]

The Moores intermarried with many of the important families in early North Carolina history. Among these were the Ashe, Nash, Davis, Hill, London, Stedman, and Waddell families. Wealthy land owners and slave holders, the Moores lost practically everything as a result of the War between the States.

"Rena" Moore's marriage to Claxton was long remembered by the women of Goldsboro, chiefly because of the "wedding trip"— the "couple" went "abroad,"[3] an unusual event in the little town in those days. They traveled by way of Washington to New York where they took passage on a 3500 ton passenger vessel of the Hamburg Steamship Line. Annie Moore accompanied them to travel, and to study painting in Germany. Mrs. Claxton, who had inherited her mother's beauty, also had an excellent singing voice,[4] which she expected to improve under the training of a German teacher.

Claxton's young wife and her sister were seasick from the time the boat was out of sight of land until it came in sight of Ireland. The navigation was by dead reckoning, as it was cloudy during the entire voyage; but the first observation of the sun near Ireland showed that the discrepancy in the reckoning was only a few yards. Claxton was not seasick but did not particularly enjoy the voyage. Almost all the passengers were German. He remembered only the very dignified captain; a very fussy, conceited, much bejewelled, wealthy old lady, who was a nuisance to the captain; and a very delightful German girl, who said "many strength" for "much strength."

Landing at Hamburg, they were conveyed to a hotel by cab for a fare of only one mark. This amazed Claxton for he had paid in

New York about twenty times as much cab fare for equal that distance. At the same time, he felt reassured at the low cost of living in Germany as his financial resources were limited. They did not tarry long in Hamburg but went directly to Leipzig, where they arrived on Christmas Eve. The manager of Lebe's Hotel, where they spent that night, invited them to attend the Christmas party which he was giving for the employees. There was a tree and there were presents, all of which Claxton noticed were useful gifts. From this hotel they soon moved to more permanent quarters in two rooms on Haertel Strasse.

Claxton chose to go to Leipzig because it was a musical center, had an excellent system of schools, and was the home of a great university, then very popular among American students, as he had learned at Hopkins. Both Dr. Adams and Dr. Hall had studied there. Claxton had not then read the latter's *Aspects of German Culture*, which gives a scholarly account of the city and its culture. "No one is fonder or prouder of his city, dialect, folk-festivals, ancient customs, etc.," wrote [5] Hall, "than the average inhabitant of Leipzig. It has been half-humorously known all over Germany for half a century as the little Paris. Since its population reached 100,000 about 1870, it is designated as a *Gross-stadt*; and as its inhabitants are descended from very varied nationalities, and its institutions attract a great number of foreigners, it is quite cosmopolitan, or a *Weltstadt*. It is, moreover, pre-eminently a *Cultur-stadt*, or the 'German Athens.' Yet it is a rather dirty, unhealthy city, with an atmosphere full of dust and smoke, and with only surface-drainage for many of its streets. It fills but a small space in the guide-books. . . . On the other hand, Leipzig is the center of the German booktrade, with nearly fifty printing-houses, over 200 bookstores, and a unique booksellers' exchange. It was the home of Bach, and here his music is best performed. It is the stronghold of Wagnerism; and the great *Maestro* himself, more than once, has personally directed the production of his Nibelungen trilogy here. The new and magnificently equipped opera house, the Conservatory of Music, the famous Gewandhaus concerts, etc., all together make Leipzig—if the verdict of its inhabitants is impartial—the musical capital of the world. Homeopathy and the German scientific agriculture originated here, and are commemorated by monuments to Hahnemann and Thaer, respectively. Its university had last semester about 4000 students, and it is rivalled only by that of Berlin. There are certain streets and restaurants where, I have been told, every other man was a professor, an author, or a critic more or less known to fame."

Claxton and his wife and sister-in-law rented rooms on the second floor of a house on Haertel Strasse. On the same floor lodged Dr. Adams, later professor of history in the University of Missouri, with his wife and four year old daughter. Across the hall roomed Dr. Duncan, afterwards professor of philosophy at Yale. He had been in Germany long enough to learn more of practical German than Claxton knew, though the latter knew more German grammar and could read the language better than the former. They, accordingly, made an agreement to read German literature together for two or three hours a day. In addition to Claxton's purpose of studying German schools and hearing lectures in the University of Leipzig, he wished to get a more practical knowledge of the German language. So for several months he and Dr. Duncan read together from the works of Goethe, Schiller, Von Kleist, Herder, Lessing, and others. Their plan was not to refer to grammars or dictionaries unless absolutely necessary and not to translate into English. By turns they read aloud to each other to accustom their ears and voices to the German. If a word or phrase was not understood at first, they made for it the best meaning they could, and waited for it to appear again and again until the meaning was revealed. Thus some thousands of pages were read.

Claxton also had an arrangement with a German university student to teach him English while he taught Claxton German. They read, walked, and talked together alternately in German and English. On one of these walks, Claxton asked him about his reading and learned that the German had not read as much of the best German literature as he had. When he asked him, however, if he had read Goethe's *Hermann and Dorothea*, he began reciting the poem and continued until Claxton stopped him, fully assured that he had read the poem.

Claxton attended a few lectures in the University. In the philosophic curriculum of the University of Leipzig at this time, physiological psychology had assumed an almost supreme position; there were also courses in the theory and history of education. Though Claxton was told by American students in Germany that he might obtain a Ph.D. in one year, and was advised to do so, he decided that circumstances were not then favorable for such intensive study. Instead he visited the schools of the city in order to study at first hand the German system of public education. As early as 1861, Henry Barnard [6] considered the Burgher class of public primary schools in Leipzig to have the most complete plan of organization of all such schools in Germany. They were designed for middle class children and those of the upper class whose parents wished them to have a public education. The system was so devised as to enable students at the age of eleven, after five years in school, to begin different courses, according to their inclination or preparation for life. Those wishing to follow a trade remained in the school for three more years and then began an apprenticeship or entered a trade school; those expecting to follow higher occupations left the school and entered what was called the "real school" for five years; and those qualified for the learned professions went at eleven to a gymnasium where they graduated at eighteen and then spent three more years at a university, being ready for a profession at twenty-one.

Leipzig was in Saxony. According to the statistics of 1889, only three years after Claxton's visit, this German state had one university with 3,583 students and 184 professors; four polytechnic and professional schools with 88 teachers and 734 students; 58 gymnasia and other high schools with 14,439 students and 958 teachers; nineteen normal schools with 2,475 students and 267 teachers; 87 industrial and trade schools with 7,618 students and 458 teachers; 28 industrial high schools with 7,912 students and 316 teachers; twelve art schools with 3,288 students and 242 teachers; 32 commercial and nine agricultural schools with 7,179 students and 260 teachers; eleven special schools for young ladies with 1,081 students and 81 teachers; three military schools with 789 students and 39 teachers; 4,139 public schools with 654,732 pupils; eleven schools for defective children, eleven reform schools, and 90 parochial and private schools with 6,732 pupils and 593 teachers. The total cost for these schools was nearly $7,000,000. The elementary and high public schools cost $4,500,000, more than half of which was paid by local taxes and the rest by the state government. The entire population was about 3,500,000, about twice that of North Carolina at that time, though its area was equal to only about ten central counties of that state. This amazing support of education was given in spite of the heavy burden of a monarchical government and a large standing army, though natural resources were limited.[7]

"Some of my best lessons in education," declared Claxton,[8] "were learned in the schools of Leipzig." One morning he visited the third district school, a Burgher school attended by about 1500 boys. At the age of eight, boys and girls were placed in separate schools. Claxton was permitted to observe the teaching of a class in the seventh grade. As he entered the room, the teacher was asking, "Who remembers anything that has happened which has affected the way the people are acting and thinking in Leipzig at the present time?" The boys recalled one thing after another. One remembered the conquest of Constantinople. Everything was brought down to Leipzig as the center of book publishing. The recitation lasted forty-five minutes, the last five minutes being devoted to summarizing, unifying, and applying the knowledge which had been brought out in the discussion. The class had no textbook, but the 4th, 5th, and 6th grades had little reading books. Claxton asked the teacher if the students remembered all they read. He replied with a question, "What do they read it for?"[9] The teacher was familiar with all that the students had covered up to the time they entered his classes, and examinations were devised to cover everything the student had learned. This school gave Claxton the same feeling he would have had in entering a room where there was an electric dynamo.

Claxton was also favorably impressed by the other schools he visited. He liked particularly the great thoroughness of the work and the skill of the well trained teachers. They were mostly men who had completed preparation in normal schools and been given temporary licenses to teach under supervision and inspection from two to five years, meantime following courses arranged by training school and state school officials. Then if they satisfied an examination in subject matter, theory, and practice of teaching, they took the oath of office as professional teachers. Their tenure of office was practically permanent, and they were highly respected by students, parents, and people in general. On a Sunday afternoon Claxton walked with a teacher in a small town where he taught, and every person they passed bowed respectfully and said, "Abend Herr Lehrer" [9] (Good evening, Professor). The high school (gymnasium) teachers all had the Ph.D. degree or a government certificate, the requirements for which were as high as for that degree.

The class time was for teaching and not chiefly for recitation as in American schools. The German children gave strict attention and kept busy. They learned to listen and remember. Seldom was there evidence of inattention. Only once did Claxton see a child whisper to another during a lesson. There were forty-five minutes of intense work and then fifteen minutes of rest. There was no recreation period, as in American schools. Health seemed to be well cared for and Claxton noticed that more of the children wore glasses than in American schools. Though he had never seen schools so well equipped nor such skillful teaching, he felt that both teaching and discipline were too much *auf commando*. Mark Twain once said that they brand the German boys as we brand Texas ponies.

W. S. Learned,[10] who spent a year as an exchange teacher in a Leipzig gymnasium a few years after Claxton was there, thought the teachers emphasized too much the drilling of facts into the heads of their students. Discipline was easy, he stated, because the students were anxious to do well as their whole future depended on passing the examinations. A common method he noted was lecturing, interspersed with questions answered in concert by all who knew the answers. Claxton, more favorable, thought that the German schools were influenced greatly by the philosophy of Pestalozzi, and that the teaching was consequently both inductive and deductive and not characterized by mere memory drills. The great lessons he learned about German teaching, however, were the value of definite preparation for teaching as a profession and the importance of thoroughness. He had never before seen such power and definiteness in teaching.

Annie Moore meanwhile was taking art lessons with an artist of some ability who had a studio in an old castle in the city. Mrs. Claxton was having music lessons, vocal and piano, with the second violinist of the Symphony Orchestra of the New City Theater, who was also a good vocalist.

Fortunately that winter the best singers in Germany gave all of Wagner's operas, except those of the Nibelungen Ring group, to raise funds to erect a monument to the great composer, who was born in Leipzig and had died in February, 1883. The operas were given in the New City Theater. The orchestra of 99 pieces from this theater was said to be the best in Europe. Claxton and his wife and her sister heard most of these operas. The best seats cost only seventy-five cents; Claxton heard the "Flying Dutchman" from a gallery seat for about twelve cents. Sitting next to him was a woman who made her living carrying coal up several flights of steps.

They also saw Goethe's *Faust*, five hours for the first part and four hours for the second; Schiller's *Wilhelm Tell*; and other great plays. The theaters were required to give plays and music at low prices for tickets for the masses of the people on Wednesday evenings and Sunday mornings. They presented Italian as well as Wagnerian operas and plays by Shakespeare in addition to those by German playwrights. The theaters were usually crowded with standing room only. In Leipzig, then, the average working man and woman had better opportunities for this kind of culture than anyone in the United States could get at any price. One morning Claxton asked Frau Lange, who sublet to him the rooms which she herself rented, did their laundry, and cooked their dinners, if she had heard a certain opera advertised in the morning paper. "Yes, three times," she replied. He then asked her about other operas as well as plays and oratorios, and found that she was better informed about these than any of his friends and acquaintances in America. Her husband was a locksmith who worked for seventy-five cents a day, but they managed to see the best plays and hear the finest music in the world. She was studying English with the hope of going to America sometime, not realizing how well off she was at home.

The Claxtons and Annie attended services at the Thomas-Kirche and the Matthew-Kirche more often than at other churches. At the latter they heard an oratorio sung at Easter by a large chorus of more than 300 of the best singers in Germany. One of these, Frau

Materna, Austrian court singer, Claxton thought, had the richest voice he had ever heard. The same day they witnessed, at Peters-Kirche, the confirmation of children who had finished the eighth grade of the folk schools—a beautiful and impressive ceremony. Occasionally they went to the Thomas-Kirche on Saturday at noon to hear the Motett singing by the boys of the Thomas-Schule, of which Bach was once "cantor." All these musical services were of the highest order, but the sermons seemed to Claxton to have been committed to memory and reminded him of the oratory of American school boys.

The common people were very religious, religion being required as a subject of study in all schools. Most of the people attended church early on Sundays. After services, they went to the theaters, parks, or beer gardens. On winter mornings the young folks took their skates to church so they would lose no time on the frozen ponds, some of which were the old moats outside the walls of the old city.

"It is very difficult for an American to understand the religious conditions of Germany," wrote G. Stanley Hall,[11] a few years before Claxton went to Leipzig. "There seems everywhere to be a strong reaction against the naturalism of the founders of the Tübingen school. The cruder and undiscriminating forms of unbelief, which are intolerant of Bible, church, and creed, are found no longer except among Socialists. Among the clergy of the Lutheran Church, there is the greatest diversity of sentiment and opinion, ranging from the philosophical rationalism of Strauss to the straitest sort of orthodoxy. A prominent clergyman lately complained to the writer that during the last twenty years, while Berlin had doubled in population, only two new churches had been built."

"Although the religious sentiment in the Teutonic heart is strong and ineradicable," continued Hall, "it exists there independent of, and indifferent or else positively hostile to, even Scriptural dogma. A cultivated mother of a large family, e.g., a clergyman's daughter and a very constant church-goer, rather surprised her husband the other day by saying in answer to the writer's questions that she never had believed in the miracles of the New Testament nor in a personal immortality. Religious belief and rites are considered as aesthetic formulizations of pious feeling, and as a most essential part of the ideal side of life and culture, identified in its essence with the higher forms of art, and in its interests (as opposed to the modern materialistic philosophy of science and the understanding) with the idealistic and absolute philosophy of Fichte, Schelling, Hegel, etc. Methodism, represented here by a little chapel with a congregation of less than forty, is absolutely unintelligible to the German mind."

Claxton did not discover this Methodist chapel. For Americans of all denominations except Roman Catholics, services were held in one of the Leipzig school buildings. There was, however, an English chapel, where the Claxtons attended worship one Sunday. By a strange coincidence, they sat just behind a pew marked with the nameplate, "Mr. and Mrs. Claxton." They did not, however, become acquainted with these English "cousins." The Claxtons did not come in contact with spiritualism, then "extensively cultivated in private social circles in Leipzig especially in families of comfortable business men." [12]

Nor did Claxton hear or read of the Socialist leaders, Bebel and Liebknecht. "The fiery little Bebel, when he is neither in the Reichstag nor in prison," wrote Hall,[13] "has always been ready to leave his lathe, don his coat, and talk earnestly by the hour to any interested visitor about the injustice of the government to the cause he represents. Liebknecht also lives here, and collects abuses, edits his paper, and pushes his propaganda as far as circumstances and the laws permit." Claxton recalled, however, that the people of Saxony were not very enthusiastic then about Prussian domination, resenting particularly the militarism of the domineering Prussians. Emperor William I then ruled Germany, with the able assistance of "blood-and-iron" Bismarck. By that time the strong arm of the government was being felt even in the universities. "The state now [1881] regards the universities," according to Hall, "as one of the means for the accomplishment of its ends, which they are too unpractical to be trusted to determine without guidance or even dictation. Hence no complaint is more common in university circles than that of the absoluteness of the state, which, although generally leaving the universities to manage their own affairs as of old, has not scrupled on several conspicuous occasions of late to assert its supremacy, reversing the decisions of academic senates, and even deposing professors and suppressing their works. Teachers of political or philosophical subjects who show their loyalty by zealously espousing the cause of the Government are generally promoted rapidly."

Goethe's *Faust* being Claxton's favorite literary work, he visited the Auerbach's Keller on Grimmaische Strasse, the setting for one of the scenes in this drama, with its curious murals of the sixteenth century portraying the traditional background of the play. Goethe was for awhile a student at the University of Leipzig. Accompanied by Annie Moore, the art student, the Claxtons visited many other points of interest in the city, among which was the museum where they saw the sculptures and the picture gallery.

When Claxton went to Germany, his plan was to study there two years and then to return to Hopkins to finish the requirements for the Ph.D. degree. But for reasons, chiefly financial,[15] he was forced to return home after six months. Near the end of April, he and his wife and her sister left Leipzig and went to Dresden, where they spent a week. Here they found better architecture and more beautiful parks than in Leipzig, and one of the greatest picture galleries in the world. From there they traveled by way of Hof to Munich, where they remained about two months. They found this capital city of Bavaria filled with interesting palaces, churches, educational institutions, museums, and art galleries, the Old and New Pinakothek for pictures and the Glyptothek for sculpture. On the Isar River they saw the English Garden, laid out by Count Rumford in imitation of an English park, and two or three miles outside the city the magnificent grounds of the summer palace of King Louis II, the mad king of Bavaria.

Early in June, they went by train across Germany to Mainz, and from there took the scenic boat trip down the Rhine to Rotterdam, where they went aboard the *Rotterdam* for Philadelphia. Arriving here about the first of July, they went down to Baltimore, where Claxton was planning to secure a position in the public schools to support his family while he continued his graduate work at Hopkins. At the office of the Superintendent of City Schools he found the Assistant Superintendent in charge, to whom he explained the purpose of his visit and gave an account of his professional qualifications and experience. After he had recounted these details, the

[59]

Assistant inquired if he had any special influence with any member of the Board of Education. "No," briefly replied Claxton. "Have you any friend or relative on the City Council?" queried the Assistant. "No," Claxton repeated and then added, "My only recommendation is that I can teach." The reply was, "That counts for very little here. I advise you not to pursue your application further." Claxton accordingly continued his journey to North Carolina.

Though his studies of German schools had not advanced him any nearer the Ph.D. at Hopkins, which Claxton estimated would have taken him three years to secure, yet he returned home with new and valuable practical knowledge of pedagogy, a greatly increased knowledge of German literature and facility in speaking the language, and a much broader cultural background. For the great work he was destined to do, it was just the preparation which he needed.

In recognition of his studies in Germany and at Johns Hopkins, The University of Tennessee in 1887 conferred the master's degree on Claxton. No residence work was required, but he submitted a thesis on Goethe's *Faust*, his favorite book.

VI

North Carolina School Superintendent

◇◇

ARRIVING IN North Carolina, Claxton and his wife spent the summer at Morganton in the western part of the state. Miss Annie Moore went to visit relatives in Goldsboro. During the summer Claxton was offered the superintendency of the schools of Greenville, South Carolina, and of Wilson, North Carolina. He accepted the latter position at a salary of $1200, mainly because his wife's uncle, Dr. Duncan Moore, lived there and she had many friends in that town.

The Wilson graded school had been organized after a mass meeting of citizens was addressed on July 8, 1881, by Superintendent Alexander Graham, of the Fayetteville graded school, on "Graded Schools, Their Organization and Management." A committee of five secured enough money by private subscription to supplement the local public school apportionment for supporting the school for a year. It was opened the following autumn about the same time the one in Goldsboro was organized. In 1883, Wilson was one of the fifteen towns in North Carolina which were fully supported under the provisions of the Dortch Act.

From the beginning, the school had been warmly supported by the local newspaper, The Advance, edited by the boy editor, Josephus Daniels, a native of Wilson. In his Tar Heel Editor,[1] Daniels lauds Wilson as "a community free from caste or social chasms, as true a democracy as the world has known," and as "the loveliest village of the plain," a town of beautiful trees. "If there is a more beautiful and restful-looking street anywhere in the world than Nash Street, I have not seen it," he continues.[2] It was strictly a cotton town with two carriage factories, one foundry, a plow factory, and a cotton mill.[3] In 1884, however, the farmers in that vicinity raised their first crops of tobacco experimentally, for which they received four times as much per acre as for cotton; and then tobacco soon dethroned cotton as king.[4] The chief amusements were church festivals, fish fries and picnics at Contentnea Creek, participation in politics, and reminiscing about the late war and reconstruction.[5] For young men the chief cultural feature was the Shakespeare Club which had been organized by Henry Blount. He had spent some time as a salesman in New York, and aspired to be an actor.[6]

When Claxton went to Wilson as superintendent of schools, Josephus Daniels was in Raleigh where he had gone the previous year to become editor of the *State Chronicle*. His brother Charles then took over the Wilson *Advance*. Claxton had roomed with Charles Daniels in Kinston, where he was editor of the *Free Press*, and had known the oldest brother, Frank, a young lawyer, in Goldsboro. One summer in Wilson he boarded with their mother, whom he characterized as "a strong, fine, courageous woman with a good mind."[7] The Daniels brothers, Governor Charles B. Aycock, and many other distinguished North Carolinians were educated at the Wilson Collegiate Institute. At the time Claxton was in Wilson, the reputation of this school had declined; President Hassel was scholarly and much esteemed but old and quite peculiar in his habits.[7]

Claxton's memories of Wilson were not so nostalgic as those of Josephus Daniels. Among its population of 2,500 were many wealthy old families, landowners, and merchants. There was much leisure among the whites; the Negroes did most of the work. The culture was of the kind derived from local female colleges and academies for boys. The women played the piano and sang in fairly good church choirs. Churches of various denominations were quite strong. There was a small opera house or hall for plays. The lawyers, graduates of Wake Forest, Trinity, or the State University, had little business and much leisure. Oratory was popular.[7]

The first superintendent of the Wilson graded schools was

Julius L. Tomlinson, who had been a member of the Normal School of the University of North Carolina.[8] He was succeeded by E. C. Branson, and he in turn by Claxton. When the Dortch Law was declared unconstitutional, the school at Wilson was supported by private contributions to supplement the regular state, county, and district funds. That was the condition of affairs when Claxton took over the superintendency.

The school was housed in an old building, which had once been used for a woman's college. The campus was large and beautiful. There were only eight grades. Claxton thought the most important function of a superintendent was the promotion of good teaching and not chiefly taking care of the finances and material affairs of the school. He accordingly spent a large part of his time in the schoolrooms observing and helping the teachers and in teachers' meetings, discussing the principles and methods of education and their practical application. He contended that practical teaching must be related to the environment in which the children lived and probably would work when they left school. As an example of impractical teaching he recalled the old and much respected primary teacher, who had taught the parents and some of the grandparents of the children in her room. When the circus came to town and the parade passed the school, she kept all the children in the room, and some time later punished them because they could not describe large animals in Africa.

While visiting the classrooms, Claxton tried to find out just how much real knowledge the children were getting. One day he went into a fourth year room just as a lesson in geography ended. The teacher said she wished he had come earlier, for the children had recited the best lesson they had had, and every child knew it well. She then asked him if he would like to hear them recite it again. "No," he said, "but I should like to ask them a few questions." The lesson which was on Moscow went somewhat like this: "Imagine yourself approaching the great city on a fete day. You look down on the many domes covered with burnished gold and on the towering spires piercing the blue sky, etc." Then the book related how the citizens burned the city in order to drive Napoleon's army out into the cold and snows of a Russian winter to perish. Claxton's first question was, "What is a dome?" No answer. To the forty pupils it was merely d-o-m-e. Finally a small boy in a falsetto voice replied, "Mr. Claxton, one of them things what's on the capitol at Washington." "What is burnished gold?" was the next question. This seemed easier to them. They remembered the city had been burned. So "burnished gold" must be burnt gold used for covering domes. Wrong association of ideas. Then he asked the meaning of "spire." Silence again for awhile. Then the boy with the falsetto voice, encouraged by his first display of knowledge, squirmed in his seat and answered, "One of them men what goes about seeing things." To him it seemed a reasonable supposition that one who spies was a "spire." These simple questions indicated to Claxton that the children had little real knowledge of their "perfect" lesson.[9]

At the close of the school year, the school was discontinued temporarily until the citizens were willing to vote the necessary local school tax under the new law providing schools for Negroes and whites from the same funds. At a meeting of the Board of Education Claxton made a plea, arguing [9] that, "though some of the members of the board and some of the richer men might pay taxes more than the tuition of their children in private schools would cost, they could afford to pay the taxes for the general welfare and for the advantages which their children would have in living in a more intelligent and prosperous community." The Chairman of the Board, a lawyer and a politician, remarked, after the meeting adjourned, "I do not understand you. If other children are educated as well as mine, what advantage will my children have over them?" The main basis of the opposition was that many "respectable" people did not believe in educating the "white trash" and the Negroes. Throughout the state and the South generally, the people of property naturally objected to paying such a school tax, and besides there were some private school teachers who feared that they would lose their jobs.

During the summer Claxton taught four weeks in a summer normal in Wilson and in county institutes of a week each in eastern and central North Carolina. While he and Alderman were holding one of these in Asheville, an election was held to decide whether a local tax would be levied for the support of schools. The measure was approved by a majority of only one vote. It had failed in the two previous elections. The favorable impression Claxton had made in Asheville led to his election as superintendent of schools there. The salary was $1200. The schools were not to open until the following January. Meanwhile Claxton taught in the Goldsboro schools, of which Alderman had become superintendent when Moses went to Raleigh as head of the schools.[10]

Shortly before Christmas Claxton went to Asheville with his family. During the summer his wife and daughter Claire, born the previous September 19, 1886, in Wilson, had visited Mrs. London, an aunt in Pittsburg, North Carolina; afterwards they had been living in Goldsboro. Asheville, the largest of North Carolina mountain towns, then had a population of about 7,500. Surrounded by magnificent scenery, it had already become a summer resort for Southern families of wealth and culture, and a winter resort for Northerners of similar social standing. There were several good hotels, and most of the private homes were boarding houses. There was considerable money in circulation, but the natives spent more than they should in trying to keep up with the visitors.

Before Claxton's arrival, most of the teachers had already been chosen, some on his recommendation. The Board of Education, composed of four white men and one Negro, was a progressive one, seriously interested in the development of the schools. There had been no public school buildings; so the Board purchased a small brick building in which Captain Venable, a graduate of the University of Virginia and then an engineer and architect, had conducted a small school for boys, known as the Venable Academy. The following year a new building was erected, composed of ten classrooms and a large study hall. For the Negro school a building was purchased by the Board. Only one of the buildings was fit for use as a school, according to modern standards.

Claxton indoctrinated his teachers, untrained but of good native ability, with his pedagogical methods and aims, which by that time he had rather definitely formulated. Everything was made ready for the opening, it was thought; but the first day 500 white children and 250 Negro children applied for admission. This was about three times as many as the Board of Education had expected, and it became necessary to limit the schools that winter and spring to five grades. Both the schools were filled immediately, and the

Negro school was overcrowded, with ninety-five children in one room. As there had been no public schools in Asheville for several years, the average of the children in the first grade was twelve years. The teachers, all women, were paid only $25 to $30 a month; but, intelligent and co-operative, they were the best that most Asheville people had ever known. The principal of the white school was a graduate of the State University, but received only $50 per month. In the spring of 1888 bonds were voted for the erection of another building to replace the old Academy. Later a new schoolhouse was built for the Negroes and later still two more for the white children. An increase in the tax rate and the city appropriation made possible the doubling of the number of the teachers and the adding of the sixth and seventh grades the second year. The following year the eighth grade was added, and two years later the ninth grade.

The elections approving the issuance of bonds for new schoolhouses were hotly contested. In one of these, close co-operation developed between the supporters of schools and those interested in street improvements, and Claxton found himself standing by the side of the owner of the principal barrooms in the city, each handing out ballots for schools and streets. Thus grew the interest of the people of Asheville in public education.

Claxton and his teachers were largely responsible for this. They worked hard. Teachers' meetings for all were held twice a month, and group meetings almost every day. Papers were read and discussed on Froebel, Rousseau, Pestalozzi, and other pioneers in education, and on the principles of the kindergarten, Greek education, psychology, and the methods of teaching special subjects. Claxton's office was usually closed during school hours; he spent most of his time in the classrooms, observing, advising, and helping the teachers. According to Julia Johnson,[11] one of his teachers, "He was most inspiring to his teachers; we would attempt *anything* for him. He simply surcharged us with the desire to carry out his ideals. . . . I have known him to come into my classroom, take the children in hand and teach them as well as it possibly could be done— first year children! . . . He would sometimes come in, take charge of the clay-modeling class, make models, and teach the modeling as if it were an everyday affair with him."

[66]

For the new school the second year more teachers had to be employed. Among those recommended by Claxton were a Jewess and a Roman Catholic, both brilliant and able. A good Baptist on the Board suggested, "We had better stay within our Protestant groups." Claxton replied, "I never ask about religious applications. I do not know officially about the church membership of any of the teachers." The Jewess was elected as the music teacher, and the schools gained such a good reputation in music that the winter tourists from the North frequently came to hear the children sing. The following year, Claxton again submitted the name of the Roman Catholic, remarking, "You remember; she is a Catholic." The man who had objected to her the previous year replied, "That is none of our business." [12]

Claxton introduced many innovations and tried many experiments in the schools. He employed special teachers for music and for drawing—almost unheard of then in the South. Systematic courses in nature study were introduced. These included much outdoor work; such as, excursions to fields, forests, and brook basins; to stores to find out what they had and from where; to mills and other industrial plants to observe their processes and learn about their raw materials and products; and to railway freight stations to study the exchange of goods. First hand information thus gained made more vital what the students read in their textbooks. With the aid of Northern residents in Asheville Claxton was able to establish kindergartens in the schools and later a school for preparing kindergarten teachers.[13] Later still, Mr. Pack, a wealthy man from Cleveland, Ohio, gave a kindergarten building. Only one other school then had a kindergarten in the South. That was in New Orleans. The Asheville schools soon gained the reputation of being the best in the state, and Claxton's salary was raised to $1500.

Another innovation was the introduction of good literature in all the grades—altogether thirty-five books in the nine grades. Very ingeniously Claxton had the children buy one set of these books, which they read and then gave to the school in exchange for another set purchased by the school without cost to the children. In this way books were accumulated until there were enough for all to read. The reading of entire books instead of disconnected selections in "readers" was encouraged. Also "phonics" was introduced as a means of giving children the ability to read without having to be drilled on new words.

The time devoted to arithmetic was reduced by cutting out the unused applications of subjects carried over from earlier days. Thus time was saved for the study of inductive geometry and algebra in the sixth and seventh grades.

Claxton also tried the experiment of promoting the teacher with the children from grade to grade up to the fifth when departmental teaching was begun. The experiment was tried first with one teacher, who was told that the first grade children she then had were to be hers for the next three years. She could group them and regroup them in each subject as she thought desirable, visit their homes and become familiar with their home environment, and at the beginning of the next year would know "what the teacher did with these children last year." The experiment worked so well that when the children were in the middle of the third grade they were well ahead of other children in the fourth grade, in advancement and in power.

Claxton then requested the Board to apply the principle to all the teachers. "All right," they said, "if my children are in Mrs. H's room, but what if they are in Miss Y's class?" "You employed them all," Claxton answered. "If the teacher is not good enough to teach the same class three or four years, why let three or four groups of children in turn waste their time with her for one year each?" He also suggested that a teacher who was only fairly good in the old system would do better teaching in a system which enabled her to learn the children better. "You seem very earnest. Try it," the Board agreed. It was put into effect and resulted in great improvement in the teaching.

The practice of grading by percentage figures was abandoned, and instead letters were sent monthly or bimonthly concerning the work and conduct of each child with suggestions as to how the parent might aid in improving the child's school work. "There was no ranking of children by term grades, with tears from the children and expostulations from the mothers," Claxton wrote.[13] "Teachers and children worked more for love of subjects and joy of knowing; less from artificial stimuli. There were no general examinations for promotion or demotion at the end of the school year. The teachers were told to promote such children as they were sure could do the work; demote those who surely could not; ask me for help about those in doubt; if parents objected to our judgment, give examinations."

Claxton's report [14] to the Board of Education for the scholastic year, 1889–1890, throws additional light on the character of his work and his pedagogical ideas and ideals. At that time there were two schools for white children: on Orange Street with a principal and eleven teachers and on Academy Street with a principal and six teachers. The Mountain Street School for the Negroes had a principal and two teachers. Besides the male principals there were only two other men teachers in all the schools. The total funds for the schools amounted to $15,435.51, more than three fourths of which came from the city tax. The enrollment totaled 1446 with an average daily attendance of less than half, which was considerably lower in the Negro school.

In his report, Claxton dealt with satisfaction and at length upon the growing respect of the people of Asheville for public schools and upon the decrease in the honest objection which some people had had to their children, particularly girls, associating with "the masses." He made a plea for an increase in appreciation of, and respect for, the teachers, and requested that the citizens visit the schools frequently to show their interest. "Rightly considered," he declared, "there is no other public enterprise in which every citizen should feel so great an interest, for on the public schools depends, to a greater extent than on all things else, the moral, the intellectual, and the business character of the Asheville of the future." Displeased with the low attendance, he logically urged the need for a compulsory attendance law with a truancy officer. For the future he recommended the introduction of manual training and physical education, and the establishment of a public high school. He registered his opposition to written examinations for determining the promotion of children to a higher grade, and to corporal punishment. Pupils who cannot be controlled by the use of other punishments, he claimed, should be removed; the public school is "not intended for a reformatory." With great warmth he defended moral education in the schools, through the proper use of the books of the Bible. In conclusion, he argued for better buildings and fair salaries for the teachers.

During the summers, while Claxton was superintendent of schools at Asheville, he helped conduct teachers' institutes. In 1889, State Superintendent Sidney M. Finger appointed Alderman and Charles D. McIver as Assistant Superintendents of Schools to conduct state institutes for teachers, initiated that year by the State Board of Education. Alderman covered the state from the sea to the foothills of the mountains; McIver from the foothills to the western boundary. The second year they exchanged territory. They were aided by Alexander Graham, J. Y. Joyner, M. C. S. Noble, Logan D. Howell, W. A. Blair, E. P. Moses, and Claxton.[15] The latter worked with his intimate friend, Alderman. McIver, a robust young farm boy, had just graduated from the University of North Carolina. He learned rapidly by experience and eventually became one of the most effective leaders for public education in his native state. According to Dumas Malone,[16] "Alderman may have charmed more audiences but McIver won more hearts."

The campaigners spent a week or two in each county, conferring with superintendents, principals, teachers, and trustees. On the last day, called *People's Day*, a mass meeting was addressed in a schoolhouse, church, court house, or warehouse. Sometimes two of these meetings were held on Wednesday and Friday. They had some of the spirit of a religious revival. The new gospel was summed up in the slogan, "Every child has the same right to be educated as he has to be free; the one right is as sacred as the other."[17] The purposes of these institutes were to carry to the people information about the schools, their needs, and means to improve them; to carry instruction in the meaning and methods of education to teachers who were unable to secure it; and to receive from teachers themselves suggestions as to the improvement of the school system.[18] These lasted from July 1, 1889, to August 22, 1892.

During the last summer, Claxton and Alderman worked in the western counties, preaching the doctrine of public education for all children regardless of race, color, or place in society—a doctrine they found to be very unpopular in some places. At Robbinsville, a mountain town in Graham County, after the meeting a group of those who had heard the addresses were overheard by Alderman to

[70]

say, "Men who talk like that ought to be lynched." [19] When he returned to the hotel, he reported this to Claxton. The next day, at Andrews in Cherokee County, some men, who were playing marbles, asked Alderman, "What'ur you fellers gittin' fur this?" Later the North Carolina mountain people became a stronghold for education.

The reports of the campaign showed that teachers, two thirds of whom were men, were inefficient and paid less than $30 a month on the average. County superintendents were paid an average salary of $175 a year. The school term was only four months long and the average attendance was 40 per cent of an incomplete enrollment of children of school age.[20]

Great sorrows came to the Claxton family in Asheville. On October 21, 1890, Mrs. Claxton's sister Annie, then a teacher of art in the schools there, died of typhoid fever. On September 12 of the next year, Mrs. Claxton, who had grieved deeply over the death of her sister, had a nervous breakdown followed by pneumonia. Claxton, who was engaged in institute work, returned home before her death. Her daughter Claire was then a few days less than five years old, and it was arranged for her great aunt, Mrs. Nellie Moore, a widow, to bring her only daughter Carrie who was a few years older than Claire, and keep house for Claxton. In September, 1890, his mother also died comparatively young, at the age of fifty-five.

Claxton remained in Asheville as superintendent of schools until the autumn of 1893, when he left to become Professor of Pedagogy and German in the newly established Normal and Industrial School at Greensboro, North Carolina.

❦ VII ❧

Normal School Professor

◇◇◇

O NE OF THE results of the interest awakened in the North Carolina public schools by the state institutes was the establishment of the Normal and Industrial School for Women at Greensboro. The bill, which was passed February 18, 1891, stated that its
objects were "to give young white women such education as should
fit them for teaching, and to give instruction in drawing, telegraphy,
typewriting, and such other industrial arts as might be suitable to
their sex and conducive to their support and usefulness." [1] Tuition
was to be free for those preparing to teach, and after an eight
months' session, the members of the faculty were to conduct
county institutes for eight weeks.

The school opened on October 5, 1892, with McIver as its president and with 176 students. [2] Alderman was Professor of History
and English Literature on the first faculty, but Claxton did not become Professor of Pedagogics and German until the autumn of the
following year, when Alderman left to become Professor of Education in the University of North Carolina. President McIver also
taught Pedagogics and Civics, and the members of the Department
of Pedagogy were then McIver, Claxton, and Fannie Cox Bell.

The courses offered were History of Education; Elementary Psychology; Science and Art of Education; and Principles, Methods of
Teaching, Discipline, and General School Management. The textbooks used in the first course were F. V. N. Painter's *History of
Education* with readings, G. Compayré's *History of Pedagogy*,

R. H. Quick's *Educational Reformers*, and Oscar Browning's *Educational Theories*. Special consideration was given to the educational ideas of Bacon, Comenius, Locke, Rousseau, Pestalozzi, Froebel, and Spencer. For the science and art of teaching the text-books were Joseph Payne's *Lectures on Education*, Wilhelm Rein's *Outlines of Pedagogy*, Charles De Garmo's *Essentials of Method*, and the McMurry books on the teaching of special subjects.

Claxton's German courses were "Reading Easy German, Reading Selections from Modern German, and German Classics," for sophomores, juniors, and seniors respectively. Speaking and writing German were taught in all three courses.

The third year McIver retired from the Department of Pedagogy and Claxton became its head. He also took charge of the Practice School which began that year with only fifteen students but grew to 126 the next year. He continued as head of the German Department, but was assisted by Bertha M. Lee who relieved him of the entire department the following year.

Claxton made changes, adopting E. A. Kirkpatrick's *Inductive Psychology* and G. A. Lindner's *Empirical Psychology* for the course in Elementary Psychology, and adding S. G. Williams' *History of Modern Education* and J. P. Monroe's *Educational Ideal* to the course on History of Education and J. Baldwin's *Elementary Psychology* and J. G. Fitch's *Lectures* to the course on Science and Art of Teaching. In 1897, he added graduate courses in the philosophy of education. These were based on K. Lange's *Apperception*, N. K. Davis' *Inductive Logic*, F. W. Dorpfeld's *Thought and Memory*, R. De Guimps' *Life and Works of Pestalozzi*, F. Froebel's *Education of Man*, and C. A. McMurry's *Method in the Recitation*. In addition to the parallel reading, two hours a week of lectures and two or three periods each day of teaching in the Practice School were required.[3] Claxton also gave normal extension correspondence courses.[3]

In his presentation of the history of education to his students Claxton emphasized the ideas, principles, and methods revealed in the practices and writings of the great educational thinkers and reformers. He began the course with a summary of education in North Carolina, ending with the question, "How has this come about?" The remainder of the course was an answer to this question. This device, used by Ben Franklin, Claxton considered a good one for teaching a subject with a historical background. In the course on psychology, application of its principles was constantly made to the methods of learning the various school subjects, to the formation of mental attitudes, desires, and feelings, to the promotion of purpose and will, and to the relation of biological and psychological development. Simple textbooks were used for beginners; Herbartian psychology for the advanced students. Special methods in teaching reading, arithmetic, geography, and language were discussed with the students, and then Claxton watched them teach in the Practice School to observe their application of the methods. A plan was worked out for the study of home geography in the primary grades and a whole year of the geography of North Carolina in the intermediate grades. Such a study was important for two reasons; one should have a comprehensive knowledge of his own state for practical purposes and for the aid thus afforded as a kind of measuring rod in learning the geography of other states. As a result of this experiment, he prepared a supplement on North Carolina geography for Alexis Everett Frye's *Complete Geography* (1896). "Believe it or not," declared Claxton, whose handwriting has long been the despair of his students, secretaries, and friends, "I also taught writing, and some graduates were paid additional salaries because they wrote so well." The method adopted was the vertical style of Newlands and Rowe.

Claxton was a very popular professor among the young women students. About forty-five years afterwards one of these wrote: "Dr. Claxton came to the school a very handsome young widower— black hair, heavenly blue eyes, as I thought them. He stood erect and walked with a stride—always seemed preoccupied. In the classroom the position I remember best was both hands in his coat pockets, thumbs out. He would rise on his toes as he grew interested in his subject. I shall never forget how he said 'Pesta*lotsi*' (Pestalozzi), placing his tongue back of his front teeth and opening his mouth on the syllable 'lot.' Pestalozzi was a favorite subject and basis for much of his teaching. Dr. Claxton was far ahead of his time in his teaching of methods. The *child* was of paramount importance. He really interpreted to us Pestalozzi, Goethe, Froebel—the great interpreters of childhood—and applied this knowledge to the schoolroom."

"I have talked with some of Dr. Claxton's former pupils who lived at the school," she continued, "and one said that he studied all the time, arriving at the school before the students had breakfast and leaving late in the afternoon. His neighbors in Greensboro said that his light burned late into the night—sometimes until four o'clock in the morning. . . . Dr. Claxton was a great teacher, as truly inspired as a great musician or artist, and he has been an inspiration to hundreds of teachers who are as grateful as I am for his teaching."

"Every year," wrote [5] another one of his students, "there were a certain number of students who fell very much in love with him. To his credit, if he knew this, he never paid the slightest attention to it; I doubt if he even knew it. He used the lecture method in his classroom almost entirely and he hated (and stated that fact frequently) to correct examination papers worse than anything in the world. When they were handed in, he sat right at his desk and read them then and there, and you had to go back and get your paper which he gave you with comments. . . . His was my favorite class while a student at the college and I unhesitatingly state that I remember more of what I absorbed under him than any other subject or teacher. I can still confound my daughter (an M.A. from U.N.C.) with bits of psychology I gleaned from Dr. Claxton's classes. I never fell in love with him but I liked him and found him one of the most original and amusing people I have ever encountered."

"Mr. Claxton was a very likable person," according to a third student,[6] "and there was a certain freedom in his classes. . . . He had quite a sense of humor. . . . I think I never saw him when he wore anything but a gray suit."

"It is hard to speak with restraint," wrote still another student,[7] "when I remember his brilliancy, his charm, and his magnetic personality, or when I think of his ability as a teacher. We in his class were inclined to be decidedly worshipful. Later we heard that our adoration displeased some members of the faculty. I am sure he did not try to invite this worship. By nature dignified but never stiff, he was perhaps a bit cool, not cold but necessarily cool. Otherwise his extreme grace and good looks—he was the handsomest man most of us had ever seen—would have been a handicap in a class of girls who, then as now, need to idealize some one. He was the scholar, and looked it. He must have been the patrician for he looked it and never stepped out of that character. For some reason he never overawed us. He was easily approached and always helpful in any subject pertaining to his work. He gave respectful attention to our ideas no matter how half baked they were—made us feel we were quite worthwhile folks."

Of this same period in Claxton's life, another[8] wrote, "As a student I was greatly impressed with his forward look and his progressive attitude as were all of the students who had the high privilege of sitting before his magnetic presence during those years. His thinking was far in advance of the times; consequently his methods were sometimes startling and frequently questioned by other professionals who *thought* they knew. . . . His class, no matter what his subject, was full of inspiration and sometimes good fun. Frequently after making a point on the blackboard he would find the faces of his students wreathed in smiles. Quickly he would scan the board and say, 'Now what word did I misspell?' His spelling was influenced by teaching the sound of word method. This little incident will show his spirit with his class. One day he asked his class to look around the room and draw the most conspicuous thing we saw. One student with very limited training prior to her entrance had a decided gift for drawing. She drew a splendid picture of Dr. Claxton. We were numbered but he learned in some way who the artist was. He sent for her and commended her by telling her that her drawing was the best likeness he ever had made."

"At one time in his career," she related, "he had much to say about mind over matter. He would startle us by telling us we were not sick—the trouble was in our minds. A serious outbreak of smallpox made it necessary to vaccinate every one. The virus that was injected into Dr. Claxton's arm must have been very bad. His arm turned dark and serious looking, so much so that there was real alarm among the students lest he might lose his arm. We never heard him discuss 'no pain' afterwards."

"Dr. Claxton was the students' ideal as a man and as a teacher," she declared. "His popularity was not so unanimous among the faculty members. There were those who felt the sting of jealousy as is common when a personality stands out in such decided prominence. He, however, was unconscious of it or did not allow it to disturb his thinking and so made himself master of the situation."

She closed with this very human touch regarding the young lady whom Claxton was soon to marry: "As students we thought he was deeply in love with Miss Elizabeth Porter, judging by an unexpected visit from her in his class one day. That was the only time any student ever saw him ill at ease or not up to his usual high level of self-possession."

Of Claxton, one who was associated with him as a teacher in the Training School wrote,[9] "As I recall him, he was a man of striking personality, tall and slender, erect, with a rather proud bearing, head held high. His hair was dark and his eyes were animated, glowing. His step was quick like 'Greatheart of eager face and fiery grace.' His dress was always neat and simple. In the classroom, where he excelled, he reminded me of some prophet with glowing message. He was far ahead of his times, and for that reason not always understood by some of his fellow teachers, those of the college group. The young women whom he taught were devoted to him—'crazy about him,' in school girl language. He taught them to think and inspired them to their best effort. He was the most inspirational teacher I have ever known. Dr. Claxton was a man of high ideals, pure minded and single in purpose. In the formative period of the Training School he gave an uplift, a forward movement, and left an impress which has remained throughout the years. One of my fellow teachers in the Practice School, who was appointed to visit the various public schools of the state, said to me on her return, 'The girls trained in the Practice School under the leadership of Dr. Claxton are different from other teachers; his earmarks are upon them. Their teaching is dynamic.' I remember so well a remark he made in speaking of some formal teaching he had observed. He said, 'It was like putty, heavy, or like dough without leaven, lifeless.' His teaching, indeed, was different. Like the Great Teacher whom he studied, his work had the leaven of life— vital and inspirational."

The only adverse criticism of Claxton from his former students related to the fact that some thought he was visionary and unpractical, and a few regarded him as conceited. These adverse opinions of him were more generally held by fellow faculty [10] members than by his students.

When Claxton first came to Greensboro, he and his daughter Claire lived in the home of Robert Glenn, a prominent business man, on West Market Street. He was a widower with three children that were under the care of his sister-in-law, Miss Dora Jones, a highly cultured woman with a brilliant mind.

On September 26, 1894, Claxton was married to Anne Elizabeth Porter in the Methodist Episcopal Church South in Tarboro, North Carolina, her home. He had first met her at some entertainment in Wilson, North Carolina, and had later seen her frequently in Asheville where she was teaching vocal music in the College for Women. She was "a beautiful woman, tall and graceful, with delicately modeled features and large expressive hazel eyes. Her hair was brown, her complexion fair with delicate coloring." [11] She had a large circle of friends, both men and women, who admired and loved her. When Josephus Daniels was asked by the editor of the Tarboro *Southerner* to explain his frequent visits to Tarboro, he replied that he had come "to see a stately and beautiful young lady whose voice made my admiration compare her to what I had heard of Jenny Lind and her 'notes almost divine.'" [12] This was Elizabeth Porter.

After completing her formal education at the Tarboro Female Academy, established soon after the War between the States by the widow of the famous Confederate General, William Dorsey Pender, her beautiful soprano voice had won such recognition through her singing in the choir and participation in all the musical affairs in that town that her parents sent her to New York for the best available training in instrumental music and in singing. She was not related to William Sydney Porter (O'Henry), who was born in Greensboro, North Carolina, but left for Texas in 1882 at the age of twenty. Her parents were Joseph John and Cynthia Ann Patience Porter. Their home, one of the show places of Edgecombe County, was known by the town folks as "Solomon's Temple." Mrs. Porter was a direct descendant of Sir Herbert Jeffreys, the second appointed governor of the Colony of Virginia. Both

Porter and Jeffreys families were large land owners and gentleman farmers.[11]

Claxton's salary was then $1800 a year, considered rather good for a teacher at that time, and in a year or so he bought a large house and lot on the corner of West Market and Mendenhall Streets. Greensboro, then a small town, was a pleasant place to live, and in the summer time quite came up to its name with its well kept green lawns and well shaded tree-lined streets. It was a town of wealth and culture, the Greensboro College for Women as well as the Normal School being located there. The town was really named after General Nathanael Greene, whose army fought that of Cornwallis five miles west of the town during the American Revolution.[13]

According to an act of the legislature, all teachers at the Normal and Industrial College were required, as a part of their work, to hold teachers' institutes during the summer. For this work they were to receive no extra salary and were obliged to pay their own traveling expenses. Each institute usually lasted a week. Claxton was one of the few who obeyed this law. He usually worked alone; sometimes one other accompanied him. On the first four days he instructed forty to seventy-five teachers for six hours a day. On Friday he addressed a gathering of teachers, school committees, and the public generally on the importance of public education, and the need for more money, better prepared teachers, better school-houses, better equipment, and longer school terms. Frequently he spoke on Saturdays also and in churches on Sundays. He also had to help read the examination papers of teachers seeking certificates. To save time he read the arithmetic papers first, for more than half failed to make the required grade of 65% in this subject and were thus disqualified no matter how good their other papers might have been. These institutes were very helpful to the teachers, and also to their conductors in giving them a firsthand knowledge of the abilities and needs of teachers. Such an experience was very valuable to Claxton as a professor of education in the Normal School. On the other hand, his work during the summer no doubt contributed materially to increasing the popularity of the Normal School throughout the state.

The private and denominational colleges in North Carolina organized the Christian Educational Association to oppose state appropriations for higher education. Dr. Kilgo, President of Trinity College and later a Bishop of the Methodist Church, was the leader in the movement. The association claimed that state schools took students away from their colleges and diminished their income. In 1893 Claxton was asked to address a meeting of this Association at Charlotte. In his speech he recounted all that the churches had done for education before the state became interested enough to appropriate money or otherwise foster education—especially in colleges. Then, he declared that, since the state, representing all the people, was ready to support public education on all levels, the churches ought not to try to oppose the work of the state, which was greater than any smaller group of people could accomplish. There was hearty applause from one side of the audience; complete silence from the other side.[14]

"During the campaign of 1894," according to Josephus Daniels,[15] "the antagonism of denominational colleges to appropriations for the university and other state colleges blazed forth." At Rutherfordton in the western part of the state, Claxton spoke not long after President Kilgo had spoken there. Kilgo had declared that the state schools were "godless." To this accusation Claxton replied, "The statement that the state colleges are godless is a lie out of hell, and those who make the charge know it!"[16] A yell of applause, such as one frequently hears at political speakings, was the response.

The Fusionists (Republicans and Populists) defeated the Democrats in the 1894 election, and during the session of the legislature the following year the religious leaders reopened their "war on the university" and other state-supported schools. The attempt to undermine the state support of institutions of higher learning was led by the Reverend Columbus Durham, a prominent Baptist preacher, and President Kilgo. They failed, however, in all their efforts, and somewhat larger appropriations than ever before were made. The Superintendent of Public Instruction, Charles H. Mebane, also succeeded in getting the Fusion legislature to pass an act requiring every school district to hold an election in August of that year to vote a ten cents tax increase on each $100 of taxable property and a thirty cents increase on the poll tax to provide more school funds.[17]

Josephus Daniels, then editor of the Raleigh *News and Observer*, strongly advocated in his paper public school improvement on all levels. At the breakfast table in the Yarborough Hotel, he heard a legislator remark that he did not know whether the classes ought to be taxed to educate the masses. Immediately Daniels with note-book and pencil was ready for action. "To which do you belong, the classes or the masses?" he asked. The lawmaker was caught in a dilemma and began to hedge. He knew that, if he said he belonged to the classes, Daniels would have a scathing editorial on him in the next issue of the *News and Observer*.[18] The opposition of the Christian Education Association was motivated by sympathy for the "classes" from whom the denominational schools and colleges drew their patronage. Alderman, then President of the University of North Carolina, argued that state and church colleges were like two lighthouses on two sides of a harbor entrance lighting ships to safety. Claxton frequently used the less ornate simile that education was like measles or smallpox, for the more there was the more likelihood there was that it would spread and increase.

From April to November, 1896, Claxton traveled in Europe and attended lectures at the University of Jena in Germany. This further preparation for the more roles he was to play in the great drama of educational development is the subject of the following chapter. He returned home after the spectacular Bryan campaign of 1896 had come to a close. In North Carolina he found that the Fusionists were still in control of the government. The people were not ready for the advanced school law which the Fusionist legislature had passed the previous year and only a few towns had voted the increased taxation for schools.

According to the law, elections were to be repeated every two years until such support was approved in every district. In the campaigns incident to the election in August, 1897, Claxton participated. His first speech was at Apex in Wake County. A speaker's platform had been prepared; but the crowd of farmers and farmers' wives had to sit on crossties which had been laid on the ground for seats. In his speech Claxton emphasized the relation of education to wealth and wealth producing power, and compared North Carolina to Massachusetts in this respect. Though few men were willing to make a public plea against public schools, he found to his surprise that he had an opponent. He was a Mr. Penny, the secretary to the Congressman in that district. He replied to Claxton by pointing out the conflict between science and religion. "Talk about Massachusetts!" he exclaimed. "I had rather have North Carolina with its simple faith in my mother's Bible and its poverty than Massachusetts with its wealth and its isms. When I was a student at Wake Forest College, the professor of geology wanted me to believe that the world was not made in six days of twenty-four hours each. I told him that before I would give up the faith in my mother's Bible, I would quit his classes." When he had finished, Claxton asked, "Mr. Penny, do you mean to say that the faith of these good North Carolina people in their religion is so weak that ten cents worth of education would destroy it?" With a dry grin, he replied, "I guess it would do some toward it." [18]

Claxton's last speech was on the evening of August 9 just before the election at Burlington in Alamance County. He spoke in a large, poorly ventilated hall, but there was such little interest in the improvement of schools in the town that there were only six people present when he began to speak. At the close, there were only twelve. Needless to say, the increased tax was not voted in Burlington the next day, but two years later a liberal tax was voted and Claxton liked to think that his speech bore some fruit.

At the 14th Annual North Carolina Teachers Assembly at Morehead City in June, 1897, the private school teachers were given one day on the program. Captain Morton, co-principal of the Morton and Denson Academy, read a paper which bitterly assailed the advocates of public high schools—particularly in Raleigh where the academy was located. "Are you going to take the bread out of the mouths of the men who bared their breasts to the shells of the enemy in the War between the States?" he asked. In a later reply, Alderman remarked, "It was a beautiful thing when Sir Galahad went forth to protect the weak against the strong. But since when has it become necessary for grownup men to be protected against the children?" [18]

This same summer at the Greensboro Normal School on May

19, Walter Hines Page made the commencement address on "The Forgotten Man." Claxton heard this speech and was greatly and favorably impressed by it. Page, he thought, was a very forceful speaker because of the simplicity, earnestness, and sincerity with which he spoke. He made no attempt at oratory. It was his subject matter rather than his platform manner that challenged attention. His speech revealed that the forgotten man was the uneducated man. "The forgotten man," he declared,[19] "remained forgotten. The aristocratic scheme of education had passed him by. To a less extent, but still to the extent of hundreds of thousands, the ecclesiastical scheme had passed him by."

"The forgotten man was content to be forgotten," he continued. "He became not only a dead weight, but a definite opponent of social progress. He faithfully heard the politician on the stump praise him for virtues that he did not have. The politicians told him that he lived in the best state in the Union; told him that the other politicians had some hare-brained plan to increase his taxes, told him as a consolation for his ignorance how many of his kinsmen had been killed in the war, told him to distrust any one who wished to change anything. What was good enough for his fathers was good enough for him. Thus the forgotten man became a dupe, became thankful for being neglected. And the preacher told him that the ills and misfortunes of his life were blessings in disguise, that God meant his poverty as a means of grace, and that if he accepted the right creed all would be well with him."

The forgotten women, Page thought, were even more tragic. These he portrayed as "thin and wrinkled in youth from ill-prepared food, clad without warmth or grace, living in untidy houses, working from daylight till bedtime, the slaves of men of equal slovenliness, the mothers of joyless children—all uneducated if not illiterate."

This speech created a furor throughout the South. Those who felt the sting of the attack called him "renegade," "Southern Yankee," sacrilegious "intruder" desecrating his old home and its traditions and religion. Particularly vocal was the clerical wrath. One newspaper declared that he had befouled the nest in which he was born and reared. But the net result of his speech was greatly beneficial. The better newspapers and more liberal people throughout the state supported him. The speech was particularly stimulating to the young men like Claxton, Alderman, McIver, and others who for several years had been laboring to decrease the number of forgotten men and women in North Carolina.

Claxton heard many other good commencement addresses at the Normal School. William Jennings Bryan gave the address in 1894, and during commencement week that year General John B. Gordon spoke on the "Last Days of the Confederacy." The next year President Nicholas Murray Butler of Columbia University was the principal speaker. Claxton considered Butler no orator like Bryan, but clear and convincing. In 1898, James Wilson, Secretary of Agriculture, delivered the address. Other speakers at various times were governors of North Carolina, Josephus Daniels, Conwell on his famous "Acres of Diamonds," and President E. Benjamin Andrews of Brown University on "Robert E. Lee." [20]

The Fusionist Party was defeated and disrupted in 1898; but against the strong opposition to state supported colleges and public schools progress was made but slowly, until Charles B. Aycock was elected governor in 1900. The chief plank in his platform was equal opportunities for education for all the people; he lived up to his pledges and became a great educational leader not only in North Carolina but throughout the South, dying in 1912 on the platform in Birmingham, Alabama, while making a speech on popular education. In bringing about a more sympathetic feeling toward public education in North Carolina, Claxton greatly aided Alderman, McIver, and Aycock, and received valuable experience and training for leadership in later campaigns in his native state.[21]

Claxton found time also to participate in the activities of the Southern Educational Association, which was organized in 1890 after the wife of the President of the National Education Association wrote a private letter condemning racial discrimination at the meeting of the association in Nashville, Tennessee. The letter got into print and provoked bitter feeling and a secession of Southern teachers from the National Education Association.

At the meeting of the Southern Educational Association at New Orleans (Dec.-Jan., 1898, 1899) Claxton read a paper on "The Training of Teachers for Elementary Schools," and was elected secretary of the association—a position which he held until 1903.

This entailed much work incident to the arranging of the programs for the annual meetings at various cities in the South. As far as possible he influenced the selection of subjects for papers which would bear on the educational needs of the South. As secretary, he for the first time had the proceedings of the meetings published, —a great task as much of the material had to be edited and practically all of it had to be condensed.

At the Memphis meeting, in 1899, he was Chairman of the Division of Normal School Training, and the only member present from North Carolina. At the tenth meeting of the association in Richmond, Virginia, in December, 1900, he read a paper on "The Function of the Normal School," beginning,[22] "As is the teacher, so is the school. In a very true sense, the teacher is the school." He further declared that the training of the teacher must give him "an exact and masterly knowledge of the subjects which he is to teach and the related subjects." At the same meeting, he spoke on "Education for Production with Some Considerations of the Question of Scientific and Technical Education for the South." In this address he emphasized the cultural value of scientific study and contended that the study of languages, literature, and philosophy was only one part of cultural knowledge, and that God is also revealed in nature as well as in the Bible.[23]

At the meeting in Columbia, South Carolina, in December the following year, Claxton read a paper on "Arithmetic and Geometry in the Elementary Schools" and discussed a paper by Dr. Alexander L. Phillips on "The Pedagogical Treatment of the Bible." Claxton outlined the work he had done in the Sunday School of the West Market Street Methodist Church in Greensboro.[24] With all his other work, he had found time to serve as superintendent of this Sunday School, having previously been assistant superintendent and teacher of the men's Bible class in Asheville, and had introduced systematic graded lessons and advanced methods of teaching, similar to those used in the Practice School of the Greensboro Normal School. Dr. Phillips, Secretary of Sabbath Schools of the Southern Presbyterian Church, was the representative of that church on the International Sunday School Committee. After learning of Claxton's methods during a lengthy conversation with him on a train, he influenced the liberalizing of the International

Sunday School lessons.[25] At the Columbia meeting Claxton also discussed a paper by J. W. Thompson on "The Importance of the Training School in Normal Work."

Claxton was, while in North Carolina, also an active member of the National Education Association, and at the meeting in July, 1894, at Asbury Park, New Jersey, he discussed a paper by James L. Hughes on "The Relation of the Kindergarten to the Public School System." Hughes was Inspector of Schools of Toronto, Canada. In his discussion, Claxton gave an account of the development of kindergartens in the Asheville school system. The kindergarten, he declared, influenced the primary teachers in improving their methods. "Joy is the sunshine in which grow all things save vice," he said.[26] ". . . If the children might ever thus rise above their work, doing it for the very joy and love of doing rather than from compulsion and fear, how different would be the life of the child and the atmosphere of the school room! Then might the joy of childhood pass into manhood, and, their work no longer regarded as tasks, they might escape the slavery of enforced and joyless labor, carrying with them through life the kindergarten spirit of freedom."

Always interested in this subject, Claxton read a paper on "The Need of Kindergartens in the South" at the meeting of the National Education Association in Charleston, South Carolina, in July, 1900, emphasizing the influence the kindergarten had upon the parents, the home, and the whole public school system. "I have known the entire school system of a city to be reformed and vitalized through the influence of kindergartens," he said.[27] ". . . In many homes of wealth and refinement the Negro nurse is the child's most constant companion. This does not mean what it did when the old black 'mammy', true and tried, cultured and refined by years of the most intimate association with her mistress and the mother of her mistress, and mellowed into the finest sympathy by the care of more than one generation of children, cared for the children with a mother's love and devotion, and the watchfulness developed by family pride and a strong sense of personal responsibility. She has gone with the days that are no more, and her successor, a half-grown Negro girl, hired for a few weeks or months at most and then replaced by another of whom you have probably never heard before, is of a different type. The cultured and refined white woman, with her mother heart and patient care in the kindergarten, certainly might well replace the Negro nurse. Shall we of the South never learn this lesson?"

During this productive period, Claxton in collaboration with M. Winifred Haliburton edited *Grimm's Fairy Stories, Supplementary to First Reader* (1900). He also adapted and arranged *From the Land of Stories: a book of stories for children of the first and second reader grades, mostly from the German of Fräulein M. Meissner* (1902). He began as well the publication of the *North Carolina Journal of Education* in the autumn of 1897. After four years it became the *Atlantic Educational Journal* with Claxton as editor. These journals were so important that an entire chapter has been devoted to them.

Claxton resigned his position at the Normal School early in the year 1902 in order to take charge of the Bureau of Investigation and Information for the Southern Education Board. By that time this school had grown to over 400 students, and its Practice School had about 250 pupils.[28] It had survived a terrible tragedy in 1899 when a typhoid epidemic caused several deaths and necessitated the suspension of the school for three months, beginning the middle of November, for making improvements in sanitation.[29] It had survived all the attempts of those who tried to have its appropriations decreased or completely stopped. It was destined to grow and develop until it eventually became the Woman's College of the University of North Carolina.

Of Claxton's work in North Carolina Josephus Daniels wrote,[30] "I knew Dr. Claxton very well. He was one of a group of dynamic educators who, in the days before and during the administration of our educational Governor Charles B. Aycock, changed the attitude of North Carolina toward public education. Early in my life when I became an editor in Raleigh and was a member of the Watauga Club, composed of young men who were trying to broaden the education of the State and give equal educational advantages to all the children, a wise old philosopher who had a seat on the grandstand said of us, 'They are conspirators against complacency.' That truly would have applied to the educators among whom Claxton was one."

The Second Trip to Europe

◇◇◇

IN APRIL, 1896, Claxton went to Europe again, primarily to hear the lectures of Dr. Wilhelm H. Rein, professor of education in the University of Jena, who was then the recognized authority on the Herbartian philosophy and method of education.

Landing at Liverpool, Claxton spent a day there visiting the Bray Street School. Though the equipment, including a swimming pool, was excellent, the teaching was done with the assistance of students, who were taught one day the lesson which they were to teach the next day. This was not approved by Claxton; and with his dislike of corporal punishment, neither was he pleased when the headmaster gave a demonstration of discipline by whipping two lads, stating that an average of fifteen were punished that way every day.[1]

From there Claxton went to Chester to visit the Teachers' Training College, where he was favorably impressed with the work being done by the students. The tuition, he found, was in proportion to the parents' ability to pay. Henry Wadsworth Longfellow, he learned to his surprise, was the most popular poet among the students.[2]

At the famous Rugby School, which Claxton next visited, he presented his credentials to the headmaster, Dr. James, who refused him permission to observe the teaching methods, as there was no rule allowing it. He cordially invited him, however, to come back later in the day to see a game of cricket. Claxton asked Dr. James which he considered more valuable, the Latin, Greek, and mathematics taught at Rugby or the football and cricket. In a rather gruff voice he replied, "One is worth as much as the other, sir." [2] Somewhat disappointed, Claxton went on down to London, where he visited the art galleries, museums, and other places of interest. After a few days he left for Holland, crossing the Channel from Harwich to the Hook (Hoek van Holland). From here he went direct through Germany to Jena.

Claxton found Jena to be a city of about 20,000 population with interesting medieval buildings, quaint narrow streets, and promenades replacing the old fortifications which once surrounded it. Located on the Saale River in the Grand Duchy of Saxe-Weimar, it was about fifty miles southwest of Leipzig, where he had formerly resided for several months. The University of Jena, which early in the nineteenth century had had as members of its faculty Fichte, Hegel, Schelling, Schlegel, and Schiller, had considerably declined in prestige, but Dr. Rein had the reputation of being the leader of the Herbartian movement and was probably the most widely known lecturer on education in Europe. Several of the more progressive American professors of pedagogy, such as Charles De Garmo and Charles A. and Frank McMurry, had in recent years gone to Jena to hear his lectures.

The Herbartian movement originated in the pedagogical doctrines of Johann Friedrich Herbart (1776–1841), a student under Fichte at Jena. Herbart met Pestalozzi while he was in Switzerland as tutor of the sons of the governor of Interlaken, and was influenced by his psychological methods of teaching at first hand and not from textbooks. His chief doctrines were that education was a distinctive science, that its aim was morality, and that it was to be obtained through the process of apperception. [3]

Dr. Rein was a rather prolific writer. With Pickel he collaborated in writing the *Encyclopedia of Education* in eight large volumes. He was an excellent classroom lecturer, reading his clear, thoughtful lectures in the German professor style. There was usually hearty applause from his rather large class. He was equally effective in his seminar, or practikum. Connected with his department was a practice school, of which Dr. Lemensick was principal. After teachers had heard Rein's lectures and attended his seminars, they would put into practice in the school what they had learned and be prepared to justify the method employed by them. There were no textbooks, and each teacher was required to make up his own lesson. Three or four times a year Rein gave an original lesson in the school himself.

An important feature of the practice school was the trips taken by teachers and pupils to study the surrounding country and gain by direct observation material for use in the schoolroom. Short excursions were made during school hours and on the afternoons of half holidays. During Easter, Whitsuntide, and other holiday seasons longer excursions were arranged. All these were systematically incorporated in the school program.

When Claxton arrived in Jena in May, the second class of the practice school was preparing for a Whitsuntide excursion [4] across the Thuringian forests to the Rhoen Mountains and the sources of the Fulda River. For some weeks Principal Lehmensick and other teachers had talked to the boys about the routes of travel and the places were located on a wall map. All additional information had been imparted that would make the excursion more pleasantly educational.

Early on the morning of May 27, Claxton left Jena on the train for Weimar with the eleven eager boys, nine or ten years old, and twelve teachers, three of whom were from England, three from America, one from Bulgaria, and the rest from Germany. In Weimar they visited the museum, a monument to soldiers who fought in the war with France in 1870–1871, and Goethe's theater, before which stood heroic statues of both Goethe and Schiller. Stopping next at New Dietendorf, a Moravian village, they entered a church, sang to the accompaniment of the organ, and listened to a prayer by Principal Lehmensick. They then visited the cinnabar works, the chief industry of that village.

Arriving at Saltzburg in the Thuringian forest, they climbed up to the ruins of an old castle, whose history was related to the boys on the spot. The next place, Neustadt, was the first Catholic town the boys had seen, and they were there taught lessons of religious tolerance. At Bischofsheim, a poor mountain town, they slept on straw at the inn, and the next morning saw coal miners at work and other laborers in a stone quarry. Many lessons were thus afforded. After tramping across the mountains through magnificent beech forests, keeping time to the music of "In the Fresh Green Woods," "The Lovely May," "The German Fatherland," "The Watch on the Rhine," and other favorites, they arrived at Kreutzfeld and spent the night in a stone-built hospice kept by Catholic monks. The four women teachers in the party were cared for in an inn.

At Schmalnau they took the train for Fulda, where there was a convent, an abbey, and a cathedral, modeled after St. Peter's in Rome. Then they proceeded to Bebra and climbed to the top of the Milseberg, the highest of a group of cup-shaped mountains. Many lessons on geology were thus afforded. After climbing Grosse Wasserkuppe (Great Watercup) the next morning, a Sunday, they tramped on to Waestensachsen, arriving in time to witness a religious procession at the head of which images of Christ and the Virgin were borne through the town. Halts were made at various shrines where the priests blessed the fields. From there they went across the moors by way of Frankenstein, "the poorest village in Germany," and then across the mountains the next day to a health resort, Salzungen, where they had lunch on the veranda of a fashionable hotel. At the last stop at Eisenach they saw the Luther monument in the great square and the Wartburg where he was concealed after the Diet of Worms and where he translated the Bible. Before returning by bicycle to Jena, Claxton again visited Weimar where he saw the impressive monuments to Goethe and Schiller at night. At a later date he saw Goethe's *Faust*, complete, presented at the Goethe Theater in Weimar. Back home in Jena, the young lads and their teachers had rich materials for further study in history, geography, geology, and many other branches of knowledge.

Claxton found this experience most interesting and valuable. Many German schools, he learned, employed this method of instruction, which helped the children form what was called "vital cores of apperception." As on his previous visit to Germany, he was impressed by the high regard with which teachers were held in the country. But their salaries were small, as compared to those in the United States. The regular salary of a professor in the University of Jena was then only $1000, though a few hundred dollars might be added from fees paid by students. One day he asked Dr. Frantz, Professor of English, why he and others did not go to

America, where he might be paid a salary of $5000 or more. He replied, "We could not live on it. We would have no social standing; some of our professors have been induced to go for this larger pay. Most of them have returned." Teachers in German schools of all levels were then the most honored of all people, with the exception of those of royal blood and possibly army officials.

After several weeks at Jena, Claxton and Richard J. Tighe, then principal of one of the schools at Asheville, who had joined him at Jena two or three weeks after his arrival, went on a bicycle tour of Europe together. They had brought bicycles with them from America. They went to Paris by way of Halle, Weimar, Erfurt, Fulda, Frankfort on the Main, Heidelberg, Mainz, Bingen, Koblentz, Köln (Cologne), Worms, Mannheim, Karlsruhe, Strassburg, and Nancy. Everywhere en route and in Paris, they saw everything of interest and significance, particularly museums and art galleries and places of literary and historical importance. In Paris they saw *Hamlet* presented as an opera. They also went to Versailles to see the royal palace of Louis XIV.

At Weimar Claxton saw everything connected with his favorite poet Goethe, including his house and his tomb in the New Cemetery. In the Ducal Vault, both Schiller and Goethe were interred in coffins of oak covered with laurel wreaths, placed on each side of the more elevated and ornate coffin of Duke Charles Augustus. The Duke thus intended to honor the poets; but indirectly was bringing honor to himself.

From Paris, Claxton and Tighe continued by bicycle to Geneva by way of Dijon. At that time the Quinquennial Intercantonal Exhibition was being held in Geneva. Wandering through the exhibit, Claxton observed evidence of the prosperity of the people. Then looking out at the snow-capped mountains with their glaciers and narrow little valleys, he could only wonder as to the source of such wealth. Finally he came to the educational exhibit, which was the best he had ever seen. In a prominent place was the statue of an old man with a kindly face; one hand rested on the head of a barefoot boy and the other on the head of a little girl. Both children looked up hopefully into his kind face; he looked down on them with loving sympathy. On the base of the statue were these words, as translated into English: "To our father, Pestalozzi—a grateful

Switzerland. All for others; nothing for himself." [5] That, Claxton thought, was the answer to his question as to the source of the prosperity of Switzerland. "The only way to help any people," Pestalozzi wrote, "is to help them help themselves." His famous prayer was as follows: "Would God some archangel would fly through the hills and valleys of this country and proclaim in thunder tones, 'There can be no freedom without the education of man!'" His own voice was that archangel.

From Switzerland, Claxton and his friend went by way of Chamonix, Tête Noir, and Martigny and up the Rhone River. They spent a night at a hospice on the Simplon Pass. Claxton climbed to the top of the highest ridge near the pass, some three or four thousand feet above the hospice. The top of the range was narrow and sharp, and from there he looked down on the wildest, gloomiest scene he had ever witnessed. Going down, he lost his way and did not reach the hospice until near midnight.

They then crossed Lake Garda to Como. After spending a day on Lake Como, they went by bicycle to Milan. Here Claxton climbed to the top of the great cathedral with its roof of flowers carved in stone. He noted that the back of the statue on the highest peak of the roof had been carved as perfectly as the faces of the great statues at the front of the cathedral. He was thus reminded of these lines:

> "In the elder days of art,
>   Men wrought with extremest care
> Each minute and unseen part,
>   For the gods see everywhere."

From Milan they continued by bicycle to Florence by way of Bologna. After visiting the Pitti and Uffizi galleries and other places of interest in Florence, they traveled by train to Rome. Here they spent a week seeing the ancient ruins, St. Peters and other great churches, and the museums. Returning to Florence, they bicycled across Italy to Venice, where they saw St. Marks and other celebrated places. Then by way of Verona and Lake Garda they reached a small village near the Italian-Austrian boundary, where they spent the night. It was a wild looking place, and Claxton locked the door of his room—an unusual thing for him to do. The next morning through the window he saw a church and a schoolhouse, and was reassured. Here they took train for Munich, where they spent a day or two, and then continued by train to Jena by way of Nürnberg, Bamberg, Eisenach and Wartburg Castle, Gotha, and Erfurt. Altogether they had traveled by bicycle alone more than 2000 miles, a method of cheap travel which Claxton considered most delightful and instructive.

At Jena, Claxton and his friend separated. Tighe went to Ireland to visit relatives, where he learned on arrival that he had inherited the title of Sir Richard Tighe. He declined, however, to accept it. Claxton, having been invited by Dr. N. C. Lagerstedt of the Royal Gymnasium in Stockholm to attend the Quinquennial Meeting of the Pan-Scandinavian Education Association, went by train to Askov, Denmark, the place of meeting. About seventy-five of the most prominent teachers of Norway, Denmark, Sweden, and Finland were in attendance. At one session they discussed child study, and asked Claxton to speak on Dr. G. Stanley Hall and his work. Dr. Otto Salomon interpreted, retelling in regular order the substance of Claxton's twenty-five minute talk. Practically all present, however, understood, and could speak, English.

The meetings were held in the oldest and most important of the Danish Folk High Schools, which was located at Askov. To such schools were admitted young men and women above the age of eighteen from rural Denmark. There were no definite courses of study, no examinations, and no diplomas. The principal, instructors, and students lived democratically under the same conditions, ate together, walked and talked together. They sang at their meals, and all classes and lectures began and ended with songs. The principal was Dr. Schroeder, a rather large person with a strong voice, who was a man of learning, vision, and statesmanship. He was President of the Danish Society for reclaiming waste lands, and also an author of note. Dr. La Cour, a learned mathematician and scientist, was a member of the faculty. He had been offered positions in some of the great universities of Europe but he preferred to study and work among his own people. Because of his many inventions, he was known as the "Edison of the North." The school buildings were substantial but not costly; the library was adequate. There were sixty-five of these schools in Denmark and many more in other Scandinavian countries. They were private schools with government subsidies.

The meetings of the Association continued throughout a week. One afternoon Claxton went with a group to Skiblung, a natural amphitheater on the southern border of Denmark overlooking the country taken from Denmark by the Germans after the War of 1864. Around the elevated edge of the amphitheater had been placed monuments of Danes whose work had been really beneficial to Denmark in modern years. Here, the Danes held one of their periodic patriotic meetings, which was very impressive.

On the last day of the conference, the members went by train to a seaside town called Esbjerg for a meeting and picnic. After speeches were made by all the representatives of the Scandinavian countries, Claxton was called upon to speak as a representative of the "fifth" Scandinavian country. The introducer explained that one fourth of all Scandinavian people lived in America.

During the week, Claxton had a room at a little hotel in the nearby village of Vejen and daily bicycled out to the school. He had lunch and sometimes dinner at the school. When he was preparing to leave, he asked an official of the school how much he owed for the lunches and dinners. He went in to see Dr. Schroeder and returned with the reply, "Think of us kindly while you are away." Claxton left with the conviction that he had never seen a school with so good a spirit and with methods so well fitted to prepare young men and women for life. "Further knowledge has convinced me," he declared,[6] "that these Folk High Schools of the Scandinavian countries are probably the best in the world."

At Askov, Dr. Otto Salomon, principal of the Sloyd School at Nääs, Sweden, invited Claxton to be his guest for a week. On the way, he spent two days at Copenhagen, and then went by boat from Elsinore to Gothenburg, and thence to Nääs, situated on a beautiful lake. Salomon, a young lawyer, was the nephew of a wealthy Jew who had purchased a large estate on which was the castle of a former Danish king, when Denmark ruled this part of Sweden. The nephew, employed to manage the estate, established schools for the tenants and their children where they could learn how to make the simple household furniture and farm equipment. Such schools became so popular in Sweden that teachers were needed for them. Dr. Salomon then established a school for teachers near Nääs, which was called Sloyd, this being the Swedish word for "skill."

At the time of Claxton's visit, there were about fifty teachers from thirteen different countries at the Sloyd Training School. Claxton was lodged in one of the cottages on the grounds and spent the week, observing the methods of teaching, watching the Swedish gymnastics in costume in the late evening twilight, and enjoying interesting conversations with Dr. and Mrs. Salomon in their home. Dr. Salomon, he thought, was one of the few real philosophers he had ever known in the flesh. On leaving at the end of the week he asked what he should pay. "Come again!" was Dr. Salomon's reply.[6] Then as a further expression of kindly hospitality the Salomons and the whole school accompanied him to the lake shore where he took a small boat for the village and the railway station.

Returning to Gothenburg, Claxton took boat for Edinburgh, where Tighe rejoined him. Here they spent several interesting days seeing this beautiful old city. Claxton was impressed with the observance of Sunday, there being no street cars or cabs and all the people walking to and from church. Also he long remembered the soap box orators in the park on Sunday evening. The largest group gathered about a speaker with a banner, "No Ballot, No King, No God." Police protected him while he delivered his wild, anarchistic speech. The next day, Claxton wrote his wife that there would be a revolution in England within the next twenty-five years. He did not then fully understand the value of free speech as a safety valve for pent up feelings of discontent. Similar freedom of expression was enjoyed by the professors at the University of Edinburgh, among whom was Patrick Geddes, then already known for his socialistic and other radical teachings.

From Edinburgh Claxton and Tighe rode their bicycles to Glasgow by way of Stirling and Loch Katrine. In Glasgow Claxton was greatly impressed with the many editions of Burns' works and the hundreds of books about the poet in the Hunterian Library. Upon leaving that city, they traversed the "Burns Country" in Ayrshire and the "Lake District" of Northern England. Thence by way of Lincoln and Cambridge they proceeded to London, where they spent a week, visiting the British Museum, Parliament Houses, Westminister Abbey, Saint Paul's Cathedral, the Tower of London, the British Empire Exhibit at Wimbleton, art galleries, and other places of special interest. Trips were also made to Windsor and Oxford.

Sailing from Liverpool, Claxton reached Greensboro by way of New York in November, after an absence of about six months. He left home in April with $400 and returned with thirty-eight cents, after paying all expenses. He had traveled and lived comfortably. The trip was of the greatest value to him, not only in enriching his general knowledge but especially in the formation of his educational ideals and philosophy.

❧ IX ❧

Editor of School Journals

◇◇◇

UNDISMAYED BY his other many duties, Claxton, in the autumn of 1897, commenced the publication of the *North Carolina Journal of Education* in partnership with Clinton W. Toms, then superintendent of the Durham schools. The first number appeared in August. Before it was off the press, Toms withdrew to take a position with the Duke Tobacco Factory at a salary of $5,000, more than three times as much as he had received as school superintendent. Claxton then secured another partner, Logan Howell, superintendent of the Raleigh schools, but he did not invest any money in the journal and soon retired in June, 1898, to join the Army. For awhile Claxton employed T. Gilbert Pearson as agent, but he was more interested in studying birds and in writing about them than in securing subscriptions for the journal. He, however, wrote some good articles for it on birds. Claxton induced B. F. Johnson and Company to publish Gilbert's first book on birds, and he later became secretary of the National Association of Audubon Societies.

Claxton had long known Toms and Howell and the previous June and July had been associated with them on the faculty of the summer school of the University of North Carolina, of which Toms was the superintendent. Claxton lectured on educational psychology; Howell taught geography. Among the eight other members of the faculty was E. P. Moses, who was in charge of primary instruction.[1]

The Journal of Education was published at Greensboro. The subscription rate was fifty cents a year; single numbers cost five cents a copy. The first issue had sixteen pages, which was doubled in the next number. In April, 1898, it was further increased to forty-four pages, and exactly one year later the yearly subscription rate was raised to one dollar. On the cover of the first number was a photograph of the statue of Pestalozzi by Lanz, and significant excerpts from his writings or concerning him; such as, "It is a chief business of education to pass from distinctly perceived individual notions to clear general notions." Besides a rather long editorial by Claxton the first issue contained seven articles by prominent North Carolina teachers.

In his first editorial, Claxton set forth the purpose of the journal. His creed he declared to be "Better schools and wider opportunity for all." He would work for the upbuilding of all schools, private, corporate, denominational, but particularly for the schools of the people, "free to all, supported by all, for the good of all and each." Some of the things he would advocate were "longer school terms for town and country, better schoolhouses, more adequate support, better supervision, a higher standard of preparation for teachers, a more ample provision for their professional training." "It will point out the need for a better system of high schools and academies," he continued, "and for industrial and technical schools. It will plead for larger endowments for our colleges and universities and for the more liberal support of all state schools. It will fight for public libraries in every city, town, village, and country schoolhouse. It will have no enemies except such as fight against the light and the great democratic, Christian doctrine of the fullest and freest opportunity for all. To such it will give no quarter." The *Journal* would, of course, attempt to bring to its readers the "best that is being said and done in the teaching world" regarding theory and method.

Next, Claxton strongly defended the method of local taxation as a logical way to support a public school system adequately. In discussing the needs of such support, he declared, "An ignorant man is a slave wherever you find him. Untrained communities are in a state of servitude to trained communities all over the world. Character and intelligence are the true creators of values. Ignorance is a curse. It has never done any good thing. It has never written a great book or enacted a wise law or sung a great song or invented a new machine."

Comparing conditions in the South with those in the North, he wrote, "Our money flows in a golden stream to the states to the north of us, whose skill enables them to make things that we need and cannot make. Four fifths of the improvements in productive machinery is the result of their trained mental acuteness. Among them an inventor is an ordinary citizen; with us he is a celebrity. Their per capita wealth indicates prosperity. Ours indicates poverty. All this is equally true of our intellectual life. If large literary talent arises among us, it must die or depart elsewhere. Our school textbooks come to us in bales from other states. All that reflects our inner life in poetry, history, or biography is done by alien pens and unsympathetic minds. It is difficult to sustain our public journals and magazines and impossible to create a really great newspaper, though we have men of power, brains, and energy who devote themselves to the task. The readers are lacking; and that is a fundamental problem."

From month to month, Claxton wrote editorials, sometimes critical but always informative, encouraging, and hopeful. In commenting on the general failure of the election of August, 1897, to vote increased local taxation for schools, he declared,[2] "To see a man deny his four children the benefit of greatly increased school facilities that he may, perchance, leave each of them two or three dollars more when they are men and women grown; to see those who should lead the people in their communities to better things and wider life play away the eternal interests of the children and the prosperity of the community for the sake of gaining a brief partisan advantage; to hear men who stand in holy places, and should know better, proclaim that darkness is better than light and death better than life and, by skillful sophistry and false appeal to nobler passions, make truth a lie to an all too confiding people; to see the honest people of a great state cursed with ignorance as are no other people of Teutonic blood, elect a continuation of ignorance, poverty, helplessness, and narrow darkened life for themselves and their children—all this is enough to arouse to pity or righteous anger."

In the fact that seven townships voted the tax, he saw hope for the future, and eloquently prophesied, "North Carolina will provide schools, well equipped and taught by trained, skillful teachers, ten months in the year, free to all children within her borders. The stigma of illiteracy will one day be removed. The nations will cease to point the finger of scorn and say, 'Poor old North Carolina.' Our children shall no longer be deprived of their birthright. But to an unexcelled native ability they will add the training and culture of the schools and the knowledge and control of the laws of nature made possible by modern science. Then shall poverty give place to wealth, the hovel to the home; the face of the mother shall wear a smile; the father no longer toiling like a slave, dragging his chains of ignorance, shall walk with an elastic step; the voice of children, released from the hard lot of bearing the burdens of age in tender youth, shall ring in mirth on our streets, and the 'forgotten man' will walk upright in the image of his maker."

Very early, Claxton came out strongly for consolidation of small schools in the country. "We cannot have a school at every man's door," he wrote.[2] "It is better to send children three miles to a good school for five months than to have an inferior school just across the road for three months." If children cannot walk the increased distance, he suggested that it would be cheaper to convey them at public expense, as was being done in many states.

Upon the increase of the students at the University of North Carolina after Alderman became president, Claxton declared,[3] "This gives hope for the future. . . . North Carolina might well afford to double her present appropriation to her University. It pays to buy trained minds and rightly educated men at any price." He expressed his pleasure also at women's beginning to seek a higher education. There were then four or five at the University and more than a dozen at Trinity. He pled for dormitories and other opportunities for them equal to those afforded men.

In an editorial relating to Thanksgiving, Claxton wrote,[4] "North Carolina should give thanks not only for abundant harvests and other material blessings, but also for that all her schools, high and low, public, private, and denominational, are filled to overflowing with earnest students, eager for the light of knowledge, the power of training, and the grace of culture. This means much more for us as a people than do acres of golden grain or whitening fields of cotton. For a state becomes great only through the right education of all its people."

Sometimes a very practical lesson in teaching was derived from an editorial. This is an example:[5] "To keep a bicycle steady keep it moving. If you stop the revolution of the wheels to steady it, you may expect it to wobble and fall; and the greater your efforts to hold it erect, the more disastrous will be the result. The only way to control a bicycle is to keep it moving. So must the teacher gain and maintain control of her class. . . . Bicycles and classes are most easily ridden at a good steady pace, and are most difficult to control when brought to a standstill."

In the form of New Year's Resolutions to improve the *Journal*, among other matters he wrote,[6] "While recognizing our present poverty and backward condition, we believe in the South and its people, with no sectional prejudice or false pride, but with a faith born of a knowledge of the history of the past, of the native ability of our people, and of our unbounded natural resources. Only the full development of this ability and these resources is needed, and then will the South assume its rightful place among the sections of the Union, and its people among the peoples of the world. It is our home; we love it and shall live and labor for its higher interests—

'The South whose gaze is cast
No more upon the past,
But whose bright eyes the skies of promise sweep,
Whose feet in paths of progress swiftly leap;
And whose fresh thoughts, like cheerful rivers run
Through odorous ways to meet the morning sun.' "

With great breadth of view and fairness, during a period of bitter controversy in North Carolina, Claxton thus paid [6] tribute to private schools: "Next to a better system of public schools, we need more good academies and private schools of a high grade. Nothing can ever take the place of these. As our public schools increase and improve, these will increase and improve. In those states where the public schools are best, the academies are most important. They saved North Carolina and other Southern states from ignorance and aided in building up an excellent, though limited, culture when public schools were an unknown factor in the educational life. While the *Journal* believes in public schools first, last, and all the time, from the Kindergarten through the University, it will always rejoice in the growth of these private institutions and will gladly lend its aid in helping to build them up in every way."

He pays tribute [6] also to the work of city school superintendents, but points the way toward other needs; such as, high schools with well equipped laboratories and schools of manual training and a higher standard of efficiency and training for teachers. He never lost an opportunity to advance the cause of public libraries, and congratulated [7] Durham on its public library supported by city appropriation, the first of the kind in North Carolina. "All honor to Durham," he declared, "for this progressive step, and may other towns make haste to follow her example! What a small item will this $600 be on the list of the town's annual expenses—not more than the pay of one policeman; yet what a power for good it secures. How poor indeed—poor with the worst kind of poverty—is the bookless town!" He praised the work of Dr. J. L. M. Curry in connection with the Peabody and Slater funds. "These funds are doubly helpful," he wrote, [7] "in that, while they send the gifts of money so much needed, they also send Dr. Curry with his inspiring words and earnest pleadings that we can and should help ourselves by appropriating more money for education." He lauded also the Teachers College of New York, just incorporated in the educational system of Columbia University, as "probably the best equipped school for the training of teachers in the world." [8]

Again and again, Claxton emphasized the need for development of country schools. The entire issue of the *Journal* for May, 1898, was devoted to this subject. "Larger Districts, Fewer Schools and Better" was his slogan. He wrote frequently of the importance of Summer Schools and Educational Meetings for teachers. He also frequently emphasized the moral side of education in the public schools, and never ceased praising the kindergarten.

After the "White Supremacy" campaign of 1898, the legislature the following year was mainly concerned with legislation that would curb the Negro political power in the state. [9] With his accustomed fearlessness and foresight, Claxton wrote [10] in his *Journal*,

"The wisest legislation possible in North Carolina just now is that which looks toward the more complete education of every child in the state—white and black alike. . . . The schools must be of equal efficiency for all regardless of race or the financial ability of the parents. The state that begins to make a division in the educational opportunities of its children must expect, sooner or later, to find a fatal division in its citizenship. The destinies of North Carolina are in the hands of the present General Assembly. It must make the provisions necessary for carrying out the democratic ideas of the founders of the state."

Perhaps, Claxton's most beautifully written editorial was entitled "The Greatest Master of the Art of Teaching." This is so unusual that it deserves complete quotation. "The greatest teacher the world has ever known," he wrote,[11] "not only in what he taught but also in his method of teaching was he who spoke as never man spoke. His doctrine has revolutionized the life of the world, individual and national, and is revolutionizing it. Truly did he say he came that men might have life, and that more abundantly. But his doctrine is no more wonderful than his method of teaching— wonderful in its clearness, simplicity, and perfection, as measured by every known pedagogical principle. With that perfection of art which conceals art and escapes the notice of all but the closest students, he taught the most difficult lessons to the Galilean, Samaritan, and Judean peasants; taught to fishermen, carpenters, outcasts, to the great multitude, those sublime truths which men had always held (and many still hold) should be entrusted only to the chosen few; taught in such a way that the common people heard him gladly, and understood him; taught with such power and clearness that by no other means than his teaching he has gradually destroyed, remodeled, or given new meaning to every fundamental doctrine of individual and social life; taught in such a way that his teaching stands for all time the model for all teachers who would attain to the highest perfection in their art. No teacher can spend a few hours or days of the spring vacation better than in reading one or more of the Gospels, and studying carefully Jesus' method of teaching and the great principles underlying the method. Who is the greatest in the kingdom of heaven? What shall I do that I may inherit eternal life? Study the answers. Read, over and again, the conversation with the woman at the well, the parable of the sower, and others, and see how they illustrate the best known principles of pedagogy. If you have read Froebel, Pestalozzi, Herbart, note how Jesus is the master of them all. A few hours of reading will open up a new world to you; and having once begun, you will certainly be led on to ever deeper and deeper study of the method, until these four brief books will become your greatest textbooks on teaching. Thirteen years ago I began studying them for their pedagogical value, and every year has revealed new truths and new applications. No teacher can afford to neglect this vital study."

Claxton continuously associated education with religion. For example, he wrote,[12] "This [education] should be the chief concern of the modern democratic state, just as has been seen and understood by all the greatest democratic leaders of our own country and of Europe for more than a century, and by all great reformers since Luther proclaimed the freedom of conscience at Wittenberg and Worms. . . . The educational fund is the most sacred of all public funds, the office of the teacher is the most sacred of all public offices, and those in whose hands are the duty and power of electing and dismissing teachers should guard the office most sacredly from incompetency, and with perfect freedom from all political or sectarian partisanship, and from all individual fanaticism." Recollecting the vision of Nebuchadnezzar, he later wrote,[13] "The glory and splendor and wealth of statues and nations may be in the brass and silver and fine gold of other parts of the body, but their strength is in the feet; and their glory and splendor and wealth are as naught in the day of trial, if the feet break by reason of the clay that is in them. No state is stronger than the strength and virtue in the lowest stratum of its citizenship; and especially is this true of the democratic state."

Arguing for a universal system of education, Claxton explained,[13] "Mitchell's Peak, hidden in cloud or bathed in the sunlight of the upper atmosphere, rises from a basal plateau 3000 feet above the tidewater of the east. Mont Blanc, covered with eternal snows, rises from a plateau high as the top of Mitchell's Peak—a plateau from which flow the rivers of central Europe. Mt. Everest, lifting its summit five miles into the heavens, the prince of mountains, rises from a plateau high as the top of Mont Blanc, from which the

[105]

mighty rivers of a continent spring. And so it is the world over. Great mountain peaks never rise from the lowland marshes, but always from broad and high plateaus and great mountain ranges; the higher and broader the plateau the greater the mountain peak it will support. Would men of education and culture reach their fullest stature and secure the fullest results from their enlightened labors, they must have the support of an intelligent and cultured people. Men whose heads are to tower among the clouds and catch the sunlight of the upper air cannot stand with their feet in the marshes of ignorance and helplessness. They can attain their full stature only by a general upheaval producing a broad and elevated plateau of intelligence and culture and strength."

Claxton wrote frequently on the relation between education and crime, on the problem of educating the children of the cotton mills, on child labor, on practical technical education. He always opposed war. He took no notice of the War with Spain, while it was being fought; but after it was over and the Philippine Insurrection was in progress, he wrote,[14] "The Philippine war costs the U. S. $1,000,000 a day, which is twice as much as the average daily cost of all the public schools of the United States. . . . But great is war and the road to glory is wet with human blood." Again he wrote sadly of how the money spent in war, for pensions, and in preparation for war was sufficient to bring education to every child in the civilized world. "Some day," he declared,[15] "the Christian nations of the world will learn that there is a better way of spending their money and energies." Then he quotes from Longfellow,

> "Were half the power that fills the world with terror,
>   Were half the wealth, bestowed on camps and courts,
>   Given to redeem the human mind from error,
>   There were no need for arsenals and forts."

Frequently Claxton compared conditions in North Carolina with those in other states or in European countries to show the relation between education and wealth. For example, "In Switzerland the price of farm lands is from $600 to $1600 an acre, and farming pays in spite of these high values. Switzerland has no pauper class, no slums in the cities, and no tramps. The roads are almost perfect, the streets are clean, and there is little need of police or soldiers. It is a country of universal education, and the best house in any village or town is the schoolhouse. Effect and cause. . . . Denmark, almost exactly one third the size of North Carolina, with sterile soil and severe climate, exports $30,000,000 worth of butter every year. North Carolina, with its rich lands and genial climate, buys butter. But Denmark has universal education; public high schools for the sons and daughters of farmers are found at a rate which would put two or more in every county in North Carolina, while industrial and technical schools, public libraries, and farmers' clubs are liberally supported and attended. Denmark knows on which side her bread is buttered and how to butter it. We have not yet learned the lesson; but we will, sooner or later." Very early Claxton came out strongly for the study of forestry in colleges and universities, and for school gardens as laboratories for the study of agriculture in the public schools.

When his friend Alderman resigned the presidency of the University to become president of Tulane, Claxton wrote a glowing tribute to him and his work for education in North Carolina.[17] It would be difficult to exaggerate the importance of Claxton's editorials not only in the struggle toward universal public schools in North Carolina and elsewhere in the South but also in raising the standards of teaching. His ideas were indeed seed thoughts which bore rich fruit in the minds of hundreds of teachers. Other seed thoughts were implanted by another interesting feature of the *Journal*. On the cover of each issue was the picture of some great educational leader with several inspiring quotations from his writings. Other significant passages were printed elsewhere in the issue. Space is inadequate for quoting any of these here, but one can readily imagine the richness of such material in the writings of Pestalozzi, Horace Mann, Froebel, Herbert Spencer, Joseph Payne, Comenius, Herbart, Jean Paul Richter, Rousseau, and John Locke, all of whom were featured. Washington, Jefferson, and Robert E. Lee were similarly treated, as well as the Southern poets, Lanier and Timrod, and the English authors, Milton and Ruskin—all because of their interest in education. Many teachers in this way heard of some of these men for the first time, and were led to read more widely in the field of their profession. Also featured were philanthropists like George Foster Peabody and John McDonough,

U. S. Commissioner of Education William T. Harris, Zebulon B. Vance and more recent North Carolina educators like Alderman, and J. L. M. Curry of the Southern Education Board.

In each issue of the *Journal*, there were, on the average, ten or twelve signed articles. Most of the authors of these were from North Carolina, but as the *Journal* became more widely known articles appeared by writers from Louisiana, Texas, Georgia, Kentucky, Tennessee, New York, South Carolina, Virginia, Alabama, Pennsylvania, and West Virginia. The more frequent contributors from North Carolina were Charles D. McIver, T. Gilbert Pearson, R. J. Tighe, E. P. Moses, Charles L. Coon, J. D. Eggleston, M. C. S. Noble, J. Y. Joyner, Edward S. Joynes, Logan D. Howell, and Miss M. W. Haliburton. Among the more prominent contributors outside the state were Professor C. Alphonso Smith, then at Louisiana State University; President George T. Winston of University of Texas; Supt. Lawton B. Evans of Augusta, Georgia; Reuben Post Halleck of Louisville, Kentucky; William H. Mace of Syracuse University; J. L. M. Curry; U. S. Commissioner of Education Harris; President Charles W. Dabney of University of Tennessee; and President Eliot of Harvard. Professor Edwin Mims of Trinity College; Professor W. L. Poteat of Wake Forest College; Dr. Thomas Hume, Professor Charles Baskerville, Dr. Kemp P. Battle, and Professor Eben Alexander of the University of North Carolina also wrote for the journal.

The subject matter of the articles varied greatly. They related both to the methods of teaching and the knowledge to be imparted. All the courses in the curricula of schools were covered and probably every new idea in pedagogy was presented. Claxton himself wrote several articles on the teaching of elementary arithmetic.

Other features were poetry, particularly poems suitable for reading to children; programs for Thanksgiving and New Year's and the birthdays of Washington and Robert E. Lee; pictures of new public school and college buildings and of libraries; digests of teachers' magazines by Charles L. Coon; notices of teachers' meetings, state, sectional, and national; and brief reviews of books relating to teaching. After the issue of the *Journal* for August, 1900, Claxton found it advisable to suspend publication for six months "to readjust its business management";[18] there were on the books more than $1000 of unpaid subscriptions. After the appearance of the February and March, 1901, numbers, he found it necessary to sell the *Journal* to the B. F. Johnson Publishing Company of Richmond, Virginia, on April 20, 1901. Claxton was to remain sole editor at a salary of $50 a month and to receive ten per cent of the profits for three years and double that amount for the following two years. He was to have an assistant at $50 per month, and all expenses of publication and distribution were to be paid by B. F. Johnson and Company. The name was to be changed to *South Atlantic School Journal* and the first issue was to be published on June 1, 1901.[19]

Claxton had edited the *North Carolina Journal of Education* as a labor of love for the cause of education in the South. Most of his leisure time went into this editorial work, and he often sat up late at night reading manuscripts and editing them for publication. Most of the time he had the assistance of a stenographer, and some of his students also helped him with the clerical work. "One of my early memories," wrote[20] one of these, "is helping Claire and the second Mrs. Claxton mail out issues of an educational journal Mr. Claxton edited." Though the circulation was not large, its influence extended beyond the borders of North Carolina. U. S. Commissioner of Education Harris said it was one of the best educational journals in America.[21] "I do not know whether the paper paid all expenses, probably not," declared[22] Claxton, "but it was a lot of fun and filled a needed place. . . . Income might have been greater if I had had time to look after the business side of it better." For most of the time he had been not only owner of the journal but also its editor and business manager.

The name of the new magazine was changed again, before its first issue, to *Atlantic Educational Journal*. It was essentially the same as the other journal; its format was slightly different but its editorials were aimed at the same target, improvement of educational standards in the South. In the first issue Claxton made a strong plea for better country schools, technical schools, and school libraries, and praised the leadership of Dr. Curry.

In another issue he advised[23] teachers to read Dickens' works "and learn the indomitable power of love and intelligent sympathy, the unreasonableness of harshness and cruelty, the ugliness of selfishness, the crime of attempting to destroy individuality, the importance of the culture of the imagination, the cruel absurdity of the old doctrine of child depravity, the uselessness of cramming, the life-giving effect of childish joy and happiness. Read him and learn how empty and dry are all methods and forms unless filled by the spirit of love and right devotion."

Upon the death of Dr. Curry on February 12, 1903, Claxton wrote [24] this very beautiful eulogy: "Soldier, statesman, author, diplomat, teacher and friend of man, he was honored, respected, and beloved by all. Born of the Old South, tried in the furnace of a lost cause, he was an apostle of education to a newer and grander South. He was a prophet of hope. Living in three generations, active and useful in many fields, he was a great American whom the South will ever honor with love and affection. Tender, honest, courageous, he loved all the needy and ignorant of both races. But he hated meanness and small politics. He was truly great. His life will ever remain an incentive to noble deeds and heroic sacrifice in the promotion of the deathless cause of popular education."

There were numerous other editorials, informational as well as inspirational; but they dealt largely with the same problems he had editorialized upon in the earlier journal. The signed articles also were as varied in subject matter as were those in the *North Carolina Journal of Education*. Many of the same contributors continued to write for the new journal. They represented more states, however—twenty-eight in number from Maine to California, Illinois to Florida. Two foreign countries, Sweden and Canada, also were represented. Pictures of educational leaders continued to appear on each cover, but most of them were contemporary figures; such as, state superintendents of education, heads of normal schools, professors of pedagogy, and superintendents of city schools. U. S. Commissioner of Education Harris, President Charles W. Dabney of University of Tennessee, Dr. Curry, Governor Aycock of North Carolina, Governor Frazier of Tennessee, George Foster Peabody, and Walter Hines Page were also thus honored. There were four rather important features under the headings: "Educational Progress," "News and Comment," "Summaries and Extracts from Journals," and "Book Notices."

Though the *Atlantic Educational Journal* cost only one dollar a year and was decidedly a valuable periodical for every teacher in the South, it never received the patronage it merited. Finally in the double number of July-August, 1903, the publishers found it necessary to make this announcement: "We secured the services of perhaps the best equipped educational editor in the South. . . . Applause—abundant applause—came from every section. Subscribers—a few subscribers—came from here and there. We were glad to get the applause. We are grateful for every kind word that was said about the *Journal*. We would have been glad to get the subscriptions—not for our own sake, for we expected no profit, but that the permanence of the *Journal* might be secured." Consequently, the journal was sold to E. L. Kellogg and Company, publishers of *Teachers' Institute* and *School Journal*.

By this time Claxton's time and energy were taken up very largely in the promotion of other important educational work, and he found, no doubt, a somewhat welcome relief in the suspension of a publication upon which he had expended so much labor.

X

The Southern Education Board

E ARLY IN JANUARY, 1902, Claxton was invited by Dr. Charles W.
Dabney, President of The University of Tennessee, to come to
Knoxville as chief of the Bureau of Investigation and Information of
the Southern Education Board, at a salary of $1800.[1] His wife and
children arrived a few months later and were taken by him immediately to "Bleak House," which he had rented from Mrs. Robert Armstrong. This large red brick house on the Kingston Pike in the out-
skirts of the city overlooking the Tennessee River had been built
by slaves of the Armstrong family before the Civil War. Its walls
of solid brick were a foot thick; its rooms were large with high
ceilings, and with walls frescoed with paintings by the late Mr.
Armstrong and his daughter Adelia. During the war while Knoxville was under siege, it served as General Longstreet's headquarters
and from its tower a sharpshooter killed the Federal General
Sanders. Here they resided happily until the autumn following the
death of Mrs. Claxton on February 14, 1905; then they moved to
"Hill Crest" just off Kingston Pike, a large house purchased from
Mr. C. C. Sullins. Here they lived until the family moved to
Washington about eight years later.

President Dabney was the Director of this Bureau, and his attention had been drawn to Claxton by his work in the Normal
School and by his *Journal of Education* which showed both scholarship and public spirit. He also had known of his excellent work as
superintendent of the Asheville schools, and had learned of his

early years from Dr. Eben Alexander who had believed that he would go far in the profession of teaching. "Partly as a result of these things," Dabney wrote,[2] "but chiefly because from my earliest acquaintance with him I formed a great admiration for his zeal and devotion to the cause of Southern education, we called him."

The Southern Education Board originated in the Conference for Education in the South, which held its first meeting, June 29-July 2, 1898, at Capon Springs Hotel, West Virginia. The idea of such a conference was suggested by Dr. Edward Abbott of Cambridge, Massachusetts. He was present along with twenty-six other gentlemen from the North and the South. Among the latter was Professor James A. Quarles of Washington and Lee College. The following year a second meeting was held at the same place, seventy-five being present, forty of whom were Northerners. J. L. M. Curry was president, Robert C. Ogden vice president, and A. B. Hunter secretary and treasurer. Among the prominent members were George Foster Peabody, Dr. Albert Shaw, and Dr. Charles W. Kent. A third meeting was held the next summer also at Capon Springs Hotel. Only forty-four were present, eighteen of whom were from the North. Ogden was made president and Quarles became vice president.[3]

The fourth meeting at Winston-Salem, North Carolina, April 18–20, 1901, was a much more ambitious undertaking. Ogden brought a train load of about seventy men and women from the North and the South, who were interested in improving education in the South. Among the prominent members of the conference were Governor Aycock of North Carolina, Dr. McIver, Dr. Dabney, Dr. Lyman Abbott, George Foster Peabody, Walter Hines Page, Albert Shaw, and John D. Rockefeller, Jr. Claxton was among the less prominent members. He had been invited to attend some of the meetings at Capon Springs but was too busily engaged to accept the invitations.

Many stirring addresses were delivered on fundamental problems. Dr. George S. Dickerman of New Haven, Connecticut, declared, in substance, that Northern men and women should make it possible for Southern men of education, understanding, and ability to do what they knew better than any Northern man or woman could know. Dr. Curry delivered an inspiring and prophetic speech. President Dabney made an effective address, recommending the formation of a permanent committee.[4]

Dabney's suggestion was approved by the conference, and a board of seven was appointed. They were authorized to conduct a campaign of education for free schools for all the people and to establish a Bureau of Information and Advice on Legislation and School Organization. This board was also authorized to raise funds to carry out these purposes. The original membership comprised Curry, Dabney, Alderman, McIver, H. B. Frissell, Wallace Buttrick, and George Foster Peabody. At its first meeting in New York the following November these men were added: William H. Baldwin, Jr., Albert Shaw, Walter H. Page, and H. H. Hanna. Robert C. Ogden, president of the conference, became president of this board. McIver was elected Secretary and Peabody treasurer. Curry was made Supervising Director; Dabney, the Director of the Bureau of Information and Investigation (revised designation). District Directors were McIver, Alderman, and Frissell. Curry, Dabney, McIver, Alderman, and Frissell composed the Campaign Committee. The Field Agents were G. S. Dickerman and Booker T. Washington. Edgar Gardner Murphy was the Executive Secretary.[5]

According to Dr. Dabney, it was the educational campaign in North Carolina carried on by McIver, Alderman, Claxton, and others that led to the Conference for Education in the South and the establishment of the Southern Education Board.[6] It is significant that the meeting which organized that board was held in North Carolina, where the movement for the advancement of public schools originated.

On February 2, Claxton established an office at 21 McNutt Building in Knoxville. There Joseph D. Eggleston, who had been for several years superintendent of the Asheville schools, joined him as his assistant. Each, with a good secretary, went energetically to work and soon a mass of information, statistical and otherwise, pertinent to public schools in the South began to accumulate.[7]

For the expenses for the first year, George Foster Peabody supplied $30,000, and $10,000 was raised from various other sources.[8] One fourth of the money was appropriated for the maintenance of the Bureau of Information and Investigation; the rest was to be used for the educational campaign in the South—especially in Virginia, North Carolina, Georgia, and Louisiana. "The proper use of this fund in these directions," wrote [9] Claxton, "will mark the beginning of a new era in the South." To raise funds for future expenses a committee was appointed, out of which grew the General Education Board, chiefly supported by the munificence of John D. Rockefeller.[10]

For the Bureau of Investigation and Information, Claxton collected valuable statistical material relating to school attendance, length of terms, preparation of teachers, normal schools, higher education, taxes, and legislation. This information was distributed through circulars, notes, and bulletins.[11] Circulars containing statements and arguments for campaign workers were printed in editions varying from 15,000 to 25,000.[11] *Southern Education Notes* was published bi-weekly at Knoxville, beginning with March 10, 1902, and continuing until February 20 of the following year. The first issue numbered 1400 copies; later issues were increased to 2000. These "notes" contained all kinds of information suitable for republishing in newspapers, to which they were sent with permission for their use without acknowledgment of source. For the convenience of editors they were printed in the narrow format of a newspaper editorial.[11]

Bulletins contained extensive reports on investigations of problems. The subject of the first of these, published in May, 1902, was "Educational Conditions in the Southern Appalachians." It explained the historical background, the racial purity, and the educational needs of these white people who were, in 1900, 16 per cent illiterate. The bulletin of December, 1902, discussed "Educational Conditions in Tennessee." On its cover was a picture of Jefferson, around which were printed the great statesman's words, "Preach a crusade against ignorance." This gave statistical facts regarding school buildings, enrollment and attendance, school term, and number of teachers and salaries.[12]

"Fortunately," declared Claxton,[12] "this information met opposition and adverse criticism enough to help get the attention and thoughtful consideration of people, including politicians." Assistance and support were rendered freely by educators and educational officials throughout the South, where similar investigations on a small scale were being carried on. The harsh criticism came from the conservative, backward-looking opponents of progress and real democracy. Claxton's figures and statements began to be used in educational campaigns and before legislatures. "For the first time," he wrote,[12] "speeches and writings on education and educational legislation began to be based on definite knowledge of conditions and needs. For the first time people at large began to have definite ideas of those conditions and needs."

Claxton left his office frequently to make speeches in campaigns. He spoke at the school rally, held at Hickory, North Carolina, August 13, 14, 1902. It was a convention of the school superintendents of the western counties of the state. Other speakers were Governor Aycock and Ex-Governor Thomas J. Jarvis, State Superintendent of Schools Joyner, and Ex-Superintendent Mebane, President Winston of the Agricultural and Mechanical College, President Venable of the University, and President McIver of the Normal School. Traveling expenses of the speakers were paid by the Southern Education Board; local expenses by the community. "Educational rallies," wrote [13] Claxton, "have come to be more common than Sunday School picnics or protracted meetings. Scores of speeches are made every week, and one can hardly get off or on a train without meeting an educational campaign orator. People come to these rallies in wagons and carriages, driving miles and bringing their dinners with them. Nor do they come because of idle curiosity. They listen eagerly to the speeches, of which there are usually two or three." On November 7 following, he spoke on "The Outlook of the Public High School in the South" before the Association of Colleges and Preparatory Schools of the Southern States at the University of Mississippi. Just a week later he attended the meeting of county superintendents at Raleigh, North Carolina, as one of the representatives of the Southern Education Board.[14]

The Conference for Education in the South continued to meet annually, with a larger membership, of course, than the Southern Education Board. Its meeting in April, 1902, was at Athens, Georgia. There were addresses by President Ogden, Governor Hoke Smith, McIver, Alderman, Dabney, Aycock, Hamilton W. Mabie, Lawton B. Evans, Felix Adler, and Albert Shaw. Claxton read a report on the work of the Bureau of Information and Investigation.

After touching upon the educational needs and improvements in the South and the history of education in other states and other countries, he said, "The great problem in the South is the education of the children who live in the country and who must be educated in the rural public schools or none. The strength of the South is in its rural population, where it must remain for many generations." [15] The bureau, Claxton explained, planned to study the problems of education in mill towns as well as in the rural sections.

Because of his additional duties as Superintendent of the Summer School of the South and Head of the Department of Education of The University of Tennessee, described in the following chapters, and because he was still editor of the *Atlantic Educational Journal* and Secretary of the Southern Educational Association, it was thought best to relieve Claxton, at the end of the year 1902, of his work in the Bureau of Investigation and Information. Eggleston was promoted to his position, and Charles L. Coon of North Carolina was employed to take Eggleston's place. At the end of the following year Eggleston resigned to become superintendent of schools of Prince Edward County, Virginia, and Coon then became Chief of the Bureau.

A few months after the establishment of the Bureau of Investigation and Information, it was moved from its office in Knoxville to quarters at The University of Tennessee, with free light, heat, water, and rent. Here Claxton and his staff in the Department of Education unofficially assisted Eggleston and Coon. The second year the bulletins were continued under the title of *Southern Education*, a weekly publication beginning on March 12, 1903. This lasted throughout the year until December 21. Published irregularly, the issues numbered only twenty, totaling 420 pages and costing fifty cents a year to subscribers.[16]

The meeting of the Conference for Southern Education for 1903 was held at Richmond, Virginia, April 22–24. Its attendance was over 2000. President Ogden brought 112 distinguished Northerners on his private train. There were thirty-seven college presidents, thirty-nine college professors, and ten state superintendents present. Governor Montague of Virginia welcomed the conference which held its meetings in the Academy of Music. Speeches were given by President Ogden, Professor Wickliffe Rose of The University of Tennessee, Josephus Daniels, Chancellor Kirkland of Vanderbilt University, President Venable of the University of North Carolina, Professor Mims of Trinity College, President Houston of the Agricultural and Mechanical College of Texas, Dr. Bailey of Cornell, and Chancellor Hill of the University of Georgia.[17] Claxton spoke on "A Model School." This school was the Farragut High School, then being established at Concord, Tennessee, within sight of the birthplace of Admiral Farragut. It was established to demonstrate what a model industrial rural school should be. It was a practical experiment in the "new education," and eventually was visited by hundreds of superintendents and teachers from all over the South. It was connected with the Department of Education of The University of Tennessee and received funds from the General Education Board.[18] Claxton was a member of its board from 1903 until he became U. S. Commissioner of Education. In his address, he declared, "All people must be prepared for two things. First, they must be prepared for life. . . . The second thing to be remembered is that all people must make a living." [19]

On April 25 the entire conference went to the University of Virginia, where addresses were delivered by Ogden, Dr. Charles W. Dabney, and Dr. Charles W. Kent and Professor Richard H. Dabney of the University of Virginia. The keynote of the speeches was the great interest Thomas Jefferson had in public schools for general education. On the following day, a Sunday, a memorial service was held in Richmond for Dr. Curry, the great leader in the educational crusade who had died the previous 12th of February.[20]

Claxton did not attend the meetings of the Conference on Southern Education at Birmingham (1904), Columbia, South Carolina (1905), and Little Rock (1910). They were quite similar to the others, but the majority attending were from those respective states.

In 1905, a significant pamphlet, *Facts about Southern Educational Progress: A Study in Public School Maintenance* by Charles L. Coon, was published by the Bureau of Investigation and Information for workers in the field. Its statistics were based on the census for 1910 and upon the school reports of eleven Southern states for 1903–1904. Negroes, it declared, constituted 40 per cent of the population in 1900; the average amount of property behind each child of school age was only $1,837, less than half of the average for the entire United States; the average salary of teachers was $150 and the value of rural schoolhouses averaged only $285; the average school expenditure for each child in the South per year was $3.89, about one third of that for the whole United States. The statistics were also low for enrollment, attendance, and length of school term and high for illiteracy.

Dr. Wickliffe Rose of the Department of Education of The University of Tennessee assisted Claxton in studying schools for teachers. Before leaving in 1907 to become agent for the Peabody Board he also carried on an investigation into available educational funds and existing school laws. Two years later his findings were published in his *School Funds in Ten Southern States.*

In 1904, Claxton was assigned the work of directing the activities of the School Improvement League in several Southern states, most of which had either this organization or one under a different name which did the same kind of work. Claxton called meetings of the paid leaders of these associations, usually twice a year, for the discussion of methods, aims, and problems. At his suggestion, they soon took for their motto the same that had already been adopted in Tennessee: "For Our Schools, Health, Comfort, Beauty." In September, 1908, Claxton as chairman of the executive committee of the Co-operative Education Association in Tennessee employed Miss Virginia P. Moore of Gallatin as state organizer of school improvement leagues in that state, and by 1912 they were flourishing in practically every county in the state.[21] They worked for longer school terms, better school buildings, better sanitary conditions, and a better understanding and co-operation in providing for education. This work was aided by the Southern Education Board.

At the Conference for Education in the South, which met at Pinehurst, North Carolina, April 9–11, 1907, Claxton made a report on the campaign which he and Superintendent Mynders had made in Tennessee in 1905 and 1906 with the aid of the General Education Board. This was a part of the general report of field work, called "Educational Progress in the South: A Review of Five Years." Addresses were given by Governor Glenn, Dr. Bruce R. Payne of the University of Virginia, Chancellor Kirkland of Vanderbilt, Richmond Pearson Hobson, Professor Mims, and Josephus Daniels. A letter was read from President Ogden, who was prevented from attending by illness.[22]

In 1906, Claxton became a member of the Southern Education Board, which by that time had received many millions from Mr. Rockefeller for carrying into effect the work inspired by the Southern Education Board. For two years, 1908 and 1909, Claxton was chairman of the campaign committee of the General Education Board, and helped to direct this work in several states in so far as this was connected with the work of the Southern Education Board. The money appropriated by the General Board for this purpose was paid to these states according to Claxton's recommendations. Practically all the Southern states were carrying on educational campaigns at this time. In many of these campaigns Claxton himself participated.[23]

At an educational meeting at the University of Kentucky in Lexington, a patriotic Kentuckian spoke at the morning session and assured the audience that the schools of Kentucky afforded ample opportunity for all Kentucky youth, and that if any boy in that state failed to get a good education, it was his own fault. Of a man sitting beside him, Claxton inquired, "How would it do for me to tell the truth in my speech tonight?" He replied, "Go to it." Claxton was the principal speaker that evening, and spoke as honestly and truthfully as he could of the educational conditions in that state. The Louisville *Courier Journal* in an editorial, declared, "An unusual thing for a guest speaker to do, but unfortunately true."

In the audience were Mrs. Desha Breckinridge, C. C. Cherry, and other forward looking men and women. Out of this meeting came plans for the "Kentucky Whirlwind Campaign." This campaign in the summer of 1909 provided for speakers to go in pairs, and so divided the state that all counties could be visited and education rallies held in them in two weeks. Before beginning, the twenty-eight leaders met for a two days' conference in Lexington, and Claxton was invited to meet with them. In the campaign which followed immediately, he spent a week, speaking two or three times a day in the counties near Lexington.[23] The speakers addressed about 60,000 people at 300 public meetings. State Superintendent John G. Crabtree led the campaign. Mrs. Breckinridge, great granddaughter of Henry Clay, was, according to Claxton, "one of the firebrands setting off the conflagration." [24]

In Louisville, Claxton received mixed praise and criticism for a speech he gave at the meeting of the Kentucky Industrial Convention. His speech, printed in the *Courier Journal* and other papers and in pamphlet form, became a kind of textbook for the Kentucky campaign. Early in 1908 he addressed the Kentucky legislature at Frankfort on the same subject. This became known as the "Educational Legislature," because it passed a law which completely reorganized the school system, authorized the establishment within two years of high schools in every county, and made liberal appropriations for institutions of higher learning in the state—all resulting from the "Whirlwind Campaign." [25]

The other states in which Claxton assisted by speaking in educational campaigns were Alabama, Mississippi, South Carolina, Louisiana, Texas, Arkansas, and Georgia. With twenty-eight other speakers he participated in a two weeks' campaign in the latter state, speaking five or six times each week day and also preaching education on Sunday. This campaign stirred up the people's interest in county high schools.[25] During a similar campaign in South Carolina, he spoke in January, 1909, in the State Capitol at Columbia, attempting to show as clearly, forcefully, and truthfully as he could the real condition of public education in that state. Senator Ben Tillman was in the audience, and after Claxton left he spoke at the night meeting. "I was told," Claxton wrote,[26] "he used his pitchfork on me very vigorously, for my rudeness as an invited guest. But I found later that the speech was effective. South Carolinians of better manners avoided offending their fellow South Carolinians by suggesting that their schools were not so good as some of their neighboring states. Much of what I said seemed to be unknown to members of my audience."

Also, in April, 1908, Claxton spoke at Memphis during the annual meeting of the Conference for Education in the South, on "Methods of an Educational Campaign," based on recent experiences in Tennessee and Kentucky. There were many other addresses, among which was one by Ambassador James Bryce of Great Britain on "English Experience in Education." [27]

Claxton continued to be active in the affairs of the Southern

Educational Association. At the meeting in Chattanooga in July, 1902, he gave an address on "Local Taxation" and an impromptu speech as president of the Department of Normal Instruction. At the Asheville meeting the following summer he spoke extemporaneously on "The High School." At the Nashville meeting in November, 1905, he was made a member of the Board of Directors, and at the Lexington, Kentucky, meeting two years later, he was elected president of the association. At this meeting he made some remarks approving a paper by C. B. Gibson on "A Brief Account of Industrial Education at Columbus, Georgia." Claxton declared [28] that Pestalozzi was right when he said, "I will turn the car of education around. I will make these children intelligent in regard to the life that they must live." "In an industrial age, an age of universal education, an age when the whole public school system, from bottom to top, is accepted as a necessary fact and as a proper burden on the public revenues," he said, "we must get beyond the old time way of preparing a few elect boys and girls for professional life and for lives of culture and leisure."

Claxton also read [29] a paper on "The Rural High School," the thesis of which was that "the high school must be the heart and center of any vital school system." "Without good public high schools our Southern colleges and universities must remain small and weak," he declared. Continuing, he discussed the needs of the children of rural communities and the curriculum best adapted to meet these needs. "The South is now able to do for its children whatever it will," he affirmed. At this same meeting a paper on "Co-operation of School and Library" [30] was read by Miss Mary H. Johnson, Librarian of the Carnegie Library of Nashville, Tennessee. Five years later she was to marry Claxton.

At the Atlanta meeting in December, 1908, Claxton's Presidential Address was entitled "A Review, A Condition, A Task." [31] Great progress had already been made, he admitted, but he declared that all should continue to work for a nine months school, total attendance, better schoolhouses, consolidation of schools, better teachers and higher salaries, good public high schools in reach of all, reorganization of courses of study, sufficient normal schools, and industrial and agricultural schools.

At the meeting of the Conference for Education in the South, at

Atlanta, in April, 1909, Claxton presided over the Conference of Supervisors of the Women's School Improvement Work and also over the Conference of Campaign Managers of the Southern States. Among the addresses were those by U. S. Commissioner of Education Elmer Ellsworth Brown and Gifford Pinchot, Chief of the Bureau of Forestry of the U. S. Claxton spoke on "A School for Grown-Ups," which was based on his visit to the folk high school at Askov, Denmark. At the following meeting at Little Rock, though not present, he was elected secretary, a position which he held for two years.

In the summer of 1910, following his election as secretary, he was invited with other members of the Southern Education Board by George Foster Peabody, also a member, to a meeting at his famous home, Abenia on Lake George. Claxton spent three or four days as a house guest in this large mansion surrounded by beautiful grounds. "Mr. Peabody," Claxton wrote,[32] "was always a gentleman of distinguished appearance—very fine manners, hospitable, cordial, and generous to a fault. His own living was very simple. A friend of mine who knew him well said he was the only man he ever knew who was constantly looking for some good altruistic purpose for which he might spend his money."

As secretary of the Conference for Education in the South, Claxton arranged the meetings in Jacksonville in 1911 and in Nashville in 1912. At each of these meetings he was chairman of the Executive Committee. At the former he arranged for papers by Count Carl Moltke, Danish minister to the United States, by Dr. Paul Ritter, minister from Switzerland, and by Mr. John Christian Bay on "Folk High Schools of the Scandinavian Countries." While arranging the program for this Conference, Claxton went with a friend to the home of William J. Oliver in Knoxville to invite Theodore Roosevelt to speak at the Jacksonville meeting. Roosevelt was then in Knoxville as the principal speaker at the Appalachian Exposition. Roosevelt declined Claxton's invitation, saying that it would take too much time as he would have to stop often en route to make speeches. Claxton suggested that he take the boat from Washington to Jacksonville. The conversation ended without a reply.[34] At Nashville, the important speeches were made by Ogden, Alderman, David F. Houston, Walter Hines Page, and Dabney.[33]

From the commencement of his work for improving Southern education, Claxton had been interested in Negro schools, for improvement of which he had spoken and written frequently and persistently. When he was President of the Southern Educational Association in 1908, he arranged the program of the Atlanta meeting so as to give one session to a discussion of Negro education.[34]

The meeting of the Conference for Education in the South at Richmond in April, 1913, was practically the last one. Mr. Ogden was too ill to attend, and Walter Hines Page presided. There were over 2000 in attendance. Claxton, among many other speakers, made an address on "The Country Church and Good Literature." [35]

The next meeting was combined with that of the Southern Educational Association at Louisville, in April, 1914. Claxton, a Life Member of the Board of Directors of this association, gave an address on the "Improvement of the Rural School through Demonstration Schools." He was then U. S. Commissioner of Education, and was chosen to give the address at the memorial service for Mr. Ogden, who had died on August 6, 1913. The service was held on Tuesday evening, April 7, in the First Christian Church. He had been present, Claxton said, at the meeting of the Conference at Winston Salem, his first; though invited to attend the Capon Springs meetings, he had been unable to be present. He then gave a summary of the work of the various conferences and of the Executive Board, of which he had been a member more than half of the time. In conclusion, he said: "The heart and soul of the conference, and under God, above all others, the leader and inspirer of the movement, has been a simple, honest, lovable, great man, Robert C. Ogden. His annual addresses as president of the Conference have inspired us all to better things. His masterful and inimitable presiding, his wit and good cheer, his self-sacrifice, his patience, his interest in details can never be forgotten. His benediction rests on this conference and all its work. Whatever their first impressions and attitudes toward the Conference and its work, all who knew Mr. Ogden came to love him. His memory will long be cherished by thousands of people of the South, and the lives of millions who may never hear his name spoken will be richer and fuller because he lived." [36]

After the death of Dr. Ogden, resolutions were adopted by the

Conference for Education in the South to merge with the Southern Educational Association. The Southern Education Board, however, provided for the continuation of its agencies until July 1, 1914, when all its work was transferred to the General Education Board.[37] Thus ended, after thirteen years, an organization which gave immeasurable aid to the development of public education in the Southern states. In this great work Claxton had the distinction of playing an important role.

The merger was effected in April, 1915 under the name of the Southern Conference for Education and Industry. Claxton became a member of the Executive Board of seven members, and at the meeting in Macon, Georgia, in March the following year, he gave an address on "The Relation of Federal Government to Public Education." Since May, 1912 he had been one of the twelve trustees of the Southern Industrial Educational Association. Among the other trustees were Richmond Pearson Hobson and Thomas Nelson Page.

XI

The Summer School of the South

◇◇

IN MARCH, 1902, soon after Claxton came to Knoxville, he was
asked by President Dabney of The University of Tennessee to assist him in organizing a summer school, and to serve as its superintendent. Though summer schools had been held in connection
with some Southern universities, there had been no such school of
a rank commensurate with those in the North and West. A few
Southern teachers had attended these better summer schools, but
the low salaries had prevented most of them from doing so. Dabney,
therefore, decided to establish a summer school of the highest
grade in the heart of the South. Knoxville, Tennessee, was approximately the geographical center of the region south of the Ohio and
Potomac Rivers, and was an important railroad center.[1] It had a
population of about 35,000. Being situated 1100 feet above sea level,
it had a salubrious summer climate and beautiful mountain scenery.

Dabney succeeded in interesting the General Education Board,
the Peabody Board, George Foster Peabody, Robert C. Ogden,
Albert Shaw, and friends in Knoxville in affording financial aid to
the extent of about $6000. Though the school was to have no or-
ganic connection with The University of Tennessee, its board of
trustees donated free of charge the use of its buildings and grounds
and light, water, and janitor service for a period of six weeks. A
small board, of which Judge Edward T. Sanford was chairman, gave
the summer school a legal status.[1]

Claxton asked Dabney if he were willing to take the financial risk

[126]

involved in making the school better than any summer school for teachers then known. This would cost more money than had been promised by friends, but Dabney replied that he was willing to undertake anything for the good of education in the South. Claxton then suggested that the school be called the Summer School of the South, and that it be made such in reality—especially adapted to Southern needs for instruction, inspiration, and propaganda.

With his accustomed enthusiasm and energy, Claxton went to work to prepare for a session of the school in the summer of 1902.[2] His chief concern was to secure a faculty of distinguished educators. In this he succeeded beyond expectation. "At first, I was somewhat alarmed at Claxton's grand plans," wrote Dabney,[3] "but he had won my confidence and I let him go ahead and get the faculty he proposed. I remember that only once did I find it necessary to ask him to stop hiring professors, as I was on the verge of bankruptcy." Somewhat later, Dabney wrote[4] generously of Claxton, "He deserves the credit for organizing one of the most marvelous faculties ever brought together in a summer school in this country."

According to Claxton's bold plan, he proposed to assemble some of the greatest educators in the country. Among the fifty-one distinguished teachers whom he engaged for the first session of the school were eight presidents of Northern normal schools, colleges, or universities, three or four ex-presidents of such institutions, four or five deans, two or three of the best known superintendents of city schools, and a large number of professors, who were widely known as specialists in their chosen fields. The faculties of educational institutions in fifteen states were represented. His was a faculty of experts; no work was left to tutors and inexperienced teachers. Some of the members were President Alderman of Tulane University, President G. Stanley Hall of Clark University, President Charles D. McIver of North Carolina Normal and Industrial School, Ex-President Emerson E. White of Purdue University, President Henry Louis Smith of Washington and Lee University, Dean Brown Ayres and Dr. Alceé Fortier of Tulane, U. S. Commissioner of Education William T. Harris, Professor T. W. Jordan of The University of Tennessee, Walter Hines Page, Professor C. Alphonso Smith of Louisiana State University, Superintendent Edward P. Moses of the Raleigh schools, Superintendent B. C. Gregory of the public schools of Trenton, Superintendent E. H. Mark of the Louisville public schools, Professor Eben Alexander of the University of North Carolina, President E. C. Branson of Georgia State Normal School, Professor Austin C. Apgar of New Jersey State Normal School, President Arnold Tompkins of the Chicago Normal School, and Inspector of Schools James L. Hughes of Toronto, Canada.[5]

The courses of study were grouped under three divisions: Common School Subjects and Methods, High School and College Subjects, and Psychology and Pedagogy. The first included kindergarten, primary school organization, primary and elementary reading, expression, elementary and advanced arithmetic, elementary geometry, geography, grammar and rhetoric, United States history and civil government, nature study, ornithology, elementary agriculture, elementary horticulture, school gardening, elementary astronomy and meteorology, elementary physiology and hygiene, elementary physics, manual training, drawing, school music, physical culture, and school games. The second division comprised Greek, Latin, German, and French language and literature; modern European history, English history, history of the growth of religious tolerance in the sixteenth century; algebra, plane geometry, trigonometry, analytical geometry, and calculus; chemistry, physics, botany, geology and mineralogy, physiography of North America; mechanical drawing and popular science. In the third group were psychology, history of education, principles of education, philosophy of education, school management, and the art of teaching.[6]

General lectures were also scheduled to be given by many members of the faculty, publicists, statesmen, and distinguished men of affairs interested in Southern education. These, together with the members of the faculty and the courses of study, were detailed in an attractive bulletin, prepared by Claxton. This included a statement as to expenses. Tuition was free; only a registration fee of $5.00 was to be paid. Lodging and board averaged about $30.00 for the six weeks. All the Southern railroads offered a round trip rate of one fare. The total necessary expenses for each student amounted to $40 or $50 for the entire six weeks. Also advertised was the nearness of Knoxville to Asheville and Chattanooga with their scenic and historic attractions for excursions by the teachers.

Early in March, a preliminary statement was mailed to some

35,000 teachers. In this it was stated that the purpose of the school was "to help the teachers of the South to better scholarship and to greater power in teaching," and to this end "to offer here as good opportunities as can be found in any summer school in any part of the country." [7] In April 40,000 copies of the bulletin or complete announcement were mailed. To county superintendents and principals of schools 20,000 large posters were sent to be posted. Several thousand copies of these were distributed and posted by officials of the Southern Railway. Ten thousand copies of a condensed statement were also distributed. [8]

There appeared in the March issue of the *Atlantic Educational Journal* a general announcement of the school in two columns. Also in the next three issues of April, May, and June, there was a full page advertisement. In April and May, Claxton made a trip through the Carolinas, Georgia, Louisiana, Mississippi, Arkansas, Oklahoma, Texas, Alabama, and Tennessee, and talked with school superintendents, principals, and groups of teachers. In some states he spoke at meetings of state associations of teachers. No attempt was made to persuade teachers to attend the Summer School of the South rather than any other school they thought might be more profitable to them. [9] While on this tour, Claxton wrote Dabney that he thought there might be eight or nine hundred students in attendance and that a larger place would be needed for general assemblies than the University auditorium. Chairman Sanford of the Summer School board had predicted an attendance of only three hundred.

As a result of Claxton's letter, Dabney ordered a large open air pavilion, called Jefferson Hall, to be erected. It provided seats for about 1000. Improvised seats along the sides and the rear accommodated a few hundred more. The following year the pavilion was enlarged to seat under shelter an audience of about 1700. Five or six smaller pavilions for classes were later built on the shady hill sides of the campus. [10]

When the school opened on June 19, the registration for the first day was more than 1600. [10] From Georgia 150 teachers came on a special train with streamers marked "Summer School of the South." [11] The low cost of expenses had much to do with the large attendance. One teacher who had traveled more than 400 miles to attend said, at the close of the session, that he had saved enough on board to pay for his registration fee and his railroad fare. Of course, the chief attraction was the faculty of distinguished professors and lecturers, but teachers receiving the low salaries they were then paid could not have come in large numbers if the expenses had been high.[12]

The teachers began their work with great enthusiasm and eagerness. "There was upon the part of some an almost too eager desire to get the full measure of return from every hour," wrote E. G. Murphy.[13] "Upon the part of all there was, for the serious instruction, the response of genuine intellectual enthusiasm—not only the desire for light but also the joy of a co-operative sympathy—a desire for the best and a desire to put it at once to work. There was not merely a zeal for admiring things, but a zeal for using them. The dominant note, the constant and heroic note, was, therefore, practical. All in all, I have never witnessed anything finer in American life." The classrooms became places of eager, clear-cut discussion. The teacher-students were characterized by intelligence and refinement, and the seriousness of their purpose shone in their faces.

By the 4th of July, this enthusiasm had mounted to a high peak. Daily assemblies were held in Jefferson Hall each morning from eleven to twelve and in the evenings, at which lectures by distinguished men were heard or cultural entertainments were enjoyed. Independence Day was made a special occasion in the great hall named after Jefferson. The teachers, preceded by a band, marched to the hall by divisions according to states with national and state flags and banners with mottoes waving in the summer breeze. There was much singing of state songs, as the procession moved along the winding road under the green trees, the summer dresses of the women lending color and beauty to an unforgettable occasion.

The audience was seated by state groups, twenty-five in number. A unique feature of the program was the reading by President Dabney of the "Declaration of Principles," written by a committee from the school. This has been appropriately called "the Second Declaration of Independence for the South, a declaration of educational policy for the entire South." [16] These ten principles are so pregnant with meaning and significance that they demand to be quoted in full. To the great audience of Southern teachers, Dr. Dabney, a large man with dignified bearing, read these in a clear voice with ringing tones, as follows:

"1. We bear grateful testimony to the great sacrifices made in behalf of education by the people of the South, who, in their desolation and poverty, have taxed themselves hundreds of millions of dollars to educate two races.

2. Notwithstanding these efforts, we are confronted with the appalling fact that the large majority of the 3,000,000 white children and the 2,500,000 black children of the South are not provided with good schools. In 1900 ten Southern states having 25 per cent of the school population of this country owned only 4 per cent of the public school property and expended only 6½ per cent of the public school moneys. We must recognize these conditions and frankly face them. We therefore declare ourselves in favor of a public school system, state supported and state directed, in which every child may have the open door of opportunity.

3. Conscious of our dependence upon the God of our fathers, and believing that the highest and truest civilization can be attained only by following the precepts of the great teacher, Jesus Christ, we favor the recognition of the Bible in our public schools.

4. We regard local taxation as the foundation upon which a public school system should be built, and therefore favor an agitation in behalf of such taxation in every community.

5. If an increased expenditure of money is to be of lasting value, a more intelligent public interest must be brought to bear upon our schools. But even greater than the need of money and interest is the need of intelligent direction.

6. A mere extension of the present school term with the present course of study will not meet the needs of the children. The lines of development in the South must be both agricultural and mechanical. Our people must bring a trained brain and a trained hand to the daily labor. Education should be a means not of escaping labor but of making it more effective. The school should be the social center of the community, and should actively and sympa-

thetically touch all the social and economic interests of the people. In addition to the usual academic studies, therefore, our courses should include manual training, nature study, and agriculture.

7. To secure more efficient supervision, to encourage grading, and to broaden the social life of the children, we favor the consolidation of weak schools into strong central schools. It is better in every way to carry the child to the school than to carry the school to the child. We indorse the movements recently made by the women of the South for model schools, built with due regard to sanitation, ventilation, and beauty.

8. Teaching should be a profession, and not a stepping-stone to something else. We therefore stand for the highest training of teachers and urge the school authorities of every state to encourage those who wish to make the educating of children a life profession. We call upon the people to banish forever politics and nepotism from the public schools, and to establish a system in which, from the humblest teacher to the office of state superintendent, merit shall be the touchstone.

9. We express our hearty appreciation of the noble work of the Southern and General Education Boards, which by their earnest sympathy and generous means have made possible this great Summer School of the South, and in numerous other ways are strengthening the patriotic efforts of the Southern people to improve their educational conditions.

10. With gratitude to our fathers for the heritage of a noble past, with thankfulness to God for the many blessings bestowed upon our people, with due recognition of our present problems and their deep importance, we face the future with a faith which we shall endeavor to make good by our works, to the lasting glory of our Republic." [14]

The principles were seconded by speeches by Dean Henry St. George Tucker of the Washington and Lee Law School and by Superintendent Lawton B. Evans of Augusta, Georgia. These practical and inspiring addresses exemplified the fact that the highest form of patriotism was a preparation for the defense and progress of the country through the right education of all the people. Responses followed from the leaders of state groups, interspersed by the singing of state songs and college yells adapted to the occasion.

Finally the "Principles" were adopted unanimously by the assembled teachers. The celebration proved to be so inspiring and fruitful that it became an annual event as long as the Summer School functioned.

The organization of the school was wholly democratic; all met and mingled in perfect equality; teaching was enthusiastic and effective.[15] "It is small wonder," wrote H. W. Terry,[16] "that on the 4th of July, when the long procession opened to let the faculty and directors march through, the faces of the leaders wore a look of almost boyish delight. The appearance of that expression in the early days of the school was much in its favor. The biggest men, many of the biggest occasions have that quality. This biggest thing that has happened in the New South has it always latent. It is the delight in the game, the tingling of the blood, the perfect assurance that everything is going to turn out all right. . . . It was, in fact, when the whole school gathered together in the auditorium on the top of the hill, that their connection with the great campaign became manifest. . . . The fine speakers who gave the general addresses in the auditorium every morning were met by an audience that man after man declared the most inspiring he ever addressed. Out from this school are going to go men and women on fire. Their spirit is the spirit of the man who said, 'It's a pretty hard thing. But I'm the man to do it.' . . . It was all so healthy, so happy; the audience was all so frankly at one with the speakers that it was like a great family reunion at Thanksgiving time. It was a patriotic, a religious occasion. One never heard speaking more to the point and to the heart, more real; it was earnest, eager, sober, buoyantly hopeful; it bubbled over with fun, it was live English. It was filled with that spirit of thanksgiving which is also a bugle call."

There were twenty-five or thirty popular lectures by distinguished educators and supporters of education. Among the former was U. S. Commissioner of Education William T. Harris. Others were Dr. Eben Alexander on "Modern Greece," Professor Fortier on "Louisiana and France," Dean Ayres on "Physics of the Sun," President McIver on "The Education of Women," President Branson and Superintendent Evans on the poor white and the country schools, Dr. John Campbell Merriam on the "Physiography of North America," and Dr. Henry Louis Smith on "Popular Science."

Among the latter speakers were Governor Aycock of North Carolina and Governor McMillin of Tennessee, William H. Baldwin, Jr., of the Southern and General Education Boards, Secretary Wallace Buttrick of the General Education Board, Editor Albert Shaw of *Review of Reviews*, and Editor Walter Hines Page of *World's Work*. Page gave five lectures on "How to Write Clear English." Besides giving lectures to classes in psychology and pedagogy, the following also spoke at general assembly: President Arnold Tompkins, Superintendent B. C. Gregory, Dr. Emerson E. White, President Alderman, and President G. Stanley Hall.

The Summer School of the South was the first institution in the South at which Dr. Hall spoke. His class lectures were on child study, education of motor centers, evolution and education, value of different studies, high school and higher education, school and home, education of women, religious education, and preparation of teachers. "Without offense to any," Claxton wrote,[17] "it may be claimed that these lectures by Dr. Hall constituted the most important and most popular feature of the school."

Other important features of this first session were the frequent meetings of school officers and institute conductors, the educational campaigners convention of July 4th and 5th, and meetings of Sunday School workers on Sunday afternoons and evenings, led by Claxton and others.

When the school closed on July 31, the total enrollment had reached 2019, the students coming from 28 states and one territory.[18] The largest registrations, not including those from Tennessee, were, in this order, from Georgia, Alabama, North Carolina, South Carolina, Louisiana, Kentucky, Florida, Texas, and Virginia. There were 687 men and 1332 women. Two thirds were graduates of colleges or normal schools.[19] About 900 came from Tennessee, 250 of whom were from Knox County. The Summer School of the South would indeed not have been able to accommodate the flood of teachers but for two factors: the railway fare was too much for many who lived at great distances from Knoxville, and many states, such as Virginia, South Carolina, Texas, and Louisiana, had summer normal schools which that year had a larger attendance than ever before. Still, according to G. Stanley Hall, "It is the biggest one in the world. In numbers and interest it has never been surpassed. From what observation I have been able to give the class work, the character of the work being done is of the best. . . . This school is sure to have a tremendous influence upon Southern civilization."

The total expenses of the first session of the Summer School of the South amounted to $14,795.75. The General Education Board gave $750; Robert C. Ogden $1000; and George Foster Peabody $2000.[20] Subscriptions were also received from the Peabody Board, Albert Shaw, and friends in Knoxville.[21] According to Dabney, the total expenses exceeded all receipts by about $1500, which he paid with money borrowed on his life insurance policy, this being repaid to him from receipts of the second session.[22] "Such was Claxton's enthusiasm for setting up a great school," he continued, "that I had to hold a tight rein on him, having as president of the University undertaken the financial management of the school on my own personal responsibility." And he added, "I give Claxton chief credit for the remarkable success of this school."

Encouraged by the success of the first session, Dabney and Claxton expanded the work of the next year, with the aid of an appropriation of $10,000 from the General Education Board. There were 91 members of the faculty who offered 149 courses to 2,150 students: 662 men and 1488 women, from 31 states and territories and from Canada, Puerto Rico, India, and Japan.[23] Two professors from Columbia University, whose names were well known to all students of pedagogy, joined the faculty; they were Edward Lee Thorndike and Charles A. McMurry.[24]

The school followed the pattern of the previous year. There was the same eager enthusiasm; the same beehive activity on the "Hill"; the same interest in the inspiring lectures at the daily assemblies. An attractive new feature was a model school library of 1250 volumes on display, and also exhibits of textbooks, school apparatus, and school supplies.[23] In addition to the registered students, 703 visitors attended the lectures, conferences, and conventions.[25] The total expenses rose to $30,398.15, which included the cost of some additional buildings.[26]

And so continued the Summer School of the South during the eight succeeding summers while Claxton was its Superintendent, holding to its double purpose of giving the best possible opportunity for teachers to improve their culture and their preparation for teaching, and of promoting the cause of democratic public education in the Southern states. During this time it ranked with the Conference for Education in the South as one of the two great agencies for the promotion of universal Southern education.

The courses of study continued to be wide in range of subject from kindergarten to college. Besides the psychology, philosophy, history, and methods of education, which were stressed, there were courses in Latin, Greek, and modern languages, advanced mathematics, the sciences, history, music, art, physical education, and Swedish gymnastics and games. Two summers, courses were given in Russian literature. There were courses in Jewish history and literature given by Rabbis, sent to the school without cost. The faculty was maintained at an extraordinarily high level. Some continued to return from summer to summer. Among the names appearing from time to time on the anual summer school announcements of faculty and lecturers were John Dewey, C. Alphonso Smith, Richard T. Ely, Charles W. Kent, Edwin E. Sparks, Hamilton Wright Mabie, Paul Monroe, J. W. Redway, Henry Lawrence Southwick and Jessie Eldridge Southwick of Emerson College of Oratory, George Herbert Clarke, Edward Howard Griggs, Archibald Henderson, Arthur Radclyffe Dugmore, President John Duxbury of Manchester (England) School of Elocution, John Holladay Latané, Ernest H. Shackleton, and William Jennings Bryan.[27]

Beginning in 1905, concerts were given by famous musicians, including Reinald Werrenrath, baritone; Thaddeus Rich, violinist; Giuseppe Campanari, baritone; Daniel Beddoe, tenor; Henry Witherspoon, basso; Janet Spencer, contralto; Violet Waterhouse, soprano; Henri Ern, Swiss violinist; Lillyn Sheila Powell, Celtic ballad singer; and Maude Powell, the greatest woman violinist in the world. Witherspoon and Miss Powell returned again and again for many summers. An idea as to the low cost of these concerts may be formed from the fact that in 1908 Miss Powell was paid only $600 for four concerts.[28] Each summer, concerts were given every night throughout "music week," usually by a group of six artists—four singers, a violinist, and an accompanist. Frequently one or more of these took part in the morning assembly program.

Claxton received no extra salary for directing the work of the school. "The summer school was simply vacation work," he wrote.[29] "After Dabney had left and the entire burden of the summer school had fallen on me, I sometimes paid myself a few hundred dollars, if there was a surplus after all other expenses were paid. Usually there was no surplus. If there was a deficit, I gave my personal note at the City National Bank for the amount needed to pay all debts. This amount was considered as a legitimate charge against the income of the next summer. One year, as I now remember, I paid myself approximately $750; most of the years, nothing. The deficit was frequently more than this. . . . For myself, the summer school was a labor of love, as it was to a large extent for most of the fine men and women who served as teachers and entertainers."

Originating at the Summer School of the South were the following significant organizations: Southern Kindergarten Association, National Story Tellers' League, National Guild of Play. Many other organizations met there from year to year; such as, Interstate League for the Betterment of Public Schools, School Improvement Conference, Southern High School Conference, and the American School Peace League.

During the ten years of Claxton's superintendency the enrollment varied from 1312 in 1904 to 2529 in 1911. During this period over 22,000 teachers registered from about forty different states, including all those of the South, from which the larger portion of the teachers came.

The faculty varied in number from 125 to 150, and approximately 750 lectures and entertainments of cultural and professional value were given. The cost averaged about $25,000 a year. The General Education Board continued to donate $10,000 annually, and the Knox County Court $2,500 for free registration of its teachers. Friends in Knoxville subscribed from $3000 to $4500 a year. The registration fee was raised to $6.00 in 1905 and the next year it was increased to $8.00; in 1909 it reached $10.00. The University of Tennessee continued to give free use of its grounds, buildings, and other facilities, but because of the objection of some members of its faculty it did not give credit to the work of the school. The University of Chicago, however, and many state universities accepted its work at face value.[30]

After leaving Tennessee to be the United States Commissioner of Education in 1911, Claxton returned the following year to give round table conferences at the Summer School, July 2–5, on rural education and vocational and moral education. Also he was a lecturer at the school on July 22, 1914. After Dabney left Knoxville in 1905 to become President of the University of Cincinnati, Claxton alone continued the administration of the school. In addition to managing the school, he taught courses three or four hours each day.

Dabney was always eager to acknowledge the importance of Claxton's work in the Summer School. In closing his report for 1904, he wrote, "I cannot close this report, however, without expressing my personal feeling of gratitude to Professor P. P. Claxton, superintendent of the school throughout its whole career, who deserves the credit for its detailed management. He has been wise in directing, faithful in managing, and self-sacrificing in personal service to a degree that none can ever know who have not had the opportunity to watch his work as I have done. More than any other man he made the actual school what it was and to him, therefore, I wish to extend my most hearty thanks." Over forty years later Dabney wrote,[31] "I give Claxton chief credit for the remarkable success of this school. It was his idea to get a large faculty and to call it the Summer School of the South and then make it deserve the name."

"There were many men and many women who made marvelous contributions to this summer school," wrote Willis A. Sutton,[32] then Superintendent of Atlanta schools, who attended the summer school in 1911 and 1912, "but the guiding spirit, the genius of the institution, the inspirer of all students, old and young, and the leader of our thinking as well as the source of our information was Philander P. Claxton, who seemed to be almost everywhere at the same time. During the two years that I attended the school, I met him often on the walkways, in the passages between buildings, and at the lunch hour. At any and all times he could be seen; everybody had access to him. They could tell him their troubles, their anxieties, their worries and cares with the assurance that they would be patiently listened to and that their problems would be astutely judged and that the right kind of guidance, advice, and information would be given. Regardless of whether he was on the platform at the great assemblies where all received inspiration at the same time, or whether he sat behind his desk, or whether he conversed under the magnificent trees or gave advice as we walked about, it was always the same inspiring, informative, and guiding hand of a great genius that directed us while there we labored together. . . . The leader in it all was Philander P. Claxton, one of the nation's greatest educators and one of the choicest individual spirits it has ever been my pleasure to know."

Another interesting impression of Claxton's work in the Summer School of the South comes from Dr. Ambrose L. Suhrie, then a professor in New York University. "I have in mind very vividly the picture of the Summer School of the South," he wrote,[33] "under his inspiring leadership in the days of the truest educational renaissance which this country or any section of it has ever had. Judged by its immediate and long-term practical results, I do not think that we have ever had an educational movement launched in any one of our colleges or universities in any part of the country or in any period of our history, which accomplished so much as did the Summer School of the South under Dr. Claxton's leading."

Of the Summer School of the South, Henry Nelson Snyder has written in *An Educational Odyssey*,[34] "To the very end the school was a combination of the campaign mood of the early crusaders of popular education, of the patriotic fervor of the Ogden Movement, of a passion to know conditions and improve them, and of the close application of men and women who desired earnestly to add to their knowledge, learn better methods of teaching, and come to a clearer understanding of the subject matter of their profession. I doubt whether there will ever again be such a combination of high and noble human emotions as those that fused into an enthusiastic unity that miscellaneous group of nearly 3000 people, coming as they did from 34 American states, 90 per cent of them from the Southern states. . . . I count the three weeks spent at the Summer School of the South, coming as they did so close upon the session of the Conference for Education in the South at Athens, Georgia, and following immediately my acceptance of the presidency of Wofford, as a most valuable experience."

At that time, Claxton was in the very prime of life, and a more handsome man it would have been difficult to find. He was then a widower, his second wife having died in 1905, and he was accordingly much sought after as an eligible husband by some of the women attending the Summer School. It is not an exaggeration to state that he received baskets full of "fan" mail by such admirers. But his behavior was always proper, dignified, and decorous. He was too preoccupied with his many duties as Superintendent to take any "campus courses" himself.

◆§ XII §◆

Head of Department of Education
University of Tennessee

◇◇◇

A FTER GAINING the approval of the Board of Trustees, President
Dabney asked Claxton in July, 1902, to organize and head a
new Department of Education at The University of Tennessee.[1] His
salary was to be $1800, which was the same as that of other pro-
fessors on the faculty. He accepted the position, and at once began
to assemble a faculty and organize the courses of study.

It was not until January 6, 1903, that the new department began
to function with a faculty of four full time members and seventy-
five students from six different states. Claxton was chairman of the
department, and taught the science and art of teaching. Wickliffe
Rose, M.A., was professor of the history and philosophy of education. Lilian Wycoff Johnson, Ph.D., was assistant professor of
history and the methods of teaching history. Anna Monroe Gilchrist was instructor in manual training and domestic science and
art. Burtis Burr Breese, Ph.D., was professor of psychology and
ethics. He also gave courses in psychology in the Literary Department (now called the College of Liberal Arts) in the University.
Samuel McCutchen Bain, professor of botany; Florence Skeffing-
ton, assistant professor of English and instructor in the methods of
teaching English; and Emilie Watts McVea, instructor in the
English language and literature, also taught in the Literary Department as well as in the Department of Education. Andrew Mc-
Nairn Soule, professor of agriculture and instructor in nature study,
and Charles A. Keffer, professor of horticulture and instructor in

plant culture and school gardening, also were attached to the Department of Education. Mary Read Comfort, instructor in free-hand drawing, was assisted by Alexander C. Lanier of the Department of Engineering. In this way the new Department of Education was intricately connected with the other departments of the University. The total number of its students in Knoxville was then only 481.[2]

The subsequent careers of members of this new department indicate their unusual ability. Miss McVea afterwards became dean of women at the University of Cincinnati and later was president of Sweet Briar College. Miss Johnson became president of Wesley College in Oxford, Ohio. Miss Gilchrist later went to New Zealand as head of the department of home economics at Otago College and later still to Baroda College in India for similar work. Amanda Stoltzfus, who later joined Claxton's staff, afterwards went to the University of Texas Extension Department. Dr. Breese afterwards became professor of psychology at the University of Cincinnati. Dr. Rose became, in turn, dean of Peabody College, general agent of the Peabody Education Fund, secretary of the Rockefeller Sanitary Commission, and president of other important educational foundations.[3] The others remained at The University of Tennessee.

Besides being head of this Department of Education, Claxton was the director of the practice-demonstration school, a Knoxville city school on Rose Avenue under the principalship of a Miss Fletcher.[4]

Claxton soon made his department the largest of its kind at the time except that in the University of Chicago and Teachers College of Columbia University. The work of his department was given equal rank with others in the University and led to the same degrees. "It is not the purpose of this department to compete with the normal schools of the South," wrote [5] Claxton, "but rather to become a school of education of higher grade and to prepare men and women of scholarship for superintendents, principals, and responsible positions as teachers in public and private schools of cities, towns, and country districts." This aim was reached, for during the eight years he was its head it became the most widely known department of education in the universities of the South, both in its plan of work and in its staff. With a more hearty co-operation of the other professors on the faculty of the University, it might have taken a prominent place among the leading departments of its kind in the entire country.

There was a lack of sympathy among the University professors not only for the Department of Education but also for the Summer School of the South, though an average of a dozen or more taught in the school each summer. They had little sympathy also for the movement for universal education in the South, taking the point of view of the church and private school teachers in the South. Even the Board of Trustees were unsympathetic to the work of the Southern Education Board. One of these, in an address before this Board at a banquet given in honor of Mr. Ogden on his visit to the University, made an attack on the Board, charging that they were "meddling with Southern education" and trying "to put the Negro on top in the South."

When Dabney left the University to become president of the University of Cincinnati, he suggested to one of his best friends on the Board of Trustees that Claxton be made president of The University of Tennessee because of his great success with the Summer School of the South. But the Board refused to consider him for the presidency because of his connection with the Southern education movement. Dabney thought it very noble of Claxton that he stayed on at the University after this, and did such a magnificent work both in the Department of Education and the Summer School, and for the school system of Tennessee.[6] After the death of McIver, president of the Normal and Industrial School for Women in Greensboro, in 1907, Claxton was offered the presidency because of his excellent work at Greensboro and elsewhere in North Carolina, but he chose to remain in his native state.

While Claxton was connected with The University of Tennessee, he was also offered the superintendency of the schools of Knoxville, and of Memphis, Tennessee; the head of the College of Education of the University of Virginia, and of the University of Cincinnati; and the presidency of the North Carolina College of Agriculture and Mechanic Arts, the Greensboro College for Women, the University of Vermont, the Virginia Normal School at Farmville, and the Peabody College for Teachers. These were not accepted because he was then engaged in educational work in Tennessee which he could not well leave. One of the offers he did not consider because he had determined to give his life and energy to the South. But in 1906 he accepted the degree of Doctor of Literature, conferred upon him by Bates University in Maine in recognition of aid rendered by him to Dr. Stetson, Superintendent of Public Education, in an educational campaign.

After Claxton became United States Commissioner of Education, the Department of Education of The University of Tennessee was continued and eventually became the College of Education, an enduring monument to his pioneering work.

Very soon after coming to Knoxville, Claxton began to plead for public high schools throughout the state. His first speech on this subject was made at Bearden, near Knoxville, in 1902. There was then only one high school for country children in the entire state. This was at Tiptonville in Lake County. There were, of course, high schools in the towns and cities, though their curriculum was limited; and there were several very good private academies. But no progress had been made in establishing county high schools, though a law had been passed in 1899 permitting county courts to levy taxes for this purpose.

The year 1902 was an important one for public education in Tennessee. In November of that year James B. Frazier was elected governor. He was to play a role in Tennessee similar to that of Aycock in North Carolina. In his message to the legislature in January, 1903, Frazier declared, "Universal education is the only safeguard for universal suffrage. It is the very bedrock of our civilization as well as of our prosperity; it raises the standard of citizenship, while it decreases crime and cheapens government; it increases the productive energy of the people and it augments the wealth of the State; it encourages healthful immigration and adds desirable citizens to the Commonwealth. It has come to be universally conceded in all the American Commonwealths that public education is a function of the State." [7]

At that time great improvements had already been made in the public school system from what it was when Claxton attended the country schools of Bedford County. In 1902 there were 6,758 primary schools and 1,069 secondary schools in the state. The average school term, however, was still only 95 days, varying from

[144]

50 to 168 days in different counties. Only 62% of the scholastic population was enrolled, and of these 484,663 children only 341,538 were in regular attendance. Of 7,136 schoolhouses, about one seventh was of log construction, while only 164 were built of brick or stone. The average monthly salary paid to county teachers was $28.36. The certification of teachers by examination was left to the county superintendents. County institutes, for which the state appropriated $10,000 in 1901, were the chief means for training teachers. There were only 274 students from Tennessee in Peabody College for Teachers in 1902. There was no provision for consolidation of schools, no school libraries, no free textbooks, and no teachers' pensions at that time, and nothing was contributed by the state legislature to the support of The University of Tennessee. The total fund for public schools in 1902 was $1,883,744.66, all but about $300,000 of which was derived from the poll tax. The schools in the towns and cities were, of course, very much better as their state allotments were supplemented by local taxation.[8]

In February, 1903, at the meeting of the Public School Officers Association, Claxton proposed a resolution requesting the association to approve, and work for, a state appropriation for the state university. Bitterly opposed and debated, it was carried by a small majority. This support had no immediate results, though the 1903 legislature made an appropriation to purchase an addition to The University of Tennessee farm—the first appropriation from state funds for the use of the University. In the following April, an education conference, called by the State Superintendent of Schools, met at Peabody College. Eighty per cent of the county superintendents attended, their expenses being paid by the General Education Board. Dr. Buttrick, Dr. Glenn of Georgia, Dr. McIver, and Dr. Alderman were present. For three days the conditions and needs of education in Tennessee were freely and frankly discussed before an enthusiastic crowd of "friends of education."[9]

Governor Frazier made an excellent choice for the office of State Superintendent of Public Instruction in Seymour A. Mynders, a graduate of The University of Tennessee who had had long and practical experience in the public school system of the state. This official was then paid only $2000, and by law was required to disseminate "statistical information," make tours of inspection, and see "that the school laws and regulations" were faithfully executed.[10] Mynders and Dabney drew up a bill which was passed by the 1903 legislature, providing that the balance in the treasury at the end of the year would be distributed to the counties according to population for increasing their public school funds. Surprisingly, there was a balance of $250,000 for that year and a larger balance of $375,000 for the next year.[11]

This was the first faltering step toward the practical improvement of public schools—an improvement which was rapidly accelerated as a result of the educational campaigns in which Claxton played the leading role. These were so interesting and so important that the detailed account of them has been reserved for the following chapter.

In connection with his many other duties while head of the Department of Education at The University of Tennessee, Claxton accepted membership on the Sanitary Commission for the Eradication of the Hookworm Disease in 1909 when it was established to administer a gift of one million dollars from Mr. Rockefeller for that purpose. He remained a member during the entire existence of the Commission. It became a great health education movement.[12] On the day it was organized Walter Hines Page, another member, wrote [13] in his diary, "The one greatest single cause of anaemia and stagnation in the South will by this fund be ultimately removed and two million inefficient people be made well." This turned out to be no vain prophecy.

In addition to the many addresses which Claxton made at the meetings of the Conference for Education in the South, the Southern Educational Association, and the National Education Association, he spoke on education very frequently in cities particularly in the North and West.

For example, in March, 1908, Claxton spoke at Teachers' College of Columbia University at a meeting arranged by Professor Munroe. This speech called forth a favorable editorial in the New York Times.[14] "A very remarkable exposition was made at Columbia University last Sunday of the advance in education in the South by Dr. P. P. Claxton, head of the Department of the History [sic] of Education in The University of Tennessee," declared the editorial. "The very existence of such a department in a Southern university is a fact of much significance. According to Dr. Claxton it would hardly be an exaggeration to say that until the past twenty years the history of education in the South, certainly the history of general public education, would be like an account of the snakes in Iceland [sic]. We emphasize this point with no wish to make invidious comparisons, but solely to bring out the very great progress made by the South."

After giving Claxton's statistics showing the increase in high schools in Southern states during the past five years, the editorial concludes, "The increase is thirty-fold. We know of no such record in the North. It is true that the increase seems more impressive because so little had been done in the past. But it must be remembered that this fact also rendered the work of establishing schools so much more arduous. Very much the same achievement has taken place in the establishment of good normal schools, of schools for the training of teachers, a special work in itself, and a very difficult one. To estimate these tasks at their true value, two facts must be borne in mind, the absolute poverty of the people of the South at the close of the Civil War, and the enormous difficulties imposed by the presence of the enfranchised slaves and their descendants."

Claxton also spoke on "Temples of the People" (adult education) at the Labor Temple School on the East Side in New York, with which Will Durant, the author of the *Story of Philosophy*, was connected.

Early in April following, Walter Hines Page wrote Claxton, suggesting that he come to New York for a month's vacation in the autumn. As a postscript he wrote the clause, "If you don't rest," after which he drew the outline of a grave with this explanation: "This is a mound where the daisies grow!" [15]

Claxton replied that it would give him a great deal of pleasure to "loaf around New York for a month next fall under your direction," and that he was planning to take a vacation of at least two weeks after the close of the educational campaign in Tennessee. "Some people are arranging for a meeting at Cooper Institute on the evening of May 11," he added,[16] "at which I am to speak. I am going to present the question of the possibility of practical education for the grown up young men and women of the Southern mountains."

In answer, Page advised [17] Claxton, "Don't confine your May 11th address wholly to the mountaineers, if you will accept a suggestion from a man who conscientiously takes a month's vacation every year before he feels tired, and makes it the habit of his life to loaf all he can between times. By the way, you must come up and spend some time with me then—that is, come out to my house."

During the summer of this year, Claxton spoke at the home of a wealthy woman in New York City to an invited group. His subject was education in the South, particularly in the mountains. When he had finished, the hostess asked in surprise, "Do you have public schools in the Southern mountains?" She was the author of several books on Russia but was not familiar with her own country.

Not long afterwards he spoke on the same subject on a Sunday in Chicago at Lincoln Place Church, of which Dr. Jenkin Lloyd Jones was pastor. In his address, Claxton declared that the Southern mountaineers were not degenerate but possessed great native intelligence and only needed education and training so that they might develop the natural resources of that region. After the address, while standing in front of the pulpit and shaking hands with the people, he saw a distinguished looking man with an apparently benevolent face approaching and he said to himself, "He is going to make a generous offer of help." Instead, the man asked, "Why do these people need help, if the natural resources are as abundant as you say and the people are intelligent?" Claxton thought his question "not a bad one." [18]

As an illustration of the extent of Claxton's speechmaking while in Knoxville, during the first six months of the year 1911 he addressed teachers' meetings at Danville, Illinois; Oshkosh, Wisconsin; Oklahoma City; Forest City, Arkansas; Indianapolis; and Macon, Georgia. Besides, he delivered five commencement speeches in Tennessee, two in Indiana, and five in Wisconsin. He also spoke on "Universal Education as a Factor in International Peace" at the National Peace Conference in Baltimore on the 5th of June, and addressed many teachers' meetings in Tennessee. "Education for Democracy" was the subject of many of his speeches during those years. This was a broad subject with many ramifications.

"Claxton used to say," declared [19] Judge Albert Williams, "that he had only one speech, which he thought would be about eight hours long if he ever delivered the whole of it, and that he only took such parts of it as each occasion seemed to call for most strongly and as time permitted. Although this was subject to the inaccuracy which attends all general statements, it was noteworthy because it reflected the fact that he conceived the cause of public education as an indivisible unit and the interest of its organs inseparable."

◄§ XIII §►

Educational Campaigns in Tennessee

◇◇

IN 1904, under the direction of Dr. Dabney, President of The University of Tennessee, Claxton and State Superintendent of Education Mynders organized a systematic campaign for improving the public schools.[1] Claxton was the manager of this campaign. "At first," wrote[2] Claxton, "we took advantage of all possible opportunities to speak and write for education and to get others to do so. We used school commencements, picnics, churches, Sunday schools, farmers' meetings, Decoration Day assemblies, lodge meetings, etc. I wrote to all colleges and high schools asking that they request their commencement speakers to speak on education, to preachers asking them to preach on education, to editors asking them to write on education, to women's clubs asking them to put education in Tennessee on their programs, to labor unions asking them to discuss education and to give their help, to county superintendents asking them to have the purposes and programs of the educational campaign discussed in all their teachers' meetings, and to all other available organizations and publicists asking their aid."

The 1905 legislature passed the Tollett Bill which limited to $300,000 the amount the state school fund might receive in any year from the "surplus act" of 1903, $50,000 of which was to be used as an equalization fund for poorer counties. A bill appropriating $105,200 for two years to The University of Tennessee was written by Claxton. He had difficulty in getting the faculty to approve it; they feared that, if the state supported the University, the state would control it. After much lobbying, the appropriation was scaled down to $25,000 for two years, a part of which was to be used for paying the traveling expenses of students from West and Middle Tennessee, and the bill then passed. This was the first appropriation by the state for the support of the University. This legislature also appropriated $25,000 a year for ten years to Peabody College.

Early in 1905, Dabney with the financial aid of the General Education Board established at The University of Tennessee a professorship of secondary education. Combined with it were the duties of high school inspector. At Dabney's request Claxton accepted this new position, giving courses in secondary education, high school organization, and curriculum, while he continued as head of the Department of Education.[2] An additional salary of $2,250 was paid him by the General Education Board for this extra work.[3]

Early in the spring of 1905, Claxton wrote to Mynders suggesting that they plan and conduct an educational campaign in all the counties of East Tennessee. Mynders agreed with the understanding that Claxton make the plans, arrange and advertise the meetings, and pay all necessary expenses. He could pay only his traveling expenses from state funds and send postcards to all county superintendents, teachers, and district school committeemen, directing them to announce a holiday if the schools were in session at the date set for the meeting in their county and also requesting their attendance. Claxton had sufficient money from the General Education Board to pay for advertising and his traveling expenses.

Rallies were arranged in thirty-six counties, one each week day in order to reduce traveling expenses to the minimum. Large posters were printed and sent to school officials to be displayed in conspicuous places. Notices were also sent to the newspapers. The superintendents were asked to arrange for picnic dinners. They were requested to speak themselves and to ask prominent lawyers, preachers, and other influential persons to participate in the programs. If the schools were in session, it was requested that the children march to the place of assembly. A new United States flag and a Tennessee flag, then but recently adopted by the legislature, were purchased, and a dozen appropriate mottoes were stenciled in large letters on strips of white cloth approximately eighteen inches by five feet in size. These were all to be displayed on the speakers' platform, the walls of buildings, and on trees if the meetings were held outdoors.

Soon after the close of the session of the Summer School of the South, the campaign was begun. The attendance was larger than had been anticipated. In some counties two or three thousand people assembled to hear the speakers. In one county more than one thousand children marched with banners and mottoes. After this parade, Claxton in his speech reminded the audience that they had been watching the future march by and that they were responsible for the character of that future. Mynders spoke in most of the counties; Claxton in all of the thirty-six in East Tennessee. Frequently he spoke two or three times on Sunday, and on week days in the evenings at other places than the county seat, where the rally was held. As the average per county was more than a thousand in attendance at the meetings, he probably addressed about 50,000 people during the campaign. His principal subject was the improvement of schools at public expense and under public control.[3] He had plenty of material for these addresses—ideas on which he had elaborated in his editorials in the school journals and on which he had frequently spoken in similar campaigns in North Carolina.

These rallies usually lasted all day, interrupted by picnic dinners or barbecues. In season, there were wagon loads of watermelons for sale,[4] and the number in attendance could be predicted by the number of watermelon wagons en route to the place of meeting. As previously in North Carolina, the people listened to the speakers with an earnestness only to be observed at religious revivals, and responded with an enthusiasm only to be witnessed during a heated political debate. This East Tennessee educational campaign was very important in its later effects as well as in its encouragement to the leaders. It also served as a testing ground for the methods soon to be employed throughout the state.

In the winter of 1905–1906, Claxton proposed to Mynders that a similar campaign be made in all the 96 counties of Tennessee. He agreed on the same terms as for the East Tennessee campaign. All expenses were to be paid through the Southern Education Board.

These included the necessary traveling expenses of a few prominent speakers. Mynders' traveling expenses were paid out of state funds.

The Summer School of the South closed its session in 1906 on Friday, July 28. Claxton spent the following Saturday and Sunday in settling accounts and writing his report, and left his office just in time to catch the evening train for Memphis, where the first rally was to be held on Monday evening. In the previous campaign no definite legislative program had been presented to the people. After advising with Mynders and Rose, Claxton decided to correct this omission. On the train to Memphis he drew up a program under seven headings in the form of a resolution, as follows: [5]

"We do hereby petition the general assembly at its next session to make the following appropriations, and we request our representatives in both houses to give their support and influence to the enactment of laws providing for such appropriation:

1. 75¢ per capita per child of school age.
2. Continuation of the Tollett Bill appropriation of $50,000 to help weak schools [passed in 1905].
3. Annual appropriation of $25,000 to encourage and assist the establishment of public high schools.
4. Annual appropriation of $75,000 for the establishment and maintenance of three normal schools.
5. Annual appropriation of $50,000 for The University of Tennessee.
6. Annual appropriation of $5,000 for encouraging and assisting rural schools to establish school libraries.
7. The establishment and maintenance of an agricultural high school in each Congressional district."

In Memphis, Claxton had approximately 750 copies of the resolution printed on long sheets of paper with lines at the bottom for the signatures of the secretary and chairman of a meeting. Beginning with the rally in that city, at the close of the speeches, Claxton requested that the meeting be organized with a secretary and presiding officer. Then he read the resolution and asked for its adoption. It was adopted unanimously in every county but one, where there was one negative vote—the only opposing vote recorded in the entire state. After the adoption of the resolution, he always asked the chairman and secretary to sign enough copies for all the local papers and three or four others for later use. "Of course we managed," wrote [6] Claxton, "to have prospective legislators elected chairmen and secretaries. Later this was found to be quite helpful."

There were two hotly contested political campaigns in Tennessee that summer, but the educational rallies drew much larger attendance than the politicians had at their meetings. The flags and motto banners with local bands and singing groups of children gave more glamor to the educational rallies than the political meetings had. The banners bore such mottoes as "Education Makes Wealth," "Education, A Debt Due By The Present To The Future," "Education Of All The Children Of All the People," and "No Freedom Without Education." The average attendance was more than a thousand, making a total of more than 100,000. There were 95 rallies, one in each county except Houston and Stewart for which a joint meeting was held in connection with their joint county fair.

The first rally was held at Memphis on July 31; the last at Crossville, Cumberland County, on November 16. The following is a sample of the advertising posters:

"GREAT EDUCATIONAL RALLY

HOLIDAY FOR ALL PUBLIC SCHOOLS IN SESSION
TEACHERS AND ALL GOOD CITIZENS URGED TO BE PRESENT
SPECIAL INVITATION TO SCHOOL DIRECTORS AND MEMBERS
OF COUNTY COURT

Addresses by Prominent Speakers

HALTER'S CAMP GROUND, FRIDAY, OCTOBER 17TH
ALL COME, BRING YOUR DINNER AND MAKE IT THE GREAT DAY
OF THE YEAR." [7]

About 200 of these were printed for each of the 96 counties. They were on lightweight paper about 16 by 20 inches in size, and were posted in court houses, school buildings, town and cross-roads stores, at the forks of roads, and along highways.

President Ayres of The University of Tennessee spoke in about twenty counties; Superintendent Mynders in 87; Claxton in all of them. As in the East Tennessee campaign he frequently spoke at night and on Sundays at other places than those in which the rallies were held.[8] Meetings were held in the daytime in courtyards, picnic grounds, school campuses, and fairgrounds; in the evenings, in schoolhouses, court houses, opera houses, public auditoriums, dance halls, and churches.[9] "Education and public schools," declared [10] Mynders, "have been preached from the pulpit, the bar, the stump; at picnics, barbecues, circuit and county courts, school commencements, county fairs, race tracks, and even at a wedding ceremony." Claxton capped this statement with the following: [11] "I have myself made an address on public occasions when the people met to strew flowers on the graves of their ancestors. . . . Then, of course, there are women's club meetings, and there are patriotic societies, Daughters of the Confederacy and camps of the Confederate soldiers."

At Rogersville in Hawkins County, the campaigners found themselves in competition with a circus. The manager, however, was induced to give up the morning to the educational speakers who promised to advise the crowd to attend the circus in the afternoon.[12]

"When we arrived at Pikeville in Bledsoe County," declared [12] Claxton, "we found that the campaign material had not been distributed and that the County Superintendent of Schools was not there. I telephoned him at his home some miles away and asked him if he were coming to the rally and why he had not distributed the material. He said he was not coming and that he had not distributed the material because he thought he had already done as much as he was paid for. His salary was only $64 a year. Mynders and I met and spoke to the few people who came to the meeting in the court house before noon. At the hotel a man of middle age who owned a large number of cattle on the mountain range said he was sorry he did not get in in time to hear us. 'I wanted to hear what you men had to say for education,' he added; 'I am agin it.' On the train that afternoon I tried to think out what we might have said to convince this man; his only interest was in money. The result was a formulation of material in a speech on the money value of education and the formula: material resources $\times$ native ability of the people $\times$ the acquired ability that we call education = wealth

[155]

and wealth-producing power. This speech has been helpful in persuading many county courts and state legislatures to make more generous appropriations for public education."

The schedule of rallies was arranged so that Mynders and Claxton could travel from one county seat to another between the close of an afternoon meeting and the beginning of another at ten o'clock the next morning. Before the days of good roads and automobiles this sometimes required driving late at night and occasionally spending the night at some farm house on the road. In dry weather these roads were traveled in a cloud of dust; in wet weather, in deep mud.[12] Claxton devoted himself every day of the week to the campaign, and did not resume his duties at The University of Tennessee until the campaign was completed in the middle of November.[13]

The Tennessee newspapers did not make an outstanding contribution to the success of this and the other educational campaigns in the state. "We had very little help from the newspapers except in Knoxville and Chattanooga," declared [14] Claxton. "The Nashville papers were definitely against our program, and the Memphis papers were indifferent." In this, he had reference to the editorial policy of the press. As to the news space devoted to the rallies, the papers were fairly liberal. In recognition of this, Claxton wrote,[15] "Local newspapers and city papers, except the Nashville *American*, gave us good publicity." Even the Nashville *American* carried a story under this headline: "Big Educational Rally Held at Cookeville." [16] County weekly newspapers usually not only freely advertised the meetings but also reported the programs in as much as half a page. The city newspapers also reported the rallies freely. In the 1906 campaign the Memphis *Commercial Appeal* had ten such articles, the Nashville *Banner* forty-six, the Knoxville *Journal and Tribune* twelve, and the Chattanooga *Times* four.[17]

An example of an announcement appearing in the *Commercial Appeal* of Memphis is as follows: "Much interest is being manifested in the educational rally to be held at Ellendale. Special trains will leave Memphis at special excursion rates.

The educational rally to be held at Ellendale is one of a series of such meetings being held over the state under the direction of Superintendent Mynders. The object of the meetings is to awaken new interest in educational matters and to consider certain educational legislation which is to come before the general assembly when it convenes at Nashville in January.

The program includes a number of addresses and barbecue and basket dinner. It will be a legal holiday for county schools and teachers. Invitations have been extended to County Court, the Legislative Council, Board of Education, Woman's Public School Improvement Association, Candidates for the General Assembly, and all persons interested in educational topics.

Speakers are to be Ex-Governor Bob Taylor, K. D. McKellar, Superintendent Mynders, P. P. Claxton, and Wharton Jones. Invitations have also been extended to Malcolm Patterson and Senator Carmack." [18]

The speakers who assisted in the campaign were mostly experienced platform orators and many were veterans on the "stump." Claxton stood high among the best of them. One report [19] declared, "Dr. P. P. Claxton . . . delivered the address. . . . It was one of the most eloquent and forceful speeches ever heard in this county." Among the prominent school superintendents who spoke at a few places during the campaign were P. L. Harned of Montgomery County, R. L. Jones of Hamilton County, and S. G. Gilbreath, former State Superintendent of Public Instruction. At Centerville, as at some other places, the additional feature was a spelling contest; [21] in most of the programs there were songs and instrumental music. Indeed the variety of entertainment gave the rallies sometimes a resemblance to a carnival or school fair.

Claxton showed himself to be a master propagandist and strategist as well as orator in the campaign. He had boundless enthusiasm, imagination, and forceful eloquence. "His speeches and written articles," in the opinion of Holt, [22] "abound in comparisons, contrasts, and persuasive arguments. His style is clear, concise, and forceful, and reports of his addresses indicate that he possessed the power of oratory necessary to carry an audience with him in his enthusiasm and sincerity." Holt might have added that his speeches contained many statistics for he always had the figures and the facts at hand to prove his points. In spite of the dominant role played by Claxton, this crusade for education was generally referred to in the press as "Mynders' Campaign of 1906." This gave Claxton no concern, as he preferred to work under the official leadership of the state superintendent rather than solely as an agent of the Southern Education Board. But it was he who planned the campaign in its every detail and who directed it from beginning to end.

Claxton's work did not end with the close of the campaign, the real fruit of which would be the legislative enactments by the general assembly of 1907. To see that some fruit was harvested, a "school lobby," of which Mynders and Claxton were the principal leaders, had to be on the alert. Claxton's general plan in dealing with legislatures was to be constantly on hand during sessions to see that the proper persons introduced the bills, that committees were correctly informed about them, that the bills did not remain in the hands of committees, and that the legislators were kept informed as to their status.[23]

Bills, covering each item of the campaign resolutions, except the establishment of agricultural high schools, were written by Claxton, a separate bill for each item. That providing for an appropriation of $50,000 a year for the University was introduced by John R. Neal of Knoxville. Within a month after its introduction it was passed by the majority of 57 to 31 in the House and 19 to 11 in the Senate. This was four times the appropriation given the University in 1905.[24] The Chestnutt Bill, providing for an appropriation of fifty cents per capita for each child of school age for the following year and seventy-five cents per capita for each year thereafter, and for a continuation of the appropriation of $50,000, provided under the Tollett Bill, to help weak schools, also passed after strong opposition from the supporters of the Baldridge Bill. This latter bill provided for a one and one-half mill property tax for schools to be apportioned among the counties on a per capita basis of children of school age. The Chestnutt Bill added an estimated increase of $50,000 to the annual public school appropriations.[25] Three out of the seven items in the platform of the 1906 educational campaign were thus made into law by the 1907 legislature.

"I remember," wrote Claxton,[26] "asking a member of the Legislature, a senator, a rather cold-blooded one, about a certain resolution: 'If that bill is introduced into the Legislature, do you think it will pass?' He was busy reading. He looked around and said: 'Is it one of those that you resoluted about?' and I said, 'It is.' He re-

[158]

plied, 'Of course, it will be passed if it is, because that is the voice of the people.' "

Another bill was also passed, which replaced the district boards with county boards. This naturally had the opposition of the school directors throughout the state. In order to avoid having the disgruntled directors oppose the other objectives sought by Mynders and Claxton, this item was not included in the platform but Superintendent Harned of Montgomery County was sent by Mynders throughout the state during the campaign to explain how well the plan was already operating in Montgomery County.[27]

While the fate of most of Claxton's bills was uncertain, some of the legislators who wished to improve the public schools complained to him that there were too many school bills pending, some educators supporting one and some supporting another. In the Tulane lobby one evening Mr. Dickens, a member of the House of Representatives, asked Claxton, "Why don't you school men agree on what you want? Why are you here fighting each other? We want to do what we can for schools, but we do not know what is needed. You ought to agree and inform us." "We are not fighting each other," Claxton replied. "I wrote all seven of the bills now before the legislature. Some of us are more interested in some of the bills; others of us more interested in others." These did not include the Baldridge Bill; but after getting the principal proponent of this bill to agree that he would be satisfied if a certain per cent of the state's gross income (school taxes on public utilities, insurance companies, etc.) were apportioned to the counties on a per capita basis, Claxton conceived the idea of the General Education Bill.[28]

Returning to his room at the Maxwell House about ten o'clock, he wrote before going to bed the outline of a bill providing for appropriating one third of the gross revenue of the state for public education and apportioning the amount, thus secured, on a percentage basis among the different objectives. The next day he called Mynders and Harned to his room and read the outline to them. They approved it in principle and asked him to write it in the form of a skeleton bill for introduction in the legislature. After doing so, Claxton asked Henry Horton, later Governor of Tennessee, to introduce it in the House. This was done, not with any expectation of its passing at that session but with the idea that it might become the basis of the next educational campaign and be given standing for the legislature of 1909.[28]

After the highly successful campaign of 1906 and the partially favorable legislation resulting from it, Dabney wrote,[29] "Professor Claxton has been one of the hardest and most successful workers in the Southern educational campaign and since McIver's death is the chief leader in this cause. He is a modest, unselfish, unassuming man, but a devoted and indefatigable worker. He is not a scientific man, in the narrower sense, though he is in thorough sympathy with scientific and technical education. He is a man of fine physique and robust health and has altogether an attractive personality. Professor Claxton is a fine speaker and the best campaigner I ever knew. He has had a great deal of executive experience and I have perfect confidence in his success in that line. Having been associated with him in The University of Tennessee, it is proper for me to say that he deserves the chief credit for the success of that institution before the legislature and in the state. He is the man who organized all of this work and put it through. He is highly esteemed by the students and teachers and is the most popular man before the people we ever had in Tennessee."

The previous summer Dabney had written [30] of Claxton, even before the campaign, "I think he is one of the greatest educational forces in the South and will, when his work is known, be ranked with the foremost school reformers of our country. . . . Professor Claxton's ideals of education are fully abreast of the times and far ahead of those commonly current in his part of the country. Although far in advance of his time and of most of his colleagues, he knows how to organize them and has made himself a most successful leader. He is an indefatigable student and is growing steadily both in scholarship and in power. . . . [He] has done a good deal of literary work and published a great many papers. He is a fine public speaker, as you know, and a noble teacher."

At the invitation of State Superintendent Robert Lee Jones (appointed by Governor Malcolm R. Patterson who was elected in 1906), a representative group of educators, statesmen, and business and professional men met in the Senate Chamber in Nashville on May 3, 1907. Addresses were delivered by Governor Patterson, Mynders, Claxton, and others, and as a result of the meeting the

Co-operative Education Association was organized, with an executive committee of seven, of which Claxton was chairman. The association adopted the General Education Bill as its chief objective, and its executive committee, of which Superintendent Jones was a member, directed the campaign of the Co-operative Education Association, which was sometimes referred to as "Jones's Campaign." As previously, however, it was Claxton who planned and directed the activities.[31]

Claxton rewrote the bill, which was approved by his executive committee at a meeting at The University of Tennessee while the Summer School of the South was in session in 1907. He then made an abstract of the bill and had fifty thousand copies [32] of it printed for distribution to newspapers and for use in the campaign which was planned for August and early September, 1908.

Claxton wrote to the heads of all the colleges in the state, requesting that public education be the subject of all commencement addresses in 1908.[32] Most of them assented, and thus hundreds of thousands of people were reached. On every available occasion Claxton himself spoke in churches, at picnics, at commencements, and before county courts, labor meetings, women's clubs, and celebrations of various kinds throughout the year.[33]

When the campaign got under way in August, 1908, rallies were held throughout the state as in 1906. "The people in the Southern States," wrote [34] Claxton, "were raised on camp meetings, and when they go and carry their dinner with them it is an offense to speak a half hour and dismiss them. A man who has come twenty miles to hear a speaking wants to hear a good deal of it, and they have the power to sit and hear it; so you can appeal to them morning and afternoon and they will remain." These audiences wanted more than mere entertainment. "The appeal must be made," continued Claxton, "not to the sentiments for higher culture alone, but to the sentiment for the dollars and cents, because it will make money, because education and wealth and wealth-producing power go together, because it is better to pay the money to the children now for their education than to leave it to them when you die."

The counties of the state were divided among several groups of speakers. This made possible a shorter campaign than the one two years before. The headquarters of Claxton's executive committee was in the offices of State Superintendent R. L. Jones, who participated vigorously in the campaign. As in 1906, Claxton had resolutions printed embodying the abstract of the bill, which were presented for adoption by the audiences organized with chairmen and secretaries. This was another election year; so prospective legislators were chosen for officers of the meetings in order that their signatures might be recorded at the bottom of the adopted resolutions. "Our people in the South here," declared [33] Claxton, "with their blue eyes and soft hearts, can be moved, but after a time they will forget; so, while they are sympathetic, the resolutions are read and are usually voted unanimously." Copies of these resolutions were sent to women's clubs, boards of education, city councils, P.T.A.'s, pastors' associations, labor groups, patriotic orders, county courts, farmers' meetings, and other organizations. Practically all of these approved the resolutions and returned the copies signed by the appropriate officers. Also petitions for the passage of the bill, with 90,000 signatures, were later presented to the legislature.[35]

During the session of the General Assembly of 1909 the General Education Bill was introduced. Briefly, it provided that 30 per cent of the state's gross revenue be appropriated as an education fund. Sixty-one per cent of this amount was to be distributed to the counties according to scholastic population. Ten per cent was to be an equalizing fund for aiding weak schools, $33,600 of which was to supplement the salaries of county superintendents. Eight per cent was to encourage and assist in the establishment of county high schools. One per cent was for the establishment and maintenance of public school libraries. Thirteen per cent was for the establishment of normal schools in each of the state's three grand divisions and an Industrial Normal School for Negroes in Nashville. Finally, seven per cent was apportioned to the University for maintenance and improvement.[34]

On the first day of the session of the legislature the bill was introduced in the Senate by John R. Neal and in the House by Representative Stewart of Cannon County, and referred to their respective education committees. With others Claxton appeared before these committees. Neal was a member of the Senate education committee which soon approved it by a small majority. "Governor Patterson opposed the bill to the extent of saying that it could not become law," according to Claxton.[35] "But he did not object to Jones working for its passage. Jones had been a member of the committee that wrote the bill and he had helped to campaign for it. He hoped to be able to induce the Governor to sign it if it passed both houses." The Speaker of the House opposed the bill and the large House Education Committee of thirty-six members was packed against it. After about three weeks, this committee finally granted a hearing at night in the Tulane Hotel. Including the chairman, there were twenty-five members present.

Jones, Mynders, Gilbreath, Harned, and Claxton appeared before the committee in support of the bill. After presenting their arguments, they retired to the lobby, and the committee went into executive session. Soon it was reported that they had voted to recommend the bill for rejection. Twelve had voted for it; twelve against it. The chairman, a former school teacher, had cast the deciding vote against it. Jones remarked that they had done well to tie so large a committee on so comprehensive a bill of that nature. All except Claxton were in favor of letting the matter rest there and trying again two years later, since it was known that absent members of the committee were against the bill and the House was organized for its defeat. He, however, went to his hotel room, and spent most of the night addressing large envelopes to each member of the House. In each envelope he placed the resolutions adopted by mass meetings and various organizations in the county or counties represented by each respective member. When the House met the next morning, each member found one of these envelopes on his desk. Some of the opponents of the bill found that they had signed the resolutions as chairman or secretary of a mass meeting, and were angry at thus being reminded of their obligations.

As a result of this maneuver, Jones and Mynders and Harned were able to persuade the chairman of the Education Committee not to report the bill for rejection and to permit it to be referred to the Committee on Finance, Ways, and Means. The Prohibitionists opposed the bill because they feared that, if 30 per cent of the gross revenue were allotted to education, the treasury would be so depleted that the sale of whiskey would be permitted as a means of raising revenue. Governor Patterson, learning that the Prohibitionists, with whom he had had a bitter struggle, were opposing the bill, joined his forces to those supporting it.

When Claxton and the other school lobbyists finally secured a hearing before the Committee on Finance, Ways, and Means, they saw to it that all the members from Shelby County, close to the Governor, were present as well as all other friends of the measure. As a consequence, the committee voted to recommend the bill for passage. Immediately afterwards, the chairman called a "rump" meeting of a few members who rescinded the action and voted to report the bill for rejection. But Jones and Harned, who came from the same county as the chairman, persuaded him not to report the bill at all but to allow it to be called out of the hands of the committee without prejudice. He agreed. After several hours of bitter debate on the floor of the House and several attempts at adjournment to prevent a vote, the bill was passed. Of the 99 members of the House, 65 voted for the bill. There were some amendments, which its supporters had agreed to. Among these was the reduction of the percentage of the gross revenue to be allotted to education from 30 per cent to 25 per cent.

Knowing that the legislature was to recess in three days, Claxton went to the Clerk of the House and asked that the bill be recorded at once so that it could be sent to the Senate for action before the recess. But he found that the clerk had been already ordered not to do this. During the recess the opponents of the bill were very active. The Tennessee Bankers Association opposed it because it required the distribution of school funds twice a year, in July and January, and thus deprived the banks for six months of their free use of the state's money deposited with them, then without interest. In spite of this and other opposition, the bill passed the Senate a few days after it was re-assembled, 23 of its 32 members voting for it.

Believing that the Governor would sign the bill, Claxton prepared to return to his work at the University. But in the lobby of the Maxwell House, he met J. W. Barton of Paris, a supporter of the bill and leader of the Prohibition group, who asked,[36] "Where are you going?" "I am going home," Claxton replied. "Well, I don't believe you'd better," he said; "I've just come from a Prohibition meeting where it was planned to practically kill the bill by amending it so as to render it effective only after two years following its passage." Deciding to remain longer in Nashville, Claxton met John R. Neal, an able constitutional lawyer, and learned from him that a bill which had passed both houses and been sent to the Governor could not be amended while it was in his hands. A quick counting of days showed that, if the Governor held the bill the full limit of time permitted by the consitution, there would not be time enough left to permit its amendment that session. Claxton accordingly telephoned Jones and asked him to request the Governor to hold the bill as long as possible. Patterson did so, and there was no time for further interference. Thus the bill became law, and a real foundation was laid for the development of public education in Tennessee.

This bill had a helpful influence on the educational legislation in other Southern states. A prominent professor of education in Teachers College of Columbia University thought it "the most statesmanlike education measure ever passed by any legislative body in America." [37]

In the campaign of 1910, Claxton's work was done principally as chairman of a committee of ten, appointed by the Public School Officers Association in January to revise and codify the school laws of the state. This committee prepared a bill, most of which Claxton wrote and all of which he put in its final form. Its aim was to do as much for the administration and effectiveness of the schools as the General Educational Bill had done for the financial support and integration of the school system. In August, 1910, he met in Knoxville the campaign speakers to make final arrangements. Those present were President Ayres, Superintendent Jones, Mynders, Gilbreath, Harned, and Claxton. According to the Knoxville *Sentinel*,[38] "They expect to put before the people in a forcible way the absolute need of improvement in all grades of the state's schools and ask that they urge legislation to that end as well as support legislators who will make it their express duty and pleasure to see that such legislation is passed. They expect to urge the need of more and better county high schools, ask the support of the three state normal schools about to be established, urge upon the patrons better attendance in the common public schools, the establishment of school libraries, school improvement associations, the establishment of courses of study, longer school terms, and to show the needs of education along general lines." There was, however, no specific set of objectives as in the previous campaign of 1908.

Rallies were held as before. Railroads offered special rates and in Memphis the street railway company provided a special service for the meeting.[39] At Cleveland, a farmer offered a prize of $20 to the school having the largest attendance.[40] In Jackson there was a great parade of floats. These were wagons decorated with each school's colors in bunting, hand-painted banners, pennants, and flags.[41] At Fountain City, every man who had been county superintendent since 1868 was invited to sit on the speaker's platform, as a means of arousing local pride in school leadership.[42] The educational rallies of this year, however, seem to have been considerably overshadowed by the bitter political campaign which was raging throughout the state. The Democratic party was split and the Republican candidate, Ben Hooper, was elected Governor, the first since 1880.

Because of details in the bill "To Revise, Amend, and Codify the Public School Laws" which might have confused the masses of the people, the speakers did not discuss it in the campaign. For its passage in the legislature, the plan was to present it intelligibly to the key members of the General Assembly. The bill was introduced early in the session of 1911 in both houses and its passage seemed assured. But on the night before it was to be considered in the House, the quorum was broken by the departure of 34 "fusion" members to Decatur, Alabama, to prevent the passage of an "elections law" which would have placed the balance of power in the hands of the Prohibitionists. When they at last returned, there was not time for its consideration. "I considered this the most important piece of educational writing with which I have had to do," declared [43] Claxton.

The bill provided for a State Board of Education with no ex-officio members but with large powers and responsibilities, among which was the appointment of a non-partisan State Commissioner of Education with a long term of service with no reference to the fortunes of partisan politics, and at such a salary as would enable the Board to obtain and retain the services of men of great ability. All appointments of his staff were to be made on his recommendation. Another provision was the election of members of county boards of education by the people of the county at large. This board was to have large authority and responsibility in the administration of the elementary and high schools, and was to elect the county superintendent for a long term and at a salary sufficient to hold a man or woman of ability. The bill also provided for a permanent professional textbook commission with power to adopt not more than 30 per cent of the textbooks in one year. Publishers and their agents were permitted to submit their books for examination with briefs explaining their merit. They might even appear before the commission in open session, but by other activities they would forfeit their right to have their books considered for adoption. The bill also regulated the issuance of teachers' certificates and fixed a minimum length of school term and minimum salary for teachers. Though the bill failed of passage in 1911, several of its provisions have since been enacted into law.

Another important bill failed to be passed, through a technicality. This was a bill for raising the percentage of the gross revenue to be allotted to education from 25 to 33⅓ per cent. Bills for this purpose were introduced and passed in both houses but by an oversight neither house took over and passed the bill of the other.[42] This bill became law, however, two years later.

This was the last of the educational campaigns which Claxton directed, as he became U. S. Commissioner of Education in the summer of 1911. In addition to the legislation already considered, Claxton was responsible for an amendment fixing the requirements for a county's participation in the equalizing funds; for bills providing for compulsory school attendance in Knox County in 1907 and in 1909 in about twenty-eight other counties, resulting eventually in 1913 in a compulsory attendance law for the entire state; for aiding in preparing a bill for substituting county boards for district boards of education in 1907; and for bills which improved the administration of public high schools.[43] By the time Claxton left Tennessee there were about 45 county high schools in the state.[44] A few years later, a law was passed requiring every county to maintain at least one four-year high school. "When I travel over the state," wrote [45] Dean Charles E. Ferris of The University of Tennessee, "and see the fine brick high school buildings on the hillsides, I say that there is another monument to Dr. Claxton." The establishment of high schools in Tennessee probably did more for the cause of education in the state than any other one thing.

The General Education Bill in 1911 allotted $67,236.32 that year to The University of Tennessee. In 1917 the University gave up its part in the General Education Bill for a much larger amount from a five-cent General Property tax and a million dollar building program. When that legislation was pending, Claxton met a committee of the alumni and others in Nashville, and addressed a joint session of the legislature in behalf of the University and other educational interests.[46]

Well could President Hoskins of the University of Tennessee write,[47] "Dr. Claxton has meant a great deal to the University and especially to the State of Tennessee. . . . He has done more constructive work for the benefit of the schools of the state than any one man, and the University is proud of him." There was no exaggeration in the statement of J. W. Brister, Governor Hooper's State Superintendent, before the Fifteenth Conference for Education in the South,[48] in 1912, that Claxton was "Tennessee's most distinguished educator." At Dabney's invitation, Claxton gave the commencement address at the University of Cincinnati in 1909 on "A City and Its Schools." In a letter complimenting him on his "splendid address," Dabney wrote,[49] "I have just received another copy of your general education bill as passed and wish to congratulate you again upon one of the most splendid pieces of work that has been done in our country."

✥ XIV ✥

United States Commissioner of Education: Up to World War One

◇◇

IN MAY, 1911, Claxton received a letter from his intimate friend, President Dabney of the University of Cincinnati, which was to lead him into a wider field of educational service. "Within the last few weeks," wrote [1] Dabney, "I have taken the liberty of mentioning your name, first in connection with the Iowa State College; and secondly in connection with the Commissionership in Washington. Dr. D. W. Fisher, the father of the new Secretary of the Interior, Walter W. Fisher, is a dear old friend of mine. He is a Presbyterian minister of distinction, whom I have met frequently in church councils. At a recent meeting of the Board of the McCormick Theological Seminary in Chicago, he asked me to suggest the name of a good man for the U. S. Commissioner of Education, saying that he would see that the information was brought to the attention of his son, the Secretary. I have, therefore, taken the liberty of writing to Dr. Fisher and mentioning your name. As you did not know of either of these, I suppose I have done no harm, even if I have not done any good."

After deliberating a few days, Claxton replied [2] that he appreciated Dabney's kindness in mentioning his name for the two positions. As to the Iowa State College presidency, he wrote, "This is a good position and an opportunity for great service, but I confess it does not appeal to me very much. This is because of my interest in the educational work of the South. The Commissionership does appeal to me, since it offers an opportunity to serve the whole country, and my knowledge of educational conditions in the Southern states would enable me to do this section a special service without neglecting the interests of other sections. I have written letters in regard to this position in behalf of Dr. Suzallo of Columbia, but, if the position is offered to me, I will accept it and will appreciate anything that may be done in regard to it."

A little later when President Taft, on a visit to Cincinnati, spoke to Dabney about Claxton and said he wanted a Southern educator who would not mix in politics, Dabney strongly recommended Claxton as the best man in the whole country for Commissioner.[3] Claxton's father after the war had usually voted the Republican ticket in state and national elections. Claxton himself grew up as a Republican but changed his party affiliations after going to North Carolina, becoming a Democrat chiefly because he believed in low import taxes rather than high protective tariffs.[4] The rotund President Taft had been in office since March, 1909. Dr. Elmer Ellsworth Brown resigned as Commissioner of Education to become chancellor of New York University, a position to which he had been elected in April, 1911. He had been Commissioner only five years.

Toward the end of June, Claxton received a letter from Secretary Fisher inviting him to come to Washington for an interview. During lunch at Fisher's club, Claxton was asked some pertinent questions regarding the Commissionership. At the close of the conversation, Fisher asked him if he would accept the position. "If some 'bite' can be put into the work," he replied,[4] "and if we could have some assurance that we could get sufficient appropriations to enable us to do the work in a worthwhile way, I would consider it and give you an answer within a week." Fisher then asked Claxton to see President Taft and Congressman Fitzgerald, chairman of the House Ways and Means Committee.

Claxton found Taft at the Chevy Chase Golf Course and rode with him back to Washington. He assured Claxton that he was interested in the Bureau of Education and would do all he could for its improvement. Claxton was unable to see Fitzgerald, but did see Champ Clark, then Speaker of the House. Claxton told him he had been offered the Commissionership of Education and asked him if he thought adequate appropriations could be secured for that

Bureau. He replied, "The Bureau ought to do something or quit. I will talk to Fitzgerald about it."

Returning to Knoxville, where the Summer School of the South had already begun its session, Claxton gave further consideration to the matter. The salary of $5000 was only a little more than his combined salaries at Knoxville, not including his income from lecturing and other activities.[5] He considered that he was then engaged in worthwhile work for Tennessee and the South, where much remained to be done. "Possibly the deciding argument for the acceptance of the position was made by a friend," wrote [6] Claxton; "the position would offer opportunity for personal education."

Accordingly, a few hours before the expiration of the week, Claxton telegraphed his acceptance to Secretary Fisher, and early in July he took the oath of office in Washington. After a few days at the Bureau, he returned with leave of absence for the remainder of July until the close of the session of the Summer School of the South. As a parting gift, members of the Summer School presented to him a beautiful gold watch, suitably engraved, which he still cherishes. To the speeches of good will at its presentation, he replied with an expression of sincere thanks and the assurance that they would be able to find him in Washington "in the Bureau of Education, top drawer, upper righthand corner." [6]

Soon after taking up his duties in Washington, Claxton wrote Dabney, thanking him for his 4th of July address at the Summer School and enclosing a check for $75. "Let me thank you again for what you did for me in regard to the Commissionership," he continued,[7] "and for all you have done in the many years of the past. . . . I wish you would, at your earliest opportunity, write out for me at some length any suggestions you may have for the improvement of the Bureau so as to make it more serviceable. The more I see of it, the more I am convinced that there is an opportunity to do something and a great need of some kind of reconstruction."

To this Dabney replied [8] with his usual generosity, "You know, I have always had the highest regard for your abilities and the greatest admiration for your patriotism. I feel that I have not rendered you a service, but the country a good service in helping to put you in a place where you can do the most good. I shall see you or write you some time about the Bureau's work."

Claxton wrote similar letters, requesting advice, to Joseph D. Eggleston, Walter Hines Page, and others. Page replied,[9] "Make a plan to do some active work. I have no doubt you have a dozen. For instance, select two or three regions where the best rural public schools are—people that are working intelligently towards making a real country school of a new sort in the world. Make a plan to help them and to report them. Work towards the creation of a perfect country school. Then you'll have something to make a report about—a report that will be read all round the world. Then the Congressmen from those districts will stand by you. Then you'll have a plan, too, to make a comprehensive program to find a way whereby your Bureau can be of direct help in planting or developing such schools everywhere. You can take this great movement, organize it, report it, direct it—manage it.

Then if you ask for $10,000 to do this particular job with—showing precisely how you'll use the money—you'll get it; then you'll get $20,000; then $100,000—then any sum you want.

With no plan, nobody cares for the Bureau. If it does something, then everybody'll care. I'd like to talk this over with you."

Of the many letters congratulating him on his new position, probably none gave Claxton more pleasure than one from Dr. Wallace Buttrick of the General Education Board, who wrote,[10] ". . . First of all let me felicitate you and congratulate the whole educational world that you have been made Commissioner of Education. . . ."

As head of the Bureau of Education, Claxton was chiefly interested in the promotion of elementary and high school education particularly in rural communities. But he did not follow the plan suggested by Page. "I had learned the great truth," he wrote,[11] "that the educational system of any state or country is an organic thing, and like all other organisms, must, for effectiveness, develop harmoniously like a tree, a boy, or a state. It is not a mechanical thing to be constructed piecemeal." He therefore planned a reorganization of the Bureau so that it might do more than collect and publish statistics. The aim was to help actively in the promotion of education of all types on all levels. This plan called for an increase of at least 200% in the appropriations for the Bureau.

While this plan, which was approved heartily by Secretary Fisher, was awaiting the necessary appropriations by Congress, Claxton appointed a large number of "dollar-a-year" men, prominent educators many of whom had been already interested in the improvement of rural schools. He thus secured several thousand dollars worth of work for a very few dollars. He also began a series of rural education conferences in several states, chiefly in the South. These were held under the direction of the rural education specialists of the Bureau. Some of these Claxton attended personally.

Commissioner Brown had already appointed a specialist in higher education, Dr. Kendrick Babcock. At the request of deans of graduate schools which were members of the American Association of Universities, he undertook to evaluate the work of institutions from which these universities drew their graduate students. Early in the autumn of 1911 he submitted to Claxton his report on about 250 colleges and universities with the request that it be printed and submitted in proof to the institutions interested. This was done and the proof was marked "confidential for consideration and correction." In some way this was made public, and a storm of criticism roared across the country from coast to coast, which echoed on the floor of each House of Congress. "The trouble was," according [11] to Claxton, "that it was too nearly correct." President Taft was requested to forbid its publication. He held it over for Wilson who decided not to release it for publication. It had already become so widely known that publication was hardly necessary. The Carnegie Foundation took it up, and the American Association of University Women made it the basis of their classification of colleges. It marked the beginning of a widespread raising of college standards.

Soon after becoming Commissioner, Claxton increased the number of bulletins per year from six to sixty and began a series of mimeographed sheets which were sent to school officials particularly interested in such information.

From the beginning of his administration, Claxton traveled more widely and made more speeches than all the other Commissioners of Education had. During the last five months of 1911 and the following year 1912, he made over two hundred addresses. A few examples will illustrate the nature of this work. On September 25, 1911, he spoke at the opening exercises of New York University [12] on "Some Ideals in Education Which Our Democracy Must Realize." Dr. H. H. Horne thought the address was "a great success." [13] But Claxton was not pleased with it and wrote him that it was "an entire failure." "I ought not to have attempted to do it," he explained. "I had a slight nervous collapse in my office the day before, and I felt it coming on Saturday morning again. I have been knocked out entirely since that time." He further explained that he had had no vacation in fourteen years and had expected to take one in August, but that his coming to Washington had made this impossible. On November 2 following, he spoke to teachers at Worcester, Massachusetts on "The Holiness of Teaching and the Divinity of Children." On the 15th of that month he addressed the Association of American Agricultural Colleges at Columbus, Ohio. Early the next year, on January 20, he gave an address at Cooper Union in New York on "Democracy in Education." On Sunday, March 31, he spoke at the morning religious service in Howard Houston Hall at the University of Pennsylvania. At the 21st Annual Meeting of the Louisiana State Public School Teachers Association, which met at Alexandria, April 12–13, he gave four addresses, one of which was on "International Peace." [14] A week later he spoke to the Central Missouri Association at Warrensburg.

Frequently during his long administration of the Bureau of Education, Claxton spoke on the relationship of democracy to education. In an introduction to *The Educators* by Eliza Taylor Cherdron, he wrote at the request of the author, December 21, 1911, this opening paragraph: "The public school has come to be one of the most important factors in our civilization. As our political, social, and industrial life becomes more democratic and its problems more complex and difficult, the school must increase in importance." This was the central idea of many of his speeches.

It was the last of March, 1912, when the *Report of the Commissioner of Education for the Year Ended June 30, 1911* was ready for publication. This, of course, covered the work of his predecessor. In the introduction, Claxton dealt first with the great progress made in education in the United States during the past ten years. He then showed by statistics the great need for further improvement in every department of education—in common schools as well as institutions of higher learning and particularly in school buildings, salaries, libraries, length of term, and student attendance.

Lastly, he quoted in full, from the annual statement made by his predecessor to the Secretary of the Interior, the specific recommendations for increasing the scope and the effectiveness of the Bureau. The report comprised two large volumes. The first contained about twenty different divisions which discussed various phases of education in the United States and in foreign countries. The second volume was devoted entirely to educational statistics. The two volumes totaled about 1400 pages.

On April 23, 1912, Claxton, who had been a widower for about seven years, married Mary Hannah Johnson of Nashville, Tennessee. She was the daughter of George Sterling Johnson and Hannah Iredell (Spottswood) Payne Johnson, and was related to many prominent families in Tennessee and other states. Miss Johnson was the first woman in Tennessee to be included in *Who's Who in America*. She was a brilliant, hard-working young woman, who had been the leader in establishing the Nashville Public Library and in obtaining a donation from Andrew Carnegie for the erection of a large library building. As a wedding present Mr. Carnegie sent her a check for $1000. She and Claxton were married in Christ Church Episcopal by Bishop Thomas F. Gailor, assisted by the Rector, Dr. H. J. Mikell. A reception at the Maxwell House was attended by several hundred guests. On their wedding journey the Claxtons spent a few weeks in Puerto Rico, where the Commissioner, never forgetful of his work even on a honeymoon, assisted the Puerto Rican Commissioner of Education in solving some difficult problems. After returning to the United States, Claxton brought his family to Washington and established them in a large house next door to the British Embassy.

The first attempt Claxton made to secure adequate appropriations from Congress for the Bureau was largely a failure. He first appeared, on June 11, 1912, before the House Education Committee and read a statement. In this he traced the development of the Bureau since its founding in 1869 and pointed out the need for an appropriation of $220,000. For lack of personnel the publication of statistics was two years behind time. There was only one $1800 a year clerk to administer two and a half millions of dollars for the Agricultural and Mechanical Colleges under the Morrill Act. There was need for a traveling expense fund; Claxton had traveled that year about 80,000 miles and been away from his office two thirds of the time. An assistant commissioner was greatly needed. Rural school education, vocational education, and school libraries needed the attention of experts. "I am asking for money for men and women to study the great fundamental problems affecting the great masses of children and of interest to all," Claxton declared.[15] When he finished, Chairman Asbury F. Lever said, "I think the committee will agree that the morning has been well spent, and we thank Dr. Claxton for his remarks."

Though Secretary Fisher took with him the heads of all the bureaus and other divisions of the Department of the Interior to the hearing by the House Ways and Means Committee, he was unable to secure a recommendation for any increase in the appropriation for the Bureau of Education. Though the administration was Republican, the House was Democratic; but the Democrats were not interested in supporting anything which would give credit to the administration, for they as well as many Republicans were bitterly opposed to Taft. Besides, the chairman of this committee, Fitzgerald of Brooklyn, a Democrat and a Roman Catholic, was not interested in public education. The only increase of appropriation allowed was a small amount for rural schools, which was largely due to the efforts of Monahan, specialist in rural education in the Bureau. His being a Roman Catholic probably aided him in gaining this much from Fitzgerald. Claxton was, however, undaunted by his first failure to secure a larger appropriation, and continued to make known the needs of his Bureau.

In his introduction to the *Report of the Commissioner of Education for the Year Ended June 30, 1912*, he wrote, "The lack of preparation of teachers is one of the greatest evils of our school system. In no other country that pretends to provide an opportunity for universal education is the condition in this respect so bad as in the United States. This condition must be remedied, or the schools must continue to be much less efficient than they should be. The state or country that assumes the responsibility of educating its children at public expense in schools under public control must assume the corresponding responsibility of preparing at public expense a sufficient number of teachers, and must refuse to license persons not having sufficient native ability, education, and training to use to good advantage the time and money of the children."

The statistics showing the decrease of illiteracy, he declared, "are more interesting than any baseball or football score, and more thrilling than the reports of a great war."

"Despite all the crudities and all the difficulties attendant on the task unprecedented for magnitude, method, and purpose," he continued, "the public schools have probably accomplished more for the good of humanity within forty years than has ever been accomplished by any other agency in a like number of years."

This voluminous report, as for the previous year, occupied two volumes totaling about 1300 pages. The first contained educational articles; the second was filled with statistics.

Claxton continued to make speeches far and wide. On December 3, 1912, he spoke at the Academy of Music in Philadelphia in the interest of Tuskegee Institute. Among the others who spoke were Booker T. Washington and Ambassador James Bryce. On December 28, he made an address on "The Place of Music in Education" for the Illinois State Teachers Association. On February 26, 1913, he spoke in Philadelphia again. Of this address, Bird T. Baldwin of Swarthmore College wrote [16] Claxton, "Since I am a Quaker, I believe in certain forms of inspiration, and I wish to take this opportunity to say that your Philadelphia address before the Department of Superintendence was the best I ever heard given before this body. It sounded as if you were educationally inspired."

On May 13, Claxton spoke at a banquet of the Women's North Carolina Society of Baltimore on "North Carolina and Education." Two weeks later he was speaking at the commencement of the North Carolina Agricultural and Mechanical College for Negroes at Greensboro.[17] On June 13, he gave the commencement address at the State Normal School in Richmond, Kentucky.

Claxton attended the meeting of the National Education Association at Salt Lake City, July 5–11, 1913. Since 1911 he had been a life director of this Association. He was scheduled for addresses on kindergartens, the high school, industrial education, rural schools, the library and the rural community, and the National Bureau of Education, "always expressing himself forcibly and in a most interesting manner." "He is a public servant of the highest type," continued the newspaper report.[18]

On Sunday, he spoke to over 5000 Mormons in the Tabernacle. According to a newspaper,[18] "His human appeal, strong personality, and felicitous words won for him a most attentive audience. He is one of the few visitors who have been able to speak intelligibly in the Tabernacle for his voice is strong and well pitched."

He also spoke in the Tabernacle at a meeting of the American School Peace League, arranged by its secretary, Mrs. Fannie Fern Andrews of Boston. Governor Spry presided. In 1910 at the meeting of the National Education Association in Boston, a resolution had been passed requesting the Commissioner of Education to take appropriate steps for the formation of an International Education Conference. After becoming Commissioner, Claxton attempted to put this resolution into effect. In his efforts he had the assistance of Mrs. Andrews, whom he appointed as a special collaborator. Her wealthy friend, Mrs. Forbes of Boston, agreed to finance the conference and deposited $10,000 in bank at the Hague to pay local expenses. The co-operation of the Dutch Minister in Washington and of his government was secured for holding the conference at the Hague in 1913. Later it was postponed for good reasons until September, 1914. The Netherlands Government extended invitations to all governments officially represented at the Netherlands capital, and all accepted except the German Empire. Ten delegates, including Claxton, were appointed by President Wilson. But the commencement of the First World War made the holding of such a meeting impossible.[19]

At a conference on rural education at the University of Georgia Summer School (July 21–24, 1913) Claxton spoke at a civic luncheon given in his honor at the Georgian Hotel. On September 3 following, he gave an address at the Music Hall in Cincinnati on "The Public School and Democratic Freedom." Dr. Dabney presided at the meeting which was held under the auspices of the State Council of Entertainers of the Daughters of America. Ex-President Taft introduced Claxton as follows: [20] "Ladies and gentlemen, when I was President of the United States, it became my duty to appoint a Commissioner of Education. I looked the nation over to find the person best qualified for that position. I selected

Dr. Claxton. He has filled the position with honor to himself and credit to the nation. If I had the job to do again, I would not change my appointment, therefore I take great pleasure in presenting him to you."

On November 25, Claxton spoke at the Elks Theater in Albuquerque at the 28th annual convention of the New Mexico Educational Association on "Literature in Our Schools." "To call him merely an orator would be unfair," declared a reporter.[21] "Saturated with his subject, he held the attention of his hearers while he told in faultless language his theories for the benefit of education throughout the nation." Two days later he was at Dallas, addressing the Texas State Teachers Association on "An Efficient Democracy." During the entire year 1913 Claxton made more than 150 addresses.

When Woodrow Wilson became President in March, 1913, it was rumored that Claxton would be removed from the Commissionership. The following is an example of the numerous letters of confidence that Claxton then received. "I saw in some paper a recommendation of someone as your successor," wrote [22] George Foster Peabody. "I do hope that you are not going to withdraw. I can not think for a moment that President Wilson could think of substituting anyone for you, except upon your insistence. If anything has happened and I can be of service, do let me know, please." Mr. Peabody was quite correct. The rumor was not well founded. Wilson kept Claxton at the head of the Bureau.

In the introduction to his report for the year ending June 30, 1913, Claxton pointed out that only two items of his report covered the statistics of the school attendance of more than twenty-five millions of children and the expenditure of approximately three-quarters of a billion dollars. "Because of the importance of the information contained in these statistics, for which there is no other source, it is very desirable that the Bureau should be enabled to make its statistical reports complete, accurate, and up-to-date." But this could not be properly done, he complained, until adequate funds were provided by Congress.

As an indication of the work in his Bureau, Claxton reported that, during the year, forty-four bulletins, three circulars, a medical handbook for the Alaska school service, and more than 200 multigraph circular letters to school officers, teachers, and the press had been issued besides his voluminous report in two volumes. He and his assistant specialists had visited many more schools and attended more teachers' meetings than ever before and had thereby secured accurate first hand knowledge of educational conditions. Members of the Bureau had even been sent to Switzerland, Denmark, and the British Isles to gather information. Divisions of Negro Education, Kindergarten Education, and Home Education had been established.

For improvement of schools and school systems he suggested more kindergartens, an apportionment of six years each to elementary schools and high schools, the advancement of the teacher with pupils to next higher grade in entire grammar school, the consolidation of rural schools with better buildings and a small model farm attached, summer schools for four hours a day during mornings, part-time adult education in the schools, expansion of vocational education, more county libraries, more definite standards for admission to and graduation from colleges, and better teachers.

"Since in a democracy everything waits on the education of the people," he wrote, "since the school is the most important agency of education, and since the character and results of the school depend on the teacher, the selection and preparation of teachers for its schools become therefore the most important task and function of a democracy. If democracy succeeds in this, then it succeeds; if it fails in this, then it fails in all and must soon give place to some form of government, society, and industrial organization less dependent on the intelligence, virtue, skill, and good will of all the people. Civilization and progress have long halted and still go forward more slowly than they should because too little attention has been, and is, given to this all-important factor."

After giving a very complete and impressive characterization of a good teacher, he declared, "I think we may not expect to get and retain for our schools the services of men and women of the type I have indicated for less than the wages of a washerwoman, less by half than the wages of a mail carrier, and less by two thirds than the wages of a carpenter, a bricklayer, or a plumber. We profess to believe in education and talk of our teachers as the standing army of the Republic, and of our schoolhouses as the fortifications which hold back the invasions of ignorance, vice, anarchy, and economic inefficiency, but the salaries of teachers are still criminally low, and the sum total of expenditures for schools pitifully and absurdly small."

Several pages of Claxton's introduction were devoted to suggestions for modifying the policy of education for the natives of Alaska. He had traveled extensively there the previous summer. It would be better, he thought, to consolidate the native people in fifty or sixty communities, and give them an education which would enable them to increase their earning capacity and which would improve their health and well being.

In commenting on this report of the Commissioner of Education, the *Journal of Education*[23] stated, "We say without the slightest reservation that the current volume of Dr. P. P. Claxton as United States Commissioner of Education is by far the best educational year book in the world, now or in the past. Indeed it makes all other official reports look amateurish. . . . The treatment of every vital American problem is faithful and fearless, while the survey of the educational problems of the world is clear, definite, and helpful."

On January 26, 1914, Claxton appeared at a hearing before the House Committee on Education on a bill to investigate adult illiteracy and another bill limiting editions of publications of the Bureau of Education.[24] Claxton informed the committee that in 1910 there were four million persons above ten years of age who were illiterate, and that the number had probably risen to 4,750,000. The committee voted $10,000 as an appropriation to investigate the question and prepare a report for Congress. It voted also to remove the limit of 12,500 on a publication and to authorize the Secretary of the Interior to print as many copies as he thought necessary to meet the demand.

In February, Claxton sent out 1300 letters to city school superintendents inquiring how school buildings were used in the evenings.[25] In March, he addressed the Supervisors' Conference of Pittsburgh (March 22–26) on "The Place of Music in National Education." A few days later he spoke to the University Club of Washington on "Improvements in Washington Schools." [26] On April 2 he spoke at the 20th annual session of the Southeastern Iowa Teachers Association at Burlington chiefly on education and democracy.[27] On April 4 he was in Sioux City, speaking on rural education to the Iowa teachers.[28] At the conference of the American Library Association in Washington, May 24–29, he spoke on the need for the extension of library facilities among the rural population. On June 5, he gave the commencement address to the Altoona, Pennsylvania, High School, on "The High School as the Heart of the Educational System." [29]

Claxton attended the meeting of the National Education Association at St. Paul, Minnesota, July 4–11, 1914. He opened the session of the Kindergarten Department with an address on "The Readjustment of the Kindergarten and Primary Grades to Conform to the Same General Principles." [30] He gave another address on the teaching of science, in which he said,[31] "I am interested in the plan that is being put into operation by the University of Cincinnati, where the young men work in the shops and factories for a week and then go to the University and learn the theory that makes significant the experience that they have had in the shops. I look forward to the time when everywhere in all schools we may have students who, for a few hours a day, work at some gainful occupation and for the remainder of the day attend a school where the full significance of their experience may be brought out. It may be true that for all communities this may not be practicable. If this is so, we must have, instead, school rooms, shops, and laboratories in which the economically valuable products are made and later are put to their full economic use. We have talked about schools as being somewhat apart from life. We have talked about culture and cultural education, until we have, by unfortunate association, come to think that the attainment of culture as a process is apart and removed from the realities of life. I want to say to you that culture is not that, but it is that intangible something that comes only from intelligent labor rendered in the service of our fellowmen."

At this meeting of the National Education Association, Claxton was asked by the nominating committee to permit them to nominate him for the presidency, chiefly because the next meeting was to be held at Oakland, California, and was to be international in character, as representatives from other countries were to be invited to take part in the program. He refused because he did not believe the Commissioner of Education should hold this office. He is probably the only man who ever refused the presidency of the National Education Association. At his suggestion, President David Starr Jordan of Leland Stanford University was nominated and elected. When the Oakland meeting was held the following year, Germany and France were at war, and it became Claxton's duty to entertain German delegates at one end of the platform while some one else took charge of the French at the other end.

In July, Claxton spoke twice at the Summer School of Peabody College in Nashville, Tennessee—in the morning on kindergartens and in the evening on education in the primary grades. The following day he spoke in the morning and the afternoon on the grammar school and the high school, respectively.[32] Two days later he was at the Summer School of the South, speaking on "The Democracy of Education." According to a Knoxville reporter,[33] "As usual, the address by Commissioner Claxton was bristling with figures. He has the most prodigious faculty for assembling lists of figures with which to answer and defeat any contrary argument that is offered. He has computed the number of waking, sleeping, and idle hours in the life of children from birth to a given age, and he has figured out how much of that time could be profitably spent in leisure and in work to the benefit of that child as an individual and to the benefit of the community in which he lives. . . . His visions are so large, his ambition so great, and his confidence in the future so deeply rooted that he paints his pictures in bold, dashing colors, and it is sometimes difficult for the mind of the layman, centered upon other things, to catch the vision and to comprehend just how all these problems are going to be worked out."

The very next day he was at Athens, Georgia, addressing a conference of superintendents and teachers on "The Ideal Equipment of the Rural Teacher." At a civic luncheon at the Hotel Georgian he spoke on "Co-ordination between City and Country." That afternoon his third speech was delivered in the University Chapel. The theme was the cost of ignorance and its remedy, compulsory school attendance.[34]

In November, Claxton spoke on "College Surveys" at a meeting of the National Association of State Universities in Washington. On the 25th of this month he was at Charlotte, speaking to the

North Carolina Teachers Assembly on his favorite topic, "Education and Democracy." [35] Two days later he was in Nashville, addressing the Tennessee State Teachers Association on "An Ideal School System," one that would give every child a chance and exemplify the democracy of education. In November he also spoke to the Maryland State Horticultural Society in Baltimore.

On the preceding October 12 he had delivered the address on University Day at the University of North Carolina, and on the same day had received the degree of LL.D.

Also in 1914, Claxton wrote an introduction for *Sketches of Froebel's Life and Times*. "No other educator," he declared, "has realized so fully the unity of nature, man, and God. No other has seen more clearly the vision of redeemed humanity, living in harmony with nature, governed by love, and rejoicing in ever-progressing creative work. No other has ever understood better that the Kingdom of God is the kingdom of love, of light, of truth, and of intelligent, skillful, effective service. For him, all roads lead to God. For him, God is the all-pervading, creative spirit of the universe. The soul of man is a part of the divine essence. The education of man consists in the unfolding and revelation of this divine essence, through well-guided, spontaneous, creative activity. . . ."

Early in Claxton's administration, the National Congress of Mothers agreed to pay the salary of a woman in the Bureau to assist in the organization of Parent-Teacher Associations and in other things in which this National Congress was interested. Miss Lombard was selected for the position, the Bureau paying her the nominal salary of one dollar a year, as the Federal Government may not accept free services. All persons working for it must be paid by it and be subject to its control. One of the valuable things done by the Bureau through this co-operation was the preparation of National Reading Courses. The first was a course in great literature, including the *Iliad* and *Odyssey*, the *Divine Comedy* by Dante, *Faust* by Goethe, and certain plays by Shakespeare. Claxton made out the first reading list. These were widely advertised through public libraries and newspapers. The Chicago *Tribune*, for example, frequently gave a whole page of its Sunday edition to a new course, when it was announced. The first course was sent out early in

November, 1914.[37] Certificates were awarded to persons who gave evidence that they had read intelligently and appreciatively all the books of a course. They were intended primarily for people in rural communities and some towns and cities where this kind of guidance and stimulation was needed. But individuals and groups in all parts of the world read the books.

Soon after Claxton went to Washington, an agent of the Southern Railway System called his attention to the need of a more general knowledge of Spanish. The railway was interested in Spanish-American commerce. A manufacturer of plows in Chattanooga, Tennessee, wanted clerks and salesmen who had a practical knowledge of Spanish. On inquiry, Claxton found that only fourteen high schools in the United States taught Spanish. He undertook then to create more interest in Spanish in high schools, and made some progress, which was accentuated when the war began and Spanish replaced German temporarily.[38]

As in previous reports, Claxton's introduction to that for the year ending June 30, 1914, mentioned repeatedly the lack of funds, though an increase in appropriations of $30,600 had been made that year by Congress. "It is not necessary," he wrote, "to emphasize the importance of having once each year a complete and accurate interpretative survey of all important work in education in all parts of the world. Without it we may not hope to obtain the best results from our systems of schools and other agencies of education nor to obtain the fullest results from the money invested in them. Every problem in education has come to be international. The work of the humblest district school should be done in the light of all the knowledge of education the world has been able to gain." This reflects the interest Claxton then had in the proposed conference on international education.

Claxton further reported that the divisions of Civic Education and Education of Immigrants, of Vocational Education, and of School and Home Gardening had been added to the Bureau during the year. Also, a half million copies of 53 bulletins, totaling 4,122 pages, had been distributed. Six hundred thousand copies of various multigraphed articles had been mailed out. An average of three statements a week on educational matters had been issued to newspapers. The library was reported to have become one of the most important of its kind in the world. It contained 150,000 volumes, and should be better housed, Claxton declared. During the year, 84,332 letters, not including returns to blank forms of inquiry, had been received.

Included in the introduction were the nineteen recommendations which Claxton had previously made in the annual statement to the Secretary of the Interior. Particularly needed was an appropriation of $275,000. "To enable the Bureau to perform satisfactorily the function for which it was created and to respond to the demands for a clearing house for accurate information, well-matured opinion, and sound advice in regard to all phases of education and for assistance in promoting democratic education throughout the country," he wrote, "there will be need in the near future for an annual income of a half million dollars and for an education building with ample room for the library of the Bureau and a complete educational museum in which school officers, teachers, and students of education may find, properly arranged and catalogued, typical specimens of all forms of school furniture and equipment, with outlines of courses of study and whatever else will enable them to gain a comprehensive view of purposes, methods, and results of education in this and other countries and assist them in forming ideals for the improvement of their own schools and work."

The report comprised, as usual, two volumes, the only change being that the Educational Directory was issued for convenience as a separate publication. This was Claxton's last peacetime report before the world was plunged into war in the summer of 1914. Much that he had planned for the Bureau was thereby rendered impossible.

XV

United States Commissioner of Education: World War One, 1914-1916

◇◇

A FTER THE commencement of World War One and before the
actual participation of the United States in the great conflict,
Claxton continued his plan of attempting to vitalize the public
schools of the United States so that there might be a well developed
system, each part performing properly its function and being supported by all other parts. The aim of this was that all the people
might be prepared to share in the development of material wealth,
to constitute an intelligent and right minded citizenship, and "to
enjoy the largest amount possible of the sweetness and light, known
as culture." [1]

In 1914, the Bureau was asked to make a comprehensive survey of
the schools of San Francisco. For this work Claxton selected several
specialists from the Bureau and, with the $10,000 contributed by
San Francisco for expenses, employed a half dozen able men and
women as assistants. He went to San Francisco himself to get the
survey started, and then left it under the direction of W. T.
Bawden, specialist in manual training. When the survey was completed, he helped the committee interpret the findings and write
the report, which provided for a comprehensive reorganization of
the entire school system of that city. [1]

This was followed, in 1915 and the spring of 1916, by other surveys of the school systems of Jamestown (North Dakota), Webster
Groves (Missouri), Nassau County (New York), Richmond (Indiana), and the State of Wyoming. Surveys were also made in Sep-

tember, 1915, of the University of Oregon; in October, November, and December of the same year, of three colleges of higher education in Iowa; in the winter and spring of 1915–1916, of similar institutions in North Dakota; and in March and April, 1916, of such colleges in the state of Washington. By the middle of 1916, a three years' survey of Negro private and higher public schools was completed, and others had been begun of the schools in the Appalachian counties of Virginia, West Virginia, North Carolina, South Carolina, Tennessee, Georgia, and Alabama, as well as of the states of Delaware and Tennessee.[2] This was a very important practical work of the Bureau. Thirty-six surveys in all were made by him during his Commissionership.

Claxton was a member of the executive committee and chairman of the Education Division of the Second Pan-American Scientific Conference, which met in Washington in December, 1914, and January, 1915. On the 27th of December, he delivered an address of welcome to the delegates. He emphasized the importance of education in new countries like those of the Western Hemisphere in developing natural resources and creating material wealth, in preparing citizens for democratic governments, and in contributing to the literature, art, and philosophy of the world. He proposed a Pan-American policy of education, as follows:

"1. Equal opportunity for all children for that quantity and quality of education that will prepare them most fully for life, for making a living, and for the duties and responsibilities of citizenship. No child born among us or coming to us from any other part of the world should lack opportunity for preparation for the fullest life, the best living, and the largest service.

2. A closer relation in all educational matters through (a) an exchange of professors and students of higher institutions of learning; (b) some kind of Pan-American office or bureau of education to serve as a clearing house for information regarding education and as a center and means of educational propaganda; (c) an intelligent co-operation in educational experimentation to the end that we may finally have a larger body of definite and scientific knowledge of educational principles and methods; (d) a Pan-American educational association or congress meeting once in two or three years in some important city in one of these Republics."

"We meet in the Christmas time," he said. "The dominant religion in all the countries here represented is the religion of Christ—a religion not of darkness, superstition, blind faith, mechanical obedience, or wild fanaticism, but a religion of life and light and truth and love and service. . . . Our religion is a religion of love and service to man and to God, and we have come to understand that service to God can be rendered only through service to man. Our religion is a religion of righteousness and justice and peace and abounding joy. It recognizes as no other religion does the dignity and worth of the individual. It holds that the human good is above all other good; that it is the only absolute good. It is impatient of all human waste." [3]

This was probably one of Claxton's most impressive and significant addresses. It might even be considered as an important preparation for the later establishment of the "Good Neighbor Policy" with respect to the Latin-American countries. Some of the resolutions,[4] passed by the educational section of the conference, particularly that regarding the exchange of professors and students, have borne fruit.

In 1915 Claxton called a conference on Foreign Service Education. This was suggested by Dr. Glen Levin Swiggett, specialist in commercial education in the Bureau. He noted that little was being done in American schools and colleges for the preparation of men and women to serve the government or commercial and industrial enterprises in foreign countries. The conference met in Washington for two days. It was attended by college presidents and professors, businessmen, and many connected with the United States Consular Service. The conference was worthwhile in revealing, among many things, the great need for the study of the Spanish, French, and Portuguese languages. It was followed by a number of regional conferences which further awakened an interest in the problem.

Claxton continued to travel far and wide to make speeches. The following are representative. On March 5, 1915, he addressed the House and Senate of the State of Washington at Olympia. On April 21, he spoke at the Conference of Southern Mountain Workers at Knoxville, Tennessee, the central idea of his speech being the importance of normal schools and model schools.[5] On May 13, he gave an address in Washington at the New Willard Hotel before a convention of the American Federation of Arts on "Art Education in the Public Schools." [6] On May 20, he gave the commencement address at the Carlisle Indian School. On June 3, he delivered the commencement address for the Pennsylvania Museum and School of Industrial Art in the Broad Street Theater in Philadelphia on "The Place of Art in Democratic Education." Five days later he was in Bay City, Michigan, giving the commencement address to the High School on "High School Education for All." [7] On June 23 he was back in Pennsylvania, attending the 100th anniversary of the founding of Allegheny College at Meadville. Among the papers read by distinguished visitors was one by Claxton on "The American College in the Life of the American People." [8] On June 29 he arrived at Salt Lake City as the "outside lecturer" for a week in the University of Utah summer school.[9] June was indeed a busy month for Claxton the orator.

In July he journeyed still further west, and on the 12th he spoke on education day at the fair at San Diego, California, on "The Progress of Education and Its Influence on the American Republic." [10] Remaining in California until August, he attended the meeting of the National Education Association in Oakland, August 16–27. Here he delivered an address on "The Organization of High Schools in Junior and Senior Sections." [11] Each section, he thought, should cover three years of work, totaling six years for the high school. The length of the elementary school should be decreased to six years. He spoke on this same subject later at the meeting of the Michigan State Teachers Association at Saginaw on October 30. "Money spent for schools," Claxton declared,[12] "no matter how large the sum, is the best investment the public can make." Five days later, he spoke also on "The Place of the High School in American Education to the North Dakota Education Association at Grand Forks.[13]

Some disturbing incidents happened in 1915. In the March 22 issue of the New York *Times*, under the headline, "Catholics 'Robbed' for Public Schools," appeared the following: "The Reverend T. J. Shealy, S.J., a professor in the Fordham Law School and director of the Catholic laymen's retreat on Staten Island, declared at the solemn high mass at St. Patrick's Cathedral yesterday that Roman Catholics were being robbed by a despotic government when taxed for the maintenance of public schools from which the doctrines of God were excluded, compelling them to build schools of their own. He asserted that in many instances Catholic politicians were responsible for the existence of this state of affairs. The address of Father Shealy was delivered in the presence of Cardinal Farley and a congregation of more than 5,000 persons." Though this was not a personal attack on Claxton, he felt keenly the injustice of the criticism, for throughout his career he had never made any religious distinctions in administrative policy and had strongly supported religious non-sectarian teaching in the public schools.

The second incident, coming later in July, was an entirely personal attack, made by the Sons of the American Revolution during their congress at Portland, Oregon. Criticism of Claxton was embodied in the report of President General R. C. Ballard Thurston, on July 19, and the same day the matter was referred to the resolutions committee. The resolutions adopted the following day were as follows: "Whereas, The United States Commissioner of Education, P. P. Claxton, is reported to have expressed sentiments derogatory to the American flag and criticized its defenders in an address delivered before the American School Peace League; and

Whereas, Although his attention has been repeatedly called to the matter, he appears to regard it of little importance and has never, so far as we can learn, denied the accuracy of the report, as the expression of his opinion, nor repudiated its sentiments; and

Whereas, The Sons of the American Revolution take sentimental pride in the work of the builders of the republic and hold in highest honor the defenders of the flag that symbolizes the United States of America; and

Whereas, No man is worthy of the privileges of American citizenship who insults the flag or defames its defenders; therefore be it

Resolved, That the executive committee be instructed to present the matter to the attention of the President of the United States, with the firm belief that his high patriotism and devotion to duty will permit no man holding such sentiments to remain at the head of one of the most important bureaus of our Government. Be it further

Resolved, That we protest against any further printing or reprinting of the publications of the American School Peace League under the authority of Commissioner Claxton at the expense of the nation." [14]

Claxton, then in Bellingham, Washington, immediately issued a denial of the charge. "Five or six years ago in Boston," he declared,[15] "I delivered a lecture in which, among other things, I said: 'In modern times the flag must stand for larger things than it did for the ancients. People are drawn from all corners of the earth to live together. They are born in one place, live in another, travel much, and thus come nearer to the ideal universal fatherhood of God and brotherhood of man, and in this connection the flag, in the broader sense, must serve all. The time has come when men do not revere the flag alone for its material or combination of colors, but for what it symbolizes.' I never said a derogatory word about the flag in my life."

The speech, which aroused such a tempest, was delivered by Claxton at Boston University on "The Larger Patriotism and What the Schools May Do to Bring It About," on July 8, 1910, during the sessions of the National Education Association at a meeting of the American School Peace League, which was endorsed by that association. A report of the speech in the Boston *Transcript* gave the following résumé: "After all, the people of the world care very little what flag they live under. A flag means nothing. It is not a reality. They can live under one combination of colors as well as another. Those people who go from our great Northwest to the Saskatchewan and other parts of Canada, what do they lose by the change to life under another [flag]? Their wheat will grow just as well, they can live as well, and they can make as much money for their welfare. We no longer think of our country as we used to do. State boundaries have little meaning for us. We do not mean patriotism to stick to the strip of land where one chances to have been born through thick and thin. The Germans who have come to our shores do not pine to live under the German colors; at least I have not found it so." [16]

Preceding this résumé, the report declared, "The Stars and Stripes, or the flag of any other nation amounts to nothing in particular. It is merely a combination of colors with only a mistaken sentiment clinging to it, according to Professor P. P. Claxton who addressed the American School Peace League at Boston University today. What is said about flags was intended to show that they represent only the old-style patriotism for each particular nation, whereas men should consider the whole world instead of splitting it up into nations. Incidentally, he criticized soldiers who willingly accepted positions, pensions from the Government, whether they need them or not. The latter part of his address, wherein he told of the greater benefits from peaceful employments, and showed how, if wars had been done away with centuries ago, the world would have been inestimably better off, was frequently applauded."

After Claxton returned to Knoxville, this item appeared in the local *Sentinel*: [17] "When approached on the subject, Dr. Claxton said he had been too busy to read the attack carefully, but that in regard to the statements about the flag he had been misquoted. What he did say was that it was not the mere colors or combination of colors that should incite patriotism, but what that flag stood for. A flag standing for righteousness should be revered wherever it is seen, and a flag standing for oppression and tyranny can never command the respect and patriotism of a people, he declared. Dr. Claxton had no written context of the speech made in Boston which aroused the indignation of the *Army and Navy Journal*, but declared he had made no such attack on the American flag as has been accredited to him."

Without verifying the report in the Boston *Transcript* or communicating with Claxton as to the truthfulness of the report, the *Army and Navy Journal*, in its issue of July 23, printed an editorial bitterly criticizing the American School Peace League and Claxton in particular for trying to replace nationalism with internationalism and destroying the respect and veneration for the Stars and Stripes. The speech was called to the attention of the Governor of Tennessee in order that Claxton might be removed from his position at The University of Tennessee.

On July 26, Edwin D. Mead, author and lecturer, and member of the executive committee of the American School Peace League, wrote a letter to the *Army and Navy Journal*, in which he defended the league as a patriotic organization. Incidentally he wrote, "Claxton . . . said some very extravagant—I think very unwise and untrue—things about patriotism and the flag in connection with some unwarranted and wholesome things about the bastard patriotism that is mere brag and bluster and the political superstition which makes a fetish of the flag." The *Journal* published this letter in its issue of July 30 and another editorial condemning Claxton, in which great praise was given to the Japanese for their veneration of their flag and their *unmilitaristic* patriotism.

The following week the *Journal* renewed the attack in an editorial, which quoted the Knoxville *Sentinel's* report, in which Claxton had stated that he had been misquoted and had given the substance of his remarks regarding the flag. Using Mead's letter, the editorial attempted to prove that Claxton was not misquoted and called on him for a repudiation of "his views or a manly reavowal of the sentiments expressed in Boston." [18] He will not be allowed to escape, it declared, "under cover of the common trick of saying, 'I was misquoted.'" "If Claxton will send us a copy of his speech we will print it in full," it continued, "but first we wish to submit it to Mr. Mead and ascertain whether it is exactly the speech that was delivered in Boston." Then Claxton is belabored as Superintendent of the Summer School of the South, a position in which he is capable of doing great harm. A parting shot is taken at Mead, in this sentence: "We believe we are disclosing what is really behind the peace movement, however much some of its members may beat the air in clamorous protestation." [18]

This editorial aroused Mead's anger, and he replied with another letter of August 17, in which he said that he was not present in the auditorium and did not hear Claxton's speech. "My criticisms, like other criticisms which have come to my ears," he wrote,[19] "were based upon the newspaper report which has been quoted, and which I took at its face value. I ought undoubtedly to have written to Professor Claxton about it before participating in the controversy. Every man in public life knows only too well, without any necessity of impeaching reporters, a six-inch report fails to do justice to an earnest half hour's talk; and if Professor Claxton, one of the noblest gentlemen and scholars of the country, says that the report was partial and misleading, I trust that I am not so little of a gentleman as to ask him to prove it. . . . The whole thing would seem farcical, if it were not so mournful. When you undertake to accuse Professor Claxton, of all men in this country, of lack of patriotism you are barking up the wrong tree. You have singled out the worst subject in the country for your purpose. Patriotism is Professor Claxton's very religion; it happens that he has ten times as much concern with it as with internationalism. If you do not know this, and if you and the War College of Rochester, New York, will take the trouble to look a little, with willingness to learn, into the work of the Summer School of the South, Professor Claxton's presidency of which you fling at as a 'sonorous and high-sounding title,' you will learn that his position is 'lofty' because he has made it so, by creating the most remarkable and most beneficent and most patriotic summer school in the United States, doing more to make good Americans of the great mass of Southern teachers than any other institution known to me. If I may add one particular bit of advice, it is that you go there on the 4th of July, that you may see, in that most impressive of all annual Independence Day celebrations in the United States, an exhibition of patriotism that is patriotism indeed. If 'flags' are what you are after, you will see—with one waving in the hand of each of those 2,000 teachers—more of them than have been seen in Vesey Street,[20] New York, in the last 100 years. Permit me, in conclusion, a personal word. You say that in my letter to the *Journal* the other day I 'challenge Professor Claxton's veracity.' I did nothing of the kind. The sentence which you quote shows clearly that the word 'untrue' is used in a sense which warrants no such inference. It ought not to be necessary to say this; but since you choose to make the inference I desire in your columns sharply to disclaim it."

This practically ended the battle of words, the *Journal* making only brief references to the matter in the issues of September 3 and November 12, 1910. Indeed the attack was shown to rest on such an unstable foundation that, when Claxton was appointed Commissioner of Education the following summer, no mention was made of the appointment in the *Journal*. Certainly this would have been the time to press home an attack of this kind on a man with "dangerous" ideas.

It was thus a practically dead issue which the Sons of the American Revolution revived at Portland, Oregon, five years later. For this action they received much more criticism than endorsement. An editorial in the Worcester (Massachusetts) *Gazette*,[21] entitled "A Teapot Tempest," declared in part, "Many Worcester people remember hearing Mr. Claxton deliver a most entertaining and instructive address before the Parent-Teacher Association less than two years ago in Mechanics Hall and any disloyal sentiment on his part is worse than nonsense. On the contrary, his language really expresses just what the flag is for and why we should revere it." The Salem (Massachusetts) News [22] declared, "The real objection to Claxton on their part is not what he said about the flag but because he believes in circulating world peace literature in the public schools. The Sons want it suppressed and only Roosevelt war talk circulated among the people. It means more money for arms and ammunition."

An example of unfair criticism is this from the Trenton (N. J.) Gazette: [23] "A flag may mean nothing to Commissioner Claxton, but occupying the position he does in the public service, he ought to smother his disregard for the Stars and Stripes and encourage adoration for them in the minds of those men, women, and children whose education he is expected to improve and advance."

The Army and Navy Journal took advantage of the opportunity to renew the attack which had formerly failed and, in an editorial reprinted the resolution of the Sons of the American Revolution and rehashed the facts and arguments of 1910. "If this same society had taken action in 1910," it petulantly complained,[24] "we should not now perhaps have a national Commissioner of Education against whom such a resolution has to be drafted. The anti-military organizations for so long have had a clear field that they have gone to unheard of lengths, such as having the literature of the American School Peace League published at the expense of the Government. We trust this broadside from the Portland congress will be followed by action by other patriotic societies until the whole sinister movement to undermine the manhood of the country is crushed."

At the request of Secretary of the Interior Lane, Claxton prepared a statement of about 2,000 words giving the facts regarding his Boston speech, and its substance as far as he could remember. This is a very interesting and extremely well written statement. "I said a flag rightly considered is not merely the material, the piece of bunting, of which it is made, or merely a combination of colors. It is rather what it symbolizes and stands for," Claxton wrote.[25] "Love and reverence for any flag will in the long run depend on its significance. If it symbolizes tyranny, autocratic rule, oppression of the people, and disregard of their rights, burdensome taxation and military domination, then there is danger that it will not be either loved or respected. If it stands for individual liberty, for democracy, for equal opportunity, for progress, for freedom from unnecessary burdens of taxation, and from military domination, the people will learn to revere and love it more and more. In witness of this fact and of the fact that people change allegiance more readily now than formerly, I called attention to the fact that millions of people come from all the nations of the earth to our own country and learn to revere and love the flag of the Republic which stands for liberty, democracy, progress, opportunity, and hope of better things than we have yet been able to attain. I also called attention to the 40,000 people (this was about the number at that time) who each year migrate from the Northwestern States across the Canadian border, leaving the territory of the American flag, and 'seem to be reasonably happy under another combination of the same colors,' symbolizing many of the best things for which our own flag stands. This last phrase seems to be the objectionable part of my speech, but I am still unable to see that it implies any suspicion of treason if rightly understood."

As to not replying to the *Journal*, further than as reported in the Knoxville *Evening Sentinel*, Claxton explained to Lane that he had an aversion to newspaper controversy and was too busy teaching, lecturing, and performing administrative work. "I was less inclined to correct this report or reply to anything that was said about it then," continued [25] Claxton, "because having been taught by my father, who was a staunch Union man in a state that had seceded, I learned in my childhood to regard the United States flag with a feeling of sacred reverence which I have not cared to flaunt in the face of the public. For one, whose ancestors have for generations been of the purest American stock and is closely related to those in a half dozen states who helped to determine the destiny of this country in the days of the Revolution and the early days of our national life, and who has held the principles of American democracy as sacred as his religion, and who has of choice devoted his life to the task of making these principles mean still more to the men and women of this country in the next generation, to be called on to assert his patriotism is very much like asking one to assert his devotion to his mother. Some things may well be taken for granted."

As to the request from the editor of the *Army and Navy Journal* that he would send him for publication what he really did say, Claxton declared,[25] "This I should have been glad to do had he made the request before publishing the articles. Since he had published them before trying to learn if I had been correctly reported, I did not reply. It looked too much like asking for evidence to be used in a trial after the execution."

Touching upon the accusation that he had authorized the printing or reprinting of publications of the American School Peace League in the Bureau of Education, Claxton declared this was not true. He explained that his predecessor, Commissioner Elmer Ellsworth Brown, had designated the 18th of May, the anniversary of the meeting of the first Peace Conference at the Hague, as Peace Day in the schools of the United States, and that in the autumn of 1911, after he became Commissioner, he asked Mrs. Fannie Fern Andrews, Secretary of the American School Peace League and a special collaborator in the Bureau of Education, to collect and prepare appropriate material for the celebration of this day. This was published as *Bulletin* (1912), *No. 8, Whole Number 476*, and distributed among school principals and superintendents. A similar bulletin was prepared and distributed the following year. "Inasmuch as a right understanding of the principles of international peace and a proper attitude of mind toward other nations are not unimportant in the education of a people of a democratic Republic like ours, which cultivates good will toward all the world," Claxton asserted,[25] "I am of the opinion that the publication and distribution of these two bulletins by the Bureau of Education was perfectly legitimate."

Claxton took the statement personally to Secretary Lane and sat near him while he read it. When he finished, the Secretary remarked, "This ought to satisfy one who is 'too proud to fight' [President Wilson]." On that same day some harsh criticism had been made of Lane, and to his first remark he added, "Isn't it hell anyway?" [26] That was the end of the Claxton Flag Incident.

The details of this affair have been recorded, as the whole incident reveals Claxton's character very clearly. Particularly evident is his courage. "His middle name is courage," wrote his wife; [27] "I have never seen him afraid. Little men have attacked him, have lied about him, but he never even answered." Evident also is his belief in the interrelation between education and world peace. "I have always been interested in world problems of government and international law," he wrote.[28] "I very early began to understand that the world is one, that all peoples are interdependent and all are 'bound up in the sheaf of life together.' From my earliest youth I have hated war as an insane, barbaric, and anachronistic institution. Intelligent civilized people should be willing to pay for peace as much in thought, energy, and money as war costs."

While in Washington, Claxton was a member of the executive committee of the American Peace Society, and in 1915 he made a series of twenty addresses for the Carnegie Peace Foundation. These were delivered chiefly in the states of Nevada, Washington, Oregon, and California, Claxton receiving $100 per speech. The theme of the addresses was as follows: [28] "Peace is more important than war and more valuable. We should, therefore, be willing to pay for peace in money, time, energy, thought, and emotion as much as war costs. Peace is not passive, but positive and constructive. Pacifist is not spelled 'passivist.' Preparation, military preparation, by one nation causes the same in another nation. There is no more relative safety. Heavily armed nations are more sensitive to possible insults. If a nation has costly armies and navies, the tendency is to use them. Any nation may trust itself not to use preparedness for offense, but other nations will not trust it. All military preparation is supposed to be in defense, but it may come about that the best defense is thought to be offense. Armies and navies never have assured lasting peace. All military people are finally destroyed by their own armies and navies. The cost of these leads to such economic exhaustion and such discontent as results in internal division and dissolution.

'Tis said that human nature never changes. We have always had war and therefore always will have war. Human nature does change slowly. But the most characteristic and persistent quality of human nature is: when people's minds and ideas broaden and their ideals change, when they think more accurately and obtain new visions and form new ideals and new purposes and set for themselves new goals, they first become impatient of and then intolerant of whatever stands in the way of obtaining these purposes and goals. We have extended our knowledge to worldwide proportions, have set for ourselves higher ideals of service, of health, of education, and fuller and better living and equality of opportunity for all people. War is now the greatest obstacle to the attainment of these purposes and ideals. Most people and all right-thinking leaders of the people are becoming impatient of and will soon become intolerant of this obstacle. There is no possibility of the highest civilization or of the fullest and best living until war is done away with."

Claxton was also a charter member of the American School Peace League, later reorganized as the American Citizenship League. He was a member of the executive committee of both these leagues, and in the latter capacity he helped to prepare, with the authority of the National Education Association, a series of books on American history and citizenship with the idea of eliminating war. Dr. Wilbur Fisk Gordy was the chairman of this committee.[29]

In 1916 Claxton continued his speech making. A few examples will show the extent of his travels. On April 17, he spoke at San Francisco to the California Teachers Association on "The Place of the High School in Our Public School System." [30] Three days later he was in Spokane, Washington, speaking to the Inland Empire Teachers Association on the theme of rural education. A couple of days later he was at Billings, Montana, speaking on school democracy, better rural schools, and vocational training.[31] On June 7, he was at East Las Vegas, New Mexico, addressing a state educational conference in the Duncan Opera House on "The Relation of the Town and Country Schools to the Welfare of a State or Government." The next morning at a breakfast in his honor he spoke on "Efficiency in Education." [32] About a week later he was in Nashville, Tennessee, delivering the baccalaureate at Peabody College on "George Peabody College for Teachers—as a Unique Institution." [33] Two days afterwards, he delivered the commencement address at the Kansas State Agricultural College at Manhattan on "The Value of Land." [34] On July 5, at the meeting of the National Education Association, he spoke on the progress of public instruction throughout the nation. He registered his disapproval of compulsory military training in the public schools and declared that, if real preparedness were desired, a commission should be appointed to devise a national system of education "which will be democratic, flexible, and practical." [35]

"Just think of the situation," said [35] Claxton; "not for twenty years can any big nation think of invading us, and then we shall be 150,000,000 strong. If we are well prepared and our minds are conscious of our might, we will be unconquerable." He then related that the Japanese Minister of War, in speaking of war with the United States, had declared, "We probably could take the Philippines and perhaps Hawaii too. We might land an army on the Pacific coast, but by that time the big nation would be awake and soon there would be no more Japan and our early successes would be of no avail." "Preparedness was the main topic of educators" at this meeting, according to the Philadelphia *Public Ledger*.[36]

At a Citizenship Convention in Washington, July 10–15, 1916, Claxton spoke on "Preparation for American Citizenship and Life." On September 1, he addressed the Somerset County Teachers Institute at Johnstown, Pennsylvania, on "Vocational Education." [37] At the 25th anniversary celebration of the Philadelphia School of Pedagogy he spoke on October 13 on "The Teacher and the Nation." At the dedication of the Emerson High School on December 7, in West Hoboken, New Jersey, he was the principal speaker.

During these busy years as Commissioner, Claxton did not find time to do much writing for periodicals. An article by him, entitled "Keep the School Open All the Year," appeared in *The Advance* of August 6, 1914. *The Social Service Review* for February, 1916, contained an article by him on "Immigration after the War." Since 1912 he had been employed as chief editor of an educational encyclopedia which was under preparation by the Hanson-Bellows Company of Chicago. The war caused the postponement of the work and the later financial failure of the division of the reorganized company, which had taken over the publication of the encyclopedia. Some of the material which Claxton had secured from his able contributors was transferred with the editorship to another company, who published the *World Book Encyclopedia*. Claxton also was collaborating with James McGinniss in the writing of the textbook, *Effective English*, which was published in 1917.

The Commissioner's report for the year ending June 30, 1915, differed in form from the previous ones only in the omission of disconnected general studies which were to be published later as separate bulletins. The different chapters of the first volume were designed to give "such an account of the growth of institutions of learning and of school systems, of the working of all the more important agencies of education, and of the development of educational ideals and the progress of educational thought as will enable the reader to gain a knowledge of all that has been most worthwhile in the educational life of the world within the year for which the report is made, and to understand something, at least, of the trend of educational theory and practice." [38] The second volume, as previously, contained statistics only.

In the introduction to his report for the year ending June 30, 1916, Claxton stated that there was an increasing interest in the United States in education in foreign countries and that the Bureau had, accordingly, collected more statistics than previously on this subject. To those who might misunderstand, or be discouraged with, the unequal development of school systems in different parts of the country, Claxton declared, "All must recognize that schools, school systems, and all other agencies of education in such a country as this are forever in the making. If it were possible to perfect them today to such an extent that they would be adapted in every particular to all our needs, by that same token they would be imperfect and in need of readjustment tomorrow, for in democratic freedom life flows on unfettered and is never still."

XVI

United States Commissioner of Education: World War One, 1916-1918

◇◇◇

WHEN THE United States finally joined the Allies on April 6, 1917, in the war against Germany, much that Claxton had planned for the Bureau was impossible. His main objective became keeping the schools open, well taught, well supported, and well attended. As President Wilson announced in a letter (which Claxton wrote), "No boy or girl should have less opportunity for education because of the war." [1] On May 22, *Suggestions for the Conduct of Educational Institutions during the Continuance of the War* was issued by the Bureau.[2] This made the plea that all students should remain in school as long as possible and take full advantage of all educational opportunities because more educated men and women would be needed than could be supplied if the war were long, and after the war still more educated men and women would be required for the work of reconstruction at home and abroad.

Claxton also publicized the plan of establishing school gardens to aid in counteracting food shortages. He had for many years advocated school gardening, and in 1916 he had written a chapter, "Home Gardening Directed by the School," in *Our Public Schools the Nation's Bulwark*, edited by John F. Murray. In the May, 1917, issue of *Review of Reviews* appeared an article by Claxton on "School Gardening in the Food Crisis." On April 3, he spoke at the Wilson Normal School in Washington to the Columbia Heights Citizens Association on "Educational Training of Garden Work to Be Taught in the Public School System." Through explanatory leaflets sent out by the Bureau and the aid of newspapers, school gardening became popular throughout the country. At least one parody of a song appeared, as follows:

"It's a long way from Chattanooga,
　　It's a long way to go;
　It's a long way to Mr. Claxton,
　　From Dixie's Dynamo.
　Yet he must hear our praises
　　In Washington, D. C.
　It's hurrah-rah-rah for Mr. Claxton,
　　Phil-an-der P!" [8]

Soon after American entrance into the war, there was a general hysterical movement to stop the study of German in schools of all levels, especially those supported by the state. It began in Ohio and other states where there was a large German population and German was the language of instruction in the schools, but the opposition to the teaching of the language soon became general. The first appeal for advice from Claxton came from the Brooklyn board of education. He advised against excluding German, but recommended that the language of instruction in all schools should be limited to English.[4] Through the Bureau of Education in 1917 he issued *City School Circular No. 4*, suggesting this policy: "There is general agreement among educators and public men, both in this country and abroad, that there should be no interference with the existing high school and college provision for the teaching of German; that a knowledge of the German language is more important now than it was before the war. The upper elementary grades, especially where organized as junior high schools, may quite properly offer foreign languages, including German, but educators generally look upon the teaching of foreign languages as of very questionable value in the lower grades."

The legislature of Iowa prohibited the teaching of German in any school receiving any part of its support from the state. The board of trustees of the state university asked Claxton's opinion and advice. He replied, "Just now you need to know German." A strong protest came from former Senator Lafe Young. Claxton answered that his advice was in keeping with the policy of the administration.

Young then wrote him, "If that is the policy of the administration, it makes me very sad." Claxton dictated a detailed reply of three pages. Before signing the letter, he went to lunch at the Cosmos Club where he met the Third Assistant Secretary of War, who told him he had just received a cable from General Pershing asking for 600 men who knew German and whose loyalty could be trusted.

The legislature of Kentucky passed a similar act. The governor requested Claxton's opinion and advice, and he advised him to veto the bill. He did this, and later in a political campaign for the Senate he was defeated because of the veto. He then communicated with President Wilson and asked his opinion. Wilson replied that he supposed that the Commissioner of Education knew his business when he advised the veto.

Early in March, 1918, President Robert L. Slagle of the University of South Dakota wrote Claxton for his advice with regard to the dropping of German from the curriculum of that university. In reply Claxton wrote [5] a long letter fully expressing his views. "It is, of course, desirable now and always is," he declared, "that nothing should be taught in any language in our schools or elsewhere that would tend to create a spirit of disloyalty to our country or to the American ideals of freedom and democracy. . . . The United States is at war with the Imperial Government of Germany and not with the German language or literature. The President has tried to make it plain to all people that we are not at war with the people of Germany as a people, that we have in our hearts no hatred or bitterness toward them. For our own sake and for the sake of the future of the world let us hope that we may finish this task for the establishment of freedom and safety of democracy without learning to chant any hymn of hate."

He then pointed out how a knowledge of German would be needed after the war. "For practical, industrial, and commercial purposes we shall need a knowledge of the German language more than we have needed it in the past," he added. "We should remember also that there are many millions of German speaking people outside of Germany and the number of such persons will probably increase rapidly after the war regardless of the way in which the war may end. . . . The culture value of the German language and the writings of Lessing, Goethe, Schiller, and a host of other poets and of novelists, historians, and essayists remains the same as it was before the war and it is too great for us to lose out of our life, national and individual. The value of the scientific and technical writings of the German people will no doubt continue to increase. To rob ourselves of the ability to profit by them would be very foolish."

In conclusion, he stated, "I sincerely hope that school officers and teachers everywhere will take the broad and sane view of this subject. To do so can, I believe, in no way be interpreted as a lack of loyalty to the United States, nor can failure to do so in anyway strengthen our position in the war or enable us to bring it to a successful end more quickly. I have reason to believe that the views and sentiment expressed in this letter are fully in harmony with those of the Administration at Washington."

V. M. Henderson, president of the Council of National Defense at Cleveland, Ohio, read an excerpt from Claxton's letter which had been published in a newspaper, and wrote him a rather violent letter favoring the elimination of German from the schools. He declared [6] that he had sat "under the magic of your matchless oratory as you lectured before the teachers of Cincinnati and Hamilton County, and I have not yet ceased always to think of you as my ideal school man. If you are correctly quoted, I must reluctantly wreck my ideal and seek to rear in its stead another whose words more nearly typify all that is near and dear to all loyal 100% Americans in the present world crisis."

To this Claxton took the trouble to reply,[7] stating that his letter had been published in an official bulletin of the Bureau with the approval of the Secretary of the Interior, and that George Creel, Chairman of the Committee on Public Information, had told him that a similar letter to another school official had been read by President Wilson and approved by him. "No attempt has been made by me or any one else to impose this as a policy on states or local systems of education," Claxton continued. "It has only been given as advice when we have been asked. The Federal Government and the Bureau of Education representing it has no administrative authority over the schools of the states."

As to the insinuation that he was lacking in patriotism, Claxton concluded, "I assure you that I am as nearly as possible a hundred per cent American and have been through many generations since the men of my family on both sides fought in the Revolutionary War. You are kind enough to refer to my series of lectures in the University of Cincinnati. If you remember them very well, you will remember that in those lectures was included much which I had gained from comprehensive reading of Goethe, Schiller, and Lessing; still more that came from the writings of Froebel, Herbart, Fichte, Kant, Rein, Pestalozzi, and others who wrote in German. Without what I had gained from those the lectures would have been comparatively poor. Those who are to become the leaders in education and literature should not be denied the opportunity of learning any language through which they may gain knowledge of whatever is good in any literature."

In reply to a letter from E. D. Monroe of Peoria, Illinois, Claxton repeated that Pershing in one cablegram had asked for 400 telephone operators who knew German. He also related that an American soldier picked up a German notebook in the trenches. He could not read the language, and several days passed before it was discovered to contain valuable information. "Is it not easy to understand," Claxton asked,[8] "that ignorance is not strength and that we shall not be able to win the great war for democracy and freedom by condemning ourselves to the disadvantage of not knowing the language of the people we are fighting and with whom we must have dealings after the war is over?"

Claxton was unable to stem the tide of opposition to the teaching of German. The American Defense Society claimed that fourteen states had abolished the teaching of German in their schools, and that sixteen others had a campaign under way to eliminate the language.[9] The National Security League had a Committee on Foreign Languages and Foreign Press, which fought a campaign for "A One Language Nation."

In September, 1918, a cartoon was widely published, entitled "Teacher's Pet." It portrayed Claxton standing in a schoolroom with his right hand resting on the helmeted head of a German boy (German language) in full military uniform including the iron cross on his chest. In his left hand Claxton holds a ruler "made in Germany." On the wall are pictures of the Kaiser and Von Hindenburg and a map of Germany. On the blackboard are written phrases, such as "Deutschland uber alles" and "Me Und Gott." On a table are books by Goethe and Schiller.[10]

At this time, George Creel, Chairman of the Committee on Public Information, wrote Secretary of the Interior Franklin K. Lane, suggesting the appointment of a committee to investigate German propaganda in school textbooks, especially in history. "This situation," he wrote,[11] "has been precipitated by rival publishers and by patriots suffering from civic shell shock." The problem was passed on to Claxton, who had already three months previously endeavored to form a committee for preparing a "white list" of textbooks for the study of the German language and literature.

In June, Claxton wrote[12] to Dr. C. Alphonso Smith, then head of the Department of English and History at the U. S. Naval Academy, inviting him to become a member of such a committee. Smith replied,[13] "I should be glad to serve you in any way that I could but I am too entirely in sympathy with the sentiment that demands the elimination of German from our schools and colleges to take part in the work that you suggest. A nation's language rises or falls in proportion to the rise or fall of the morals for which the nation stands. This seems to me the universal law of language, the law that has made and unmade the languages of history. It is a law that German scholars have expounded and by which they will have to abide. The sense of disillusionment about Germany is so acute today, the revulsion of feeling against her *kultur* is so widespread, and the certainty of her waning power and prestige is so assured that I cannot view with disapproval the increasing revolt against her language. This may prove temporary. I at least hope so. But it rests with Germany to make it temporary by reinstating herself and by restoring our faith in her and our admiration of her national spirit."

Perhaps it was Dr. Smith's own disillusionment regarding Germany which led him to write this surprising letter. He had been in 1910–1911 the Roosevelt Professor of American History and Institutions at the University of Berlin, and had been favorably impressed with German culture. Perhaps his connection with a national institution like the Naval Academy in time of war led him to shy away from a controversial commitment. However, Claxton was unable then or later to accomplish any practical results in formulating a desirable list of German textbooks.

In spite of the war, Claxton traveled extensively to make speeches. On January 19, 1917, he spoke in Carnegie Music Hall in Pittsburgh in the interest of Fisk University. He reviewed the development of Negro education, and declared that education was the only cure for the Negro problem. On February 5, he addressed the American Medical Association in Chicago on "Economy of Time," dealing with certain modifications in the college curriculum. At the 34th general meeting of the Association of Collegiate Alumnae in Washington on April 10, he spoke on "What the Government Is Doing for Women." On August 14, he spoke at the 40th annual Temperance and Gospel Meeting of the Prohibition and Evangelical Association of Loudoun County at Purcellville, Virginia. In July he attended the meeting of the National Education Association at Portland, Oregon, and discussed "Standards in Teacher Training." He was one of the speakers, October 19, in the Academy of Music in Philadelphia at the convocation of Drexel Institute, celebrating "The Service of the College to the State" (1892–1917). On October 31 he spoke in Carnegie Hall in New York at a civic celebration in connection with the 400th Anniversary of the Reformation, arranged by the Lutheran Society. Madame Gadski sang three Wagnerian arias. Two days later he was in Boston speaking on "Education for Democracy" to the Essex County Teachers Association.

In 1918 the speechmaking continued. On February 27 he spoke in Atlantic City at the Breakers Hotel on "War Conditions and War Duties of Parents and Teachers" before the National Congress of Mothers and Parent-Teacher Associations. On March 5 he was at the Hotel Biltmore in New York speaking on better music in the public schools at a dinner given by the Musical Alliance.[14] The menu had a picture of him in the upper left-hand corner. On March 16 he spoke in Washington at Twentieth Century Hall on "The Child and the War" before a combined meeting of the Twentieth Century Club and the Trustees of the Public Education Association. On April 5 he spoke on Founders' Day at Tuskegee Normal and Industrial Institute on the "Life of Booker T. Washington."

On May 2, in Washington at the Corcoran Art Gallery he gave an address at the eighth annual convention of the Drama League of America on "The Drama in Education." On May 1 he spoke at Tuskegee Normal and Industrial Institute. On May 13 he delivered the commencement address at Chevy Chase School in Washington. On July 2, he presided at the Action Conferences at Pittsburgh, called by the Bureau on mobilizing America.

At the 12th summer session of the Cotton Manufacturers Association, at Asheville, July 6, Claxton spoke at the Battery Park Hotel, on how best to train the minds of the children in the cotton mill communities. "I have no sympathy," he said, "with any kind of education or philosophy of life that will make any group of people merely good working cattle; that will make of any group of people good machines to be cast aside and thrown away when you can make better machines out of brass, wood, or metal, but we recognize that these are human beings and that they should be developed as well as possible."

During these years Claxton wrote various published articles. *Musical America* for June 9, 1917, contained one by him on music in training camps. Another appeared in *Religious Education* for August, 1917, on "Organ Recitals for Children." In *Musical America*, February 23, 1918, there was a front page picture of Claxton and reference to his plan for promotion of better music in the public schools. The Washington *Times*, September 5, 1918, an educational number, contained an article by him, entitled, "We Must Prepare for Future of Our Children." He also wrote an article on "Consolidation as a War Measure" for the July, 1918, issue of *Banker-Farmer*. "I can conceive of no finer community service for the bankers of the United States, especially of the smaller towns and villages," he wrote, "than to assist in the movement for consolidation. The interest of the bankers in this movement is a tribute to their good business judgment as well as to their civic ideals. An educated community is a prosperous community. Good rural schools will mean, when reconstruction comes, sustained prosperity; they will mean, both now and in the future, a nation strong with the basic strength of an educated citizenship on the land."

For *The Little Democracy, a Textbook on Community Organ-*

ization by Mrs. Ida Clyde (Gallagher) Clark, he wrote an introduction. In this he declared, ". . . For the welfare and safety of the democratic republic every final local community unit of it must be intelligent, virtuous, and united for the public good. In these local communities the people must come together on terms of democratic equality for mutual instruction, in regard to all things of common interest to them as members of these local communities and as members of the larger communities, of municipality, county, state, and nation." On the flyleaf of the book the author quotes this sentence by Claxton: "Every school district should be a little democracy, and the schoolhouse the community capital."

Claxton commenced, on August 1, 1918, the publication of *School Life* as the official organ of the Bureau. The editor of this bimonthly publication was W. Carson Ryan, Jr. Claxton frequently contributed articles and letters to it. In the first issue was a reprint of a paragraph from his statement of March 8, 1918, urging retired teachers to return to the profession during war time, and a reprint of his article on "Consolidation as a War Measure" in the July *Banker-Farmer.*

"Every public officer entrusted with the support of public schools," he wrote in the August 16, 1918, issue, "should know that Europe's lesson to the United States as a result of the war is to *keep the schools going;* to make education during and after the war better and more effective than it has ever been. There are before us now just two matters of supreme importance: to win the war for freedom, democracy, and peace, and to fit our schools and our children for life and citizenship in the new era which the war is bringing in."

This number also contained a letter by Claxton, addressed to the officials of labor unions, requesting them to aid in Americanization. ". . . Will you not therefore help our foreign-born industrial soldiers over here," he wrote, "who are so valiantly standing back of our Army and Navy over there, to better understand America and its ideals, and in your local celebrations [Labor Day, September 2] urge them

To obey cheerfully the American laws and regulations, especially those made necessary by the war;

To learn to understand the language of America;

To prepare themselves for an understanding of American citizenship;

To secure a home stake in America and buy Liberty bonds; and

To be American in thought, in heart, in speech, and in the will to win the war."

The same issue reprinted a letter by Claxton to college presidents and superintendents of city schools, calling to their attention the importance of studying the Spanish and Portuguese languages.[15]

In the following issue of September 1, was a letter by Claxton to the 200,000 members of the Boys' Working Reserve, congratulating them on their splendid summer work and advising them to return to school. Another letter addressed to the heads of public and private educational institutions explained how the American Council on Education and the French High Commission had arranged to furnish French teachers where they were needed.

In the October 1 number Claxton had articles on the "School Garden Army" and "The Schools and the Fourth Liberty Loan." In the latter, he wrote that this issue of *School Life* would be sent to half a million teachers. Two weeks later, he wrote an endorsement of the appeal of the American Library Association for textbooks for army camps, another letter urging school boards to co-operate with the Boys' Working Reserve, a third letter to school boards concerning the convention in St. Louis (November 20–22) of the National League of Compulsory Education officials, whose aims he approves, and a fourth letter on the "Wartime Needs of Colored Schools."

The number for November 1 contained a letter by Claxton to superintendents of schools regarding their co-operation in English instruction for non-English-speaking men in the Selective Draft, and another to the "Victory Boys" in regard to raising $170,500,000 for the comfort and health of men in the service and the relief of their families.

In the second issue for November, Claxton wrote on the Conference on Industrial and Technical Training in High Schools, which he had summoned to meet in Washington, and also a letter to the National Child Labor Committee, in which he declared, "Humanity and good government alike demand that no child shall be exploited to its hurt, that the health of none shall be neglected, and that none shall fail to be instructed in those things that pertain to its industrial, social, and civic efficiency."

Claxton was a contributor to the *National School Service*, a bi-monthly organ of the Committee on Public Information. The first issue appeared on September 1, 1918. In this was an article by him, entitled "Commissioner of Education Greets Teachers."

At its meeting at St. Paul in 1913 the National Education Association adopted a resolution requesting the Bureau of Education to authorize an official version of "our national songs" for use in schools. Claxton appointed a committee of five, of which Walter J. Damrosch and John Philip Sousa were members, to submit to him a version of each of these songs. In November, 1917, a version of the "Star Spangled Banner" arranged by Damrosch was submitted. Claxton approved it on December 1, and Damrosch played it at a concert of the Oratorio Society in New York. Then the members of the committee began to disagree; some thought the harmonization was "punk"; Sousa wrote a version preferred by one committeeman; and no agreement was later reached.[16]

In 1916–1917 a contest was inaugurated in the press throughout the United States to stimulate the writing of a national creed expressing "the best summary of the political faith of America." The city of Baltimore, the birthplace of the "Star Spangled Banner," offered a prize of $1000. A committee on manuscripts and another on awards were appointed, consisting of distinguished authors. An advisory committee was also selected, consisting of Commissioner of Education Claxton, Governors of States, United States Senators, and other national and state officials. After considering over 2000 manuscripts, the committees awarded the prize to William Tyler Page of Maryland, a descendant of President John Tyler and of Carter Braxton, one of the signers of the Declaration of Independence.[17]

The prize was presented to the winner on April 13, 1918, in the House Office Building auditorium and "The American's Creed" was formally accepted in the name of the United States Government by Speaker Champ Clark in the presence of members of both Houses of Congress. He then handed it to Claxton who was given the honor of first reading it in public.

Claxton very impressively read as follows: "I believe in the

United States of America as a government of the people, by the people, for the people; whose just powers are derived from the consent of the governed; a democracy in a republic; a sovereign nation of many sovereign states; a perfect union, one and inseparable; established upon those principles of freedom, equality, justice, and humanity for which American patriots sacrificed their lives and fortunes." Claxton then said, "This is a creed very fitting to be announced at this time, and the good thing about it is that it is not new, but it sums up the fundamental faith of all of the greatest of our leaders from the beginning until now; a creed that can be recommended not only to those who may come from the shores of Europe or Asia to make their home among us and become of us, but to those of our own flesh and blood who come from the shores of eternity to grow up among us and to take our places and to carry on our institutional life and to support and defend the country."

After explaining the doctrinal origin [18] of the creed, Claxton concluded, "For myself and for the department which I represent and for the educational interests of the United States, I wish to commend the author for the excellence of his selections and for the form in which he has put them together, and to congratulate him." He then handed the manuscript of the creed to Mayor Preston of Baltimore for preservation in the city archives.[19]

After the United States entered the war, many influential people became more conscious than ever before of the millions of people residing in this country who were not citizens. As early as January 19, 20, 1916, a National Conference on Immigration and Americanization, organized by the National Americanization Committee, met in Philadelphia. Addresses were delivered by Governor Brumbaugh, Mary Antin, Commissioner Claxton, Stephen S. Wise, Theodore Roosevelt, and others. The Bureau of Education took up the problem, and with funds amounting to about $100,000, made available from other sources than federal appropriations, organized a Division of Immigrant Education with offices in New York City. Claxton visited these headquarters once or twice a month to confer with the staff and direct the work. On September 1, 1916, he appointed a National Committee of One Hundred as an advisory council on Americanization. With this assistance an

"America First" campaign was launched to mobilize all forces interested in Americanization.

On February 3, 1917, a conference of prominent industrial leaders and officials met in Washington in the assembly hall of the new Interior Building. To give the conference prestige, Claxton asked Secretary Lane to allow it to be called in his name, and he readily consented. Representatives of a great variety of interests including railroads and large industries, totaling about sixty-five billion dollars of capital, were present. Secretary Lane opened the meeting with an effective speech but he continued on and on until time for adjournment for lunch. No time was left for discussion. Many members were angry and did not return for the afternoon session. Some of those who did return were in an unfriendly mood. A man from Chicago declared he would not employ any one who was not a citizen nor give him an opportunity to work. Another offered a resolution to exclude German from all public schools. When Claxton's time came to speak, he told the story of the Negro preacher who prayed, "Oh, Lord, come down; come down; oh, Lord, come down with a sledge hammer in each hand, oh, Lord, and beat religion into these Negroes' hell-fired souls." "But," continued Claxton, "neither religion nor patriotic love of country can be beaten into people. It must come in another finer and better way." [20] As a member of the committee on resolutions, he succeeded in getting the resolution on teaching German modified to recommend that the language of instruction in elementary schools should be restricted to English.

In the New York offices Claxton called a conference of representatives of the more numerous nationalities in the United States. More than sixty outstanding men and women, representing thirty-one nationalities were present. Among them was Count Tolstoy, an Armenian general, a Russian railroad magnate, and a Greek scholar from Harvard University. The meeting lasted throughout the afternoon and evening until near midnight. There were speeches, discussions, questions, and answers, all concerning Americanization. The gist of Claxton's remarks was that in the American democracy greatness was recognized only as coming through service; that there are many millionaires in the United States but no monuments to men and women merely because they were rich; that there was no such thing as original Americanism, but that Americanism, as we know it, was a summary and organization of the best of all the peoples making up the cosmopolitan population. He then asked each representative to state what his own national group had to contribute to Americanism. A Greek said he thought his people might teach us something about freedom and liberty. An Armenian said that his people could teach us something we needed to know about family life and moral purity. An Italian thought his group might help us to improve the illustrations in our Sunday newspapers. A German thought his people could continue to contribute to music, philosophy, and scientific research in America. Then Claxton asked why immigrants came to America. A Greek confessed that the aim was only to make money. The others answered that they hoped to better their condition in some way—to get rich, to get rid of militarism and army service, to secure an opportunity of education for their children.

Besides holding dozens of conferences, Claxton and his staff of assistants distributed more than 400,000 circulars, news letters and releases, enrollment blanks, "America First" posters, pamphlets, flag posters, and other Americanization material. Through the Committee of One Hundred a resolution of endorsement of the Federal program of Americanization was secured on December 13, 1917, from the Council of National Defense, which then joined forces with the Bureau of Education. Avoidance of duplication of work and correlation of effort were thus secured in the organization of Americanization committees in thirty different states. In this national plan, Secretary Lane called a conference on April 3, 1918, of all the governors, chairmen of state defense councils, and presidents of industrial corporations and chambers of commerce. About 300 persons attended the conference in Washington, at which resolutions were passed asking Congress to appropriate adequate funds for Americanization work by both Federal and State authorities. Great assistance was rendered the activities of the Bureau by the co-operation of some twenty-five patriotic societies and civic organizations.[21] In September, 1918, the Bureau of Education began the publication of the *Americanization Bulletin* for which Claxton wrote the leading article of the first issue. He contributed also four other articles to the first number and made contributions to the next nine numbers of the bulletin.

As Commissioner of Education, Claxton helped to write the Smith-Hughes Act, passed by Congress in February, 1917. This provided Federal aid to states for vocational education of secondary grade. It provided for the Federal Board of Vocational Education of seven members, including Commissioner Claxton. Several bulletins on vocational education were issued by the Bureau, which in many other ways co-operated with the work of the board.[22]

Claxton also served as chairman of the committee that wrote the Smith-Sears Act, which Congress passed in June, 1918. This provided for the vocational rehabilitation and return to civil life of disabled persons discharged from the Army or Navy of the United States. As a member of the Vocational Educational Board, Claxton assisted in the administration of this act.[23]

When the English Committee on Higher Education visited the United States in the late summer of 1918, Claxton helped to plan their itinerary and selected Carson Ryan of the Bureau of Education to accompany them on their tour of colleges and universities. When they returned to Washington, Claxton asked one of the committee what impressed them most. He replied promptly, "The good physical condition of the people everywhere." They did not see the slum districts of some of the cities they visited and naturally drew a contrast between the people of the United States in general and those of England under war conditions. The English committee traveled as far west as Minnesota and as far south as Washington University in St. Louis. When a similar larger Chinese group of fifty men came later, Claxton talked and dined with them. He gave such help and information as the Bureau had given to similar commissions from other countries. Several times he visited Canada —once in particular to speak in a campaign in Toronto for more appropriations for schools.[24]

In 1916, the Bureau published a large bulletin in two volumes (Nos. 38 and 39) on Negro education in the United States, made possible by the Phelps-Stokes Fund. This report, based on three years' first-hand study, was the most important account of Negro education ever made.[25] In August, 1917, a conference on Negro education was held in the Interior Department in Washington. As a result of resolutions adopted at the meeting, Claxton appointed a committee on Negro education, composed of religious and educational leaders interested in the improvement of Negro education.[26]

During the years 1916–1918, the work on various educational surveys was continued by the Bureau in Wyoming, Arizona, Colorado, Delaware, Nevada, South Dakota, and Tennessee, as well as in various towns and counties in California, Texas, Ohio, Illinois, New York, and Missouri. Claxton helped in interpreting the findings and in writing the reports of most of these surveys. He studied, corrected, and approved all of them.[27]

For the year ending June 30, 1918, Claxton reported that the Bureau issued 54 bulletins, five teachers' leaflets, ten reading courses, six home economic circulars, twenty-four community leaflets, six higher educational circulars, and two secondary circulars. Though the war changed somewhat the character of the work of the Bureau, its volume continued to increase with the passing years.

The amount of work which Claxton did personally was stupendous. Well could the *Raleigh News and Observer* write, "Dr. P. P. Claxton is one of those world propellers whom North Carolina has given so often to the nation." Of this the New York *Sun* declared, "Yes; and any world propeller who was inadvertently born outside of the geographical limits of smaller North Carolina is adopted, as soon as Glory garlands him, into that greater North Carolina which may be described as a combination of Valhalla, Westminster Abbey, the Temple of Fame, and the Universal Who's Who." [28]

৺§ XVII ৡ৶

United States Commissioner of Education: After World War One

◇◇

THE MOMENTUM of the war years carried forward some of the
war work of the Bureau of Education well beyond the cessation
of hostilities. An article by Claxton in *School Life* for December 1,
1918, dealt with "The School Garden Army." In *National School
Service*, published by the Committee on Public Information, appeared a letter by him in the issue of the same date, approving the
plan of the Food Administration for setting aside December 6 as
"Food Conservation Day." In this same journal of March 15, 1919,
he wrote on "America's Soldiers of the Soil." In the *Americanization Bulletin* (No. 4), also of December 1, 1918, he discussed "Co-
operation of Religious Bodies." "The more we all practice our
Americanism," he wrote, "enforcing good laws, providing just labor
conditions, actually working with those concerning whom we have
right ideals, and with tireless enthusiasm consciously building a
nobler nation, the more certainly will the hundreds of thousands of
our foreign-born American soldiers return from the trenches and
find the America worth fighting for awaiting them." In the June 1,
1919 *Americanization Bulletin*, he declared, "Education is the
fundamental thing in Americanization and of the elements comprising this fundamental the first is instruction in the English language."

Reconstruction of educational systems in 1919 became the keynote of the Bureau. In an article, entitled "Back to School," in
School Life [1] for January 16, Claxton wrote, "The war has taught

us with a new emphasis that children are a nation's greatest asset. Now that the war has ceased and the time for reconstruction has come, the work started in behalf of children must not slacken. The nation that will succeed in time of peace is the nation that puts forth every effort now to safeguard her children. Such action will be no less valuable for strength in any possible future war." To stimulate interest in industrial education, Claxton called a conference of industrial education specialists of the Students' Army Training Corps to meet in New York on April 18 and another similar conference to convene at Chicago on May 10. A third similar conference was called to meet in connection with the annual convention of the National Society for Vocational Education in St. Louis on February 19.

In the February 1, 1919 issue of *School Life*, Claxton wrote on "What the Wiping Out of Illiteracy Means." "The man who can not read and write," he declared [2] sympathetically, "is to a very large extent deaf, dumb, and blind, and bound within the prison walls of time and space. . . . For him there is no record even of his own life. For him no voice speaks across the centuries, the years, or the days. For him there is no literature of song or story, of art or science, of information or inspiration. For him the books are dumb as blocks of wood."

Two weeks later in *School Life* [3] appeared an article by Claxton concerning a letter he had sent out to the governors, state superintendents, and other prominent persons in the Southern States, asking four questions regarding Negro education. These were as follows: "Can the South develop its economic resources without educating the Negro? Is it possible to make the State sanitary so long as the Negroes are not taught the laws of sanitation? Is the moral welfare of the South safe if the Negroes are not given the essentials of an education? What should the character of the education of the masses of the Negroes be?" The twenty-four answers he received were all in the negative on the first three questions, and agreed that the education for Negroes should be largely industrial and vocational.

In the April 1 issue of this journal there was an editorial by Claxton on "Shakespeare Day, April 23." "At this moment," he wrote, [4] "when the nations of the world are straining every effort to get together to win for all time that world peace and justice for which they have fought on the battlefield, the opportunity to observe the Shakespeare anniversary comes with special significance."

In other issues he wrote on several varied subjects—particularly teachers' salaries, kindergartens, Americanization, planting trees for military heroes on Arbor Day, and adult illiteracy.

On April 23, Claxton addressed the Ontario Educational Association in Canada. The following week, at the convention of the Georgia Educational Association at Macon, April 30 to May 3, he gave two addresses on "The Special Interest of the South in Education" and "The Re-direction of the Course of Study for Rural Schools." On May 30 he delivered the commencement address at the University of Maryland.

At the meeting of the National Education Association at Milwaukee, Wisconsin, June 28–July 5, he delivered an address on "Education for the Establishment of a Democracy in the World." He stressed such needs as care of health, Americanization, moral education, improvements in curricula, training of teachers, and an international bureau of education. "All isolations," he declared,[5] "splendid or otherwise, are gone forever. . . . In our democracy there must be no forgotten man or woman, no lost waif of a child. If we would attain to our best and highest possibilities, no important talent or ability of any child, however rare, the development of which would contribute to its own welfare and happiness or to the happiness and welfare of society, of state, or of the race, must be neglected or left uncultivated. . . . Not only must society offer to all full and free opportunity for the kind and degree of education here indicated. Society must also see to it that no child at least is deprived of the opportunity offered, because of the poverty, the ignorance, the indifference, or the greed of its parents or guardians."

Upton Sinclair, in his novel *The Goslings—A Study of the American Schools* (1924), made the amazing statement that Claxton "was drunk" when he delivered his Milwaukee address. J. W. Crabtree, Secretary of the National Education Association, declined to advertise Sinclair's novel in the *Journal* for June, 1924. "Knowing Dr. Claxton as I do and being present and hearing him speak at that meeting and knowing the attendant circumstances," he wrote[6] the novelist, "I feel that you will be most fortunate to escape a suit for libel." The accusation was so preposterous that Claxton took no notice of it.

On October 2, 1919, he spoke on "The Relation of Education to Material Wealth" before the Convention of the American Bankers Association at St. Louis, and on the following November 19 he addressed the faculty and students of the University of Indiana on "A More General and Extended Study of Foreign Languages in High Schools."[7] On December 29 he gave an address to the New Jersey State Teachers Association at Atlantic City.

By 1920 the backwash of the war had caused states, counties, and cities to reduce or fail to increase their appropriations for schools. School officials began to appeal to the Bureau of Education for advice and help. To offset this backward movement, Claxton called a National Citizens Conference on Education to meet in Washington, on May 19–21, 1920, "to consider the pressing problems of education from the standpoint of statesmanship and public welfare." Governors were invited to head state delegations. About one thousand persons attended the conference, among whom were eight governors, many mayors of cities, and officers of chambers of commerce, and other organizations from the Hawaiian Islands, the Philippines, Puerto Rico, and all the states except four.[8]

Claxton had kept in touch with education also in Cuba. Dr. Ramiro Guerra wrote of having had a conference with him in 1919 at the Bureau of Education, during which Claxton talked about the democratic ideal of rural education which involved equal opportunities for education for the country and the city child. "Dr. Claxton was then about fifty years of age," wrote Guerra,[9] "and that which struck one especially was his earnest look which appeared to lose itself in the depths. That look is so remarkable as to impress on his expressive physiognomy the seal of unshakable nobility. His eyes told me, when I had hardly exchanged two words with him, that I was in the presence of a generous idealist, of powerful intelligence and magnanimous heart."

An Americanization conference was held in Cleveland, Ohio, on February 24, 25, 1920, which was well attended by representatives from many states. At this meeting Claxton reviewed the Americanization conferences of recent years and explained the Kenyon Bill, and spoke on the future of Americanization. At Minneapolis, on

May 16–18 following, a more ambitious national Americanization conference was held. Representatives attended from 218 religious, civic, educational, and industrial bodies in fourteen states. The purpose was to place Americanization on a scientific basis, and to consider every phase and relationship of the subject.[10]

Claxton continued to write for *School Life*. An editorial in the February 15, 1920 issue, entitled "For Education, $495.60," showed that the average spent on the entire education of each child in the public school system through college was not quite $500. Another editorial in the January 15 number on "How Much Are Teachers Worth?" explained that only four teachers out of a thousand were paid $1500 a year; 72 per cent were paid less than $1000; and ten per cent received less than $600 a year. An editorial by him in the July 1 issue emphasized the need for moral education.

In "The National Crisis in Education: An Interview with Dr. P. P. Claxton" by David Marboy in the June, 1920, issue of *Southern Review*,[11] Claxton demonstrated the value of education by using the economic formula: $X \times Y \times Z = W$. In this, "W" stood for wealth and wealth-producing power of all the people. The factor "X" represented the natural resources of the country; "Y" the native ability of the people; and "Z" the acquired ability produced through education in the schools and other agencies. Mathematically it was true, he showed, that, if any one of the three factors was zero, the result would be zero.

When asked, "What is the secret of the South's great opportunity today?" Claxton replied, "I can answer that by telling you the story I once heard of an old Negro preacher who was asked by his congregation to explain the meaning of free will and election. 'Yes,' said the old man, 'I understand what dat means. You see it wuz dis way. A long time befo you or me wuz born der wuz an election in heben. De Lawd he voted for you to be saved and de debel he voted fo you to be lost. And dis I say to you bredren: it depends on how you cast your vote as to what's gwine to become of you.' And that's the way it is with the South. The Lord has cast a great many votes in our favor. He has given the South a greater wealth of natural resources than any other section of the country. He has given us a climate with neither extremes of heat or cold, great forests, fertile soil, water power, etc. The Southern people are a splendid people, pure bred, of the stock of conquering races, with intellect, imagination, warm-heartedness, courage, patience, idealism. But the devil has cast some votes too. He has given us the cattle tick, the boll weevil, the mosquito, malaria, yellow fever (though we have almost conquered that), and the rest of our ills. Our material resources, though greater in extent, are very much more difficult to turn out. And not among the least of our difficulties we have the great task of working out a civilization with two distinct and widely different races, a problem that has never been solved on our scale. With opportunity comes obligation and great hazard. Where on the one hand success offers tremendous reward, the penalties of failure are equally great. And the destiny of the South depends entirely upon how it casts its vote."

To supplement the work of the National Citizens Conference on Education, which had met in Washington, Claxton arranged regional conferences. At the request of the Governor and State Superintendent of Education, one of these was held at Greensboro, North Carolina, a few weeks before the Washington conference. Later conferences for manual training and industrial education specialists were held at Cincinnati and Chicago. At Cleveland, Ohio, home economics supervisors held a conference. Rural education conferences met at the University of Virginia, the State Normal Schools of Texas, Sioux Falls (South Dakota), Cedar Falls (Iowa), Chandler (Oklahoma), Emporia (Kansas), Berea (Kentucky), Durant (Oklahoma), Tahlequah (Oklahoma), Rio Grande County (Colorado), Castine (Maine), and Montpelier (Vermont). In this way a nation-wide campaign was conducted to correct a situation which threatened the foundations of democracy.[12]

The last of June, 1920, Claxton addressed a conference of presidents and deans of junior colleges at the Bureau of Education on "The Junior College's Opportunity," showing how the effectiveness of such institutions might be increased one-fourth without additional expenses.[13] On the following 18th of December he delivered an address to the Association of Urban Universities, meeting in Philadelphia, on "American Education." At the meeting of the National Education Association at Salt Lake City, July 4–10, he spoke on "Adequate Pay for Teachers," making a strong plea for the sake of the teachers, the schools themselves, and the children. "We have come to the parting of the ways," he concluded.[14]

On January 14, 1920, Claxton spoke in the hall of the Tennessee House of Representatives before 300 delegates which had met to reorganize the State Teachers Association. Others who spoke on educational topics vital to the state were Governor Roberts, R. L. Jones, S. G. Gilbreath, H. A. Morgan, Charl Williams, and Virginia Moore.[15] On August 6, 7, he returned to Tennessee to preside over a Citizens Conference called by Governor Roberts and State Superintendent Williams to meet at Monteagle to consider the educational problems of the state. A program was drawn up which the members pledged themselves to support.[16] In October, Claxton returned again to assist the State Superintendent in sectional conferences of citizens in Memphis, Jackson, Nashville, Chattanooga, and Knoxville.[17] Favorable results of these activities followed in the work of the legislature of 1921.

Also in 1920, Claxton spoke in such cities as Waco, Dallas, and Houston in the Texas campaign for an amendment to the state constitution which would permit school districts to vote additional taxes for schools. On June 29, he spoke at the St. Louis meeting of the Junior College Conference. A month later on July 29, he addressed the National Association of Teachers in Colored Schools in Baltimore. This association had been founded seventeen years previous. Claxton had already spoken before it two or three times. On November 12, he spoke on "Education in a Democracy" to the New Jersey Congress of Mothers and Parent-Teacher Associations in Atlantic City.

In the autumn of 1920 Claxton wrote to all the principal state school officials and governors, asking them to proclaim December 5–11 as "Education Week."[18] He also wrote to the editors of the principal newspapers and magazines requesting their co-operation, as well as to county school superintendents, principals of high schools, and college presidents asking them to arrange speeches on education at assemblies. He also requested preachers to preach sermons on education, and national officers of civic associations to have speeches on education at their meetings during that week. In this way "Education Week" was successfully launched.[19]

To supplement the interest in education thus aroused, Claxton arranged another series of regional conferences which met in December and the following January in Chicago, St. Paul, Butte (Montana), Portland (Oregon), Sacramento, Denver, Kansas City, Memphis, Columbia (South Carolina), Boston, New York, Baltimore, Charleston (West Virginia), and Dover (Delaware). These conferences were all attended by large numbers of officials, prominent men and women, and educators of the states included in the respective regions. At Dover, the Du Ponts were friendly to Claxton and his educational doctrine, and as a result of the conference there they gave money toward the complete reorganization of the Delaware public schools. Claxton was present one day at each of the several conferences except the one in Boston where he spent two days. Here he met strong opposition. A large number of persons in attendance questioned everything unfavorably. In one of his speeches, Claxton declared, "If you want public utilities, you can get them through taxation. The greatest institution is the public schools, and all good citizens should be willing to pay taxes for their support." [19]

Claxton gave other addresses here and there in the first half of 1921. On January 20, he spoke in Philadelphia at the Frankford High School to the Fathers Association on "Hector's Prayer: 'May They Say This Man Was Greater Than His Father Was.'" Approximately 1500 of the 2300 members were present. On May 3, he gave an address at the First National Convention of the American Waldensian Aid Society at the New Ebbitt Hotel in Washington on "Waldensian Schools in Italy." On May 14, he spoke at the Third Closing Exercises of Americanization Classes of the Trenton Public Evening Schools. On May 26, he spoke at convocation at the University of Minnesota. He also gave the commencement address for the University of Maryland Medical School at the Lyric Theater in Baltimore on education as a factor in the production of wealth. This was his last speech as Commissioner of Education.

Reconstruction of education was even more important in Europe than in the United States, and Claxton was always ready with helpful advice and information. He spent most of a day with a group of marooned officers from Czechoslovakia, who were interested in American education. One who had long been in charge of the division of elementary education in the office of the Minister of Education in France conferred with him two or three times. "From now on," the Frenchman said,[19] "the future looks to America for educational policies." The Soviet Government of Russia wrote to inquire concerning American methods of education. More particularly were the Russians interested in the land grant colleges of agriculture and mechanical arts. At the request of the London *Times* in July, 1920 he wrote a rather comprehensive account of federal aid to education in the United States.[19]

In the spring of 1920, at the request of Roy D. Chapin, Harvey Firestone, and other automobile manufacturers, Claxton called a conference on highway engineering and transport to meet on May 14, 15 in Washington. It was well attended by professors of engineering, highway commissioners, and automobile manufacturers. At the request of the conference, Claxton appointed a permanent committee of seven members of which he served as chairman. This committee employed as executive secretary a young professor of engineering at Yale, at a salary of $7,500, paid by contributions from automobile manufacturers. The purpose of the committee was to foster research and the preparation of better textbooks in highway engineering and transport and in automotive engineering. Another result of the conference was that Firestone gave several college scholarships for the writing of essays on highway safety. The first of these was awarded to Miss Katherine F. Butterfield of Idaho on April 4, 1921, after the inauguration of Harding; Claxton assisted the President in the ceremony of presentation.[19]

The convening of an International Educational Congress in Holland having been rendered impossible by the outbreak of the World War, Claxton called a meeting of thirty prominent educators in Atlantic City in co-operation with the meeting of the department of superintendents of the National Education Association in 1917, to discuss the possibility of setting up an organization through which each country might learn what other countries were doing in education. Dr. Paul Monroe of Columbia University was appointed chairman of this committee of about 15 or 20 members, but about that time President Wilson sent him to the Near East to study educational and other conditions there in preparation for the Peace Conference after the war. After the armistice, Claxton thought best to abandon the project and try to get an effective educational "division" in the League of Nations. Only two tangible results came from the plan. A Chinaman at Yale University wrote a doctoral dissertation, in which he maintained that the Chinese know much more about America than Americans know about China. Another doctoral dissertation was written by a Norwegian woman in the University of Minnesota. In carrying out the ambitious aims of the committee, these were "like one-flake snow-storms." [19] Four years later, Claxton called the Pan-Pacific Education Conference which was held during the autumn of 1921 in Honolulu. This was called at the suggestion of Hume Ford, founder and president of the Pan-Pacific Union. Claxton was unable to attend and asked David Starr Jordan to serve as chairman in his place.

As a member of the executive committee of the Character Education Institution, from 1913 to 1921, Claxton assisted Milton Fairchild of Washington in working out his plans for moral education. The chief financial support of the institution was a donation of $10,000 a year from Spencer Kellogg, a wealthy industrialist from Buffalo, New York. He also furnished $5,000 as a prize in the National Morality Code competition, in 1915, which was won by Dr. William J. Hutchins, later president of Berea College, Kentucky. Kellogg also donated the $20,000 prize in 1919 for the Best Method of Character Education. This award was given for the "Iowa Plan." Dr. Edwin D. Starbuck of the University of Iowa received $4,000 and his eight collaborators $2,000 each. Fairchild, a wealthy man himself, served as a "Special Collaborator" without salary in the Bureau of Education during Claxton's Commissionership. [20]

Somewhat related to moral education was a book entitled *Humane Education. A Handbook on Kindness to Animals, Their Habits and Usefulness*, edited by Harriet C. Reynolds, for which Claxton was asked, January 3, 1919, to write an introduction. "The really great," he began, "are ever gentle and kind, and the greatest are the kindest and most gentle. Cruelty and indifference to the feelings of one's fellows or of any sentient beings are marks of coarseness of nature, or want of proper instruction and training. Fineness of fibre, inherited or acquired, in man or woman, as in woods and textiles and cordage, is a sure element of strength."

"He who has learned to regard the birds as little brothers of the air and to look upon domestic animals and the beasts of the field as his less fortunate kindred who need his help," he concluded, "finds a pleasure in their color and voice and motions, and a joy in the contemplation of their habits unknown to those who are without this feeling of kinship. He feels, as others cannot, the throb of the life of the world, and rejoices in the recognition of his kinship with the universe." Claxton was interested in both the W.C.T.U. and the Y.M.C.A., for each of which he wrote leaflets to aid their work.

In *School Life* for the first six months of 1921 Claxton wrote frequently. Noteworthy articles appeared in the May 15 issue on "Can We Afford the Cost of Adequate Education?" and on "What We Pay Teachers in Our Public Schools." "Even if they would do so," he declared [21] in the latter article, "teachers should not be expected to live on a lower plane socially and economically than other hardworking men and women. Neither is it good for the schools nor for society that the teachers should live the abnormal life of celibates or of homeless wanderers. Teachers should be normal men and women living a normal life as good American citizens in a normal way and under such conditions as will enable them to do their work in the best and most effective way. This can be done only when they work happily and joyously, under normal conditions, with reasonable freedom from financial care. The cheapest thing in the world is a good teacher at any reasonable price. The time and intellect and the life and character of our children are too precious to be wasted and misused by teachers who for any reason are incompetent."

For several years efforts were made to gain Claxton's approval of legislation by Congress to create a National Department of Education with a secretary who would be a member of the Cabinet. After Harding was inaugurated, he requested Claxton to prepare a bill establishing a Department of Education and Welfare, with the understanding that he would be made its secretary. With the assistance of W. T. Bawden of the Bureau, Claxton drew up the skeleton outline of such a bill. To the President's messenger, to whom he entrusted the bill, Claxton stated definitely that he did not approve of the bill nor would he desire to be the secretary of such a department. Though the bill was presented to a joint meeting of the House Committee on Education and the Senate Committee on Education and Labor, with the request that it be approved and enacted without delay, it met with no success.[22]

The plan for reorganization of the Bureau which Claxton approved was based on a National Board of Education consisting of nine members—men and women of affairs, not more than four of whom should belong to the same political party. They would not receive a salary but be paid a liberal per diem and all necessary expenses for four meetings of a week each during the year and for any other necessary meetings. All the government's educational interests would be placed in the hands of this committee, which would select an executive officer at such a salary as would attract and hold a man of the highest ability. This salary should be commensurate with that of the president of a great university. It should not be considered a political position synchronizing with a presidential term. All personnel would be employed by this board on the recommendation of the executive of the office.

The reports of the Commissioner of Education for the years 1919 and 1920 indicate the greatly increased activities of the Bureau from what they were when Claxton took charge. Since 1917, the form of his report had been changed. Instead of the two large volumes, one containing interpretative accounts of the progress of education at home and abroad and the other devoted entirely to statistical information, the annual report, in not more than 200 pages, summarized the activities of the Bureau and the progress of education in the United States. The statistics were included in one large volume entitled Biennial Survey of Education. This, Claxton believed, was better arranged and interpreted, and could be published more nearly on time. The previous voluminous reports were always two or three years late in publication. Though the report was itself briefer, the number of bulletins increased. During the years 1918–1920 these totaled 133. There were also numerous leaflets, circulars, lists of reading courses, and other miscellaneous publications.[23] Twelve surveys were made during the fiscal year 1919–1920, among which was one of the schools of the District of Columbia, with a suggested plan for reorganization of the administrative and teaching forces, and a new schedule of salaries.[24]

In spite of the fact that Claxton had been appointed by a Republican President and been continued for eight years by President Wilson, he was removed from the Commissionership on June 1, 1921, by a Republican President. Claxton's letter of resignation was dated May 12, 1921.[25]

This action aroused considerable unfavorable criticism of Harding. "It was very much to my disgust," wrote[26] Charles W. Dabney, "and that of most friends of the public schools, when President Harding caused him to be dismissed summarily from the office in which he was doing so much good work. It was a most unjustifiable act. There was no ground for it."

"It seems a tragedy for education," declared the *Child Welfare Magazine* of August, 1921, "that Hon. Philander P. Claxton, who has done more than any other man to arouse the people as to the place education should hold in the nation, should be retired as Commissioner of Education at a time when leaders of experience and knowledge are so greatly needed. . . . Dr. Claxton made the work of the Bureau an inspiration. No man ever gave himself more devotedly and earnestly to the promotion of education, not for children of school age alone, but for all the people, from birth on through life."

"Out of a clear sky after the *Journal* has gone to press," according to an editorial[27] in the *Journal* of the National Education Association, "comes the announcement of the dismissal of Dr. Claxton as Commissioner of Education and the appointment of Mr. J. J. Tigert in his place. This action will be deplored by the friends of public education throughout the nation. It is not necessary to discuss the long and faithful service of Dr. Claxton, whose work has had the approval of two successive presidents of opposite political faith, nor is it necessary to review the little-known record and untried leadership of the man who has been named for his place. It is most unfortunate that a change should be made at this time when the need for recognized national leadership in education is imperative. It is certain to be construed as having been determined by political motives and in total disregard of the growing demand for the elevation of the nation's chief educational office."

During Claxton's ten years as Commissioner, he traveled approximately 75,000 miles a year, visiting an average of 35 states a year and speaking at all sorts of educational meetings—municipal, state, and national. The only two states in which he did not speak, for some reason or other, were Arizona and Idaho.[28] During each year he delivered an average of about 200 such addresses.[29] Many illustrations of the occasions and subjects of these speeches have been cited. Beginning with one specialist above the rank of clerk, he succeeded in increasing his staff to about thirty specialists attached to approximately ten departments, which included higher education, city school administration, rural schools, kindergarten education, industrial education, agricultural education, education for home making, health education and home building, commercial education, education in civics, community organization, school and home gardening, Americanization, Negro education, and foreign education. Claxton left the Bureau with an expanded program of activities, greatly increased appropriations and staff, and a constantly growing influence throughout the country. No other Commissioner had been so widely known personally throughout the United States; no other had become so well acquainted with the schools and their needs in all sections of the country.

One of the reasons for Claxton's accepting the Commissionership, "the opportunity for personal education," [30] was fully satisfied. Washington, from 1911 to 1921, probably afforded more opportunities of that sort than any other city in the world. First, of course, were the distinguished people, both Americans and foreigners, whom he met there professionally and socially. Perhaps of equal value in his personal education were his travels all over the United States, which brought him in touch with leaders not only in education but also in many other activities.

Of President Wilson, Claxton had a very high opinion. "Wilson was probably the most constructively patriotic man in the world at that time," he wrote.[31] "If we had followed him and his League of Nations, it would have been worth the 300 billion dollars we now have as a war debt, and the millions on millions of young lives lost in war. Wilson had a vision that would have saved the world from near destruction."

Claxton was a charter member of the League to Enforce Peace, and in 1917 he went with a committee of this league to present a plea to Wilson that he would endeavor to bring about an association or a league of nations which would lead to the abolition of war. "Hamilton Holt spoke for the group earnestly and persuasively," declared [32] Claxton. "After hearing us thirty or forty minutes, President Wilson replied, 'Gentlemen, my mind is to let on this matter.' Possibly our visit and Holt's well reasoned speech had something to do with starting Wilson's thinking which resulted in the League of Nations."

"President Wilson was thought to be cold and difficult to approach," Claxton recalled.[32] "He was reserved in manner, but easy to deal with rationally. He was a scholarly idealist of a very fine type."

Claxton observed that Wilson liked to do things on time in a prompt business-like manner. When the English Higher Education Commissioners had finished their tour of visiting American colleges and universities in 1918 and had returned to Washington, Wilson gave a luncheon in their honor. "Naturally, the Secretary of the Interior, the Commissioner of Education, and Mrs. Lane and Mrs. Claxton were invited," Claxton wrote.[32] "The time of the luncheon was set at one o'clock. Secretary Lane was expected to present the members of the Commission to the President, but was late arriving. Promptly at one o'clock, Mr. Wilson came out. Not seeing Secretary Lane, he said, 'The time of the luncheon has arrived. Lane is not here. I think we shall have to penalize him. Mr. Claxton will please present the guests.' Lane arrived as the presentation was about over."

"After luncheon," Claxton continued,[32] "we all went out on the back porch, really the front of the White House, and for nearly two hours Mr. Wilson told stories and chatted and laughed in a very human way. As the party went away, one of them remarked, in high praise of the informality of the occasion, that he had never seen anything like it."

The Commission was composed of men from the universities of Oxford, Cambridge, and London, and Wilson no doubt entertained them as he would have done as President of Princeton rather than as President of the United States. One of the Englishmen who tarried behind asked Wilson on what conditions he would accept the surrender of the Germans. He replied,[32] "I do not know the conditions, but I think I will recognize them when I see them."

"Wilson was frequently accused of aloofness and stubbornness," remarked [32] Claxton. "I would say he had the weakness of all great idealists: a feeling that what had come to him as if by inspiration could not be quite so well understood or explained by others."

According to Claxton,[32] "In theory at least, Wilson was one of the most democratic of all our presidents. He had unlimited confidence in the people, but feared the politicians and the newspapers. With Socrates, he believed that, if the people knew the whole truth, they would act rightly and wisely. For this reason he was much interested in what we in those times called 'school community organizations'—the organization of all the people of a local school community with frequent meetings at the schoolhouse for mutual acquaintance, entertainment, information, discussion, and co-operation. Somewhat like the open forum of later date, but much more comprehensive and better. When the Bureau of Education was first trying to find some way of promoting such school organizations, Wilson sent to me E. J. Ward, a friend of his and of Margaret Wilson, who had been connected with the University of Wisconsin in just such work in that state, which the legislature had authorized and made appropriations for. Ward brought a brief letter from Wilson asking me to take him on as a dollar-a-year man and saying, 'You know I am interested in this more than in anything else connected with public education.' Ward's salary was paid by a wealthy friend of his and of public education. Later Wilson gave to the Bureau $50,000 out of his Emergency Fund for the promotion of these organizations."

"While Wilson was at Versailles," Claxton continued,[32] "and after the covenant of the League of Nations had been formed, Dr. Jackson, one of the group in the Bureau of Education, whose job it was to promote these school community organizations, prepared a bulletin for the Bureau of Education containing the text of the Covenant of the League, the Lodge-Lowell Debate, some comparisons of the Covenant of the League with the Constitution of the United States, and an arrangement and outline for half a dozen debates. Since the Bureau did not have sufficient printing funds for this, Breckinridge Long agreed to pay for the printing of three million copies, from three to six for each public school in the

United States. The Bureau of Education would give the bulletin its approval and mail them to the principals of the schools. A copy of the manuscript was sent to Wilson at Versailles, and he cabled the preface for it. He believed that, if the masses of the people should have such an opportunity to know of the League in this way, the adoption of the treaty and the Covenant would be assured. Unfortunately before the bulletin was printed, our entrance into the League had become so much of a partisan matter that the Secretary of the Interior would not approve of its printing as a bulletin of the Bureau."

To Claxton, Taft seemed very different. "I have seen a line of approximately fifty prominent men waiting for half an hour after the time of an appointment with him," Claxton recalled.[32] "During a portion of this time, at least, Mr. Taft was telling stories and laughing heartily with someone or a small group. Someone has said, 'A good executive is one who acts promptly and is sometimes right.' Taft was usually right. His judicial temperament and his training made him take time for at least mental discussion of all important matters before approving or disapproving them. Frequently the time for most effective action had passed before he reached a decision. Nevertheless, he was a great secretary and a great President: open-minded, genial, with high purpose to serve effectively all the people of the country."

Claxton knew William Jennings Bryan very well. He first heard him speak when he delivered the commencement address at the Normal and Industrial College at Greensboro, North Carolina, while he was a professor there. After speaking on bimetalism as a monetary standard with the coinage of silver and gold in the ratio of 16 to 1, he made a political speech to the townspeople of Greensboro in the afternoon. Claxton remembered a story he told in this speech, concerning a man who lost his property and, becoming a tramp, went to sleep by the side of the road. From this he was awakened in time to see a dog running away with his last loaf of bread. "Thank the Lord," he exclaimed, rubbing his eyes, "I still have my appetite." "The Democratic Party," added [32] Bryan, "still has its appetite."

At Claxton's request, Bryan delivered his famous lecture, "The

Prince of Peace," one year at the Summer School of the South. At a peace meeting in Washington he and Bryan spoke from the same platform.

On the day Bryan resigned as Secretary of State, Claxton went home and found his wife "sick," she said, because of Bryan's resignation. She thought trouble between him and Wilson would follow. Claxton told her that good would result, as Bryan was absent from his office much of his time on extensive lecture tours when he was needed to look after important international problems. "Bryan has high ideals," Claxton said to his wife; "he can move the masses of the people; he is a good kind of seer and prophet. It is a pity for a man like him to spend his time writing notes to the Kaiser."

When some months later he and Bryan were at the same hotel, attending a meeting in Charleston, South Carolina, Bryan invited him to lunch with him. "As we sat at a small table," Claxton wrote,[32] "I told him of this incident and what I had said to Mrs. Claxton. For a long moment the conversation stopped. I thought I had made a rather bad faux pas. After luncheon we went out into the lobby and stood and talked awhile, in the meantime our pictures being taken by a photographer. As we parted, Bryan said, 'I want to thank you for what you said. I appreciate that you think I am a seer and a prophet who can influence the masses of the people. As for writing notes to the Kaiser, anybody can sign notes to the Kaiser.'"

Claxton found Franklin K. Lane, Secretary of the Interior, an inspiring man to work with. Formerly an editor, a lawyer, and a Senator, he was broad-minded, believing that all countries were interdependent. Though he was most interested in the division of public lands, he believed wholeheartedly in public education. One day when he was telling Claxton about some plans for Alaska, Claxton remarked jokingly, "I think I have detected socialistic ideas in your mind before." He replied immediately, "The thing—not the name. Herbert Spencer is responsible for my socialistic attitude. Spencer opposed public schools because they were based on socialistic principles. I think a philosophy responsible for public schools must be pretty good at least."

The Claxton home in Washington was on Connecticut Avenue

next to the British Embassy and directly across the street from the residence of Alexander Graham Bell. Not long after the arrival of the Claxtons in Washington, the Bells gave a dinner party in their honor as newcomers in the Capital. Mrs. Claxton recalled that Dr. Bell sat at the middle on one side of the table and his wife directly across from him so that she could more easily read his lips. She had been totally deaf since the age of three, and as a young lady had been taught lipreading by Dr. Bell, who then fell in love with her. Though she could not hear, Mrs. Bell talked charmingly, read the lips of the speakers, and entered freely into the conversation. Dr. Bell had been a teacher of the deaf as a young man, and this experience led him to invent the telephone. Mrs. Claxton was so fascinated with Mrs. Bell's lip reading that she ate but little of the dinner.[33]

There were many invitations to receptions at the White House, at the imposing British Embassy where Lord and Lady Bryce received them and their daughter Claire and Mrs. Claxton's mother in a very friendly and neighborly fashion, at the attractive home of Secretary of the Navy and Mrs. Josephus Daniels, and at other homes too numerous to mention. They knew and admired both the first and the second Mrs. Wilson and knew the President's daughter Margaret most intimately; they knew very well also the Lanes, the Bryans, and the Bakers of the cabinet. The Claxtons' "at homes" were attended by Vice President and Mrs. Marshall, Supreme Court Justices Hughes and McReynolds and their wives, the Bryces and other diplomats and their wives, Senators and Representatives, and many other interesting and distinguished people.

They heard concerts at Constitution Hall, attended art exhibitions, and heard lectures at Carnegie Institute by famous scientists. They met General and Mrs. Gorgas and Robert E. Peary, and many other great men and women. When President Wilson was stricken, they joined on one occasion the group of people that gathered on the sidewalk near the Wilson home. "It was the greatest demonstration of devotion," declared [33] Mrs. Claxton, "that I have ever heard of. Day after day, night after night, they came quietly and knelt or stood; it was wonderful."

Mrs. Claxton headed a group of Red Cross workers connected with the Bureau of Education; she became president of the League of American Pen Women and first vice president of the National Congress of Parent-Teacher Associations; and was also a member of the very exclusive Washington Woman's Club. According to a wag, it was easier to get through the gates of Heaven past St. Peter than into this Washington club.[33]

Claxton became a member of the Cosmos Club in 1912, where he met socially many men of distinction. He was also a member of the George Washington–Sulgrave Institution. Besides his membership in peace societies, he was a member of the Council of the National Education Association, a director of the Playground Association of America, chairman of the executive committee of the National Story Tellers' League, and a member of the National Society for the Scientific Study of Education, and the American Association for the Advancement of Science. The honorary degree of doctor of laws was conferred upon him by Western Reserve University in 1912, the University of North Carolina in 1914, Allegheny College in 1915, and the University of Maryland in 1921.

The Claxton home was a rather lively place socially for the young folks too. The beautiful eldest daughter Claire was very popular. She married Dale R. Mayo in 1913 and went to Knoxville, Tennessee, to reside. By that time, Helen was seventeen and looked like a lovely Dresden china doll, and her younger sister, the beautiful, vivacious Elizabeth, was only twelve. The two sons Porter and Robert Edward were then fourteen and ten respectively.[34]

The youngest son died tragically on October 12, 1913. The family was on an outing on the Potomac River with Captain and Mrs. John R. Hendley on board their launch *Rosalie*. The young lad, ill of indigestion, was in some unexplainable manner overcome by gasoline fumes. Though he was rushed to the Alexandria Hospital, he died there at seven o'clock that evening.[27] Claxton was deeply affected by the loss of this son. He had had a strange psychic warning from the child's mother, then long deceased. Before coming to Washington, he had had another psychic experience, assuring him that he was to be Commissioner of Education. This was at a time when he had not thought of going to Washington but was considering the possibility of running for Governor of Tennessee, in order to have a friend of education in that office.[35]

Before the Claxtons left Washington another son and a daughter were added to the family: Philander Priestley, Jr., born December 11, 1914, and Mary Hannah Payne, born July 8, 1919. With this large family the Claxtons managed to live well in Washington on a salary of $5000, augmented somewhat by receipts from writings and speeches. Helen was sent to the College for Women at Greensboro, North Carolina; Elizabeth to Sweet Briar in Virginia; and Porter to The University of Tennessee, where he graduated in 1920. Mrs. Claxton, of course, deserves the chief credit for so successfully managing the affairs of the household.

The Washington period was by far the most significant decade in Claxton's life. Through his administration of the Bureau and through his contributions to periodicals, but chiefly through his speeches he wielded great influence for good in public school education and made a record as Commissioner which has so far not been surpassed. Though fifty-eight years old when he left Washington, he was destined to contribute another quarter of a century of valuable service to the cause of education, to which he had dedicated his life.

◄§ XVIII §►

Provost of the University of Alabama

◇◇◇

THE DAY that the newspapers announced that Claxton had re-signed as Commissioner of Education he had a telegram from President Denny and Dr. Doster, head of the Department of Education, of the University of Alabama, offering him the position as Provost. During his years in Washington he had been offered many positions; such as, the superintendency of the schools of four large cities, head of the department of education in two universities, and the presidency of twelve different colleges and universities, as well as some commercial positions.[1] He did not accept these offers, thinking that his work as Commissioner afforded him wider opportunities for educational service and not foreseeing that his Commissionership would be suddenly terminated as a political position.

After his resignation, Claxton had other offers of employment besides that from the President of the University of Alabama. Among these, he was asked to be chief editor of the Frontier Press Company of Buffalo, New York, and offered the superintendency of the public schools of Memphis, Tennessee, at a salary of $10,000. While still considering these offers, he attended commencement at The University of Tennessee, and on June 7 made an address at the dedication of Ayres Hall, the largest of the new buildings recently constructed.

Of the old university he knew as a student he declared [2] reminiscently, "To the boy from the backwoods of Tennessee that group of buildings seemed indeed magnificent, the greatest thing that he or most of us of that day had ever seen in the way of a schoolhouse. . . . My mind goes back to a day, not forty years but a little more than sixteen years ago, when I sat one day in the gallery of the Lower House of the Legislature of Tennessee by the side of the President of the University, at the time Dr. Ayres, and watched a bill which I like to remember I had written, for a $100,000 appropriation, a magnificent sum we thought; extraordinary and exorbitant, members of the Legislature thought. After we had worked for a month, we compromised on $65,000. We sat and watched it go from $65,000 to $50,000 and $40,000 and $25,000. When a friend from West Tennessee came and said that, on condition that a portion of that magnificent sum of $25,000 for each of the next two years might be devoted to the traveling expenses of the students from the other parts of the state, he would vote for it and thought he could hold it at $25,000, I remember how eagerly we accepted the compromise. I also remember that I said to President Ayres, 'If we don't get a cent, we have won a victory. The Legislature of the State of Tennessee has done what it has never done before; for a whole day it has debated the University of Tennessee' (the 'high school of Knox County' they called it in some other parts of the state; they did not dignify it by the name of college).

"I remember also that, though my hide had grown rather tough by that time in battles with legislatures in more than one state, tears came to my eyes, and I think they did to the eyes of President Ayres, only sixteen years ago, when by a narrow majority, after a fight of a day on a compromise of giving a certain amount of the little appropriation for the traveling expenses of boys from other parts of the state, we got $12,500, the first sum ever appropriated by the state for the maintenance of the University. . . . Only these sixteen years have gone by, and I believe, by a fairly good majority with all the forces of this state favoring and with the Governor leading in it, you have approximately $1,000,000 today for the University for each year." Continuing his address, he included most of the best things he had been saying about education for several years.

At the Alumni Banquet at the Farragut Hotel, Claxton spoke on "Tennessee and Uncle Sam, Their Common Aims."

After careful consideration, Claxton accepted, on July 1, 1921, the office of Provost of the University of Alabama with a salary of $7,500 with the understanding that he might devote one week out of each month to his own personal affairs. He was already familiar with the condition of public education in Alabama. On March 11, 1919, the Bureau of Education had been invited to make a survey by the Alabama Education Commission. This was made and submitted to the commission in the following June, and published that year as Bulletin No. 41, entitled "An Educational Study of Alabama." This comprised 522 pages. Chapter two was reprinted the following year as "Fundamental Educational Needs of Alabama as Indicated by Its Character and Resources." This was written by Claxton himself.

"Through the very nature of her resources," Claxton stated,[3] "Alabama calls aloud for a well-devised, liberal, and well-supported system of practical and vocational education for the great masses of her people, both white and colored. Nowhere will such education yield a richer material reward or the want of it bring more disastrous results. . . . If either race has possibilities beyond the other for service in any particular field, these possibilities should be fully developed for the good of both races and of the state. This does not mean social equality or social mixing. The figure of speech, wise as eloquent, used by Booker T. Washington in his Atlanta Exposition address many years ago, still holds and shall hold: 'In all things purely social, separate as the fingers, yet one as the hand in all things essential to mutual progress.' "

This survey report may have been the main reason why Claxton was called to the University of Alabama. His duties there were to help reorganize the work of the University, to integrate it more closely into the educational system of the state, and to assist in the campaign to secure a million dollars for buildings and more money for state support of the University. Claxton was also to aid in a campaign to raise funds for a school of health and preventative medicine at the University and a school of tropical medicine in Panama. These were to be a monument to General Gorgas, whose father had been president of the University and whose sister was then librarian.

The Alabama Polytechnic Institute at Auburn and the College for Women at Montevallo also had plans for raising large amounts for new buildings, equipment, and endowments, and Claxton proposed to President Denny that all three institutions unite in a single campaign. He agreed and Claxton then secured the agreement of the presidents of the other two colleges. He then joined in the campaign for the Gorgas memorial, making a speaking tour throughout the state. The British ambassador, Sir Aukland Campbell Geddes, aided in the campaign, speaking at several places. As a young man he had studied medicine and had taught anatomy and had later known Gorgas; hence his sympathetic interest. In his speeches he declared that the great task of the twentieth century should be the conquest of the tropical diseases, for which the United States was amply prepared through the knowledge, already acquired, of tropical engineering and medicine.[4]

Meanwhile Claxton delivered some speeches to increase the interest of the alumni in the University. On October 3, he spoke on its needs to a group of graduates at a meeting preliminary to the formation of an alumni association in Montgomery.[5] On November 11 he spoke at the University homecoming, and on November 18 he made an address to the Mobile alumni in that city.[6] On December 7 he spoke to the Civitan Club in Huntsville.[7] The University of Alabama *Alumni News*, November-December, 1921, published a biographical sketch of Claxton with a photograph of him on the cover. His aims as Provost were stated to be the securing of more support from the legislature to meet the rapid growth of the student body and "to help build the University into the educational life, social life, and economic life of the state." [8]

During the Christmas holidays while Claxton was in Washington where he had gone to be with his family, who had not then joined him in Tuscaloosa, he received a telegram from President Denny near New Year's Day, asking him to return at once to the University. Upon arrival, he learned that the President and Board of Directors of the Polytechnic Institute had broken their agreement as to the joint campaign because the University of Alabama had singly carried on the Gorgas campaign. Since the Polytechnic Institute was preparing to begin a separate campaign and could not be induced to adhere to the agreement, Claxton and Denny began to prepare for a separate campaign for the University also.

All through 1922, Claxton devoted most of his time to campaign-

[243]

ing for larger state appropriations for education in Alabama. He did not go from county to county, as he had previously done in the Tennessee campaigns, but spoke in all parts of the state at twenty high school commencements and to meetings of chambers of commerce, civic clubs, women's clubs, and other organizations. For example, he addressed the students of the University early in the year on the phenomenal increase in the support of education throughout the United States. "Dr. Claxton made a hit with the students at once," reported the *Alumni News*.[9] He paid "Alabama a splendid tribute," it continued, but he declared that better educational support was needed. On February 27, Governor Thomas E. Kilby called a Citizens Conference on Education to meet at Birmingham on the following April 13. Claxton wrote the draft of the Governor's proclamation, and at the meeting spoke on "Some facts about Our School System and What the Millage Tax as Proposed by Governor Brandon Will Do." Governor Brandon had meanwhile succeeded Kilby in office. On Sunday, May 7, he spoke in the morning at the First Baptist Church in Talladega on "Education," using as a text Hector's prayer from the 6th book of Homer's *Iliad*, and in the afternoon addressed the Talladega College for Colored People.

Probably his best speech of the campaign was delivered at the commencement of the University on May 22, on "The University and the State." After giving a summary of the historical development of the University during the previous one hundred years, he devoted the major part of his address to the certain future increase in student body and the consequent need for an increase in financial support and an expansion of the University in buildings and in curriculum. "The day of small things in Alabama," he said, "is past or is rapidly passing. The poverty and discouragement following the Civil War have given way to increasing wealth and to a feeling of confidence in our own powers and ability, and, with it all, we are learning something of the greater need and value of higher education in a state like Alabama as compared with some other states."

"The University is not," he continued, in explaining the relation of the University to the state, "and should not be thought of as being the school of any class or part of the people to the exclusion of any other class or part. It is not the school of the rich, as such, nor of the poor, as such. It knows no social distinction as between the 'soft-handed' and those whose hands are hardened by manual labor in field or forest, mill or mine. It is no more the school of those who live in the city than of those who live and work in the country."

To make clear the relation of the University to the public school system he used the following effective figure of speech: "The University is like a great power plant, generating the current that moves and lights up every other part of the system down to the smallest bulb of the smallest country school. If the dynamo grows weak, the whole system becomes ineffective and all the lights burn dim or not at all. Those who would gain more light by increasing the number of bulbs at the cost of dynamo current are not wise."

But the state must adequately support the University. "The duties and obligations of the state to the University are no less important than those of the University to the state," he concluded. "The state must give the University wise direction, keeping it free from all influences of partisan politics, sectarian bias, social caste, and unrighteous personal ambitions. It must also give it adequate support. The University cannot live on air alone; not even on 'hot air.' It is a great business enterprise. Lack of sufficient capital will prove as fatal for it as for any other business."

This was a characteristic Claxton speech—statistics and plain facts, a bit of humor now and then, and eloquent idealism woven together in an effective beautiful tapestry of language. It was printed in pamphlet form and widely distributed. In time, it bore good fruit.

Claxton also left Alabama occasionally in 1922 to make speeches. On June 12 he delivered the address to the graduates of the Medical School of The University of Tennessee at Memphis on "Higher Education in Tennessee." [10] He also spoke at the University of Kentucky in Lexington on "Seven Elements of Education," which he declared to be health, scientific knowledge, skill, judgment, appreciation, purpose, and will.

Probably as influential as his campaign speeches in Alabama were his articles in the newspapers of Birmingham, Montgomery, and Mobile. They dealt with various phases of the problem of education in that state; such as, "Need of Equality of Opportunity in Education and of a Large Equalizing Fund," "Geological Survey by University Is Valuable: Great Service Is Rendered to State by This Department of College," "Growing Demand for Education in Alabama, Particularly Higher Education," "What Mr. Average Citizen Receives for Taxes Paid to State of Alabama," "Education an Organic Unit," "Training Business Men and Women at the University of Alabama," "Campus of University as Extensive as State," "High School Graduates Urged to Go to College," "Rapid Growth Recorded in School of Mines at University of Alabama," "Business Man's Interest in Education," "A Plea for School Bond Vote," "Why People Should Help Raise Funds," "University Serving State Effectively in Making Teachers," "Governor's Proposed Millage Tax," "Going to College as an Investment for Profit," "What Alabama Pays for Higher Education Compared with What Some Other States Pay," "Taxes That Are and Taxes That Are Not," "Taxes for Schools, Roads, and Health Investments Not Burdens," "What We Pay for Lack of Education," "Some Needs of Southern County Schools," "Alabama Progress in Education during Past Twenty-three Years," "Why Popular Election of County School Superintendents Is Inadvisable," "North Carolina's Example," "Review of Gorgas' Personality by an Old Friend," "Money and Life Value of Gorgas School of Sanitation at Tuscaloosa and School of Research in Panama." In these last articles he urged the raising of $750,000 for the establishment and maintenance of this memorial.

On June 3, 1923, in the Sunday issue of the Birmingham *News* appeared a special article by Claxton on "Jabez Lamar Curry: Educator, Orator, Diplomat, Patriot." He emphasized the great work done for education by Curry, who said, "Universal education is an imperative duty; ignorance is no remedy for ills." Curry is one of Alabama's distinguished men in Statuary Hall in Washington.

Governor Brandon called another Citizens Conference on Education to meet at Birmingham on April 6, 1923, at which Claxton spoke. In the entire campaign subscriptions for the building program were obtained for approximately $800,000, most of which were paid.

Claxton also co-operated with President Denny in the preparation of bills for appropriations for the University which were introduced in the legislature. He spoke before the legislative com-

mittees and worked for their passage in other ways. Because of a
tactical mistake, the bills failed to pass; but the next legislature
made a much larger appropriation than had been asked for. President Denny wrote Claxton, who had then left Alabama, that what
he had done by speaking and writing was very largely responsible
for the increased appropriations. "It takes time to change the
minds of people on a question of this kind," wrote [11] Claxton, "but
the people's will is always done if they have a will intelligently
formed, firmly held, and adequately expressed."

Though one fourth of his time was to be for his own personal
use, Claxton was unable to do much of the literary work he had
planned. The corresponding secretary of the National Kindergarten
Society wrote [12] him twice, requesting his promised outline of a
plan for investigating early education. The plan was to be used in
inducing the secretary of the Commonwealth Fund to look into
the value of kindergartens as a means of education and as an
Americanization agency. The editor of the *Emerson Quarterly*
begged [13] him to send a long promised article, either a new manuscript or a speech he had already delivered. Several letters [14] came
from the president of the Frontier Press Company, urging him to
send promised material, amounting to 84,000 words on education
and ethics for the *Lincoln Library of Essential Information*.[15] The
editor of the *Book of Literature* for the Grolier Society of Philadelphia also became uneasy and wrote two letters [16] hurrying Claxton in the preparation of an introduction he had promised.

Claxton finished this introduction for the *Book of Literature* of
thirty-three volumes (first published in 1899 as *The Universal
Anthology*). "The most valuable possession of civilized man,"
wrote Claxton, "is to be found in his literary heritage—most
valuable, most indispensable and most difficult to replace if lost.
. . . Only through the records of the past, however meager, dim,
and broken, does man gain any knowledge of his long, difficult, and
uneven struggle upwards towards civilization and light. Without
them, all the past would be dark and empty. Only through the possession of these records of the thoughts, feelings, and acts of those
who have lived and wrought through the ages can men substitute
for the feeling of individual weakness and isolation the feeling of
racial unity and strength."

"The real rulers of mankind," he continued, "are not, and have not been, those who sit on thrones or lead great armies in victorious battle. Rather have they been men of vision who have stood on the mountain tops, caught the glow of the ever-dawning new day, and reported its coming to the multitudes in the valleys below; those who through patient research have pushed back the walls of darkness and let in the light; those who with a sure feeling for inherent relations and right proportions have given cosmic form to some part of the primeval chaos; those who, a little more finely organized than most of us, have felt the heart throb and pulse beat of humanity and responded strongly and sympathetically—strengtheners of hearts and healers of souls; those who have listened to the still, small voices, inaudible to those of grosser hearing, and learned and revealed some part, however small, of the eternal verities. These have been and are kings and priests to God and man."

For the Grolier Society Claxton also wrote, on December 20, 1922, a letter endorsing the *Book of Knowledge*, in part as follows: [17] "It should be in every home and school in city, village, and country, wherever the language in which it is written is read and understood. If only some good Santa Claus could bring it to the children of millions of homes that are without books! How fortunate those who have it where cold and snow shut in and the winter nights are long, and also where balmy air and sunny days invite reading outdoors on lawn or by brook or lake."

The Claxtons were very happy in Tuscaloosa. They lived in "a delightful old Southern home." [18] It had been reconditioned and painted white; there was a large comfortable porch, and the ample grounds surrounding the house were filled with beautiful shrubbery and flowers. Most of the year there seemed to be flowers everywhere in Tuscaloosa, not only in the yards but in beds between the sidewalks and the streets; particularly beautiful were the gloriously red verbenas.

Many of the teas and receptions were out-of-doors in the balmy air where the lovely ladies in their summer dresses appeared to advantage. There was much good music to hear and many cultural clubs. Mrs. Claxton organized the University Women's Club which soon grew to 75 members. They sponsored excellent outside speakers and furnished worthwhile entertainment for the University and the town. Mrs. Claxton continued her work with Parent-Teacher Associations and was elected the state vice president of this organization in Alabama.

With them in Tuscaloosa were Elizabeth and the two younger children. Helen who had married Curtis Walker of Washington continued to reside there. Porter was managing the Claxton farm near Bell Buckle, Tennessee, and serving as principal of the county high school at that place. While Mrs. Claxton left her youngest child on the campus in care of a nurse, she attended lectures in English literature. "The social life was perfect," she declared,[18] "quiet, sweet, and dignified. The people were so contented and comfortable. Nobody hurried—a bad Southern habit possibly, but so restful and calming to the human spirit. There was a graciousness about it that I thought perfect. I wanted to live there always. It was a happy time. I loved Alabama."

Superintendent of Tulsa City Schools

◇◇

NEAR THE middle of June, 1923,[1] Claxton had a long distance call from Ben H. Johnson, vice president of the Board of Education of Tulsa, Oklahoma, asking him if he would accept the superintendency of the city schools. Claxton informed him that he thought he would not be interested, but Johnson insisted that he come to Tulsa at the expense of the board for a conference. Claxton agreed, and going to Tulsa, found the board greatly interested in the improvement of their school system, for which there was ample money if rightly used. They asked Claxton to name his salary and give them an answer within a week. Promising to do so, he returned to Tuscaloosa, and at the end of a week wrote a letter of acceptance. The stipulated salary was $13,800 a year with traveling expenses, as needed up to $500. The board approved, with expressions of complete confidence in him, and on June 25 elected him superintendent for three years.

Claxton had been particularly pleased that there seemed to be no chance for political interference with the schools. The election of the board was non-partisan and the city council had no control over the school funds for either buildings or current expenses. Tulsa was then a rich oil town of about 75,000 inhabitants and was growing rapidly, and there seemed a great opportunity for doing some effective educational work.

Claxton's leaving the University of Alabama was much regretted by President Denny and other officials. "I regret to see you leave

Alabama," wrote Governor Brandon,[2] "and trust that you and Mrs. Claxton will be happy and prosperous in your new home." The Tulsa press hailed Claxton's appointment with great satisfaction. "The new board of education," declared the *Tribune*, "has executed a master stroke in securing for superintendent of schools here a man so eminent in the educational world as Philander P. Claxton, former United States Commissioner of Education. The announcement of his selection as director of the Tulsa school system will meet with the unqualified approval of all citizens, we believe. It is really a stirring announcement and one which dispels heavy clouds that have been looming upon the school horizon for many weeks. . . . His schooling in many colleges both of America and Europe qualifies him as a scholar, while his forty years' service in the field of education endows him with a great reservoir of practical knowledge about education. He knows from personal experience the problems of the teacher, the principal, and the administrator. Tulsa as a community also is to be congratulated upon the acquisition of such a distinguished citizen as Dr. Claxton. . . . He constitutes a big addition to our leaders' group."

President Denny wired the *Tribune*, "Tulsa is to be congratulated in the selection of Doctor Claxton as superintendent of its city schools. You may claim the distinction of having the best equipped and most widely known city superintendent in the country. Doctor Claxton is a great apostle of popular education. He is the ablest American educational propagandist. I ask the privilege of adding that he is an elegant gentleman, a fine spirit, and the soul of honor."

The *Tribune* took pride in the fact that Claxton's salary was greater than that of the superintendents of schools in New York, Philadelphia, Chicago, and any other city in the United States, and that no complaint had been heard at the increase in salary, his predecessor having received $10,000. "Doctor Claxton will save four times his salary increase the first year he is here," members of the board were quoted as having said. The president of the Board of Regents of the University of Oklahoma and the President of the University of Tulsa each expressed hearty approval of the appointment.

Claxton returned to Tulsa to "size up" the position he had accepted, arriving there before breakfast on July 11.[3] On the way he had stopped at Cape Girardeau, Missouri, to deliver two addresses to the students of the summer school. While having his breakfast in Tulsa, he was interviewed by a reporter of the *Tribune*, who learned that Claxton had come to attend a board meeting, get in touch with the school principals, and look over the schools before he went on a month's vacation, the first he had had in twenty-three years. "I want to know my schools, to see what conditions are so that I may be able to think while away," Claxton said;[4] "I don't want to start with a jerk, and I have no idea of inaugurating any sudden changes that might cause an upheaval. I must study the situation carefully, see what the needs are, and decide on what is to be done."

"Though 62 years of age [He was then not quite 61], Doctor Claxton has the agility of a man of 40," declared the reporter. "He is erect, five feet ten inches in height, weighs between 175 and 180 pounds. He has clear blue eyes. His manner is open and frank. He has a commanding voice and attractive personality. He asks questions in a to-the-point manner. He wears glasses when reading. His hair is gray, and is parted in the middle. He doesn't use tobacco in any form. He has every appearance of a business man. When he arrived, he wore a business suit of dark gray and a straight brimmed straw hat. He stepped lightly, like an athlete, from the train. 'You seem well preserved for a man of your age. How do you keep in physical condition?' he was asked. 'I walk a great deal. I take no systematic exercise, and my health is generally good. I just don't get sick,' he replied."

Upon being asked why he accepted the position, Claxton answered, "I have never been able to stay at home with my family. Here I can have a home to which I may go after work, and will not have to travel all around the country as I have done most of my life. . . . While I have been engaged in the promoting side of education for many years, having stood on my feet more than any man in the world advocating the advancement of the cause; this affords me the opportunity desired to perfect the system that approaches the ideal as I see it."

During his first day in Tulsa, Claxton was on the go from morning till night, talking to reporters, members of the school board and other school officials, teachers, and a number of patrons, and making two speeches at the Better Schools Conference at the University of Tulsa. He found time, however, to write a note to his wife, who had not liked the idea of going to live in that "wild spot," [5] assuring her that he was highly pleased with Tulsa. "It is clean," he declared,[6] "people alert—a little boastful of the West, but not offensively so. They are of the type that do things."

The Tulsa *World* took exception to some things Claxton said to the Better Schools Conference. In an editorial, entitled "A Disquieting Introduction," the paper declared,[7] "The *World* ventures the opinion that Doctor Claxton's first public address in Tulsa had a disquieting effect upon the public. Perhaps it was quite natural for the highest salaried school superintendent in the United States to come preaching higher taxes for school purposes. Natural, because he could scarcely escape the impression that, since this community had so much to pay for a superintendent, it would have practically unlimited wealth to draw on for the conduct of the schools along such theoretical lines as the superintendent might elect to pursue. Tulsa's new school superintendent is quoted as saying that education is the most important task this country has. 'If we succeed fully in it, all other problems are solved or solvable. If we fail in this, we fail in all.' "

Very illogically the editorial tried to show that this was the same as saying that education is an end instead of a means to an end, and devoted much space to overthrowing this man of straw. But the main ground of complaint was Claxton's statement that the "high cost of education" bogey was created by big money interests who thought more of the dollar than the child. The editorial strongly criticized "waste, crass waste, wanton waste—yea, criminal waste" of money expended by educational theorists on "various folderols." Very cleverly it continued, "It is not the multi-millionaires that make the public school system. These gentlemen, who it seems are held in a socialistic light by the new school superintendent, are amply able to take care of themselves and their children. They can give those children every advantage in the way of education. . . . For every wealthy man in Tulsa who could easily stand a doubling of the educational tax, there are 99 who are hard put to meet present demands, who want nothing but a splendid public school system devoted primarily to the teaching of the fundamentals."

This was a grim warning to Claxton that all would not be smooth sailing in his piloting the ship of education in Tulsa waters. But undismayed he busily continued his inspection of schools—"looking into everything," as one of the clerks in the office in the Board of Education Building remarked. After about a week, he returned to Alabama for his vacation. Before returning, he wrote [8] his wife, "The beauty of this city grows on me. I know none more beautiful in its business district. Good large oak and elm trees in certain parts of the residential district."

A week before the schools were to open on September 10, Claxton returned to Tulsa with his family. He immediately went to work on the multitudinous details incident to the administering of such a large system of schools. This comprised a high school and twenty-one graded schools for white children and two Negro schools with a total enrollment of nearly 20,000 students. The first change which Claxton made, with the approval of the board, was a plan for the advancement of the teachers along with their pupils from a lower to a higher grade. He found the schools over-organized but not well organized. The teachers were good but at least 100 of the 638 were not needed. Many of the buildings, particularly in the poorer sections, were not fit for use; and to these schools the poorer teachers had been sent. There was plenty of money but so used that for several years bonds had been issued annually to pay deficits. The members of the board were honest men, interested in the schools. The newer members had been elected on a pledge to dismiss the former superintendent and make certain reforms. The fight against this superintendent had divided teachers, principals, and patrons into hostile factions.

"I know nothing, and care less, of the troubles of the past," Claxton declared [9] to a reporter. "I am here as a servant of the people of Tulsa, and I will do all in my power to give your city a finer, and more efficient system of public instruction. My work and hopes are in the future."

As to the problem of buildings, soon after Claxton's arrival he requested a bond issue of $500,000, which was approved by an election after a brief campaign. With the school architect, he planned a new type of building, convenient, comfortable, and well adapted to use in Tulsa.[10] In February, 1924, another issue of two

[254]

million dollars was approved [11] by a five to two vote. "Some of the heavy taxpayers," reported the Wichita *Beacon*,[12] somewhat spitefully, "opposed the bond issue. Others, however, argued for it with almost religious fervor. If money can do it, they want to make Tulsa public schools so good that the whole world will come to Tulsa to learn how it is done."

With these funds, a building program was begun to provide five junior high schools, five new grade schools, and additions to six grade schools. The program was adapted to Claxton's proposed new 6–3–3 plan,—six years of elementary school, three of junior high, and three of senior high school. With this form of organization approximately one million dollars in buildings was saved, and the general efficiency of the schools was increased.[13]

The elementary schools conformed to the "platoon plan" which provided for two periods of one and one-half hours each with home room teachers for reading, spelling, language, and arithmetic and two periods of one and one-half hours each with special teachers of elementary science and geography, history and literature, music and art, and physical training. In the high schools the organization provided for departmental teaching entirely.[14] All schools had gymnasiums and all except the white high school had adequate playgrounds. This organization and equipment made possible the accomplishment of about 50 per cent more and better work than Claxton had seen elsewhere.

The housing facilities of the schools were also improved by Claxton's policy of grading schools carefully and increasing the number of children per teacher and by his constant improvement of the standards of qualifications for teachers. The former policy of smaller numbers of children per teacher and classroom had increased expenses to such an extent that the schools could not increase salaries, for bonds had to be issued from year to year to meet the deficit in current income. The children being better graded, the teachers generally did not find an increase in number per schoolroom a burden—particularly since their salaries were thereby increased. The average salary for all teachers increased in Claxton's first year of superintendency from $1862.03 to $1968.42.[15]

Some of the Tulsa teachers disliked Claxton for increasing the number of pupils per teacher and, forgetting that their salaries were thereby increased, thought that this policy was initiated so that he could boast of his economies. Apparently they were concerned not so much with the slight actual increase in their teaching load as they were with an imagined continuing increase which might lay upon them a staggering burden.

Claxton also raised the standard of teachers. At the beginning of the second year the board approved his recommendation that the bachelor's degree be required for all new teachers in the elementary schools and the master's degree for all new teachers in the high school. All new teachers were required also to have had two years of experience in other schools.

Directed home gardening was introduced into the schools. "I had long been interested in school gardening, for several reasons," wrote [16] Claxton. "All children should learn to do some useful work in a systematic way requiring use of mind and muscle. Work that can be done with simple hand tools and not requiring more physical strength than children have. Work, the results of which can be seen and are attractive. Gardening gives all these and more. It gives opportunity for work with feet on or in the soil, head in the sunshine, lungs filled with good fresh air, hunger for good wholesome food, physical weariness to result in good sound sleep, all ministering to mental, physical, and moral health. It also gives opportunity for learning something of the fundamental laws of nature and of observing relations of cause and effect. It also has a considerable economic value."

During Claxton's first spring at Tulsa, home gardening was started in six school districts under direction of three graduates of colleges of agriculture. During the season 1,042 children made gardens with a total net profit of $19,158. Several children made more than $100 each. Thirty-five students in the agricultural classes in the Central High School cultivated home gardens with a profit of over $1000.[17] This enterprise increased until as many as approximately 3000 children cultivated gardens and produced vegetables in a single year worth $40,000. In some districts juvenile delinquency and crime diminished, and habits of industry and thrift were formed.

Soon after Claxton went to Tulsa, many invitations to make speeches were received. He was able to accept only a few of them.

[256]

On November 4, 1923, he spoke on "The Value of an Educational Survey" in the City Hall Auditorium in Dallas. On November 12 he spoke at a Father and Son Dinner at the Second Presbyterian Church in Tulsa. At the meeting of the Louisiana Teachers Association at Alexandria, November 15–17, he made five addresses. On December 1, he spoke on "Equality of Educational Opportunity from the Standpoint of Adaptation" at the convention of the Texas State Teachers Association at Fort Worth. On December 8 at the Nowata County Educational Conference he spoke at the Rex Theater in Stillwater, Oklahoma, in the morning on "The School— The Livest Thing in the Community," and in the afternoon at the Methodist Church on "The Rural School and the Church." [18] On December 10, he addressed the Cherokee Heights Men's Club in Tulsa on the question, "Can the People Afford the Expense of Education?" On December 11, he spoke at a banquet of the Tulsa Association of Life Underwriters on "Insurance for Safety and Peace of Mind." On December 15, he spoke on "Football and School" at the Annual Football Banquet at the Tulsa Central High School.

On January 9, 1924, he addressed a meeting of Yale University Alumni at the Tulsa University Club. On February 24 he attended a Dinner Conference of the National Committee on Visiting Teachers at the University Club in Chicago. On March 19, he was speaking at Central State Teachers College at Edmond, Oklahoma, and on March 28 at the Parent-Teacher Association State Convention at Perry, Oklahoma. On April 2 he spoke on "Thomas Jefferson" before the Tulsa Chapter, Daughters of the American Revolution; on April 7 before the Oklahoma Library Association at Chickasha; on April 9 before the State Federation of Music Clubs at Ponca City; and on April 18 at the Third Annual Presidents' Day before 40 presidents of universities and colleges of five southwestern states at Fort Worth. He gave commencement addresses at Jenks (Oklahoma) High School on May 15; at Miami, Oklahoma, on May 22; at Oklahoma College for Women at Chickasha on May 28; at Tulsa Central High School on May 29 on "White unto Harvest"; and on June 3 at Central College for Women, Lexington, Missouri. He gave three addresses at Central State Teachers College Conference Week for County Superintendents at Edmond,

Oklahoma, June 9–12; and eight lectures at Oklahoma A. and M. College, June 16–20, at Stillwater.

On October 26, Claxton preached the morning sermon in Tulsa at Trinity Episcopal Church. On October 31, he spoke at Muskogee, to the Northeastern Oklahoma Education Association, and on November 8, to the Southwest Oklahoma Education Association at Altus. On December 12 he spoke at the dedication of the Community Methodist Episcopal Church at Turley, Oklahoma. On January 24, 1924, the Governor of Oklahoma appointed him a member of the State Illiteracy Commission.

Early in 1925, the Tulsa *World* took up again its critical attack on Claxton. This was occasioned by the publication of the report of the School Board for 1923–24, in which it was shown that Claxton's administration of the schools had resulted in a very marked saving to the taxpayers. In an editorial of February 16, the *World* questioned the truth of this, stating that "there is a somewhat general impression that the administration of Tulsa's schools is far more expensive than ever before."

On the following day the attack was renewed and insinuations of untruthfulness made. "Perhaps, all of the facts connected with the administration of our schools, if known, would harmonize this apparent conflict," it declared. Apparently the editor did not understand, or pretended not to understand, that the total cost of schools was bound to increase with the annual increase of students and the need for new buildings, but that Claxton was decreasing the cost of administration per pupil.

One of Claxton's great speeches was delivered at the Fiftieth Anniversary of the Founding of George Peabody College for Teachers. The ceremonies lasted three days (February 18–20, 1925). Many of the most distinguished educators in the United States attended. Claxton spoke on the morning of the first day on "George Peabody, His Life and Work in America." After giving an account of Peabody's rise from comparative poverty to great wealth, Claxton said,[19] "In the true spirit of the American business man, Peabody continued his work long after his accumulated wealth had gone far beyond his early expectations—continued it for the very joy in the work itself and for the sake of the great purposes to which he had planned to devote his fortune. Rejoicing in his work and cheered on by the vision of the results of his gifts for the relief and help of humanity, he continued in it to the end. Vision of results! Like all constructive, successful men, he had the power of the seer—the power to see and to realize. In the letter accompanying his first gift for education in the South he breaks forth almost into rhapsody: 'I see our country united and prosperous, emerging from the clouds which still surround her, taking a higher rank among the nations of the world, and becoming richer, and more powerful than ever before.' This was his vision in February, 1867, when lesser and more purely practical men could see only the abomination of desolation by which they were surrounded!"

Claxton then discussed the wisdom with which the Peabody Education Fund had been administered, paid a glowing tribute to Dr. J. L. M. Curry, and emphasized the influence of Peabody and his fund in stimulating other men to donate much larger gifts for education. "Among America's most valuable possessions," he concluded,[20] "is the example of George Peabody. Had I time, it would be pleasing to try to follow Curry in his Winston-Salem speech and to prophesy of the far-reaching influences in the next half century of this college for teachers, the now most prominent visible result of Peabody's gift. Most of you can and will do it more effectively for yourselves. The best gift to any country is a great man inspired by good will and directed by sound wisdom. Such a man was George Peabody. Render thanks to the Giver, O America, for thy son!"

On March 31, Claxton, Rabbi Morris Teller, and Colonel Patrick J. Hurley were the speakers at the Central High School Auditorium in Tulsa at a public celebration in honor of the dedication of the Hebrew University, Mount Scopus, Jerusalem. On May 6 he spoke on "Horace Mann" to the Tulsa Patron-Teachers Association at the Horace Mann School. From May 20 to June 2, he delivered three commencement addresses.[21]

On June 15 the Tulsa World made this vicious attack on Claxton in an editorial, entitled "A Pacifist Obstructer": "General Bullard, in the closing installment of his great war series of articles, which have been running in the World for several days, lodges a terrific indictment against 'Professor Claxton, federal commissioner of education,' who, the eminent general asserts, contributed mightily to the unpreparedness of the United States in the World War, as one of the most prominent of the pacifist crew who did their best to make 'I Didn't Raise My Boy to Be a Soldier' the new national anthem. For two years now this eminent pacifist, whose activities at that time so impressed a prominent figure of the war that he classed him as one of the handicaps of the United States government in winning the war, has been the superintendent of education in Tulsa's public school system. He is the man Member Johnson of the school board tells the Tulsa public the board was prepared to pay even more than $13,800 a year salary if it had been necessary. Perhaps the school board, which brought this eminent pacifist and obstructer to Tulsa to preside over its schools and instill his peculiar ideas of patriotism into the minds of Tulsa youth, cares to explain to the parents of this city what its object was. Perhaps again, it does not dare explain—honestly and completely! At any rate, there is a sentiment abroad in the city which demands not merely an explanation of this gross injustice but also a manly acknowledgment of error and a pledge that the proper remedy will be applied."

Claxton replied to this cruel attack. Writing in the Tulsa *Tribune*, he declared that General Bullard's statement was "the result of lack of knowledge or wrong interpretation or both." "I am not, was not then, and have never been, by thought, word, or deed, an exponent of such principle or policy," continued Claxton. "I have, however, long been an advocate of national justice and international peace to the extent that our own people and the peoples of the world can be brought to understand them and to embody them in their programs and policies. As a patriotic citizen seeking ever both the present and the permanent good of my country and of humanity, I have as I have had opportunity done what I could in a constructive way to help forward the cause of justice and peace in a rational way.

. . . In college I had military training at the expense of the government, and, until barred by age, held myself in readiness to serve the country as it might need or demand. With my consent and advice my son has followed the same course. With many other patriotic Americans I have long believed that peace, so far as it can be honorably and safely maintained, is better than war and that the peoples of the world, including our own country, cannot attain to the highest and best in life and civilization until they have learned to live in peace and have found some way of settling their difficulties, without resort to the destructive and disrupting agencies of war.

I have also believed that universal education, developing and training as fully as possible all the people physically, mentally, morally, and spiritually, and the unhindered pursuit of the arts and industries of peace in high patriotic spirit of service, are the surest guarantees of the strength and unity necessary for certain victory when war becomes inevitable.

In this faith I had worked for the cause of education nearly thirty years before accepting the office of Commissioner of Education in 1911. In the same faith and spirit I administered that office to the best of my ability until the shock of the World War came in 1914. From that time to the signing of the armistice the office was administered in sympathy and harmony with the policies of the government: first, the preservation of neutrality and the strengthening of the material and spiritual forces of the country for whatever task it might become necessary to undertake; second, after we entered the war, to assist in mobilizing as effectively and expeditiously as possible for the success of democracy and freedom, however long and difficult the task might be; third, that in so far as possible the schools of America should 'carry on,' that, if possible, no American boy or girl should have less opportunity for education because of the war and that they all might be prepared for the difficult tasks, the heavy responsibilities, and the splendid opportunities which all farseeing men knew would come to this generation.

After the war had been won, all the energies of the Commissioner and his staff in the Bureau were turned to the task of establishing more firmly and readjusting for their new service our educational institutions of all kinds, and the preventing loss or injury to them in the uncertainties of reaction and reconstruction.

How wisely and effectively all this was done only the future and the calm judgment of the historian can tell. But that it was done both with high patriotic motive and with the approval of the President and the Departments of State, War, and Navy, I am sure."

Nothing further came of this attack, and the following year Claxton was re-elected superintendent by the board for another term of three years.

On July 11, 1925, Claxton sailed on the S.S. *Columbia* of the Anchor Line from New York for Scotland as a delegate from the National Education Association to attend the Edinburgh meeting of the World Federation of National Education Associations. With him at his expense was his son Calvin Porter Claxton, a graduate of The University of Tennessee and at that time the principal of the High School at Bell Buckle, Tennessee. With about sixty other American delegates they arrived at Glasgow on July 19, and from there went across country by charabanc, thirty-two in each of two motor coaches. The meetings lasted from the 20th to the 28th of July.

About 2,000 delegates attended the Edinburgh conference. Claxton addressed the section on illiteracy and spoke again before the general body. But the sessions of this World Federation he found "not very interesting or instructive." [22] He recalled that an Englishman complained of the hundreds of thousands of English children under fourteen who were unemployed but he did not suggest that schools be provided for them. He asked Michael Sadler to what extent the war time promise of public schools in England had materialized. Sadler made excuses that the country was neither ready for it nor able to do it yet. One evening a Hindu official spoke, making one of the best addresses Claxton heard and using the best English. Next day he congratulated the speaker and complimented him on his excellent English. He replied, "Speech is the one thing that gives us superiority over the lower animals. It is a part of our religion to speak a language in its purity." This remark pleased Claxton very much. He recalled also that, in a departmental meeting, a representative from one of the Balkan States asked if one could be a good citizen of his country and at the same time be a citizen of the world. He was doubtful of this. At the central headquarters of the conference, a peace flag was kept flying.

The Lord Provost, Magistrates, and Council of Edinburgh gave a reception in the College of Art on the evening of July 21 in honor of the delegates. The following evening the Glasgow Orpheus Choir gave a concert in Usher Hall. On Sunday afternoon, July 26, an official service for the Federation was performed in St. Giles's Cathedral. Before leaving Edinburgh Claxton had an interesting talk with Patrick Geddes in his Outlook Tower rooms. A professor of botany in the University, he had socialistic ideas regarding city developments.

Claxton and his son then spent several weeks on a walking trip among the hills and mountains of Scotland, visiting the Scott Country, the vicinity of Stirling, and the Trossachs. From Scotland they went to London by way of Cambridge, where they spent a Sunday in the country near by and on the University grounds, missing only one of the 23 or 24 colleges of that great University. On August 15 they sailed for home from Plymouth on the Berengaria, one of the Atlantic's largest and most luxurious liners. In the absence of her husband, Mrs. Claxton spent a part of the summer at Atlantic City.

In October Claxton went to North Carolina where on the 12th he delivered an address at the Semi-Centennial of the Reopening of the University of North Carolina (closed 1871–1875). He spoke only from notes and accordingly there is no record of his speech. In the Academic Procession were representatives of nearly one hundred colleges and universities. The occasion was a notable one.

Claxton was honored on February 25, 1926, by having his portrait unveiled by his grandson Claxton Walker in the Auditorium of the Department of the Interior. The portrait, painted by Mrs. Sarah Ward Conly, of Nashville, Tennessee, was presented to the Bureau of Education by the National Congress of Parent-Teacher Associations. Commissioner Tigert thought "it a splendid likeness besides being a work of art." [23] The artist was not so well pleased with her own work.[24] Claxton was portrayed in academic gown and purple velvet hood as he appeared about the time he was appointed Commissioner of Education. Claxton was present at the unveiling and made a few remarks in response to the laudatory speeches by Secretary of the Interior Hubert Work and Commissioner of Education Tigert.

The Tulsa Tribune was highly elated over this honor accorded one of the city's adopted leaders, and declared, "It was fitting that Dr. P. P. Claxton should come to the oil capital to head its department of education—he has been 'hung in oil' as a national honor accorded his administration as U. S. Commissioner of Education." "We are aware that Dr. Claxton belongs to the Nation and to the World, as well as to Tulsa," wrote [26] the President of the Board of Education to Commissioner Tigert, in expressing regret that no member of the board was able to accept the invitation to be present at the unveiling, "and we are delighted to learn that the greatness of his contribution to his day and generation is being in some measure recognized while his work is still unfinished. We consider that the City of Tulsa and the Commonwealth of Oklahoma were signally honored when he accepted the invitation to join forces with us, and we desire to add our testimony to his singular devotion to the educational interests of youth, to his prophetic vision of the potential citizenship that is to be, and to his masterly comprehension of the necessary measures for realizing the hopes and aspirations of a free people."

In March, by unanimous agreement of the Board of Education, Claxton was offered the superintendency for three more years. He accepted at the same salary he had previously received. By this time the citizens of Tulsa had visible evidence of his work in the beautiful modern school buildings, completed or in process of construction. "Not only has the $2,000,000 bond issue created a new and modern aspect for the public school system by the completion of the junior high schools," declared the *Tulsa Spirit*, "but the bond issue has been stretched to include the new Manual Arts building, one of the most thoroughly equipped school buildings of its kind in America. . . . This building and its service to the boys of the community is a cause for real pride to Tulsans who value the dignity of labor."

In the summer of 1926, Claxton organized a six weeks' summer school for teachers in the elementary grades, costing each teacher only a registration fee of $30.[28] Even the Tulsa *Daily World* had to admit,[29] after 1000 teachers had applied for 30 vacancies in the teaching staff, "Every teacher in the United States wants to come to Tulsa, . . . doubtless attracted by the salary scale maintained by the Tulsa system." By the end of Claxton's third year as superintendent, the minimum salary for women with the A.B. degree was $1500; for men, $1800. The minimum for women with the M.A.

degree was $1750; for men, $2050. Liberal allowances for experience and for further study and educational travel made the maximum for teachers with the A.B. degree approximately $2500; and for teachers with the M.A. degree about $2900. The annual average salary of all teachers was then more than $300 above that three years before. Principals of elementary schools received from $3000 to $4000; the principal of the Central High School, $7,500, later raised to $9,000.[30]

Dental and medical clinics were established and the health department reorganized under a skilled physician. Part-time schools and night schools were reorganized and the enrollment greatly increased. A school for subnormal children, and an open-air school were housed in rooms in the Longfellow School building.[30]

Claxton spoke at the dedication ceremonies of the new schools, and at the meetings of various educational associations in Oklahoma.[31] On April 3 he was back in Tennessee again, addressing the annual convention of the State Teachers Association in the War Memorial Building in Nashville on "Education as the Most Important Business of the State." [32] At the meeting of the National Education Association in Philadelphia in July, he was elected vice president. For several years he had been too busy to attend the association's meetings.

"I came to Tulsa three years ago," Claxton wrote [33] George Foster Peabody in September, "because there seemed to be here an opportunity to work out certain phases of public school education without hampering traditions. So far the program goes on well. The schools have been thoroughly reorganized and are probably as well organized now as any schools in America. When we have done a little more work on courses of study and other details, I believe I shall be more or less satisfied with the work."

On December 14, 1926, an election was held on a bond issue of $750,000 for three new buildings, additions to seventeen others, various equipment, and grounds and a stadium for Central High School. On December 17, Claxton addressed the Tulsa Chamber of Commerce on "Progress in the Tulsa Schools," giving interesting details of the improvements in buildings, organization, and administration of the schools during the past three years of his superintendency. The bond issue was approved, and in May, 1927, contracts were let for a $100,000 vocational school, for a $100,000 playground for the High School, and for $100,000 of equipment for the schools; the rest of the money provided two new buildings and additions to other buildings.[34]

In May, Claxton gave the commencement address at the Teachers College at Pittsburg, Kansas, on "Seven Definite Aims of Education," which he declared to be development of health, scientific knowledge, skill, judgment, appreciation, a goal, and will power.[35] During the commencement season in Tulsa, a high school student, in writing of the "High School Daze," a customary occasion for razzing the teachers, thus characterized[36] Claxton: "Then Doctor Philander Priestley Claxton! Sounds terribly aristocratic, doesn't it? But he isn't. Just a sweet old gentleman—white hair, Southern brogue, and all that goes with it. He is a veritable walking dictionary of facts and figures. Knows everything. Done everything, too. They gave him half a page in Who's Who, and he's done lots since the last edition."

In June Claxton attended commencement at his alma mater, The University of Tennessee, and spoke on June 7 at the alumni dinner. In July he went to Seattle to the meeting of the National Education Association (July 3–8), and spoke on "A New Basis for Delegate Representation." For the past year he had served as chairman of a committee of twenty-five members to study the appointment of delegates and kindred problems. This committee had met in Dallas in February, and later a sub-committee had met with Claxton in Chicago. After the report was made by him, the committee was enlarged to fifty-four members under his continued chairmanship. On July 5 he spoke to the School Garden Association of America on "The Educational and Practical Value of School Gardening," and the next day on "Why Music in the Public Schools and How." On July 7, he read a thirty minute paper lauding the educational work of Governor Charles B. Aycock, then deceased.

In August Claxton, accompanied by his wife, went to Toronto, Canada, to attend the meeting of the World Federation of Education Associations. In Convocation Hall of the University of Toronto he gave an address on August 9 on "The International Aspect of Education." On August 7 (Sunday) vesper services for the delegates were held in Convocation Hall. On the afternoon of the 11th a garden party was given in the Art Gallery. The Claxtons attended this and also the banquet given the same evening by the Japanese Delegation at King Edward Hotel.[37]

In October, Claxton spoke on "Great Purposes of Education" at the meeting of North Central Indiana Teachers Association at South Bend (October 14, 15). On the way he visited the Kansas City Schools and the Gary Schools in Indiana.[38]

Another election for a school bond issue of $1,500,000 was held on January 24, 1928. This was, according to a broadside written by Claxton and signed by the Board of Education, "for the good of the children and for the continued growth and prosperity of Tulsa." "In February, 1924," continued the broadside, "the people of Tulsa authorized a bond issue of two million dollars for school buildings, sites, and equipment. In December, 1926, they authorized an issue of seven hundred fifty thousand dollars. When the first of these two issues was voted, 82 classes, more than 20 per cent of the children in the white schools, were housed in wooden 'jitneys,' unsightly, uncomfortable, unsanitary, without toilets or water. Many classes were housed in basement rooms unfit for such use, in school auditoriums, and in rented rooms. Several classes were on half time attendance. The proceeds of these bond issues have been used to provide suitable rooms in new buildings and additions to old buildings, and to provide buildings for junior high schools."

Details were then given, showing exactly how the money had been expended. The need for more funds was then explained as arising mainly from the increased school attendance which necessitated another high school building which would cost with its site about $500,000, at least three more graded school buildings, and additions to fifteen school buildings. "This expenditure is for our children," concluded the broadside, "to be paid for by them or out of moneys that might otherwise be left to them. It is to make possible for them the education without which their lives would be poor and inefficient indeed; but with which they may be able to live more efficiently and happily and produce wealth far beyond that which is expended on their education. By these expenditures we do not impoverish ourselves; we only enrich our children by

[267]

permitting them to borrow from their future richer selves to provide for themselves now what we do not feel able to provide for them out of cash funds."

At the same election the citizens were to vote on the continuance on the usual ten mills excess levy for the maintenance of the school system. "The issue was voted on," declared [39] Claxton, "without sufficient campaigning and at the time city taxes were being paid." As a consequence the bond issue failed to be approved.

An editorial in the Tulsa *Tribune*, "A No Confidence Vote," after regretting the defeat of the bond issue and detailing the excellent work Claxton had done for the schools, declared,[40] "Tulsa citizens may feel that the present city superintendent has been too liberal in using this community as an educational pedagogical laboratory. It is certainly true that his predecessor with less expenditures for auxiliaries filled the bill acceptably. Citizens, parent-teachers, and other civic organizations, going to our present superintendent of education for information or for constructive suggestions, have felt that he was evasive and difficult to work with. That is a situation that should not exist. It is not conducive to confidence to withhold information until more money is asked. These unfortunate influences have brought results. The people have voted 'no confidence.' That vote of 'no confidence' should be respected with such changes as will effect confidence."

As a consequence, the Chamber of Commerce requested Dean E. Foster, a local consulting engineer, to make a survey of the schools. After inspecting eight of the forty-three schools he reported,[41] "My study has convinced me that our schools are being administered by a conscientious board of education and well qualified superintendent. . . . However, I believe they have been much too conservative, that they should provide more space, more buildings, and perhaps reduce the size of classes in order that our children may receive more individual attention." In another article he dealt with the impression of many citizens "that a great number of new courses of study have been introduced into the grade schools of this city during the past five years at the expense of time previously devoted to the study of the three R's." "The facts, however," he declared,[42] "show that no changes in curriculum have been made and that the same courses are now being taught that were being taught six and seven years ago, and that the same amount of time is given to instruction in the three R's under this administration as was given under the preceding."

This was followed by an investigation by a committee of citizens appointed by the Chamber of Commerce, which recommended that an educational expert be employed to survey the school system.[43] Dr. Charles E. Chadsey, Dean of the College of Education, University of Illinois, and formerly superintendent of schools in Denver, Chicago, and Detroit, was employed for that purpose. After making a detailed survey, he made a report in full to the Board of Education, which he summarized; the first item was, "The Tulsa school system as it stands today is properly to be classed among the more progressive and the best of the modern city school systems." All of the other nine items approved unqualifiedly what had been done under Claxton's administration. In item number nine, he suggested the possibility of taking the tenth grade from the senior high school and adding it to the junior high schools and thus making it unnecessary to build a second high school. This he thought might possibly be more economical.

"An inspection of these summarized statements," he concluded, "justifies one in the belief that the citizens of Tulsa, far from feeling suspicious as to changes and uncertain as to the desirability of expansion along the underlying principles which have guided the present administration in the development of the Tulsa schools, are equally justified in believing that the specific types of increased educational expense resulting from the carrying out of such policies are justified and should be approved."

The Tulsa *Tribune* accepted this report with full confidence.[44] But the Tulsa *World* made a rather childish attack on Dr. Chadsey and his report, ending, "Doctor Chadsey gets $50 a day and his expenses for his eight days' work. And being an almost perfect job of calcimining, there certainly can be no objection on the part of the taxpayers to O.K. this bill. But his report will not fool those mentally alert Tulsans who are to go to the polls May 15 and choose a board of education. They will see their duty and do it."

The campaign for election of three members to fill vacancies on the school board was vigorously conducted for a month preceding the election. The main issue was school expenditures.[45] Claxton was forced to deny on May 14 the statement in the *World* that he had taken personal command in the campaign for electing members favorable to him and that he had built up a "ring" of supporters among teachers and school employees.[46] In the previous February he had felt it necessary to correct misstatements in the *World*[47] regarding the excessive number of secretaries employed in the schools and to deny that Mrs. Claxton drew a salary for mothercraft work. "Mrs. Claxton draws no salary from any source whatever," he wrote. "She gladly gives what time she can to the promotion of mothercraft and mother club work in the schools."

On May 15, the three men favorable to Claxton were elected. As the four other members of the board were strong supporters of him, the election assured his retention as superintendent. In the following September a bond issue for $1,750,000 was voted, and according to Claxton's report in the spring of 1929, plans were prepared for 116 rooms in new buildings and in additions to old buildings, including six gymnasium-auditoriums. "When they are all finished next fall," he reported, ". . . for the first time in its history Tulsa will have adequate housing for all the white children in the public schools."

On March 4, 1928, Claxton was principal speaker at Founders' Day, at Southern Methodist University at Dallas. In May, Henry Van Dyke spoke at Tulsa High School. "It is our good fortune," said Claxton in introducing him, "to have as our speaker one known and loved by all who know and love the best in American literature and the highest and finest things in our Christian idealism. He needs no introduction to any intelligent, cultured English speaking audience. With great pleasure I present to you Henry Van Dyke, scholar, preacher, teacher, author, diplomat, servant of humanity, friend and inspirer of youth."

On June 4, Claxton gave the commencement address at the University of Wichita, Kansas. In July he went to a meeting of the National Education Association at Minneapolis. He gave most of his time there to the work of the Committee on Appointment of Delegates, of which he was chairman, but on July 3, he spoke to the local Kiwanis Club.

At the meeting of East Tennessee Association of Teachers, October 25–27, he addressed both white and colored teachers on the

25th and 26th respectively on "Man's Three Great Adventures." According to an editorial in the Knoxville *Herald*, "After discussing the great adventures that had taken place in the world religiously and politically, Dr. Claxton made the climax of his address the educational advancement that has taken place within the past decade. He emphasized especially the advancement that our country and our section, the South, have made in education. While Dr. Claxton could not say it, a few men in the country and in the South have brought about this great educational awakening—one of the most prominent of whom is Dr. Claxton. Such men as Honorable Walter Hines Page, the late Dr. McIver of North Carolina, Dr. Alderman of the University of Virginia, and Dr. Claxton, have done more to advance the cause of education in the Southern States than all other agencies combined. If, within the past decade, we have entered upon a great 'Educational Adventure' in this country, Dr. Claxton has been one of the great crusaders leading and pointing the way."

On November 9, he spoke on this same subject at the session of the Iowa State Teachers Association at Des Moines (November 8–10). He also gave five other addresses to various groups of teachers. For these he received $200.[48] The following January 20, 1929, he preached a sermon on the same subject at the Congregational Church in Tulsa. In February, he went to Cleveland where he made four speeches to different departments of the National Education Association, holding sessions there.

According to the Tulsa *Tribune* of April 3, 1929, Claxton had declared "he could not possibly remain at the work here beyond July, 1930." "If the board of education feels the need of my services in correlating the courses in grade, junior high school, and senior high school classes, I am willing to remain in Tulsa for another year," he was reported to have said. The reasons for his wishing not to renew his contract were, according to the paper, "I have been offered a place on the faculty of The University of Tennessee, an administrative position, and have been urged to join a publisher of educational textbooks. Both are interesting positions and either would give me the opportunities to do the things I have been planning to do."

The following day an editorial in this paper declared, "The people of Tulsa have been able to see the motives behind most of the criticism directed at Doctor Claxton. Reaction, selfishness, pique, and not fear of school politics, was back of the fight. Followers of McGuffey, property owners who object to being taxed for the education of the children of the poor, disgruntled citizens incensed because their advice had not been asked in school management composed principally the anti-Claxton element. It was vociferous in its cry 'politics in the schools,' but not enough so to cover the real reasons for its opposition to Doctor Claxton's program. Progress, not Claxton, has been the issue in past Tulsa school elections. . . . Doctor Claxton has retained his independence. He has not been swerved by threats or derision. He has shown courage in his adherence to the policies that he believes best for the advancement of public education."

About six weeks later Claxton decided not to accept a contract for another year. "In the last year of my second term of three years," Claxton wrote,[49] "I began to get very tired and should have taken a vacation, as the Board of Education suggested. But after careful consideration, I requested the Board not to re-elect me."

Another election for three members of the board was to be held on May 25. Among these was Ben Johnson, who had turned against Claxton and was campaigning for re-election on "the Claxton issue."[50]

"Early in 1929," Claxton wrote,[51] "Ben Johnson said to me he was getting very tired of fighting the Tulsa World without much help. The World had been especially bitter against him. Others had made many false accusations; some, impugning his personal honesty, intimated that he had suggested the locations of new schools because of the effect on values of real estate in which he was interested, and other minor graftings. I do not believe any of these were true. No new school was located except on my own initiative and recommendation. I do not believe he made any money illegally out of any school contract. I still consider him one of the very best members of the Board and one of the most reliable. I can well understand his growing tired of the fight. When I told him I could take no part in any newspaper or personal fight, he said he would then have to oppose my re-election. He was a good fighter and used the laws of war. *I could have been re-elected.*"

[272]

"Rather unwisely, I think," Claxton wrote,[51] "I accepted the superintendency of the Boston Avenue Methodist Church Sunday School. This took much of my time on Sunday; so I had practically no rest." Though this no doubt contributed to his loss of health, his work was highly appreciated by the congregation. On June 25, the Board of Religious Education held a banquet in honor of the Claxtons, attended by 350 guests. Gold watches were presented to both Dr. and Mrs. Claxton. In July he attended the meeting of the National Education Association at Atlanta. A picture of him as he arrived and was greeted by Superintendent of Schools Sutton shows how impaired his health was at that time.

Socially, the Claxtons were very happy in Tulsa. They found life there very stimulating culturally. There was a great deal of wealth in the city, and each winter grand opera was sung by famous singers from Chicago and New York. The city seemed to have an unusually large number of young college graduates, and clubs, both social and educational, flourished. Many of the homes were veritable palaces planned by the best architects and furnished on the advice of the best interior decorators in the United States. The private gardens and public parks were beautifully landscaped. There were many elegant receptions, teas, dances at the Country Club, and dinners in honor of distinguished singers and lecturers.

Mrs. Claxton's only complaint was that "the tempo of the Oklahoma people ran a Southern lady a bit ragged." [52] She was an active member of the Juvenile Court Association; chairman of the council of Mother Clubs with a membership of more than a thousand women; and state vice president of Oklahoma Parent-Teacher Associations. On Thanksgiving Day each year the Claxtons were at home to the Tulsa teachers at their home at 556 North Denver Avenue.

Though some of Claxton's teachers were unsympathetic to his reforms in organization, in curriculum, and in methods of teaching, most of these found out by experience that he was right and they were wrong. Some disliked him for what they thought superficially was a proud and haughty attitude. But even these admired him as one who always took a definite stand, who was never "wishy-washy" and never "a straddler of fences."

His teachers who knew him well had no such unfavorable impressions. One of these wrote [53] of Claxton: "One never thought of his age even though his hair was gray, and his children grown to manhood and womanhood. He expressed dominion over his body and thought. His kindly blue eyes would smile as you offered to drive him back to the office when you did not see his car, and he would answer, 'Thank you, but I prefer to walk; I can think while walking.' You knew as he walked off with a light, swift step that those thoughts would illumine all who met him on the way if their eyes were open to see. Again, fairness in work and play meant everything to him. The irritating trifles, the non-essentials of daily experience which hide from view the majestic things of life, were passed by but if they involved a question of right or wrong, the eyes grew a steel gray and the mouth became firm and the rebuke was one to be remembered till the wrong was set right. 'The tree must be made to grow erect and strong,' he would say, 'even though for the moment it takes strength to bend it.' Then the wrong was never mentioned again; it seemed to have gone from his consciousness. I see him now standing tall, erect, slender, his eyes smiling from underneath the shaggy eyebrows, looking at us and saying in a full vibrant voice, 'As I walk, the Universe walks with me. Beautifully it walks before me. Beautifully it walks behind me. On every side I walk with beauty everywhere.' "

Another teacher wrote him a letter of farewell, which has all the more weight because it was signed anonymously "A Faithful Teacher." "I cannot see you bring your work in Tulsa to a close," the letter ran,[54] "without giving expression to my feeling of gratitude for the opportunity I have had for the last four years of being a part of this school system under your supervision. Your emphasis upon scholarship, idealism, efficiency, justice, tolerance, and courteous treatment of friend and foe alike have been a constant inspiration to me.

The addresses of prominent speakers you have brought to Tulsa for our benefit have been of no more practical use to me than your own lectures have been. Any time you have spoken in Tulsa at a public gathering I have made it a point to be present and have never failed to receive permanent benefit thereby.

I know great numbers of my associates who feel exactly as I do.

They may not say so in so many words but their convictions are just as strong and their feelings just as sincere. All the rest of my life I shall remember you with much gratitude and appreciation for the help you have been to me and the blessing you have been to the city in which I expect to make my permanent home."

⋖§ XX §⋗

Vacation in Denmark

◇◇

ON LEAVING Tulsa, Claxton returned to Knoxville, Tennessee, with his family. Soon after his return, he was asked by P. L. Harned, Commissioner of Education and Chairman of the State Board of Education, to take the presidency of the newly established Austin Peay Normal School, the purpose of which was to prepare teachers for rural schools. Claxton's reply was that he could not undertake any administrative duties at that time, on account of ill health.[1]

Claxton and his family took up their residence in Knoxville, and several hours nearly every day he spent during the winter and spring of 1929–1930 in an office provided for his use by The University of Tennessee, writing a book which he called *Tennessee*. It was to be a cross-section of the geography, history, industry, commerce, and general activities and interests of the people of Tennessee, and was to be adapted for use in the fifth and sixth grades. On Sundays he taught a class of men in the Church Street Methodist Church South, of which he had formerly been Sunday school superintendent.

Claxton's recovery from impaired health was much slower than he had foreseen. He was then sixty-seven years old, "a critical time in life for a busy man," he thought.[2] Though his book was not finished, it was decided that a sea voyage and a complete change of scene would be helpful in more quickly restoring his strength and vigor.

Accordingly, in June, 1930, Claxton and his son Porter sailed from New York for Bremen in a large fast boat to save time. From there they went by train to Copenhagen, where they spent two or three days sightseeing. The main reason Denmark had been chosen for a visit was to study the folk high schools and the system of rural co-operation. Porter Claxton was then the executive officer of The University of Tennessee Junior College at Martin, and like his father had developed a special interest in rural education. Since Claxton's first trip to Denmark thirty-four years before, he had had a keen interest in the peculiar system of rural schools which had been developed there, and had made some effort to secure their establishment in the United States but with not much success. Aside from the general improvement in rural education incident to his interest in this division of the Bureau while Commissioner of Education, he did influence the founding of the John C. Campbell Folk School at Brasstown, North Carolina. In giving Claxton credit for this influence, Mrs. Campbell wrote,[3] "He was farsighted enough, too, to see the great values lying in the folk-school type of education. I owe him a personal debt in first calling Mr. Campbell's attention to Denmark, and for sending over a delegation to the schools which have since become so well known." Claxton also aided Dr. Dabney and others in the establishment of the Farragut Country High School, which had some of the features of the Danish folk schools. In returning to Denmark, he was renewing an interest which he had formerly held.

Claxton and his son first visited an agricultural school and a folk high school at Lungby, near which was a summer palace of the King of Denmark, who frequently inspected these schools. Here the Claxtons saw an excellent exhibit of agricultural equipment and machinery, and a government seed farm. After spending a day or two at the excellent folk high school at Hilerod, they went up to Elsinore to see the International Folk High School.

They then walked or rode in buses and small trains at a fare of one cent a mile over the Islands of Sjaeland and Fyn and the Jutland Peninsula, visiting chiefly folk high schools and homemaking schools. One of the most interesting of the former was the Husman School for small farmers near Odense. The principal was Dr. Lange, a noted scientist who was a specialist in fungus growths. Two days were spent observing this school during the homecoming of former students. Practically all had farms of twenty to ten acres or less. Claxton was much interested in what appealed to them. The program of entertainment consisted of a rather high type of drama, a lecture on India and Ghandi, another on the English Industrial Revolution, an outdoor folk dance, and an exhibit of farm machinery.

Claxton and son also visited the school of Nils Buch, who had modernized the Swedish gymnastics, changing it into a more attractive system which was designed wholly for physical and mental health. After seeing the work done at this school and at other schools by teachers trained under this system, Claxton was convinced that it was a great improvement over any sort of gymnastics employed in the United States.

While the Claxtons were at Esbjerg inspecting a labor folk high school, they visited the home for the aged. The house, surrounded by a beautiful well-landscaped lawn, would have cost in the United States at least $750,000. It was occupied by approximately ninety people. Others preferred to live in small cottages. All were cared for by the government.

The folk high schools were all established by private groups or organizations who received definite government allowances sufficient to pay a large part of the cost of instruction. Many of the students were given help by their home communities in paying their board and other living expenses. The school year was divided into two parts, five or six months in the autumn and the winter for men and three or four months in the summer for women. The minimum age for admission was eighteen years; there was no maximum limit. The average age of students was about twenty-five years. Most of the schools were for the sons and daughters of farmers or those whose occupations were closely related to farming. There were only three such schools open to the sons and daughters of laborers in other industries than farming.

No examinations were required for admission, nor while in school, nor before leaving. The courses of study were quite indefinite. Students and teachers ate together and spent much time together. The principal lectured several times a week on subjects of importance in social, civic, and cultural life. Music, singing, physical exercises, and language study were required of all. Bishop Grundtvig called these schools "schools of life" rather than schools of knowledge. All agreed that they were the most vital force in modern Danish life.

The Claxtons visited two schools for homemakers. Young women who expected soon to be married attended these schools for practical instruction in homemaking—including cooking, sewing, housekeeping, and gardening.

Especially interesting to Claxton were the co-operative enterprises of the farming people. There were more than 1400 co-operative dairies, about sixty co-operative slaughterhouses, and many co-operative banks and factories. All buying and selling was co-operative; the middle man was practically eliminated. "Senator Carmack of Tennessee," Claxton recalled,[4] "used to say that in Tennessee there were two kinds of farmers: those who farm the farms and those who farm the farmers. In Denmark only the first kind are found." Universal education and co-operative enterprise had practically eliminated poverty in the country. Claxton asked a Dane how many millionaires there were in Denmark. He replied,[4] "As many as paupers. What is the use of either?" In all Denmark, outside the cities, one seldom saw a man, woman, or child not well fed and clothed. Within three quarters of a century, Denmark had become one of the wealthiest countries in the world per capita, though she had few natural resources; such as, minerals, forests, and water power. This small country, according to Claxton, should be studied as an example of intelligent thrift and efficiency in all her institutions.

Claxton revisited Skiblung on the southern border of Denmark and was pleased to find that statues of Schroeder and La Cour had been added to those of the great benefactors of their country around the edge of the natural amphitheater. These were distinguished teachers and scientists he had met thirty-five years before at Askov and had highly regarded.

While Claxton was in Denmark, the Board of Trustees of The University of Tennessee authorized President H. A. Morgan to employ him in work similar to that which he had done as Provost of the University of Alabama. But on returning home after the three months trip abroad, he still did not feel well enough to accept this position and went with his family to his farm near Bell Buckle in Bedford County, which he had purchased several years before to provide a home for his widowed sister. Here he spent another three months of complete rest, eating corn bread, cabbage, and other country food. This simple life completely restored his health.

Meanwhile the president of Austin Peay Normal School had died, and Commissioner Harned again asked Claxton to accept this position. Since his recent visit to Denmark, he found his interest in rural schools accentuated; so he accepted the presidency of the school with the feeling that he might aid in improving the training of rural teachers.

Austin Peay State College President

◇◇

THE AUSTIN PEAY NORMAL SCHOOL, as it was called when Claxton became its president, was then only of junior college grade, for at that time only a small per cent of teachers in rural elementary schools had as much as two years' preparation above high school. Its establishment had been authorized by the legislature in 1927 "for training of rural white teachers"[1] and named after former Governor Austin Peay, who died October 2 that year after four years of "wholehearted devotion to the school progress of the state."[2] Like an earlier predecessor, James B. Frazier, he was indeed an "Educational Governor."

The Normal School had taken over the grounds and buildings of the old Southwestern Presbyterian University at Clarksville. Later several new buildings were erected. The institution had an atmosphere of scholarly dignity and venerable age, many beautiful old trees on the rolling campus contributing to the beauty of the place. The little city of Clarksville, situated on the Cumberland River in the midst of the bluegrass section of the state, was an attractive and appropriate setting for the school, historically and culturally. Soon the erect handsome figure of the sprightly new president became well known on the streets of Clarksville as well as on the campus of the Normal School. Both he and Mrs. Claxton immediately identified themselves with the religious, social, and cultural life of the community, and the large attractive presidential home on the campus in due time became one of the social centers in Clarksville.

The school had been in session only a year when Claxton became its president in November, 1930. It was then supported by an annual appropriation of $100,000,[3] which was sufficient to justify his planning to supplement its main function with the use of a number of rural demonstration practice schools. The first of these was established at New Providence, two miles from the campus of the Normal School. Here prospective teachers gained experience in dealing with students and parents in an average rural community. Connected with the school was a small farm of twenty-two acres, stocked with farm animals, poultry, and bees and affording a good outdoor laboratory for a rural school. It was the kind of model school Claxton had dreamed of and written and spoken about for many years. Its reputation was made by a principal and teacher unusually well fitted for the work. Later he secured Pinnacle School in Cheatham County, where cadet teachers spent twelve weeks at full-time teaching under the direction of a supervisor. They received half pay as teachers and full credit at Austin Peay Normal for this practice work. Claxton also established workshop courses for teachers in the schools of neighboring counties, which were the first of their kind in Tennessee.

In the legislature of 1931, the school leaders were able to secure the same appropriations in all divisions of the public school system,[4] in spite of the financial plight caused by the failure of the large banking institutions in Knoxville and Nashville which were controlled by Luke Lea and Rogers Caldwell. Austin Peay Normal School actually received an increase in appropriation of $15,000.[5]

In February, 1931, Claxton attended the meeting of the Department of Superintendence of the National Education Association in Detroit, where at their annual dinner, the Associated Exhibitors presented him a beautiful desk set as an award for "Outstanding Service to American Education." The presentation was made by U. S. Commissioner of Education William J. Cooper, who said of Claxton, "He has served schools in nearly every professional capacity; in an intensive way he has labored in four states in this Union: Alabama, North Carolina, Oklahoma, and Tennessee; and in extent his work and his influence have covered the entire area under our flag. . . . He served ten years as United States Commissioner of Education at a time when war conditions tried men's souls. This distinguished service covers a period of almost 50 years. . . . It is with a great deal of pleasure, therefore, that I present this token given in recognition of the distinguished service in American education to Philander Priestley Claxton, doctor of letters, doctor of laws, lecturer, textbook writer, teacher, school superintendent, Federal Commissioner, and college president." [6]

Somewhat later a plaque on which were inscribed the names of the winners of this award was placed in the new National Education Association building in Washington. [6]

On April 13, Claxton addressed the students and faculty of the University of Maryland at the invitation of the honorary fraternity Phi Kappa Phi. During the scholastic year, 1930–1931, he assisted in an educational campaign in Georgia, speaking once or twice a day for a week at Statesboro, Canton, Calhoun, and other places. [7]

Some of the older leaders in the teachers' organizations of Tennessee had for some time been calling for another educational campaign, and in the spring of 1932 the State Teachers Association presented to Commissioner Harned the sum of $5,000 to be used in conducting such a state-wide campaign. "The veteran campaigner, P. P. Claxton, was chosen to direct the crusade," according to Holt, [8] "and in his usual energetic manner, he immediately began preparation for a series of rallies over the state, which were calculated to attract huge crowds." Great quantities of pamphlets and bulletins containing facts and figures on the condition of the public school system were distributed, and the assistance of various organizations and leaders of prominence was requested.

Some of these mimeographed pamphlets were entitled "Some Important Facts about Educational Conditions in Tennessee," "Higher Education in Tennessee" (statistics showing how Tennessee ranked with other states), "Illiteracy in Tennessee," "The Public Schools of Tennessee and the Teacher-Training Schools," "Public High Schools in Tennessee," "The Purpose and Task of the Austin Peay Normal School" (rural education), "The Tax Burden and Our Schools," "What Can We Afford to Pay for Education," "Election Days in Tennessee," "Our Most Important Present Duty," "For What Do Tennesseans Pay Taxes," "Tennessee's

Public High Schools Must Carry On," "Tennessee in 1900–1901 and in 1930–1931," "Tennessee's State Debt Not a Reason for Curtailing Our Schools," and "Absolute and Relative Conditions in Tennessee." [9]

These were not only widely distributed throughout the state but they also furnished material for the speakers during the campaign. A subject on which Claxton himself frequently spoke was "School Revenue and the State's Ability to Provide It." These pamphlets contained much of Claxton's best thought on public education—ideas that had been tried in the furnace of experience and found to be real gold. In brief, he demonstrated with facts and figures that the school system was in great need of improvement, that Tennessee was among the "backward" states in the support of education, that the state was financially able to greatly increase the appropriations for public education on all levels, that the public school system should be an organic whole in the service of the state (including rural sections as well as the urban population), that better trained teachers were a fundamental need, and that money invested for education was the best possible investment for increasing the wealth of the state.

During the summer a bitter political campaign incident to the Democratic primary election was being waged, and the educational campaign did not get under way in strength until after the primary. Teams of speakers, composed of members of the State Board of Education, heads of the normal schools, and influential educational leaders in various counties, held rallies, from September 19 to October 8, in ninety counties.[10] Small crowds attended most of the meetings and little space was given the campaign in the newspapers. So little enthusiasm was awakened among the people that the campaign was discontinued when only half of the $5000, generously given by the State Teachers Association, had been used. The campaign had not been well timed, for the great depression had the nation in its icy grip and the people of Tennessee were unsympathetic to propaganda which they thought might cause higher taxes.[11]

Since 1929, Claxton had been chairman of the National Student Forum on the Paris Pact. This agreement, sometimes called the Kellogg-Briand Pact, was declared in effect on July 24, 1929. The director of the Forum was Arthur Charles Watkins. The committee in charge of the Forum numbered nearly five hundred, including the U. S. Commissioner of Education and the Superintendents of Public Instruction of nearly all the states. Frank B. Kellogg was its honorary chairman; Claxton, its chairman, assisted Director Watkins in the preparation of *The Paris Pact: A Textbook for Teachers and Students in the High School (1931); America Stands for Pacific Means: A Book for Boys and Girls on the Principles and Practice of Social Co-operation (1937); Prospectus for the Ninth Year (1937–1938) for the Study of the Paris Pact and International Relations in American High Schools;* and other pamphlets containing information relative to the problem of international peace.

Claxton wrote an article, entitled "The Paris Pact in American High Schools," for the October, 1932, issue of *The Clearing House,* in which he declared, "Up to July 24, 1929, school teachers in the United States had no legal justification for teaching anti-war doctrine to public school students. Since then they have no excuse for not doing so. Before that date, if they taught the futility of war, it could plausibly be said they were setting forth 'propaganda'! Since that date, they are teaching the higher citizenship in compliance with the supreme law of the land when they expound the renunciation of war and the settlement of all international differences only by 'pacific means.' It is the Pact of Paris that has made the difference." Then he exhorted the teachers to take a fuller advantage of the great opportunity for developing a powerful public opinion favorable to the settlement of international problems by pacific means and a real disarmament by international agreement. He was also a member of the Committee on International Relations of the National Education Association from 1936 to 1942.

In the legislature of 1933 public education in Tennessee suffered serious reverses. Claxton drew up in outline form a bill for a new State Board of Education, another for County Boards of Education, a proposed act to create a permanent Textbook Commission, and a bill for additional and uniform state help for elementary schools. These were submitted, in February, 1933, to members of the Steering Committee. But none of them received any serious consideration. Instead of making progress in education, it was all the "school lobby" and the friends of education could do to prevent the normal schools from being closed for two years and The University of Tennessee from having its appropriations reduced 50 per cent. An aggressive intensive campaign by the alumni of the various institutions was carried on in Nashville and throughout the state. Claxton set forth his argument in a letter sent to the individual members of the legislature. It was entitled "Shall the Normals Close?"

"It would mean confusion in the educational life of the state for many years," he wrote. "Faculties would be disrupted; students would be forced to lose two years or go to The University of Tennessee whose facilities would be overtaxed or to George Peabody College for Teachers, which has neither buildings nor funds for a 200 per cent increase. There is already a shortage of teachers." "For twenty years," he declared, "these teacher-training schools have been the most powerful influence and agency for cultivating interest in public education, raising standards of efficiency, and supplying the schools with competent teachers. But this task is only begun. Tennessee still ranks near the bottom of the list of states in all phases of public education. Most of the gain which has been achieved would be lost by the closing of the normals. The appropriations for the schools are not as great as many seem to think, the total being less than 40 cents in every $100 of taxes paid in the state." "Good business will not permit that we let our poverty destroy us," he concluded.

Other arguments were contained in mimeographed articles, entitled, "For What Do We Pay School Money," "The Story of the Teacher-Training Schools in Tennessee," and "Close the University of Tennessee." The last was an ironical indirect argument. For example, Claxton wrote, "As for the boasted teaching of agriculture and its experiment stations, what do they amount to anyway? I have heard a member of the legislature say on the floor of the House that a man could ride a mule along the lanes through Maury County and learn more about farming than the University could teach him in four years. . . . State funds could better be used for teaching the traditional things, true or false, in the elementary schools by teachers who know how to teach by divine inspiration. Let us be reasonable and economic. We have already too much higher education. It is leading us to destruction."

In spite of all that the friends of higher education in the state could do, the legislature reduced the annual appropriation for

Austin Peay Normal to $36,000 a year. Other institutions also suffered severely. The appropriation for The University of Tennessee was decreased to $450,000; the teachers colleges at Memphis, Murfreesboro, and Johnson City and the Tennessee Polytechnic Institute to $56,000; and the Agricultural and Industrial College for Negroes in Nashville to $52,000. Indeed, for awhile it looked as though all the normal schools would be closed for two years.[12] As a consequence of the decrease in appropriation of approximately 65 per cent, Claxton was forced to reduce salaries, dismiss half a dozen members of his faculty, and discontinue the building program and the providing of adequate equipment. The student body decreased commensurately to one hundred and fifty students. In spite of this handicap he saw to it that there was no decline in the quality of the teaching and the effectiveness of the preparation of teachers for the rural schools.

In 1933 Claxton used his pen also in opposition to the repeal of prohibition in Tennessee. In one paper entitled "How Shall We Keep the Saloon Out and Prohibition In?" he graphically reminded people of the widespread drunkenness in Tennessee when the saloon was a legal institution, and showed conclusively the social improvement and decrease in drinking during prohibition. In an article, published in the Clarksville *Leaf-Chronicle*, "Have I Not a Right to Go to Hell in My Own Way?" he concluded, "No man has any right to go to hell or even to start on the journey until he can do so with entire safety to all other people nor until he has fulfilled faithfully all his obligations to himself, to his relatives and friends, to society and state, to the past, the present, and the future, and to God. Only the man who has lived wholly unto himself and can die to himself alone has a right to go to hell in any way whatever."

During this same year Claxton spoke to the Tennessee Educational Association on "Some Suggestions for a More Effective School System in Tennessee," in which he explained that, though much progress had been made in thirty years, Tennessee still ranked very low among the other states in public education, and that the wealth of the state was sufficient for the adequate support of public education.

The legislature of 1933 passed an act providing for an Educational Commission composed of the State Commissioner of Education and eight appointed members. It was to study education in Tennessee and report its findings to the legislature in January, 1935. Claxton was appointed chairman of the Public Relations Committee co-operating with this Educational Commission. There were ten other members. Sub-committees were appointed for press, radio, forum, state and county teachers associations, parent-teacher associations, women's clubs, and Tennessee College Association.[13]

On October 1, 1934, Part I of the report of the Educational Commission was published; it was a volume of 361 pages, which was acclaimed by the press as "the best real picture of the state school system ever presented to the public." [14] Claxton made a brief summary of its findings, which was printed in a pamphlet of about 4,500 words. Part II, comprising the Commission's recommendations for improving the school system, was not published until December following.[15] This was abridged by Claxton in outline form in a pamphlet of about 3,500 words.

Meanwhile early in November the Public Relations Committee of the Commission was superseded by the Public Relations Committee of the Tennessee State Teachers Association, of which Claxton became chairman. This committee continued the campaign, distributing summaries of the report of the Commission, and endeavoring to secure the adoption of resolutions approving the recommendations of the Commission by Parent-Teacher Associations, the American Legion, and other organizations. These were to be presented to the legislature. For the press and legislature Claxton prepared "A Plea for a Sales Tax for Schools," "Scrapping the Public School System and Democracy," "Teachers Colleges and the Public Schools," and "The Case of the Teachers Colleges."

The campaign was financed by appropriations of $2100 from teachers' associations in the state. Claxton was assisted by W. A. Bass, Executive Secretary of the State Teachers Association, and by N. C. Beasley, Dean of the Middle Tennessee State Teachers College. The county superintendent and presidents of local teachers' associations were appointed as a special committee to promote the campaign in each county, and were asked to furnish a list of the influential citizens in that locality. To the thousand people of distinction whose names were thus secured invitations were sent to attend a citizens' conference to be held at an accessible place at a designated time.[16]

With the assistance of members of the State Department of Education and the Educational Commission and other prominent educators, Claxton and his two assistants conducted such conferences in December in seventeen different places in the state. The average attendance was about seventy-five, approximately half that expected. Most of the conferences adopted resolutions endorsing the Educational Commission's recommendations, which had been condensed in a pamphlet to be distributed among the members.[17]

Another project of the campaign was the "Student Forum," in which a contest was to be held in each elementary and high school of the state to select the best student paper on "Educational Conditions in Tennessee." The winners were to enter in turn county, congressional district, and regional contests, and the three regional winners were to compete in a final contest, to be decided by the State Supreme Court as judges. This aroused much interest in some counties, but on the whole it failed to accomplish its purpose.[18]

Other activities of the committee included correspondence soliciting support from various organizations, preachers, and other influential persons; personal letters to legislators-elect; publication and distribution of over 20,000 copies of pamphlets explaining the recommendations of the Educational Commission; newspaper releases; and discussions of the Commission's report over the radio.[19] On January 24, 1935, Claxton made a radio address on "What the State Should Pay and Is Able to Pay in Support of Public Education."

"Ignorance is the most costly of all commodities," he declared. ". . . To make our schools of all levels what they should be will require six per cent of our annual income. Is this too much to pay for the safety and prosperity of the state and for the wealth and welfare of our children? President Eliot of Harvard University used to say that a democratic people should spend as much for education as for food or clothing. . . . When we buy education, we buy not only wealth and wealth-producing power, but also health and the prolongation of life, the possibility of the continuation of democratic government, the possibility of the beneficent functioning of the free church, civic righteousness, culture, and the permanence and improvement of our civilization. Through our children we are holding in our hands the destinies of our state and nation."

While the legislature was in session the following year, Claxton made personal appeals, on March 20 and 26, to "The Friends of Education in Tennessee" and to "The Good People of Tennessee" to use their influence on members to prevent the closing of the normal schools for two years and the drastic reduction of appropriations to The University of Tennessee. After a hard fight by the "school lobby," a general appropriation bill was finally passed, giving the public school system the same appropriations it had had the past biennium.[20] The ambitious program of the Educational Commission had failed completely, though later results were favorable.

Some noteworthy addresses were delivered by Claxton to the Philomathian Society of the Austin Peay Normal School. In 1931, he spoke on his favorite book *Faust* by Goethe. The next year his subject was "Some Thoughts about State Government in Tennessee and Suggestions for Betterment." Among these suggestions were the reduction of the number of representatives to 75 and of senators to 25, an annual session of the legislature of 100 days, repeal of the power of veto by the Governor, a single term of four years for the Governor, a five dollar poll tax, and a graduated income tax. In 1935 he spoke to the society on "The United States Office of Education." His conclusion was "that this office has for sixty years been the most useful agency in America and one of the most important in the world for the intelligent promotion of popular education."

In the summer of 1933 Claxton gave a series of five vesper service addresses at Peabody College. One was on "Man's Three Great Adventures." These, he said, were the adventure of Christianity, the adventure of democracy in government, and the adventure of universal democratic education. "Some understanding," he concluded, "of the nature and importance, and of what I believe to be the final purpose and result of those three greatest of all human adventures has given me courage and comfort. With full confidence, I appeal to you to help to carry on until they shall be far enough advanced at least to make possible the assured success of the fourth great adventure, still in the offing, the adventure in international peace and world co-operation. Then if our universe be an orderly and ethical universe, man may be free and the world shall be at last redeemed from poverty, crime, and unnecessary suffering. Such a result will be worth the price. Let us pay our part fully and courageously."

In the autumn of 1933, Claxton spoke at the Twenty-first Anniversary of the Establishment of the West Tennessee Normal at Memphis. After recalling the part he had played in the educational campaign which brought about the normal schools in Tennessee, he emphasized the important service of the normals in raising the standard of teachers in the state and concluded, "We have faith to believe and courage to hope that, despite financial depression and social and civic uncertainty and confusion, the high processes of civilization will continue unhindered; that Christianity, democracy, and public universal education working together will gradually but surely bring fuller development and more abundant life to all; that there will come about a larger degree of that fine co-operation which rises from an understanding of the fact that in a democracy like ours there can be no safety except in universal education."

Three years later, in October, Claxton also spoke reminiscently at the East Tennessee Teachers College Silver Anniversary at Johnson City on "The Founding and Early Days of the State Normal School." [21]

What Claxton hoped the rural teachers might do for country people is reflected in an article which he wrote for the Shelbyville Gazette in 1938.[22] "In our schools let us strive not only to make them [the students] wise and good, but also good for something," he wrote. "Let us teach them to do the common things and live the common life uncommonly well. Let us give them vision to see, courage to undertake, and skill to accomplish the things made possible by our still abundant resources. Let us give them the magic ability to turn potential wealth into actual wealth. Let us help them to understand the principles and practices of good citizenship in our co-operative democracy of county, state, and nation in order that constructive co-operation may take the place of destructive and self-seeking competition. Our rural schools must become rural in fact, not only in location and name. Teaching must take hold on the life and work of country people, making the future men and women more intelligent about, and more skillful in, their life and work. It should give boys and girls vision of the possibilities of the country and the knowledge, the skill, the industry, and the determination to make the vision come true. It should also give them purpose and ability to gain for themselves a larger measure of the sweetness and light we call culture, without which life is failure, regardless of what else may be gained." This was his philosophy of rural education.

On January 13, 1938, the Tennessee Public School Officers Association gave a banquet in Nashville in Claxton's honor. President James D. Hoskins of The University of Tennessee was the principal speaker, his subject being "Philander Priestley Claxton: The Horace Mann of the South." The keynote in his appreciation of the great achievements of Claxton was struck when he recalled, "I see him standing before the state legislature in 1909 and I hear his ringing appeal in these words: 'As I stand here speaking to you, pleading that you give the children of Tennessee a chance for light and a more abundant life through education, I close my eyes and visualize thousands of little children and half grown boys and girls standing outside this great Capitol, with outstretched hands and upturned faces, silently asking you to make it possible for them to have an education so that they may become better citizens and make a better living and live a better life. Right education, my friends, is the only means by which they can get these things, and it is in your hands to give it. Will you deny the children of today, the children of tomorrow, this opportunity?' And the legislature did not disappoint them. Our present system of public education was wrought in those moments and welded largely from the sacrificial fire of his devotion."

"Ability such as his," Hoskins concluded, "could not have been denied in the profit-seeking realm. But he chose instead to give—not to take. He chose the way of culture. He chose to fill the hopes of youth with a shining future. He chose to be an instrument of service. It is for this choice and for his enduring faith in this cause that I honor the man."

Chancellor George H. Denny of the University of Alabama, who was unable to attend the dinner, wrote of Claxton, "He came to us at a time when there was great and outstanding need of impressing on the people of Alabama the value of a sound system of public education, all the way from the elementary schools through the University. He did more than any other man had hitherto been able to do in laying the groundwork for the sound development of the University, and indeed of the entire school system of Alabama. My intimate association with Dr. Claxton will always remain a happy memory. I have never known a man of higher sense of honor, of greater devotion to an ideal, or of more charming and compelling personality. I regard him as one of the really great men of our day and time. Certainly I have been associated with no man for whom I feel greater admiration or for whom I cherish greater affection. He has made for himself a unique place in education, not only in Alabama and Tennessee but also in the entire South and for that matter, in the entire country." [23]

By the beginning of World War Two, the appropriations for Austin Peay Normal had been gradually increased to about 70 per cent of what they were in 1931. By that time the percentage of elementary teachers in the Clarksville section of the state with two years of preparation had increased from eight per cent to about ninety per cent. To meet the higher standards required of teachers, a third year was added to the curriculum of the Normal in 1939 and a fourth year in 1941, making it a four year school capable of conferring the B.S. degree. The legislature in 1941 increased the annual appropriation from $50,000 to $70,000, which made possible an enlargement of the faculty to twenty-nine members. [24]

At that time the name was changed to Austin Peay State College. But its main purpose continued to be the preparation of teachers for rural schools and the improvement of the economic, civic, political, social, and religious life of rural Tennessee. "Less has been done in this phase of education," declared Claxton, [25] "than in any other in the country at large. I find it the most difficult and the most challenging of all the tasks with which I have had to do."

Among the few hobbies which Claxton has had is the study of astronomy. This provides him exercise in mathematics of which he is very fond, and gives his mind relief from the problems of education and of life in general which can not be solved by mathematics. In 1940, he expressed this in a truly Miltonic sentence, which is the introduction to a paper prepared for the Philomathian Society on "Astronomy," as follows: [26] "Wearied and worried with the turmoils and confusions of undeclared wars East and West, with the reports of Japanese invasions of China, Italian conquests of Ethiopia and Albania, Nazist rapes of Austria, Czechoslovakia, Poland, and Danzig, and Russian barbarities against Finland; discouraged at the uncertainties of democracies, alarmed by the increase of automobile accidents and other evidences of the general cheapening of human life; disgusted at the follies of Hollywood; puzzled by deficits, impoundments, unemployment, and the general breakdown of our economic systems and the general upturning and overturning of the world, one may well wish for some escape to the wide open spaces, quietude and reign of law in the great universe of which we and our little earth with all its busy hubbub are but a minute and relatively insignificant part, a mere point in the sky or wholly invisible to our neighbors, if there be any on other planets of our own solar system—which solar system with all the grandeur of its powerful sun and nine revolving planets constitutes only an infinitesimal part of our universe with its 30,000,000 suns, many of which are thousands of times larger than ours, and many of which are possibly the centers of planetary systems more or less like our own; and which universe is only an island universe in the ocean of space dotted here and there with hundreds of thousands of other universes in various stages of evolution, all as parts and wholes revolving about each other and swinging through their infinite spaces obedient to a few single and unchanging laws, Newton's law of gravity, Kepler's laws of motion, the laws of light, heat, and ultra-violet radiation and vibrations, chemical combination of atoms and molecules, and electric constitution of atoms."

A very prominent astronomer came to Clarksville to lecture to the students at the college. After he had conversed with Claxton about astronomy at dinner, he said [27] to Mrs. Claxton, "Why did your husband invite me to come here and pay me to lecture on astronomy, when I have learned many things from him on the subject this evening. He should do the lecturing, not I." When Claxton was in Washington he became acquainted with the astronomer, Dr. John Brashear, who said,[27] "I have lived so long with the stars I am not afraid of the dark." Claxton concurred with this profoundly significant remark.

Before the war, Claxton secured N.Y.A. funds for the construction of an addition of twelve double rooms to Calvin Hall, one of the dormitories for men. The College paid for the material; the N.Y.A. students did all the work, under supervision, except the metal roofing. They also made all the equipment except the springs and mattresses for the beds. N.Y.A. students similarly constructed a concrete wood-working shop and made much of its equipment. This building, appraised at $25,000, cost the College approximately $3,000. At a cost of only $2,500 to the College, P.W.A. built a home for the principal of the New Providence Demonstration Practice School on the grounds of the school, which was valued at about $6,000. Claxton has long believed that such a residence should be a part of the equipment of all country schools. Through the office of N.Y.A., students were assigned to the College for regular work and also for special work in homemaking, in commercial training, and in architectural drawing and building, cabinet making, and vegetable and landscape gardening.

When the United States entered the war after the Japanese attack on Pearl Harbor, Austin Peay State College like other schools of higher learning throughout the country was confronted with another crisis. Many students were taken into the armed forces, the enrollment being reduced about sixty per cent. Claxton, however, was resourceful. He arranged with the Navy Department for the training of Navy Cadets, several hundred in number. This brought three times more funds than the receipts from all other sources.

But the most original of Claxton's improvisations was the securing in 1943 of 100 scholarships of $250 each from the Tennessee Bureau of Aeronautics, available during the summer quarter mostly to high school teachers, who were supposed to teach the fundamentals of flying to their students and thus aid in making the country more air-minded. In succeeding years the number of these scholarships was somewhat reduced. This was the first school in the United States to give such training, and Austin Peay thus received favorable publicity all over the country. Later the Link Aviation Devices Company installed a Link Trainer at the school and provided an instructor for its use, and Austin Peay College became the first school in the United States to use this device in a teacher training program.[28]

In a pamphlet entitled "Air Age and Education for it," which

Claxton prepared, he vividly portrayed the changes already in process of being made throughout the world by aviation. "When the war is over," he wrote, "and we can return to ways of peace, we shall soon become conscious of the fact that our great world is all one neighborhood. We may fly to any part of it in less than three days and phone or radio back our arrival in less than ten minutes after landing. . . . This is part of the meaning of an air age. Whether we will or not, we shall live and work in it. The schools and other agencies of education should prepare young people for it."

Claxton also applied to the Tennessee Valley Authority for scholarships in the anti-malaria educational campaign. He was not successful, but he did receive such scholarships from the Governor of Tennessee.

Off-campus classes, chiefly for teachers in service, were organized and taught in half a dozen adjoining counties. Regular college credit was given for this work. After they had proved their value, such classes were approved by the State Board of Education and recommended for use by other state colleges. These and other activities enabled the College to render a full amount of service through the war years.

On April 13, 1943, Claxton delivered a noteworthy address to the Philomathian Society at Austin Peay College on "Jefferson's Place in the Education of the People," in celebration of his birthday. After emphasizing Jefferson's struggle for an adequate school system in Virginia, he said of Jefferson, "Rich in ideals, rich in honors, rich in achievements—none richer, I believe, in all the history of the world and none having a better understanding of real and permanent values as distinguished from accidental and temporary values, when he came to write his own epitaph, which you may see chiseled on the simple shaft that rises above his grave among the trees on the slopes of Monticello, he passed over in silence the fact that he had been a member of the legislature and governor of his native state, then the most populous, the wealthiest, and the proudest of all the sisterhood; that he had been a member of the Continental Congress, minister representing his country at the Court of France, Secretary of State of the United States, Vice President, President for eight years, the founder of a great political party; that he was a musician, a linguist, an architect, a scientist, and an inventor; that he had doubled the territory of his country without the shedding of blood, and many other things, any one of which would have been remembered by smaller men—and then wrote such a combination of achievements as no other man, in all the history of the world, could claim: Author of the American Declaration of Independence, Author of the Statute for Religious Liberty in Virginia, and Father of the University of Virginia. I believe he did not consider this order an anticlimax. Political freedom, religious freedom, development and training."

On November 4, 1943, Claxton was honored by having his portrait unveiled in the Library of the Tennessee Capitol.[29] At the ceremonies Commissioner of Education B. O. Duggan read a letter from U. S. Commissioner of Education John W. Studebaker, in which he declared,[30] "He [Claxton] succeeded in securing appropriations which enabled him to add to his staff specialists in many fields of education. He not only initiated important programs of educational research, but also inspired his associates with his almost religious fervor for spreading the benefits of education everywhere throughout the United States. . . . He was in the forefront of all worthwhile educational developments and lent the prestige of the office to their promotion. . . . As the educational leader of the nation during World War One he was outstanding in the encouragement he gave to all educational activities connected with the war. . . . It is a great privilege, indeed, to be able to pay tribute to Dr. Philander Priestley Claxton, a man who for the last half century has so heroically and unselfishly served the cause of education in America."

A letter [31] was also read from Josephus Daniels, who stated that Claxton was claimed by both North Carolina and Tennessee and "like Andrew Jackson, James K. Polk, and Andrew Johnson—he brought honor to both commonwealths." Mrs. Claxton had written Daniels a summary of her husband's achievements, in which Walter Hines Page was quoted as stating, "The nation without a vision dies, and this man Claxton has a vision that will carry down the ages. He wants light, through education, for all the people, with accent on all." In reply Daniels wrote, "I am glad the words of Honorable Walter Hines Page are quoted. . . . That is honor enough for any man. . . . I value the friendship of your husband very highly, and give high honor to the service he rendered in public education in this state in a time when we were just waking up."

A letter from Dr. Willis A. Sutton, Superintendent of Atlanta Schools and Past President of the National Education Association, declared, "Philander P. Claxton found the South struggling with its economic situation and understood that only knowledge and character could regain a lost prestige and restore her to her former greatness and make her grow stronger and greater as the days go by, and so he gave himself to these two supreme duties: to live a life spotless and unblemished, becoming a great character, and to teach others knowledge and truths that would lead them to integrity, uprightness, and power. Measured in terms of my own life, he was the inspiration of my youth and has sustained himself as my major prophet in the realm of education. Personally, I can pay him no higher tribute than to say, 'He has been my inspiration and has acted as the priest at the Altar of Education to consecrate me and to send me forth as a humble evangel of the light which shone within his own life.'"

President James D. Hoskins of The University of Tennessee, in his tribute to Claxton, after enumerating his many great achievements, said, "Whether as teacher, superintendent, college professor, or college president, . . . he has created upon a large canvas designs of education that are, as has been said, 'a hundred years before their time.' And not content with vision and creative imagination, he has become the formidable champion of these issues in the public mind and in legislation. Behind him is a trail of monuments, not in bronze but in the effective operative systems of public education which he so wisely sponsored."

Hoskins then quoted from a letter from Dr. Charles W. Dabney as follows: "You know my opinion of Claxton and his work. I think he has made the greatest contribution to the cause of public education—the education of the people of this country—of any man since Jefferson." [32]

After several other speeches of high praise by state and school officials, the portrait was presented to the state by Mrs. John Trotwood Moore, State Librarian, and received by Governor Prentice

Cooper, who declared in his speech that "Claxton was indeed a missionary in the field of education, one of the greatest the nation has ever known."

The portrait was then unveiled by Claxton's youngest daughter, Mary Payne, and his grandson, Porter Claxton, Jr. It was painted by Lloyd Embry of Yale School of Fine Arts, and was the gift of the Claxton family, the faculty of Austin Peay State College, the Methodist Sunday School in Clarksville, and other friends. It is the only portrait of an educator in the State Library among those of three Presidents, and many governors, jurists, and others who have served the state and nation with great distinction. Editorials appeared in the Chattanooga *Times*, the Nashville *Banner*, the Nashville *Tennessean*, and other newspapers. "Tennessee is proud to have furnished Claxton to the nation for a long and distinguished term as Commissioner of Education," the *Tennessean* editorial concluded; [33] "but the work that he did within the state's own borders it holds in fondest memory and likes to recall him as the young evangel of educational advance carrying the campaign for a better public school system into the hills and hamlets of the commonwealth. Proverbially republics are said to be ungrateful, but it is hoped that, in the case of its distinguished son whose portrait was yesterday added to her Capitol's collection, Tennessee furnishes an exception to prove the rule."

In the April, 1944, issue of *The Tennessee Teacher* Claxton wrote an article [34] on "What the Schools Have Done to Win the War and the Peace." He first discussed the immediate war service rendered by the schools, but the main theme of his article related to the more fundamental preparatory work done by education in the past. As an illustration he recalled a visit to a Montgomery County farm where he observed two combines, cutting, threshing, and sacking the grain and distributing the straw, as the great machines were drawn over the field by tractors. As Claxton and the farmer stood watching this mechanical marvel, the latter asked, fully expecting a negative reply, "Has education progressed like that?" Claxton surprised him with the answer, "Education has produced that, has made it possible." The farmer somewhat reluctantly admitted, "I guess that is so."

In the same way, Claxton demonstrated that all the skill and resourcefulness used in preparing the wonderful weapons of war as well as their successful employment in mechanized warfare was definitely the result of education without the slightest exception. If this be true in winning a war, he argued, it must be also true in winning the peace. "A peaceful democracy," he declared, "can exist only with universal intelligence and practically universal literacy. . . . For our part in this task we shall need a much higher level of education than we now have in Tennessee."

In 1944 he delivered before the Philomathian Society in Clarksville a lecture on the book of *Job*, which he ranks next to Goethe's *Faust*, his favorite book. Claxton gave a profound interpretation of this great Hebrew drama of the soul, which deals with the origin of evil and the question as to whether every man has his price.

On October 5, 1944, Claxton addressed the Conference on Rural Education in Washington. Miss Charl Ormond Williams, formerly of Memphis, who was executive chairman of the conference, introduced him "as one of the outstanding educators of the country, whose advice on educational matters was sought by presidents." In his speech, Claxton expressed the hope that an improved educational system might some day enable all the youth to become well informed "with the right mental attitude and skill to take raw products and turn them into real wealth to serve humanity in the co-operative society that we must have." [35]

On November 17 of this year he spoke at the Education Forum, a feature of the Sesquicentennial celebration at The University of Tennessee. His subject was "The Role of Education in Tennessee. Life in Retrospect." [36] In this interesting address, Claxton spoke reminiscently of his part in the development of the public school system in Tennessee. "Good to look back on are these forty years," he said; "thrilling to look forward to the accomplishment of the next half century. Not easy, but sure, if we keep the faith, the spirit, and the energy."

The same month he issued a bulletin [37] from Austin Peay State College, entitled "What Can We Afford to Pay for Education?" Copies with a covering letter were sent to all the candidates for the General Assembly of 1947. Education, he demonstrated, could buy seven things: mental development, knowledge, skill, useful habits, and everything constituting the difference between the educated and the uneducated person; life and health; democracy and continued national unity; the continuance of a free church; civic righteousness, culture, and the promotion of civilization; winning the war and then winning the peace; and material wealth and wealth-producing power. "What then can we afford to pay for education?" he asked. "What can we not afford to pay for it? What shall we be willing to pay for it? On the answer to these last questions depends destiny."

A very enlightening article on the work done by Austin Peay College during Claxton's presidency appeared in the May-June, 1945, issue of *The Tennessee Conservationist*. "Austin Peay State Teachers College," wrote [38] Fred E. Waukan, "is a demonstration of what a college can do in a decade and a half to influence a whole county and section. This college opened its doors sixteen years ago and these years have brought great changes in the living conditions in Montgomery and adjoining counties. In fact the teaching influence of this teacher training institution is directly felt over a radius of 50 miles. Indirectly, the whole educational setup in the state has felt the impact of the teaching methods employed in this forward-looking institution. . . . The place this college occupies in the educational affairs of the state is largely due to the vision of its President, Dr. P. P. Claxton, and his group of realistic instructors. They believe, live, and teach conservation; the theory is not only taught but is demonstrated to teachers." He then explained how the campus itself had been turned into a conservation laboratory, where the leaves were not burned but turned into fertilizer, where trees of various species, flowers, shrubs, and fruit and nut-bearing trees were planted as demonstration projects, where the raising of poultry and the growing of food crops became examples of the teaching of applied agriculture, and where the landscaping showed how wornout, eroded farms might be restored to productivity.

When the war ended, Claxton began the difficult job of reconverting the college for peace time work. His report accompanying the budget for 1946–47 and his annual statement show how carefully he looked after every detail and how clearly he foresaw future needs. "At long last," he wrote,[39] "after the drastic reduction of appropriations in 1933 and the years of depression and war, the college is about to come into the possibility of doing fully and well the work for which it was established, the most important and in some ways the most difficult of all in our system of public education."

Early in June, 1946, he delivered the commencement address at the Memphis State College. "Suddenly, in the lifetime of most of you who are graduating today," he declared [40] "the world has become one. All peoples are our neighbors. We cannot ignore them. International, interracial, and cultural interests, human interests, bind us together. Under this condition, effective citizenship requires a high degree of education for all citizens. Ignorance is dangerous and deadly." Claxton then developed one of his favorite topics, the importance of education in the production of wealth and wealth-producing power, and made a plea for more adequate support for the entire school system of Tennessee.

Just about a month later, Claxton retired at the age of eighty-three from the presidency of Austin Peay State College. He had served the college long and faithfully and unselfishly. In 1933, at his request, his salary had been reduced from $4800 to $3600. After six years it was increased to only $4200.[41] He had always attempted to afford the students the best in instruction and in extracurricular activities. He was opposed to giving them anything "cheap or jazzy" in the way of concerts or lectures. In 1935, the famous sculptor, Lorado Taft, lectured there. During the war, one year, distinguished speakers from India, Czechoslovakia, France, Norway, England, and some other countries [42] lectured at the college. He had the conviction that the students should have good wholesome food and refused to allow a large container filled with coca cola bottles to be placed in a college hall; this he thought would tempt the students from families with low income to waste the money which should go for nourishing food. Everything he said and did during his administration of the college was based on careful observation and consideration without fear or favor and under conviction of right and justice.

"After all that can be done by Boards of Education, college presidents, and other officials," Claxton declared,[43] "the real work of a college, as of all other schools, is done by the teachers. The most important work of a college president, especially of the president of a small college, is the selection of teachers, relieving them of all unnecessary duties that may interfere with teaching. The high type of work done by Austin Peay State College is due to the care with which all new teachers have been selected. Here, as elsewhere, in recommending teachers for election, I have considered only their ability to teach and do other things necessary in the education of men and women. For myself I have adopted this oath which I think all democratic officials should be required to take: Officially I have no relatives, no friends, no enemies; if I owe any one anything, I will not pay it from this office; I will never prostitute the public welfare to private interests."

ᘒᏰ XXII Ᏸᘒ

President Emeritus

◇◇

C LAXTON'S RETIREMENT began on July 1, 1946.[1] Though he was then eighty-three years "young," he fortunately was still physically vigorous and had all his mental faculties unimpaired; consequently he was capable of enjoying the release from administrative duties and the opportunity to do the writing which he had wished to accomplish for many years. His eyes had always been directed toward the future. Dr. Frank E. Bass began his speech at the unveiling of Claxton's portrait in the Tennessee State Library with this parody:

> "You are old Father Claxton," the young man cried,
> "The few locks which are left you are gray;
> You are hale, Father Claxton, a hearty old man,
> Now tell me the reason, I pray."

> "In the days of my youth," Father Claxton replied,
> "I remembered that youth could not last;
> I thought of the future, whatever I did,
> That I never might grieve for the past."

This was quite true of Claxton at the beginning of his retirement; he had work yet to do; he was old only according to the calendar, for his mind and spirit were young. He had often joked about his advancing years. When the manager of a life insurance company wrote him, "Will you kindly let us have a statement to the effect that you are still living?" he replied,[2] "Pat fell from the roof of the house. Mike called and asked him if he were dead. He called back, 'No, but I'm speechless!' Fortunately I am living and have received your inquiry of November 22 in regard to the matter. The fact that I have been endorsing and cashing quarterly installments on policy is also some evidence of the fact. I am hoping to live long enough to collect in installments the full value of the policy No. 181-A."

To a reporter, interviewing him after his retirement, Claxton remarked that the rule made by the Tennessee State Board of Education for the retirement of college presidents at the age of 70 was "a pretty good thing, for, you know, some men do get old at 70." [3]

Claxton also enjoyed the somewhat rare pleasure of receiving the praise of his friends while he was still living. In a resolution adopted by the Tennessee State Board of Education in connection with his retirement, sincere regret was expressed and, after reviewing his distinguished career previous to 1930, it stated, "The benefit of all this experience and the full power of his vigorous mind have been lavished upon his work at Austin Peay State College. He established that institution and has guided its development. His interest and supreme faith in rural life and in education of rural children have permeated his own work and that of the institution. The Tennessee State Board of Education expresses sincere appreciation for his loyal and unselfish service. It also expresses high admiration for him as a man; a true and able servant of humanity."

"Though he will retire from active office," declared [3] the editor of the Clarksville *Leaf-Chronicle*, "Dr. Claxton will remain as president emeritus of the college, and that institution and the state will continue to get the benefit of his wisdom and experience. And undoubtedly he will find time to write and thereby leave a legacy for posterity. . . . At the age of 83, rich in knowledge and experience, and his mind still keen, Dr. Claxton is in position to serve the cause of education in a much broader sense than as president of a college."

Just two days before Claxton's retirement became effective, more than one hundred friends gave a banquet in honor of him and Mrs. Claxton in the college cafeteria, preceded by a formal reception in Myra Harned Hall. In the speeches following the dinner, praise was heaped upon his gray head. Governor Jim McCord said, "There have been no little things in Dr. Claxton's life. He has always been in the forefront of movements that have meant much in the state and nation." Miss Annie Laurie Huff, Professor of English in the college, praised his "sound sense, his wide experience in education, his keen sense of humor and understanding of human nature . . . and his remarkable tenacity and power to convince. . . . Above all I praise Dr. Claxton for his greatness and goodness of soul and nobleness of purpose which shine through all his works." Miss Johnie Givens, President of the Student Body, speaking for the students, said Claxton's "time was never so taken up that he could not offer a jovial, timely comment or a kindly word of counsel," and closed with a quotation from *Hamlet*, "We know what we are, but know not what we may be for having known him."

The place cards prepared by Miss Hazel Smith, college art instructor, were in the shape of Tennessee with a silhouette of Claxton's head encircled by a laurel wreath. Following the speeches, Toastmaster Felix G. Woodward presented a radio to Dr. and Mrs. Claxton on behalf of the faculty. Mrs. Claxton briefly expressed her thanks and appreciation. Claxton praised the faculty, declaring that depression and war had prevented the accomplishment of as much as he had wished. "But in quality we have done well," he said. Then he added that he was only about the same age as Moses was when he started on his mission to lead the children of Israel out of Egypt, and he did not believe his work was yet finished.[4]

Mrs. Claxton had been very happy in Clarksville, which she thought "a charming town with cultivated, sweet, gentle-spirited people." [5] She organized the College Woman's Club and the Greek letter clubs for women students, assisted in reorganizing the Montgomery County Historical Society, and assisted in organizing in Clarksville a nursery school, a community house project, the Girl Scouts of America, the U.S.O. for soldiers from Camp Campbell, and a Child Welfare Council. There were interesting changes in the Claxton family during the Clarksville period. Elizabeth married Thomas D. Lewis of Washington—her second marriage. Porter married Evelyn Mabry, Philander, Jr. married Mary Ann Watkins, and Mary Payne married Henry M. Pierce.

Though Claxton expected to devote himself largely to writing, he continued to accept speaking engagements. In the following September, he delivered the commencement address at Madison College near Nashville, an institution whose work he had long highly regarded.[6]

On October 18 Claxton spoke at a testimonial dinner in honor of Dr. James D. Hoskins, retiring president of The University of Tennessee. "Hoskins, my long-time friend and fellow worker," he said,[7] "let me welcome you to this new position of President Emeritus, a position to which comparatively few college presidents attain; a position of freedom and power, freedom from the details of administration, freedom to think and plan, to dream; and as I interpret it, power to advise and suggest without responsibility for results of such advice and suggestions if they are taken. Until recently, you and I have been limited in some degree at least to special tasks. Now the world is our parish." After praising Hoskins for his great achievements for The University of Tennessee and the state and recalling the strong support Hoskins had always given him in his educational campaigns in Tennessee, he concluded, "A last word—you and I are not old. As men, we are not primarily of the material body. We are of the mind, intellect, imagination, ideals, purposes, and will. These are dateless, ageless, ever young; at least, so long as they are in vital connection with the springs of eternal life. May you in the flesh be here many years yet to lend your wisdom to the guiding powers of the University and to enjoy the backward vision of your own good work. To all who would see Hoskins' living monument, this advice: 'Look about you over this campus and over the state from the Smokies to the Great River.'"

The words of praise which Claxton received at the time of his retirement were not merely expressions of flattery as often heard on such occasions. Already cited in this biography are estimates of his character and his achievements equally high. There were many others, some of which will now be quoted as examples.

Of very great interest is an appraisal by R. D. Douglas, now a distinguished lawyer in Greensboro, North Carolina, who knew Claxton when he was a professor in the Normal and Industrial College in that city. "In the summer of 1896," he wrote,[8] "I returned home after being a student at Georgetown University for five years, where I majored in philosophy, and our friendship soon began. I cannot remember just what first brought us together, as I was some ten or twelve years younger than he. But I think it was my George-town connection that first attracted his notice, as I later came to know that he was an ardent admirer of the Jesuits and thought that Ignatius Loyola's *ratio studiorum* was one of the most important single steps in the development of educational methods.

From then on I saw quite a bit of him for some five or six years until he left Greensboro. The times we were together were largely spent in 'bull sessions' on philosophy or education, particularly on the psychological aspects of educational methods, which was one of his chief interests. . . .

First let me say that I then had no doubt and still have no doubt of his intellectual honesty and intellectual courage, qualities which I do not think are nearly so common as financial honesty and physical courage. But his bump of diplomacy was a depression. If he had a distinct opinion he expressed that opinion in no uncertain terms, no matter who liked it or who did not like it. Both what he said and the way he said it were aggressive. But he could take as well as give and did not seem at all offended at being disagreed with. . . . He would have impressed a stranger as being emotional rather than intellectual in temperament; or, may I say, given the impression of intense feeling held in check but of intense feeling, just the same. This intense feeling was, I think, largely true if we substitute the word 'opinion' for 'feeling.' He was neutral about practically nothing regarding which he thought he had sufficient information to form a definite opinion.

In his chosen field of education he was both mentally and temperamentally an explorer and a builder and developer rather than a defender of the faith as he found it, and his stock of original ideas seemed almost limitless. At first, I thought that some of his ideas were positively crazy, but came to find out that he thought so too, and was only springing them on me to get my reactions, my objections, and my criticisms for the purpose of clarifying them in his own mind. His mental approach to a subject was scientific rather than philosophic; try to see what happens rather than employ deductive reasoning."

Another appraisal of a much later date in the *Southern Review* [9] of June, 1920, is as follows: "It has been said of Dr. Claxton that 'the more honor is done him, the more flat-footed among the people he stands,' for his greatest inspiration is the people. His is not the slogan of the politician, but a deep-rooted belief in plain 'folks' and the soundness of their principles and their sincerity. With his uncompromising idealism and a personal character of almost stoic self-control (it is said that he has never been known to lose his temper, so much a master of himself he is) there is a gentleness of heart and breadth of sympathy that reminds one of the character of Benjamin Franklin. He is never too busy to lend his counsel or material aid to those who are in need of it. He believes in clean simple living, close to nature—on a farm preferably—with a cold plunge very early in the morning and good hard work all day. In fact, he is a work fiend who has not taken a vacation for more than twenty years."

In commenting on Claxton's commencement address in 1931 at the Winston-Salem Teachers College for Negroes, the *Journal* stated,[10] "One of the initials of Dr. Claxton's name might well stand for pioneer, for that is what he was. It was obvious that he should be chosen as Commissioner of Education for the nation. His stature as an educator lifted him above the ordinary level, no matter how brilliant it may have been. His address to the colored graduates yesterday was a classic. But greater by far than the address was the man out of whose life the address had grown during the half century he has been fighting the battles of popular education."

When earlier in this same year some of his former staff wrote him a letter of congratulation on his receipt of a desk set as an award for distinguished service to education, they declared,[11] "The services you have rendered to the cause of education in this country are well known and appreciated by schoolmen as well as the general public, and you well deserve to have been singled out for recognition by the combined school exhibitors at Detroit. We shall always remember with extreme pleasure your helpful and appreciative attitude towards the members of your staff during your administration as United States Commissioner of Education and shall recall with enthusiasm the constructive work in education accomplished during your term of office."

In writing of Claxton in 1935, Josephus Daniels declared,[12] "At first he was the teacher in the school room who knew how to reach and stir the desire for knowledge in his pupils. That is the foundation of all good teachers. . . . If Dr. Claxton had remained a teacher, he could have won reputation as one of the type that drew out the best in the limited number of youths privileged to sit at his feet. . . . His contribution to university usefulness was that he helped to democratize these higher institutions of learning and caused their leaders to see that their highest mission was not merely to train the youths who matriculated but to carry the training of the university to the people of the whole commonwealth and regard itself as truly the head of and leader of such public schools as would prepare more and more youths for entrance into the higher institutions of learning. . . . Dr. Claxton was truly an educational statesman, an evangelist making straight the path in his young manhood and in expounding a philosophy of education which must be the foundation of universal education to-day, to-morrow, and for all the to-morrows. The passion to open the doors of knowledge to all dominated his life, and many in his part of the world rise up and in their gratitude call him blessed."

Probably the three men who knew Claxton best, because of long and intimate association, were Edwin A. Alderman, Charles W. Dabney, and Joseph D. Eggleston. Many expressions of the highest praise have already been quoted from Dr. Dabney. Claxton and Alderman were like brothers. Only one expression of his admiration for Claxton, however, is extant. In this letter to Mrs. Claxton he wrote [13] in 1924, "It was very good of you to send me your brief note and the little pamphlet showing how easy it was to pick up $2,534,000 in Tulsa, Okla. Alas, it is a different thing in Albemarle County, Va. In North Carolina, it is all changed, as you know. They will vote bonds in Mount Olive for a new railroad station between suns. I have been much interested in my old friend's activities in the Southwest. I congratulate those people upon the services of a man of such distinction of mind, such varied experience, and such boundless energy. Please give him my affectionate good will."

Fortunately, Dr. Eggleston, President Emeritus of Hampden-Sidney College, has written [14] more fully his estimate of Claxton's character and work, as follows: "I was for two sessions a member of his teaching corps in Asheville, when he was superintendent of schools there; and for one and a half of those two sessions I roomed with him, took meals with him, read and studied with him, discussed all manner of problems—educational and otherwise—and I discovered no faults or weaknesses in him. If that be eulogy, I am not responsible; I am stating the truth. He had a powerful will; infinite patience; a great but practical vision; good will towards all —even towards those who differed with him and tried to hamper him. I never knew him to lose his temper, even in the most strenuous fights he made in behalf of the children; I never heard him utter an untoward word; I never heard him gossip; I never heard him abuse anyone, in argument or debate, or behind one's back; and, if his heart was as clean as his lips, then he is among those of whom Christ said, 'Blessed are the pure in heart, for they shall see God.' Before his first wife died, I was as one of the family. A more beautiful family life I have never seen.

How he has had the strength, physical, mental, spiritual, to do all that he has done, I do not know. I have marveled at his resiliency, the reserve power he always has had, to 'come back.' . . .

I have heard people say that Claxton was fine on theory, but not practical; this usually meant that he was right but they were unwilling to put into practice what he wished, as the money cost might take some of their income.

His reading was wide and deep; essentials, not trivial things; and he did not confine himself to the educational field. He has always been a *radical*, in the true meaning of that much abused word. He went to the *root* of things.

Claxton's love of children has always been a passion with him; all children, not some children. And his gentleness with them, as with all others, has been one of the many beautiful traits of his character.

In the field of what is called 'religious' belief, he has been what is called a 'liberal'; not orthodox. I have differed with him in some of his interpretations of the Bible. Yet I recall what dear Dr. Seaman Knapp said on his deathbed to Dr. Wallace Buttrick: 'Buttrick, I deplore your theology, but I would rather have you pray with me here than any other man I know.' And together they prayed, as the dear old Doctor passed into the presence of his Lord."

Claxton believes that there is still much to be done in the development of universal public education, a subject on which he has spoken in "The Unfinished Task," and that there is still room for improving the methods of teaching. "Unfortunately the science of education is the most complex of all sciences," he wrote.[15] "Plato once said, 'No one should teach until he is fifty years old.' A teacher cannot have too much knowledge of the subject he is teaching; nor know too much about child psychology and the methods of teaching. The profession of teaching is far more complex than that of medicine. A teacher deals with the child's mind and body, while the physician deals mainly with the body. The best teachers are those who teach not for money but for the love of the profession." At least half of the teachers should be men, he thinks. Salaries must be sufficiently high to attract well prepared men and women to the profession, and people in general must have a higher respect for the teacher and the profession of teaching.

As to the controversial subject of teaching religion in the public schools, Claxton believes that nothing sectarian should be taught; only the fundamental principles of ethics and reverence for God. This should permeate the teaching of all subjects. Other religious teaching should be left to the churches.

At present, in the South, he believes it is necessary to have separate schools for the Negroes, towards whom he has always been friendly. It is better for the Negroes to have their own schools for they need not only courses of study but methods of instruction suited to their racial characteristics and needs. "This is one of the most difficult problems we have but it cannot be solved by keeping the Negroes in semi-slavery," he thinks.[15] In a commencement address in 1947 at the Tennessee Agricultural and Industrial State College, he said, "We now understand that the education of Negroes is a good thing for the white people of the South and of the nation as a whole. The best and fullest possible education of all citizens of our Commonwealth, of all members of our social and economic society is good for us all. . . . White and black, we are coming to understand that we are bound up in the sheaf of life together, whether we will or not, and that the welfare of the whole and of each individual unit depends on the health, strength, intelligence, skill, and mental, moral, and spiritual attitudes of all and each."

Claxton's mind is as alert as ever. Besides lecturing, he is busily engaged in writing on educational subjects. Among the manuscripts which he is preparing are *The Rights of Children*, *War for Oldsters Only* (a satire), and *A Rational Alphabet*. He has for many years been interested in simplified spelling of English words, and has devised a very ingenious alphabet of different characters for the various sounds. Several years ago he was invited by Funk and Wagnalls to serve on their Committee of Twenty-five, appointed to pass judgment on more than 3,000 words of disputed pronunciation.

Early in 1947, Claxton wrote an editorial letter for the Shelbyville (Tennessee) *Gazette* [16] on the "Ignorance Tax" in support of the recommendation of the directors of the Survey of Education in Tennessee that $71,184,110 be expended for the support of education on all levels. Statistically he demonstrated that of the 1,680,000 men and women of independent working age in Tennessee in 1940 more than 1,330,000 had less than a high school education. "Many studies have shown," he pointed out, "that the average productive earnings of men and women with high school education and adequate technical training is fully $500 more a year than the average earnings of those with less education. This indicates for Tennessee a loss of earning power of $665,000,000 a year. . . . Years ago we became conscious of the fact that our Mud Tax was greater than would be a tax for good roads and highways. This report and bills submitted to the legislature and in preparation for submission indicate that we are at last becoming conscious of the burden of the Ignorance Tax and of the means of its relief."

This editorial might be said to sum up the main objective of Claxton for more than sixty years. His long crusade has been against ignorance as the most deadly enemy of the human race. To this enemy he has given no quarter. With sharp lance and shining sword, he has led the legions of light and learning to victory on many a hard fought field. When the achievements of this crusader for universal public education shall be viewed through the revealing perspective of the years, surely he will be seen to occupy a place among the greatest men of his generation.

Notes

◇◇◇

Memoranda is used below for miscellaneous memoranda in the Claxton Papers; *Stenographic Notes* for record of conversations between Claxton and the author; *Memorandum for Dabney* for Claxton's lengthy memorandum prepared for Charles W. Dabney; and *Notes for Author* for notes prepared by Claxton for the author's use.

I. BEDFORD COUNTY BOY

1. Philander Priestley of Montgomery County, Tennessee, was the State Commander of the Tennessee Masonic Lodge about 1828. Claxton's father was not a Mason, but the name was given his son by a friend of the family who was a member of that lodge (*Memoranda*).
2. *Ibid.*
3. Genealogy of Philander Priestley Claxton, prepared for the author by Mrs. P. P. Claxton, with additional data furnished by Dr. Claxton in a letter to the author of December 6, 1946, and by Mrs. Claire (Claxton) Mayo in a letter to the author of February 9, 1947.
   5. William Claxton (b 1754) of New Kent Co., Va.; soldier Am. Rev., 1st Va. State Regiment, m Mary Ann Anderson (b 1755).
   4. James Claxton (d 1815), came from North Carolina; family originally from Va.; served in E. Tenn. militia, War 1812; wife Sarah Claxton, administrator of estate in 1817.
   3. James Claxton (1793–1871) born probably in Anderson Co., East Tenn. With Gen. Andrew Jackson in expedition against Creek Indians, War 1812; m April 26, 1819, Temperance Rathler [also spelled Rackley in Government document] (1804–1877). Had eight sons: John, Harve, Richard, Joshua Calvin, Henderson, Anderson, Mike, and Noah, and four daughters, Elizabeth, Tennessee, Adeline, and Ophelia.
   2. Joshua Calvin Claxton, born Bedford Co., Tenn., April 12, 1830; died 1907; married Aug. 16, 1854 Ann Elizabeth Jones (born Bedford Co., Tenn., Sept. 16, 1836, died Sept., 1890), daughter Dr. William Berry Jones. One of Dr. Berry Jones's sons was a Union soldier and one was a Confederate soldier, War between the States.
   Children:

1. Temperance Mahala Claxton, born May 4, 1855. Married Jan. 4, 1877 to P. M. Maxwell (born Oct. 9, 1851, died Oct. 6, 1881). Died June 8, 1945.
2. Amanda Tennessee Claxton, born Oct. 29, 1856, died Nov. 30, 1930. Married Sept. 7, 1876 to Jacob Parsons Crowell (born 1851, died June 1909).
3. Allie, who died in infancy of German measles and whooping cough caught from soldiers.
4. Philander Priestley Claxton, Born Bedford Co., Tenn., Sept. 28, 1862.
5. James Jonas Claxton, born Nov. 22, 1867, died Dec. 31, 1932. Married Dec. 25, 1891 to Emma Cleveland Shearin (born Oct. 23, 1869, died May 23, 1919).
6. Minerva Jane Claxton, born April 19, 1870. Married Feb. 18, 1891 to Robert Allen Locke (born Oct. 6, 1866).
7. Melvina Jones Claxton, born July 21, 1872. Married Sept. 5, 1886 to Thomas Russell (born June 13, 1870, died March 1, 1944).
8. Ophelia Adeline Claxton, born May 20, 1875. Married July 28, 1892 to Henry Preston Clark (born April 5, 1870, died Nov. 21, 1932).
9. Alice Cassandra Claxton, born Aug. 7, 1877. Married Mar. 23, 1893 to Samuel W. Crowell (born Oct. 9, 1872).
1. Philander Priestley Claxton, born Bedford Co., Tenn., Sept. 28, 1862. A.B., U. of Tenn., 1882, A.M., 1887; grad. student, Johns Hopkins, 1884–85; student of edn. and schs. in Germany, 1885–86; visited schs. in Europe, 1896 and 1930; Litt.D., Bates, 1906; LL.D., Western Reserve, 1912, U. of N. C., 1914, Allegheny, 1915, U. Md., 1921. Educator since 1882; U. S. Commissioner of Ed. 1911–21. Methodist; author; lecturer; Democrat; Cosmos Club, Washington, D. C. (See *Who's Who in America* for other details.)
   Married Varina Staunton Moore, Dec. 2, 1885, Goldsboro, N. C., (born Jan. 5, 1857, died September 12, 1891). Daughter Dr. William Moore and Emily Webb Moore, Goldsboro, N. C.
   Child:
1. Claire Claxton, born Wilson, N. C. Sept. 19, 1886. University of Tenn. Married, Washington D. C., April 9, 1913 Dale Redmond Mayo (born Knoxville, Tenn. Dec. 27, 1886, died Mar. 3, 1934).
   Children:
   1. Varina, born Knoxville, Tenn. Feb. 20, 1915; Salem College, University of Tenn. Married Knoxville, Tenn., Feb. 19, 1938 Dr. Harry Jenkins (born Cookeville, Tenn., Jan. 3, 1906); Vanderbilt Univ., Lt. Col. U. S. Army Medical Corps 1944–1946, Commanding Officer of 182 Medical Station Hospital, Italy.

Child:
1. Carol Claxton Jenkins, born Knoxville, Tenn., Nov. 24, 1938.
2. Daniel Redmond Mayo, born Knoxville, Tenn., Aug. 5, 1917. Univ. of Tenn. Sgt. Signal Corps, U. S. Army, 1944–1946, England, France, Belgium (Battle of the Bulge), and Germany; the Philippines and Japan (Army of Occupation).
3. Porter Claxton Mayo, born Knoxville, Tenn., Apr. 23, 1919. Lieut. U. S. Army, 1941–1945, with seven months in France. Married Knoxville, Tenn., Sept. 29, 1941 to Josephine Carmichael (born Knoxville, Tenn., March 10, 1921).
Children:
1. Porter Claxton Mayo, Jr., born Knoxville, Tenn., Nov. 23, 1942.
2. Josephine Dale Mayo, born Knoxville, Tenn. Aug. 13, 1946.
Married the second time Sept. 26, 1894 Anne Elizabeth Porter, (b. May 29, 1862, Tarboro, N. C.; died Feb. 14, 1904). Daughter Joseph John Porter and Cynthia Ann Patience Jeffreys Porter, Tarboro, N. C.
Children:
1. Helen Claxton, born Greensboro, N. C., Dec. 4, 1895. College for Women, Greensboro, N. C. Married Jan. 1, 1921, in Washington, D. C. John Curtis Walker (born Washington, D. C. on March 3, 1895; died June 23, 1939).
Children:
1. Curtis Walker, born Chevy Chase, Md., Oct. 20, 1921.
2. Claxton Walker, born Chevy Chase, Md., July, 1924. U. S. Marine Corps, World War II, 1943–1945. Iwo Jima and other invasions in the Pacific area. Married Margaret Jacquelyn Northup, Aug. 15, 1947.
3. John C. Walker, born Chevy Chase, Md., Oct. 4, 1927; Duke University, Class of 1948.
2. Calvin Porter Claxton, born Greensboro, N. C., April 23, 1898. Candidate, Central Officer Training School (C.O.T.S.) Camp Gordon, Georgia, World War I, 1918. B.S. in Agriculture, Univ. of Tenn., 1919; Principal, Bell Buckle Tenn. High School, 1919–27; M.S. in Education, Univ. of Tenn., 1927; Executive Officer, Univ. of Tenn. Jr. College, 1927–34; Asst. Prof. of Rural Ed., Univ. of Tenn., 1934–35; graduate work, Peabody College, Nashville, Tenn., 1935–37; Director of Rural Education, West Georgia College, 1937–43; graduate work, winter quarter, Ohio State University, 1943; education specialist, in agriculture, Education Division, Office of the Co-ordinator of Inter-American Affairs, Washington, D. C., 1943–46, Chief, Rural Education Section, Inter-American Education Foundation, Inc., Washington, D. C. Married March 17, 1934, Nashville, Tenn., Laura Evelyn

Mabry (born Knoxville, Tenn., May 12, 1907; B.S. University of
Tenn.).
Children:
1. Calvin Porter Claxton, Jr., born Knoxville, Tenn., Apr. 20,
1935.
2. Claire Evelyn, born Carrollton, Georgia, Aug. 2, 1937.
3. Brooks Mabry, born Carrollton, Georgia, Sept. 9, 1940.
3. Anne Elizabeth Claxton, born Greensboro, N. C., June 16, 1900;
Sweet Briar College, Va., A.B. University of Tenn. Married May
18, 1927, Tulsa, Oklahoma, to Thomas Elliott (born Aug. 21,
1897, died May 1, 1928). Married Feb. 27, 1931, Washington,
D. C., Thomas Deane Lewis (born April 23, 1900, died Oct. 26,
1947).
Children:
1. Mary Elizabeth, born Bethesda, Md., Sept. 10, 1932.
2. Helen Claxton, born Bethesda, Md., Jan. 24, 1935.
3. Agnes Chichester, born Bethesda, Md., Aug. 26, 1941.
4. Robert Edward Claxton, born July 29, 1902, died Oct. 12, 1913.
Married the third time, April 23, 1912, Mary Hannah Johnson, Nashville, Tenn. Daughter of George Sterling Johnson and Hannah Iredell
(Spottswood) Payne Johnson of Nashville, Tenn. (See *Who's Who in
America*.)
Children:
1. Philander Priestley Claxton, Jr., born Washington, D. C. on Dec.
11, 1914. Lt. Commander, U.S.N.R., 1943. B.S. 1934, Univ.
of Tenn.; M.A., 1935, Princeton University; LL.B. 1938, Yale
Univ.; Special Attorney in U. S. Dept. of Justice, Washington,
D. C. 1939; Legal Dept. T.V.A. 1940–43; Graduate Naval School
of Military Government and Administration, Columbia University,
1943; in the Invasion of France, 1944–1945. Married, April 8,
1943, Chattanooga, Tenn., Lt. U.S.N.R. (WAVES) Mary Ann
Elizabeth Watkins, born Chattanooga, Tenn. Sept. 12, 1920;
Tenn. Wesleyan College, Univ. of Tenn., Smith College; daughter
Col. Morgan Watkins and Isabelle Gettys Watkins of Athens,
Tenn.
Children:
1. Philander P. Claxton III, born Washington, D. C., Oct. 6,
1945.
2. Mary Isabelle Claxton, born Washington, Jan. 26, 1947.
2. Mary Hannah Payne Claxton, born Washington, D. C., July 8,
1919. Clarksville High School, and Ward Belmont, Nashville,
Tenn., 1937. Sorority, Gamma Phi Beta, Vanderbilt Univ.; B.S.
degree, George Peabody College, 1942. Married, August 28, 1943,
Clarksville, Tenn., Henry Maurice Pierce, Capt., U. S. Army, born
Lexington, Mississippi, March 16, 1915; Camp Campbell, Ky.

1942–1943; Capt., Pacific Area 1944–1945. Son of William Arthur Pierce and Alice Lee Watson Pierce of West Falls Church, Va. *Child:*

1. Hannah Lee Pierce, born June 7, 1947, Washington, D. C.

4. P. P. Claxton, "Bedford County as I Remember It" in *Shelbyville Gazette,* Sept. 29 and Oct. 6, 1938.

5. *Memoranda.*

6. *Stenographic Notes.*

7. P. P. Claxton, "A Return to Nature" in *Atlantic Educational Journal,* Feb., 1903.

8. Charles Lee Lewis, *Matthew Fontaine Maury: Pathfinder of the Seas,* 4.

9. Robert H. White, *Development of the Tennessee State Educational Organization, 1796–1929,* 64, 76

10. *The Rise of the Common Man,* 226.

11. Robert H. White, *op. cit.,* 113, 114.

12. Will T. Hale and Dixon L. Merritt, *A History of Tennessee and Tennesseans,* III, 774.

13. *Memoranda.* The other teachers here were Mr. Bridges and Mr. Goodrum. According to Claxton's sister (Mrs. Tom Russell), he never had any unpleasantness with any teacher except Bridges who tried once to make him "tell on" one of his schoolmates for some trifling offense. (*A Study of the Life and Work of P. P. Claxton* by George W. Rawlins, Jr. [Peabody College Term Paper], 6).

14. David Perkins Page, *Theory and Practice of Teaching or the Motives and Methods of Good School Keeping* (Albany, New York, 1847), 358. Edward H. Reisner, in his *Evolution of the Common School* (New York, 1930), speaks highly of Page. Reisner was then Professor of Education in Columbia University.

15. *Memoranda.* Steele was the principal of an academy at Elmyra, New York.

16. *Memoranda.*

17. Hale and Merritt, *op. cit.,* II, 775.

18. Autographed note owned by the author.

19. *Memoranda.*

II. University of Tennessee Student

1. *Memoranda.*

2. Edward T. Sanford, *Blount College and the University of Tennessee: An Historical Address,* 75 and footnote. On Mar. 11, 1879, Governor Albert S. Marks approved the legislative act, changing the name from East Tennessee University, which it had borne since 1840, when East Tennessee College became East Tennessee University. Former Governor James D. Porter was made the first head of the new Board of Visitors on June 18, 1879, the day following an elaborate alumni homecoming

celebration, at which Moses White was the orator. Cf. "Tennessee Calendar" by William E. Beard in Nashville *Banner*, Mar. 11, 1940.

3. Edward T. Sanford, *op. cit.*, 38.
4. *Memoranda.*
5. *University of Tennessee Catalogue, 1880–1881.* Prof. Brown was on leave for one year from June, 1880, and his place was taken by W. E. Moses, Maury Nicholson, B.S. being appointed Assistant Instructor in the Chemical Department.
6. *Memoranda.*
7. *Laws and Regulations of the University of Tennessee*, enacted by the Board of Trustees, Aug. 21, 1879, in University of Tennessee Library. These were unchanged on July 2, 1880.
8. *Memoranda.*
9. *University of Tennessee Catalogue, 1880–1881.*
10. *Ibid.*, 1881–1882. Claxton's name appeared in each catalogue with his address as "Poplin's X Roads, Tennessee."
11. *Memoranda.*
12. See bound volume of issues in the Library of the University of Tennessee. The first issue was entitled "Philo Star. Vol. I, No. I, January, 1882. Published monthly from September to June by Philomathesian Literary Society. P. P. Claxton, Managing Editor. Printed by T. Haws, Book and Job Printer."
13. *Philo Star*, Mar., 1882.
14. *Ibid.*, Jan., 1882.
15. *Ibid.*, Feb., 1882.
16. *Ibid.*, May, 1882.
17. *Ibid.*, Apr. and May, 1882.
18. *Ibid.*, May, 1882.
19. *Ibid.*, May, 1882.
20. *Ibid.*, June, 1882.
21. *Memoranda.*
22. List of the graduates:

Samuel Lusk Colville, A.B., afterwards a successful business man and outstanding citizen in McMinnville, Tenn.

Rogers Van Gilder, A.B., later a prominent glass and leather merchant in Knoxville, Tenn.

Philander Priestley Claxton, A.B.

Thomas Merriwether Humphreys, A.B., whose later career is unknown to author.

John Patterson, Jr., A.B., who became a physician and died in Florida.

Samuel Harvey Keener, A.B., afterwards a dentist in Knoxville, Tenn.

James Harman Dinwiddie, B.S., later an architect and building contractor in Chicago.

William Allison McCorkle, B.S., who was killed in Cuba during the War with Spain.

Richard Welbourne Lewis, B.S., who became an evangelist and inventor of religious games.

John Calvin Russell McCall, B.S., afterwards a lawyer, politician, and Federal office holder in Huntingdon, Tenn.

James Kennedy Meek, B.S., a spendthrift and a failure.

John Benjamin Skelton, B.S., who became a physician in Scottsboro, Alabama and died young.

Isaac Bright Hines, B.S., the oldest member of the class, who went to California where he was living at the time of the 50th anniversary of the class.

Joseph Edward Lopez, B.S., and B.C.E., afterwards president of a New York insurance company.

William Marmaduke Crutcher, B.C.E., an engineer whose career is not known by the author.

Andrew Boyd Eaton, B.C.E., who became a merchant in his home town, Lenoir City, Tenn.

Two other members of the class did not graduate. James Purdy Atkinson failed in Greek. The father of Edward Sanford decided to send his son to Harvard for a year, where he preferred to have him receive his degree, though he had satisfied the requirements for the A.B. at the University of Tennessee. He and Claxton were the youngest members of the class.

III. North Carolina Public School Teacher

1. Letter from Claxton to Charles W. Dabney, Feb. 14, 1941, a copy of which was furnished the author by Dr. Joseph D. Eggleston.
2. For further information regarding Edward Pearson Moses, see Charles William Dabney, *Universal Education in the South*, I, 193–198.
3. Claxton to Dabney, Feb. 14, 1941.
4. "The campaign for the graded schools supported by taxpayers was begun with an address by Mr. Alexander Graham of Charlotte (father of President Frank Graham of the State University), who was the superintendent of the first graded school in North Carolina" (Josephus Daniels, *Tar Heel Editor*, 70).
5. Daniels, *op. cit.*, 71.
6. *Memoranda.*
7. Edwin A. Alderman, *Charles Brantly Aycock* in H. W. Odum, *Southern Pioneers in Social Interpretation*, 75.
8. Claxton to Dabney, Feb. 14, 1941.
9. *Memoranda.*

10. *Tar Heel Editor,* 133.
11. *Memoranda.*
12. Mrs. Mela Allen Royall to author, Jan. 9, 1945, from Raleigh, North Carolina.
13. *Memoranda.*
14. Letter by Supt. W. A. Graham, Public Schools, Kinston, N. C., to author, Feb. 15, 1945. Mrs. Amelie Hardee Pridgen, another one of Claxton's teachers, spoke of him in the same vein.

IV. Johns Hopkins Graduate Student

1. Fabian Franklin, *Life of Daniel Coit Gilman,* 179, and Charles K. Edmunds, "A Half-Century of Johns Hopkins" in *American Review of Reviews* (Nov., 1926), LXXIV, 525 et seq.
2. H. E. Shepherd and others, *History of Baltimore,* 55.
3. Letters of Apr. 6 and 12, 1945, from Miss Frieda C. Thies, Chief Reference Librarian, Johns Hopkins University, to author.
4. *Memoranda.*
5. *The Johns Hopkins Circulars* [University Records]. Baltimore, 1884–1885.
6. *Memoranda.* In the *Johns Hopkins Circulars,* 1884–1885, Claxton's name does not appear in courses given by Hall, Ely, Perkins, and Todd. Such records were not then carefully kept. For example, in the alumni records Claxton is still classified as an engineering student.
7. *Memoranda.*
8. Ray Stannard Baker, *Woodrow Wilson . . . Youth,* 177.
9. *Ibid.,* 176, 177.
10. *Memoranda.*
11. Woodrow Wilson was highly critical of both Ely and Adams (Ray Stannard Baker, *op. cit.,* 178, 179, 182).
12. *Johns Hopkins Circulars,* 1884–1885.
13. Ray Stannard Baker, *op. cit.,* 174 footnote.
14. *Op. cit.,* 176.
15. *Memoranda.*

V. Student of German Schools

1. *Memoranda.*
2. Letter from A. E. Davis of Forest Glen, Maryland, to Cousin Fanny [?], Aug. 10, 1898, and letter from A. D. Moore to Claxton, Feb. 5, 1894, and *Memoranda.*
3. Letter from Mela Allen Royall of Raleigh, N. C., Jan. 9, 1945, to author.
4. Letter from Mrs. Wade Barrier (Mettie Lewis Barrier), Wilmington, N. C., Jan. 20, 1945, to author.
5. G. Stanley Hall, *Aspects of German Culture* (Boston, 1881), 73, 74.
6. *Papers for the Teacher, Third Series: German Schools and Pedagogy: Organization and Instruction of Common Schools in Germany . . . ,*

republished from *Barnard's American Journal of Education*, 158 et seq.
7. *North Carolina Journal of Education*, Oct., 1897, "Schools of Saxony" by Claxton, and *Report of U. S. Commissioner of Education*, 1889–1890, I, 301, 302.
8. *Memorandum for Dabney.*
9. *Notes for Author.*
10. *Educational Review* (Apr., 1911), XLI, 345 et seq.
11. *Aspects of German Culture*, 92, 93.
12. *Ibid.*, 75.
13. *Ibid.*, 74.
14. *Ibid.*, 116, 117.
15. According to Mrs. Claire (Claxton) Mayo, Mrs. Claxton and her sister Annie had $1000 each, and Claxton less than that for the entire trip. For the return voyage, he borrowed from a German friend. Mrs. Claxton was then with child.
16. *Notes for Author.*

VI. NORTH CAROLINA SCHOOL SUPERINTENDENT

1. P. 113.
2. *Ibid.*, 144.
3. *Ibid.*, 150.
4. *Ibid.*, 151.
5. *Ibid.*, 158.
6. *Ibid.*, 160.
7. *Notes for Author.*
8. M. C. S. Noble, *The Public Schools of North Carolina*, 403–409.
9. *Notes for Author.*
10. Charles W. Dabney, *Universal Education in the South*, I, 207.
11. Letter from Dr. J. D. Eggleston, Jan. 17, 1945, to author. Miss Johnson of Farmville, Virginia, married Eggleston in 1895.
12. *Memoranda.*
13. *Notes for Author.*
14. *Asheville City Schools: Third Annual Report*, 1889–1890. Printed.
15. Charles W. Dabney, *op. cit.*, I, 208, 209, and *Notes for Author.*
16. Edwin A. Alderman, 37.
17. Dabney, *op. cit.*, I, 209.
18. Dumas Malone, *Edwin A. Alderman*, 40.
19. *Notes for Author.*
20. Dabney, *op. cit.*, 209. For a fuller treatment of these reports, see M. C. S. Noble, *History of the Public Schools of North Carolina*, 430–434.

VII. NORMAL SCHOOL PROFESSOR

1. M. C. S. Noble, *The Public Schools of North Carolina*, 438, 439. Claxton's first legislative lobbying was done during the session of that legislature in 1891. He appeared with Miss Frances Willard and a committee

of ten, and spoke before a legislative committee in behalf of a bill requiring the teaching of the effects of alcohol and narcotics in the public
schools. The bill was passed (Letter from E. J. Forney to author, Dec.,
1944).

2. Frances Gibson Satterfield, *Charles Duncan McIver*, 45.
3. *North Carolina College for Women. Annual Catalogues*, 1892–1897.
   Extension course advertised in *North Carolina Journal of Education*,
   Sept., 1897.
4. Mrs. J. S. (Anna Meade Michaux) Williams in a letter to the author.
5. Letter from Mrs. Wade Barrier from Wilmington to the author, Jan. 20,
   1945.
6. Letter from Mrs. Charles W. Moseley from Greensboro to the author,
   Dec. 31, 1944.
7. Letter from Mrs. Robert Dick (Virginia B.) Douglas from Greensboro
   to the author, Dec. 29, 1944.
8. Letter from Miss Minnie L. Jamison from Greensboro to the author, Jan.
   15, 1945.
9. Letter from Miss Annie W. Wiley to the author, Dec. 30, 1944.
10. Letter from E. J. Forney of Greensboro to the author, Dec. 18, 1944,
    and from Mrs. Wade Barrier to the author, Jan. 20, 1945.
11. Memorandum written Jan. 8, 1947, for the author by Julia Gray Gatlin
    Moore, niece of Anne Elizabeth Porter. Miss Porter also studied music
    with Bishop in Washington after leaving Asheville (*Notes for Author*).
12. *Tar Heel Editor*, 145.
13. For a rather detailed account of the town, see *O'Henry* by C. Alphonso
    Smith, 46–94.
14. *Notes for Author*.
15. *Editor in Politics*, 102.
16. *Notes for Author*.
17. Charles W. Dabney, *Universal Education in the South*, I, 214.
18. *Notes for Author*.
19. Burton J. Hendrick, *Life and Letters of Walter H. Page*, I, 74–79.
    Though not then residing in the South, Page had come to be an im-
    portant factor in its awakening. See his "School That Built a Town" in
    Some Old Southern Commonwealths.
20. On Mar. 15, 1898, according to *North Carolina Journal of Education*
    (Jan., 1898) announcement.
21. Letter from Professor William R. Webb to Mrs. P. P. Claxton, Jan. 14,
    1935.
22. *Proceedings of Southern Educational Association* (Dec., 1900), 313.
23. Manuscript of address.
24. *Proceedings of Southern Educational Association* (1901), 159.
25. Letter from Dixie Lee Bryant of Asheville to author, Jan., 1945; letter,
    undated, from Mrs. J. S. (Anna Meade Michaux) Williams to author;
    and letter, undated, from Mrs. P. P. Claxton to author.

26. *Proceedings* (July 10–13, 1894), 493–495.
27. *Ibid.* (July 7–13, 1900), 376–383.
28. *Normal and Industrial School Catalogue*, 1902.
29. Frances Gibson Satterfield, *Charles Duncan McIver*, 50, and *North Carolina Journal of Education*, Nov. and Dec., 1899.
30. Letter to author, Dec. 22, 1944.

VIII. The Second Trip to Europe

1. *Notes for Author.*
2. Article by Claxton in *Atlantic Educational Journal*, Sept., 1902, including reduced cuts of lesson plans handed in by students on a drawing lesson in natural history. Claxton to J. S. Vandiver, Apr. 22, 1924.
3. Cf. Charles De Garmo, *Herbart and the Herbartians* (1895); Percival Richard Cole, *Herbart and Froebel* (1895), a doctoral dissertation at Columbia University; and Edward L. Thorndike, *Principles of Teaching*, 42–50.
4. P. P. Claxton, "A School Journey with a Class from Dr. Rein's Practice School" in *North Carolina Journal of Education*, Dec., 1897, reprinted from *State Normal Magazine*.
5. The original statue by Lanz is in Yverdon, Switzerland.
6. *Notes for Author.*

IX. Editor of School Journals

1. Notes in *North Carolina Journal of Education*, Aug., 1897.
2. *Ibid.*, Sept., 1897.
3. *Ibid.*, Oct., 1897.
4. *Ibid.*, Nov., 1897.
5. *Ibid.*, Dec., 1897.
6. *Ibid.*, Jan., 1898.
7. *Ibid.*, Feb., 1898.
8. *Ibid.*, Mar., 1898.
9. Cf. Josephus Daniels, *Editor in Politics*, 324 et seq.
10. *North Carolina Journal of Education*, Jan., 1899.
11. *Ibid.*, Apr., 1899.
12. *Ibid.*, May, 1899.
13. *Ibid.*, Aug., 1899.
14. *Ibid.*, Jan., 1900.
15. *Ibid.*, Mar., 1900.
16. *Ibid.*, Feb., 1900.
17. *Ibid.*, Apr.-May, 1900.
18. *Ibid.*, Feb., 1901.
19. From original copy of contract signed by Claxton and a representative of the publishers (Claxton Papers).
20. Mrs. James R. Young (Annie McIver) of Greensboro to author, Jan. 25, 1945.

21. *Memorandum for Dabney.*
22. *Notes for Author.*
23. *Atlantic Educational Journal,* Aug., 1901.
24. *Ibid.,* Mar., 1902.

X. THE SOUTHERN EDUCATION BOARD

1. *Memorandum for Dabney.*
2. Letter of Dr. Dabney to Mrs. P. P. Claxton, Sept. 2, 1937.
3. *Conference for Education in the South, Proceedings,* 1898, 1899, 1900. First called, "Conference on Christian Education."
4. *Memoranda.*
5. *A Brief Statement concerning the Origin and Organization of the Southern Education Board* [Pamphlet of four pages issued in Sept., 1901].
6. Letter of Dabney to Mrs. P. P. Claxton, Sept. 2, 1937. Cf. Dabney, *Universal Education in the South,* II, 503, 504.
7. *Memorandum for Dabney,* and *Atlantic Educational Journal,* Feb., 1902.
8. Dabney, *op. cit.,* II, 60.
9. *Atlantic Educational Journal,* Dec., 1901.
10. Dabney, *op. cit.,* II, 60.
11. *Memoranda,* and Dabney, *op. cit.,* II, 76, 541.
12. *Notes for Author,* and Dabney, *op. cit.,* II, 76, 77.
13. *Atlantic Educational Journal,* Sept., 1902.
14. *Ibid.,* Dec., 1902.
15. *Proceedings* (1902), 40–42.
16. Dabney, *op. cit.,* II, 76. A list of these is in *Ibid.,* II, 541.
17. *Proceedings* (1903), and Dabney, *op. cit.,* II, 96–102.
18. Dabney, *op. cit.,* II, 364; correspondence between Dabney and Claxton (Claxton Papers); cf. "A Model School" by Claxton in *The Annals of the American Academy of Political and Social Science* (Philadelphia, 1903) XXII, No. 2, 245–248.
19. *Proceedings* (1903), 99–103.
20. Dabney, *op. cit.,* II, 97, 102–104.
21. Andrew D. Holt, *The Struggle for a State System of Public Schools in Tennessee, 1903–1936,* 174, 175.
22. *Proceedings* (1907); Dabney, *op. cit.,* II, 284–286, 364; and *Memoranda.*
23. *Notes for Author.*
24. Dabney, *op. cit.,* II, 348, 349, 353.
25. *Ibid.,* II, 353; *Memoranda;* and letter from Claxton to author, Dec. 3, 1946.
26. *Notes for Author.*
27. *Proceedings* (1908). Dabney, *op. cit.,* II, 288, states that his subject was "Popular Education and National Efficiency."
28. *Journal of Proceedings and Addresses* . . . (Dec. 26–28, 1907), 127, 128.
29. *Ibid.,* 132–142.
30. *Ibid.,* 238–244.

31. *Proceedings* (1908), 85 et seq.
32. *Notes for Author.*
33. *Proceedings* (1909–1912), and Dabney, op. cit., II, 290–305.
34. *Memoranda.*
35. *Education in the South:* abstracts of papers read at the 16th Conference (*Bureau of Education. Bulletin No. 30. Whole Number 540.* Washington, 1913), 34, and Dabney, op. cit., II, 307.
36. *Proceedings of the 17th Conference for Education in the South and the 25th Annual Meeting of the Southern Educational Association* (Louisville, Kentucky, 1914), 10. Dabney, op. cit., II, 313, quotes the passage with some editing.
37. Dabney, op. cit., II, 315.

XI. The Summer School of the South

1. Dabney, *Universal Education in the South,* II, 105, 106; *Memorandum for Dabney.*
2. *Memorandum for Dabney,* and letter from Dabney to Mrs. P. P. Claxton, Sept. 2, 1937.
3. A memorandum by Dabney for Mrs. P. P. Claxton, Sept. 30, 1936.
4. To Mrs. P. P. Claxton, Sept. 2, 1937.
5. *Atlantic Educational Journal,* Aug., 1902; "Summer School of the South: In Retrospect" by Claxton in *Teacher-Education Journal* (Dec., 1941), III, No. 3, 135–138.
6. Report by Claxton of first session of the Summer School of the South [Manuscript copy in Library of University of Tennessee].
7. "Summer School of the South" by Claxton in *Teacher-Education Journal* (Dec., 1941), III, No. 3, 135–138.
8. Report by Claxton of first session of the Summer School of the South.
9. *Memorandum for Dabney.* In the report by Claxton of the first session of the Summer School of the South, he mentioned only the Carolinas, Georgia, Louisiana, West Tennessee, and Mississippi as the states he visited.
10. *Memorandum for Dabney* and *Notes for Author.*
11. "Summer School of the South" by Claxton in *Teacher-Education Journal* (Dec., 1941), III, No. 3, 135–138.
12. Editorial in *Atlantic Educational Journal,* Aug., 1902.
13. *Within the Year* [Pamphlet of 18 pages, without date or place of publication].
14. Dabney, op. cit., II, Appendix VII, 543, 544.
15. *Memorandum for Dabney.*
16. Of Bridgeport, Connecticut; in "The Summer School of the South: An Educational Revolution" [Manuscript in Claxton Papers].
17. *Atlantic Educational Journal,* Aug., 1902.
18. Claxton's report to Dabney (Manuscript copy in Library of University of Tennessee).
19. *Atlantic Educational Journal,* Aug., 1902.

20. Claxton's report to Dabney.
21. Dabney, *op. cit.*, II, 106.
22. Dabney to Mrs. P. P. Claxton, Sept. 2, 1937.
23. Claxton's report to Dabney (1903).
24. *Announcement and Courses of Study: Summer School of the South, June 23 to July 31, 1903 (Bulletin).* University of Tennessee.
25. Dabney, *op. cit.*, II, 109.
26. *Ibid.*, II, 110, and Claxton's report to Dabney.
27. *Announcement and Courses of Study: Summer School of the South,* 1904–1911.
28. Letter from Miss Powell's agent, H. Godfrey Turner, to Claxton, Mar. 25, 1908.
29. Letter from Claxton to author, Dec. 3, 1946.
30. *Memorandum for Dabney;* "Summer School of the South" by Claxton in *Teacher-Education Journal* (Dec., 1941), III, No. 3, 135–138; and *Announcement and Courses of Study: Summer School of the South,* 1902–1912.
31. To Mrs. P. P. Claxton, Sept. 2, 1937.
32. To Mrs. Claxton in 1940: "The Summer School of the South as I Remember It."
33. To Mrs. Claxton, Jan. 26, 1940.
34. Pp. 154–156.

XII. HEAD OF DEPARTMENT OF EDUCATION, UNIVERSITY OF TENNESSEE
1. *Memorandum for Dabney.*
2. *Atlantic Educational Journal,* Nov., 1902 and Mar., 1903, and *University of Tennessee Record,* 1903.
3. Dabney to Mrs. P. P. Claxton, Sept. 2, 1937.
4. *Memoranda.*
5. *Atlantic Educational Journal,* Nov., 1902.
6. Dabney to Mrs. Claxton, Sept. 30, 1936, and Dabney to author, Jan. 8, 1945.
7. *Message of Governor James B. Frazier to the 53d General Assembly, State of Tennessee,* Jan. 23, 1903, 5.
8. Andrew David Holt, *The Struggle for a State System of Public Schools in Tennessee, 1903–1936,* 75–87.
9. *Memoranda.*
10. *Acts of Tennessee* (1873), Chapter 25. For a discussion of Mynders' excellent qualifications for the office, see Holt, *op. cit.,* 124, 125.
11. Charles W. Dabney, *Universal Education in the South,* II, 363, and Holt, *op. cit.,* 238, 239.
12. *Memoranda.* At the Jamestown, Virginia Ter-centennial Exposition in 1907, Claxton had supervision of the awards in primary and secondary education (Letter of Peregrine Publishers, Norfolk, Virginia, to Claxton regarding the *Blue Book* of the Exposition).

13. Burton K. Hendrick, *The Training of an American*, 372, 373.
14. Mar. 8, 1908.
15. Page to Claxton, Apr. 11, 1908. "Walter Page was frequently urging me to take a vacation and warning me against a nervous breakdown. Poor fellow! The war got him." (*Notes for Author.*)
16. Claxton to Page, Apr. 13, 1908.
17. In letter of Apr. 15, 1908.
18. *Notes for Author.*
19. Judge Albert Williams to Author, Mar. 10, 1947.

XIII. Educational Campaigns in Tennessee

1. Charles W. Dabney, *Universal Education in the South*, II, 364.
2. *Memoranda.*
3. *Memorandum for Dabney* and letter from Claxton to author, Dec. 3, 1946.
4. *Memoranda.*
5. Knoxville *Journal and Tribune* (Oct. 21, 1906), 8, and *Memorandum for Dabney.*
6. *Memorandum for Dabney.*
7. *Tennessee School Report. State of Tennessee, Department of Public Instruction* (1906), 551.
8. *Memorandum for Dabney.*
9. A. D. Holt, *The Struggle for a State System of Public Schools in Tennessee, 1903–1936*, 213.
10. *Proceedings, Ninth Conference for Education in the South* (1906), 68.
11. *Proceedings, Eleventh Conference for Education in the South* (1908), 78.
12. *Notes for Author.*
13. *Memorandum for Dabney.*
14. *Memoranda.*
15. *Memorandum for Dabney.*
16. Sept. 4, 1906.
17. Holt, *op. cit.*, 197.
18. (Oct. 9, 1906), 3, 5.
19. Nashville *American*, Aug. 22, 1906.
20. *Ibid.*
21. Nashville *Banner*, Oct. 8, 1906.
22. Holt, *op. cit.*, 121, 122.
23. *Memoranda.*
24. Holt, *op. cit.*, 241, 245.
25. *Ibid.*, 244, 245.
26. *Proceedings of Conference for Education in the South* (1908), 81.
27. *Ibid.*, 239, 243.
28. *Memorandum for Dabney*; "Founding and Early Days of the State Normal School" by Claxton, an address at the East Tennessee Teachers Col-

lege Silver Anniversary, Oct. 9, 10, 1936 (*Bulletin, East Tennessee Teachers College*, XXVI, No. 2, 1936); and *Notes for Author*.

29. To Pres. J. M. McBryde, Virginia Polytechnic Institute, May 14, 1907.
30. To Dr. W. W. Stetson, Supt. of Educational Department, State of Maine, June 5, 1906.
31. Holt, *op. cit.*, 122, 171–173.
32. Address on "Methods of an Educational Campaign" by Claxton before the Conference for Education in the South (1908), 74.
33. *Notes for Author*.
34. Holt, *op. cit.*, 247, 248.
35. *Notes for Author*.
36. *Memorandum for Dabney*, and Statement of Dec. 1, 1936, as quoted by Holt, *op. cit.*, 248–250. The details of this legislative incident are from these sources.
37. *Memoranda.*
38. Aug. 22, 1910.
39. Memphis *Commercial Appeal*, Sept. 25, 1910.
40. Nashville *Banner*, Sept. 29, 1910.
41. Memphis *Commercial Appeal*, Sept. 14, 1910.
42. Knoxville *Daily Journal and Tribune*, Oct. 10, 1910.
43. *Memorandum for Dabney*.
44. *Memoranda*.
45. To author, Sept. 10, 1945.
46. *Memoranda*, and Holt, *op. cit.*, 293.
47. Pres. James D. Hoskins to Dr. Lilian W. Johnson, Mar. 27, 1940.
48. *Proceedings*, 13.
49. June 8, 1909.

XIV. United States Commissioner of Education: Up to World War One

1. May 16, 1911.
2. To Dabney, May 22, 1911.
3. Memorandum by Dabney for Mrs. Claxton, Sept. 30, 1936, and letter from Dabney to Mrs. Claxton, Sept. 2, 1937.
4. *Notes for Author*.
5. Letter from Claxton to author, Dec. 12, 1946.
6. *Notes for Author*. Claxton's telegram of acceptance was dated June 29, 1911. His appointment was confirmed by the Senate June 30, 1911 (Letter to Claxton from Acting Secretary Samuel Adams, July 3, 1911, in Archives of Office of Education). When the appointment was made public, letters of congratulation poured in to Claxton from friends all over the United States (Claxton Papers).
7. July 18, 1911.
8. July 21, 1911.
9. July 23, 1911.

10. July 17, 1911.
11. *Notes for Author.*
12. New York *Post*, Sept. 23, 1911.
13. Letter to Claxton, Sept. 25, 1911.
14. Program of meeting. The subjects of the other addresses are not specified.
15. *The Bureau of Education. Hearings before the Committee on Education, House of Representatives, concerning the Bureau of Education, June 11, 1912.*
16. Mar. 18, 1913.
17. Greensboro *Daily News*, May 30, 1913.
18. Springfield (Mass.) *Daily Republican*, July 15, 1913.
19. *Notes for Author.*
20. *The Peabody Reflector*, Dec., 1946, letter by J. O. Martin.
21. For the Albuquerque *Morning Journal*, Nov. 26, 1913.
22. Mar. 22, 1913.
23. Oct. 2, 1913.
24. *U. S. Cong. House Com. on Ed. Hearing before the Committee on Education, House of Representatives, 63d Cong. 2nd ses. on H.R. 2494, A bill to investigate adult illiteracy . . . , and on H.J. Res. 84, limiting the editions of the publications of the Bureau of Education, Jan. 26, 1914.* Washington, 1914.
25. Washington *Star*, Feb. 15, 1914.
26. *Ibid.*, Mar. 29, 1914.
27. Burlington (Iowa) *Hawk Eye*, Apr. 3, 1914.
28. Sioux City *Journal*, Apr. 4, 1914.
29. Altoona *Tribune*, June 6, 1914.
30. *Report of Commissioner of Education for Year Ended June 30, 1914,* Vol. I, 347.
31. *Proceedings* . . . (St. Paul, July 4–11, 1914), 769–771. The St. Paul *Pioneer Press*, July 6, 1914, contained a photograph of Claxton.
32. Nashville *Tennessean*, July 21, 1914, and *Peabody Record*, July 24, 1914.
33. Knoxville newspaper clipping, July 23, 1914.
34. Athens (Ga.) *Banner*, July 24, 1914.
35. Charlotte *News*, Nov. 26, 1914, and Charlotte *Daily Observer*, Nov. 26, 1914.
36. Nashville *Banner*, Nov. 28, 1914.
37. Washington *Times*, Nov. 9, 1914.
38. *Notes for Author.*

XV. UNITED STATES COMMISSIONER OF EDUCATION:
WORLD WAR ONE, 1914–1916

1. *Notes for Author.*
2. Introduction to *Report of Commissioner of Education for the Year Ended June 30, 1916.*

3. From manuscript of address (Claxton Papers). The Executive Committee numbered twelve.
4. Minutes of the Conference (Claxton Papers).
5. The original manuscript contains 40 typewritten double-spaced pages.
6. Washington *Star*, May 13, 1915.
7. Bay City *Daily Times*, June 19, 1915.
8. *The American College: a Series of Papers Setting Forth the Program, Achievements, Present Status, and Probable Future of the American College . . .* , with introduction by W. N. Crawford, President of Allegheny College.
9. Salt Lake City newspaper clipping of June 30, 1915.
10. San Diego *Union*, July 13, 1915.
11. *Proceedings . . .* (Oakland, Cal., August 16–27), 747, 748.
12. Grand Rapids *Press*, Oct. 30, 1915.
13. Grand Forks *Daily Herald*, Nov. 5, 1915.
14. *Army and Navy Journal*, Aug. 7, 1915.
15. Billingham newspaper clipping, July 20, 1915.
16. As quoted in *Army and Navy Journal*, July 23, 1910. The substance of the speech, entitled "The Broader Patriotism," was first delivered in the winter of 1910 before the Department of Superintendence of the National Education Association at its meeting in Indianapolis. In Boston, Claxton made three speeches on different phases of this subject, one of which was at a dinner in honor of the publisher, Edwin Ginn, who had given a million dollars for the promotion of peace.
17. As quoted in *Army and Navy Journal*, Aug. 6, 1910.
18. *Army and Navy Journal*, Aug. 6, 1910.
19. In *Army and Navy Journal*, Aug. 20, 1910. Dr. Mead had lectured on international peace at the Summer School of the South at the invitation of Claxton. Dr. Van Ness Myers, the historian, Dr. Walsh of Aberdeen, Scotland, and others had been invited by Claxton to lecture there on that subject.
20. Where the *Army and Navy Journal* was published.
21. July 22, 1915. See also Worcester (Mass.) *Telegram*, July 25, 1915.
22. July 24, 1915. For other examples of favorable comment see Jamestown (N. Y.) *Post*, July 22, 1915; Chattanooga *News*, July 20, 1915; and Salisbury (N. C.) *Post*, July 21, 1915.
23. July 22, 1915.
24. Aug. 7, 1915.
25. Carbon copy of the manuscript of the statement, Mar. 4, 1916 (Claxton Papers).
26. Notation on the carbon copy of the statement by Claxton for Lane.
27. To author, Aug. 14, 1946.
28. *Notes for Author.*
29. *Stenographic Notes.*

30. San Francisco *Chronicle,* Apr. 16, 1916.
31. Billings *Gazette,* Apr. 23, 1916.
32. Las Vegas *Daily Optic,* June 8, 1916.
33. Nashville *Banner,* June 13, 1916.
34. Kansas *Industrialist* (U. of Kan. paper), June 15, 1916.
35. New York newspaper clipping, July 5, 1916. New York *Sun,* July 2, in article on forthcoming convention, has a photograph of Claxton.
36. July 6, 1916.
37. Johnstown (Pa.) *Daily Democrat,* Sept. 2, 1916.
38. Introduction (p. xv) to *Report of Commissioner of Education for Year Ended June 30, 1915.*

XVI. United States Commissioner of Education: World War One, 1916–1918

1. *Notes for Author.* "Extracts from this letter, including this sentence, were quoted in large numbers of newspapers and magazines. Some publishers of textbooks sent it out with books and otherwise" (*Ibid.*).
2. *Suggestions for the Conduct of Educational Institutions during the Continuance of the War* (Cited in *Report of Commissioner of Education for Year Ended June 30, 1917,* p. 11, and quoted in large part in *Our Schools in War Time and After* by Arthur D. Dean, 146–150).
3. Chattanooga *News.* Supplement, p. 8. [Spring, 1916].
4. *Notes for Author.*
5. March 12, 1918, in Archives of Office of Education. See also his letter of Apr. 15, 1918, to Mr. E. D. Smith, Council of National Defense, Washington, D. C.
6. Sept. 17, 1918, in Archives of Office of Education.
7. Sept. 24, 1918, in Archives of Office of Education. Secretary Lane to Richard J. Biggs, July 16, 1918, ". . . I have approved the policy of the Commissioner of Education as expressed in his letter to President Slagle. . . . I believe this policy has the general approval of the more thoughtful educators of the country" (Archives of the Office of Education).
8. Sept. 26, 1918, in Archives of Office of Education.
9. New York newspaper clipping, undated.
10. As it appeared in Peoria (Illinois) *Transcript,* Sept. 20, 1918.
11. Sept. 3, 1918, in Archives of Office of Education.
12. June 18, 1918, Archives of Office of Education. Claxton had this in mind as early as Apr. 15, 1918, in letter to E. D. Smith, Council of National Defense, Washington, and in letter to C. H. Vantyne, Carnegie Institute, Washington, June 19, 1918. Letters in Archives of Office of Education.
13. June 20, 1918, in Archives of Office of Education.
14. New York *Times,* Mar. 3, 1918.
15. This was recommended in resolutions adopted by Second Pan-American

Scientific Congress, Jan. 8, 1916. In 1917 the Bureau of Education issued City School Circular No. 4 on "Foreign Languages in the Elementary Grades."

16. Claxton's Correspondence with Committee (Claxton Papers).
17. Information furnished author by Dr. Matthew Page Andrews, a member of the Committee on Awards.
18. As prepared by Dr. Matthew Page Andrews.
19. *Congressional Record*, No. 102, Apr. 13, 1918.
20. *Notes for Author*.
21. See *Report of Commissioner of Education for the Year Ended June 30, 1917*, 61–63; *Ibid.*, June 30, 1918, 132–134; and *Americanization Bulletin*, Sept. 15 and Nov. 1, 1918.
22. *Report of Commissioner of Education for the Year Ended June 30, 1917*, 53.
23. *Ibid.*, June 30, 1918, 25.
24. *Notes for Author*.
25. *Report of Commissioner of Education for the Year Ended June 30, 1917*, 64.
26. *Ibid.*, June 30, 1918, 139–140.
27. *Ibid.*, June 30, 1917, 19, and *Ibid.*, June 30, 1918, 10, 138, 139, and *Notes for Author*.
28. May 24, 1918.

XVII. United States Commissioner of Education: After World War One

1. *School Life* (Jan. 16, 1919), II, 10.
2. *Ibid.* (Feb. 1, 1919), II, 13.
3. *Ibid.* (Feb. 16, 1919), II, 14.
4. *Ibid.* (Apr. 1, 1919), II, 8.
5. *Journal of Proceedings*, 81–88. This was also published in pamphlet form by the Bureau of Education. Article on same subject in *School Life*, Aug. 16, 1919.
6. Crabtree to Sinclair, Apr. 24, 1924, in Archives of Office of Education. Many years afterwards Claxton wrote Sinclair, requesting the source of his "information." He replied that he had forgotten, and sent him a copy of his book on Henry Ford.
7. *School Life* (Apr. 1, 1920), IV, 1.
8. *Notes for Author*, and *Commissioner's Report for the Year Ended June 30, 1920*, 106.
9. *Revista de Instruccion Publica* (Cuba), Jan., 1926, "The Ideals of Rural Education" by Dr. Ramiro Guerra.
10. *Report of Commissioner for Year Ended June 30, 1920*, 100, 101, and *School Life* (Mar. 1, 1920), IV, 3, 9.
11. *The Southern Review* (Asheville), June, 1920. This contains a photograph of Claxton.

12. Report of Commissioner for Year Ended June 30, 1920, 106–109.
13. School Life (July 15, 1920), V, 1, 10, 11.
14. Proceedings . . . , 55–58.
15. Nashville Tennessean, Jan. 15, 1920.
16. Nashville Tennessean, Aug. 7, 9, 1920, and Nashville Banner, Aug. 7, 1920.
17. Knoxville Journal and Tribune, Oct. 12, 1920, and A. D. Holt, The Struggle for a State System of Public Schools in Tennessee, 1903–1936, 309.
18. School Life (Oct. 15, 1920), V, 1.
19. Notes for Author.
20. Memorandum from Miss Eunice W. Curtis, Clerk of Files and Mail, Office of Education, Nov. 30, 1946, for Claxton, and Notes for Author.
21. School Life, VI, 5.
22. Notes for Author.
23. Reports for Years Ended June 30, 1918, 1919, 1920.
24. Bulletin No. 36, 1920, Bureau of Education.
25. Copy in Archives of Office of Education. "President Harding's reason for asking for my resignation was my expressed lack of sympathy for and approval of his plan for a Department of Education and Welfare. It had been announced that any one opposing this might consider himself dismissed" (Notes for Author).
26. To Mrs. P. P. Claxton, Sept. 30, 1936.
27. June, 1921.
28. Notes for Author.
29. Statement to Secretary Lane, Mar. 4, 1916.
30. Notes for Author.
31. On the margin of the carbon copy of Claxton's statement to Lane, written in 1946.
32. Notes for Author.
33. Notes by Mrs. P. P. Claxton for author. Later the Claxtons moved to a stone house surrounded by trees on Conduit Road, up the Potomac. Later still he bought a home on Lamont Street near an entrance to Rock Creek Park, which afforded opportunity for many rambles.
34. Claxton Genealogy in note 3, chapter 1.
35. Notes by Claire Claxton Mayo for author.

XVIII. Provost of the University of Alabama

1. Superintendency of Schools of Cincinnati, Indianapolis, and San Francisco; Head of Department of Education of Universities of Virginia and Pennsylvania; and Presidency of University of Tennessee, Martha Washington College and Emory and Henry College (combined), State Normal at Murfreesboro (Tenn.), University of Miami (Fla.), American University (D. C.), Iowa College of Agriculture, University of Washington, North Carolina A. and M., University of Texas, University

of Maryland, University of Arkansas, and University of West Virginia. He was offered the position of Education and Civic Director of the State of Delaware, to be financed by one of the Du Ponts. The salary was to be $10,000, and half time was to be available for similar work in Southern states.

2. *University of Tennessee Record*, Dec., 1921.
3. P. 11.
4. *Memorandum for Dabney and Notes for Author.*
5. *Montgomery Advertiser,* Oct. 3, 1921.
6. *Mobile Register,* Nov. 20, 1921.
7. *Huntsville Daily Times,* Dec. 7, 1921.
8. P. 21.
9. *University of Alabama Alumni News,* Jan.-Feb., 1922, p. 36.
10. *University of Tennessee Record, Commencement Number,* Sept., 1922.
11. *Notes for Author.*
12. Miss Bessie Locke to Claxton, Dec. 28, 1922, and June 21, 1923.
13. Sands C. Chipman to Claxton, Apr. 26, 1923.
14. M. J. Kinsella to Claxton, Jan. 24, May 4, June 7, and July 1, 1923.
15. Correspondence with the company (Claxton Papers) and letter from B. S. Kinsella to author, Feb. 4, 1947.
16. Jan. 29 and Feb. 28, 1923.
17. Advertisement from *Oklahoma Teacher,* 1924. This contains photograph of Claxton.
18. Notes by Mrs. Claxton for author.

XIX. Superintendent of Tulsa City Schools

1. *Birmingham News,* June 27, 1923, reported Claxton's resignation and acceptance of the Tulsa superintendency at $13,800. *Tulsa World,* June 26, 1923, states that he was chosen by Board of Education on June 25. The *World* of July 28 in an editorial criticized the high salary paid to Claxton.
2. Governor William W. Brandon to Claxton, July 21, 1923.
3. *Tulsa Tribune,* July 11, 1923.
4. *Ibid.*
5. *Stenographic Notes.*
6. July 11, 1923.
7. *Tulsa World,* July, 1923.
8. July 13, 1923.
9. *Tulsa Tribune,* Sept., 1923.
10. *Memorandum for Dabney.*
11. *Report of the Public Schools of Tulsa, Oklahoma,* 1923–24, 8.
12. March, 1924.
13. *Report of the Public Schools of Tulsa, Oklahoma,* 1923–24, 18, 19.
14. *Notes for Author.*

15. *Report of the Public Schools of Tulsa, Oklahoma, 1923–24,* 21, 25, and *Notes for Author.*
16. *Notes for Author.*
17. *Report of the Public Schools of Tulsa, Oklahoma, 1923–24,* 45, 46, and *Memorandum for Dabney.*
18. Nowata (Oklahoma) *Daily Star,* Dec. 7, 1923.
19. *Peabody Journal of Education,* May, 1925 (p. 302) and *Bulletin, George Peabody College for Teachers, The Semicentennial of George Peabody College for Teachers, 1875–1925* (Nov., 1925), 32.
20. *Ibid.,* 312.
21. At Broken Arrow, Oklahoma, May 20, 1925; at Claremore, Oklahoma, May 15, 1925; and at University of Tulsa, June 2, 1925.
22. *Notes for Author.*
23. John J. Tigert to Claxton, Jan. 27, 1926.
24. Mrs. Sarah Ward Conley to Tigert, Mar. 2, 1926.
25. This article accompanies a photograph of the painting.
26. Feb. 16, 1926. At the same ceremony, a portrait of former Commissioner of Education William T. Harris was unveiled.
27. Sept., 1926.
28. Tulsa *World,* Feb. 17, 1926.
29. May 6, 1926.
30. *Notes for Author.*
31. Oklahoma Division, American Association of University Women at Sapulpa, Mar. 13; Tulsa Music Week, May 2; Oklahoma A. and M. College Commencement; Okmulgee County Teachers Association, Sept. 3, on "The Teacher and the Recitation."
32. Nashville *Tennessean,* Apr. 3, 1926, and Nashville *Banner,* Apr. 3, 1926.
33. Sept. 27, 1926.
34. Tulsa *Tribune,* May 4, 1927.
35. Pittsburg (Kansas) *Daily Headlight,* May 26, 1927.
36. Lois White in Tulsa *Daily World,* May 1, 1927.
37. Toronto *Globe,* Aug. 12, 1927.
38. Letter to Mrs. Claxton, undated.
39. *Notes for Author.*
40. Jan. 25, 1928.
41. Tulsa *Tribune,* Feb. 26, 1928.
42. *Ibid.,* Mar. 10, 1928.
43. *Ibid.,* Mar. 12, 1928.
44. Editorial, May 9, 1928. A full report was published in several issues of the paper.
45. Tulsa *Daily World,* Apr. 11, 1928.
46. Tulsa *Tribune,* May 15, 1928.
47. Jan. 29, 1928.
48. Claxton's correspondence with Charles F. Pye, Secretary, Nov. 27, 1928.
49. *Notes for Author.*

50. Tulsa *Tribune*, May 20, 1929.
51. *Notes for Author.*
52. Notes from Mrs. Claxton to author.
53. "A Personality Portrait of the Greatest Teacher I Have Known" by Blanche Cahoon, in manuscript furnished the author by Mrs. Claxton.
54. June 4, 1929.

XX. VACATION IN DENMARK

1. *Memorandum for Dabney.*
2. *Notes for Author.*
3. Mrs. Olive D. Campbell to Mrs. P. P. Claxton, Dec. 31, 1936.
4. *Notes for Author.*

XXI. AUSTIN PEAY STATE COLLEGE PRESIDENT

1. *Acts of Tennessee* (1927), chapter 50.
2. Nashville *Tennessean*, Jan. 11, 1928.
3. *Stenographic Notes.*
4. *Acts of Tennessee* (1931), chapter 85.
5. *Stenographic Notes.*
6. *School Life*, April, 1931.
7. Letter from Pres. G. H. Wells of Georgia State College for Women to Claxton, Mar. 18, 1947.
8. Andrew D. Holt, *The Struggle for a State System of Public Schools in Tennessee, 1903–1936*, 377.
9. Holt, op. cit., 377 footnote; the Claxton Papers; and material in the Library of Austin Peay State College.
10. Holt, op. cit., 378.
11. *Ibid.*, 377, 378.
12. *Ibid.*, 397.
13. Minutes of the Committee.
14. Nashville *Banner*, Oct. 11, 1934.
15. Holt, op. cit., 406.
16. *Ibid.*, 422, 423.
17. *Ibid.*, 423, 424.
18. *Ibid.*, 424.
19. *Ibid.*, 425, 426.
20. *Ibid.*, 438–442.
21. *Bulletin, East Tennessee Teachers College*, XXVI, No. 2, Sept., 1936.
22. "Bedford County as I Remember It . . . ," Shelbyville *Gazette*, Sept. 29 and Oct. 6, 1938.
23. Letter to Andrew D. Holt, Jan. 8, 1938.
24. *All State* [Pictorial Supplement of Austin Peay State College paper], 1941. The extension of curriculum was authorized by an act of the General Assembly of 1939. A similar act of 1941 authorized the change in name.

25. *Memorandum for Dabney.*
26. Manuscript of lecture, Mar. 19, 1940, first prepared for a broadcast and then read at college assembly.
27. Letter from Mrs. P. P. Claxton to author, Jan. 27, 1945.
28. Clarksville *Leaf-Chronicle*, May 30, 1945.
29. The Shelbyville *Gazette*, Nov. 11, 1943; Washington *Post*, Nov. 7, 1943; Chattanooga *Times*, Nov. 5, 1943; Knoxville *Journal*, Nov. 4, 1943; Clarksville *Leaf-Chronicle*, Oct. 29 and Nov. 5, 1943; Nashville *Tennessean*, Nov. 5, 1943; Nashville *Banner*, Nov. 5, 1943 with picture of the portrait and of Mary Payne, Porter Claxton, Jr., and Claxton.
30. Excerpts of speeches from mimeographed copies furnished to author by Mrs. Claxton.
31. To Mrs. Claxton, Oct. 26, 1943.
32. Quotations from speeches and letters are from the program furnished the author by Mrs. Claxton.
33. Nov. 5, 1943.
34. This was delivered first as a lecture to the students of Austin Peay State College, Jan. 7, 1944.
35. Nashville *Tennessean*, Oct. 6, 1944.
36. *The University of Tennessee Sesquicentennial. A record of 150 years of achievement of public education on the higher level and an analysis of future problems and responsibilities.* University of Tennessee Press, 1945. 103–110.
37. *Bulletin, Austin Peay State College, Clarksville, Tennessee*, November, 1944 (XIV, No. 2). This was broadcast over WJZM at Clarksville.
38. P. 7, "Austin Peay College Conservation Classes Improve Whole District."
39. President's Annual Statement, May 14, 1946.
40. *The Commercial Appeal*, June 4, 1946.
41. Report to State Board of Education, Apr. 26, 1946.
42. Letter from Mrs. Claxton to author Oct. 16, 1946.

XXII. PRESIDENT EMERITUS
1. Nashville *Tennessean*, May 11, 1946.
2. To T. Bultman, Manager, Jefferson Life Insurance Co., Nov. 25, 1935.
3. Clarksville *Leaf-Chronicle*, May 11, 1946. This contains photograph of Claxton.
4. *Ibid.*, June 29, 1946.
5. Notes from Mrs. Claxton to author.
6. Note by Mrs. Claxton.
7. To author, Feb. 2, 1945.
8. Letter to author, Feb. 2, 1945.
9. *The Southern Review* (Asheville), June, 1920, p. 9.
10. *The Journal* (Winston-Salem, N. C.), June, 1931.
11. Letter to Claxton from L. A. Kalbach and others, Mar. 6, 1931.

12. To Mrs. Claxton, Aug. 5, 1935.
13. Mar. 19, 1924. He was then President of the University of Virginia.
14. To the author, Jan. 17, 1945.
15. *Stenographic Notes.* On June 2, 1934, he spoke on "The Unfinished Task" to the Phi Kappa Phi at the University of Tennessee.
16. Jan. 19, 1947.

Sources and Bibliography

◇◇◇

I. Manuscripts

Claxton Papers:
  Letters.
  Speeches.
  Reports.
  Memorandum prepared for Dr. Charles W. Dabney.
  Miscellaneous Notes.
  Educational Campaign Material.
Office of Education, Department of the Interior.
  Correspondence Files of Claxton's Commissionership.
  Manuscripts of Speeches.
University of Tennessee Library.
  Reports of the Summer School of the South.
Stenographic Notes of Conversations between Claxton and Author.
Letters and Numerous Memoranda from Claxton to Author.
Letters to Author from:
  Mrs. Claxton.
  Claxton's Children.
  His Former Students and Associates.
  Term Paper, Peabody College for Teachers, *A Study of the Life and Work of P. P. Claxton* by George M. Rawlins, Jr.
    55 typewritten pages.

II. Periodicals

Albany *Herald*, Mar. 31, 1921.
Albany *Journal*, Apr. 7, 1921.
Albuquerque *Morning Journal*, Nov. 26, 1913.
Altoona (Pennsylvania) *Mirror*, Mar. 28, 1921.
Altoona *Times-Tribune*, June 6, 1914 and Apr. 8, 1921.

American Review of Reviews, Nov., 1926, "A Half-Century of Johns Hopkins" by Charles K. Edmunds.

Anaconda (Montana) Standard, Apr. 2, 1921.

Annals of the American Academy of Political and Social Science (Philadelphia, 1903), XXII, No. 2, "A Model School" by P. P. Claxton.

Army and Navy Journal, July 23, 30; Aug. 6, 20; Sept. 3; Nov. 12, 1910; and Aug. 7, 1915.

Asheville Citizen, Apr. 8, 1921.

Athens (Georgia) Banner, July 24, 1914.

Atlantic Educational Journal, July, 1902–Aug., 1903, edited by P. P. Claxton.

Augusta (Georgia) Herald, Apr. 17, 1921.

Baltimore News, Mar. 13, 1921.

Baltimore Sun, Apr. 5, 1921.

Bangor (Maine) Commercial, Apr. 18, 28, 1921.

Banker-Farmer (Champaign, Ill.), July, 1918, "Consolidation as a War Measure"; Apr., 1919, "Education in the School for the Farmer and the Farmer's Wife" by P. P. Claxton.

Bay City (Michigan) Daily Times, June 19, 1915.

Billings (Montana) Gazette, Apr. 23, 1916.

Birmingham (Alabama) News, June 27, 1923.

Bloomington (Illinois) Bulletin, Mar. 25 and Apr. 10, 1921.

Bridgeport (Connecticut) Post, Apr. 8, 1921.

Brooklyn Standard Union, Apr. 24, 1921.

Buffalo Commercial, Apr. 16, 1921.

Buffalo News, Apr. 4, 8, 1921.

Burlington (Iowa) Hawk Eye, Apr. 3, 1914.

Butte Daily Post, Dec. 2, 1920.

Butte Miner, Dec. 3, 1920.

Canton (Ohio) News, Apr. 17, 1921.

Charleston (South Carolina) News-Courier, Apr. 6, 15, 26, 1921.

Charlotte (North Carolina) Daily Observer, Nov. 26, 1914.

Charlotte News, Nov. 26, 1914.

Chattanooga News, July 20, 1915.

Chattanooga Times, Oct. 13, 1920; Apr. 24, 27, 1921; Nov. 4, 5, 7, 1943.

Cheyenne Leader, Apr. 13, 1921.

Child Welfare Magazine, Aug., 1921.

Christian Herald, Nov. 15, 1919, "Why Kindergartens?" by P. P. Claxton.

Christian Science Monitor, July 9, 1919; Sept. 10, 1920; and Apr. 29, 1921.

Cincinnati *Enquirer*, Apr. 22, 1921.

Clarksville (Tennessee) *Leaf-Chronicle*, May 16, 1941; Oct. 29, 1943; May 30, 1945; May 11 and June 29, 1946.

Clearing House, Oct., 1932, "The Paris Pact in American High Schools" by P. P. Claxton. A journal published at New York University.

Cleveland (Ohio) *Plain-Dealer*, May 1, 1921.

Colorado Springs *Gazette*, Apr. 17, 1921.

Columbus (Ohio) *Citizen*, Apr. 19, 1921.

Council Bluffs (Iowa) *Nonpareil*, Feb. 9, 1917.

Dayton (Ohio) *Journal*, Apr. 10, 1921.

Dayton (Ohio) *News*, Apr. 5, 1921.

Decatur (Illinois) *Review*, Apr. 10, 1921.

Denver *Post*, Dec. 8, 9, 1920.

Denver *Times*, Dec. 8, 1920.

Detroit *Free Press*, Apr. 17, 1921.

Duluth *Herald*, Apr. 7, 28, 1921.

Durham (North Carolina) *Sun*, Apr. 27, 1921.

Educational Review (April, 1911), XLI, "An American Teacher's Year in a Prussian Gymnasium" by W. S. Learned.

Elizabeth (New Jersey) *Journal*, Apr. 25, 1921.

Fargo (North Dakota) *Courier-News*, Apr. 26, 1921.

Galveston *News*, Apr. 4, 1921.

Grand Forks (North Dakota) *Daily Herald*, Nov. 5, 1915.

Grand Rapids *Press*, Oct. 30, 1915.

Greensboro (North Carolina) *Daily News*, May 30, 1913 and Feb. 10, 1924.

Hagerstown (Maryland) *Globe*, Apr. 8, 1921.

Hagerstown *Mail*, Apr. 15, 1921.

Harrisburg *Telegraph*, Apr. 8, 1921.

Hartford *Courant*, Apr. 18, 1920.

Hartford *Times*, Apr. 12, 1921.

Haverhill (Massachusetts) *Gazette*, Mar. 18 and Apr. 8, 1921.

Hoboken *Observer*, Mar. 18, 1921.

Huntington (West Virginia) *Advertiser*, Apr. 10, 1921.

Huntsville (Alabama) *Daily Times*, Dec. 7, 1921.

Independent (May 13, 1902), LIV, "Southern Educational Conferences" by Walter Hines Page.

Jamestown (New York) *Post*, July 22, 1915.

Johnstown (Pennsylvania) *Daily Democrat*, Sept. 2, 1916.

Johnstown *Tribune*, Apr. 11, 1921.

Kansas Industrialist, June 15, 1916. University of Kansas newspaper.

Knoxville (Tennessee) *Journal and Tribune,* Oct. 21, 1906; Oct. 10, 1910; Oct. 14, 1920; Nov. 4, 1943.

Knoxville *Sentinel,* Feb. 12, 1919; Mar. 18, June 7, 21, 22, 1921.

Ladies Home Journal, May 1920. Portrait of Claxton, p. 97.

Las Vegas (New Mexico) *Daily Optic,* June 8, 1916.

Lexington (Kentucky) *Herald,* Mar. 22 and Apr. 24, 1921.

Los Angeles *Herald,* Apr. 18, 1921.

Louisville *Courier-Journal,* Apr. 4, 17, 19, 20, 1921.

Lowell (Massachusetts) *Courier-Citizen,* Apr. 7, 1921.

Macmillan's Magazine, July, 1878.

Manchester (New Hampshire) *Union,* Mar. 21, 1921.

Maryland Historical Magazine, Mar., 1947, "Herbert B. Adams and Southern Historical Scholarship at Johns Hopkins University" by W. H. Stephenson.

Memphis *Commercial Appeal,* Sept. 14 and 25, 1910; Apr. 16, 1921; and June 4, 1946.

Milwaukee *Journal,* Nov. 4, 1920 and Apr. 27, 30, 1921.

Minnesota Daily, May 24, 1921. University of Minnesota paper.

Mobile *Register,* Nov. 20, 1921.

Montgomery (Alabama) *Advertiser,* Apr. 4, 10, 1921 and Oct. 3, 1921.

Morristown *Jerseyman,* Apr. 3, 1921.

Mt. Pleasant (Tenn.) *Record,* Mar. 18, 1932, "Improvement of Our Rural Schools" by P. P. Claxton.

Music Trades, June 18, 1921, "Why We Should Have a National Conservatory of Music" by Claxton. Portrait of Claxton.

Musical America, June 9, 1917, "Music in Training Camps" by Claxton. Issues of Feb. 23, 1918 and Nov. 15, 1919 contain portraits of Claxton.

Nashville *American,* Aug. 22, 1906.

Nashville *Banner,* Oct. 8, 1906; Sept. 29, 1910; Nov. 28, 1914; June 13, 1916; Apr. 10, 1921; Apr. 3, 1926; Nov. 17, 1934; and Mar. 11, 1940.

Nashville *Tennessean,* July 21, 1914; Apr. 30, 1921; Apr. 3, 1926; Jan. 11, 1928; Nov. 5, 1943; Oct. 6, 1944; May 11, 1946; Sept. 14, 1947; and Feb. 22, 1948.

National Education Association Journal, Oct., 1913 and June, 1921.

National Municipal Review, Sept., 1917, "The Effect of the War on Schools" by P. P. Claxton.

National School Service, Sept. 1, 1918–Mar. 15, 1919. Bimonthly published by Committee on Public Information.

New Age Magazine, Sept., 1915, "The National Bureau of Education" by Henry Ridgeway. A Masonic journal.

New Bedford (Massachusetts) *Mercury,* Apr. 7, 1921.

New Brunswick (New Jersey) *Home News*, Mar. 26, 1921.

New Haven *Journal-Courier*, Mar. 9 and Apr. 6, 1921.

New Haven *Union*, Apr. 7, 27, 30, 1921.

New Orleans *Times-Picayune*, Apr. 4, 30, 1921.

New York *Call*, Apr. 17, 1921.

New York *Commercial*, May 3, 1921.

New York *Evening Post*, Sept. 23, 1911; May 15, July 6, 7, 8, 9, 1920; Jan. 29, Apr. 2, 9, 12, 22, 30, May 2, 5, June 16, 1921.

New York *Evening World*, May 4, 1921.

New York *Globe*, Apr. 22, 29 and May 2, 1921.

New York *Mail*, Mar. 17, 1920 and Apr. 19, 1921.

New York *News*, Apr. 21, 1921.

New York *Sun*, July 2, 1916.

New York *Times*, Mar. 22, 1915; Mar. 3, 1918; Apr. 10, 17, 26 and June 15, 1921.

Newport News *Press*, Mar. 27, 1921.

North Carolina Journal of Education, Aug., 1897–Mar., 1901, edited by Claxton.

Nowata (Oklahoma) *Daily Star*, Dec. 7, 1923.

Oswego (New York) *Times*, Mar. 14, 1921.

Outlook, Sept. 24, 1919, "The Economics of the Kindergarten" by P. P. Claxton.

Peabody Alumni News, April, 1917. Memorial Number.

Peabody Journal of Education, May, 1925, "George Peabody, His Life and Work in America," address by Claxton at 50th Anniversary of the Founding of George Peabody College, Feb. 18–20, 1925.

Peabody Record, July 24, 1914.

Peabody Reflector, Dec., 1946, letter by J. O. Martin.

Pendleton *East Oregonian*, Feb. 21, 1921.

Pensacola *Journal*, Apr. 13, 1921.

Peoria *Transcript*, Sept. 20, 1918.

Philadelphia *Public Ledger*, Apr. 30, 1921.

Philadelphia *Record*, Apr. 13, 1921.

Philo Star, Jan.-June, 1882, edited by P. P. Claxton and published by the Philomathesian Society of the University of Tennessee, Knoxville.

Phoenix *Republican*, Apr. 30, 1921.

Pittsburg (Kansas) *Daily Headlight*, May 26, 1927.

Pittsburgh *Leader*, Mar. 18, 1921.

Pittsburgh *Post*, Apr. 5, 1921.

Pittsfield (Massachusetts) *Berkshire Eagle*, Apr. 9, 1921.

Plattsburg *Republican*, Apr. 6, 1921.

Portland (Maine) *Herald*, Mar. 24, 1921.

Portland (Oregon) *Journal*, Mar. 31, 1921.

Portland (Oregon) *Telegram*, Dec. 4, 1920, and Apr. 14, 1921.

Poughkeepsie *Star*, Feb. 25, 1921.

Presbyterian Advance, Aug. 6, 1914, "Keep the School Open All the Year" by P. P. Claxton, and Feb. 2, 1933, "The Forgotten Man of Saloon Days" by Claxton.

Progressive Farmer, June 24, 1916, "How We May Get Efficient Rural Schools" by Claxton.

Providence (Rhode Island) *Tribune*, Feb. 25, Apr. 17, 27, and May 5, 1921.

Pueblo *Chieftain*, Mar. 27, 1921.

Raleigh *News and Observer*, Nov. 21, 1920 and Apr. 29, 1921.

Raleigh *Times*, July 22, 23, 1915.

Reading *Eagle*, Apr. 17, 1921.

Record of the Hampden-Sydney Alumni Association, July, 1945, "Charles William Dabney" by Dr. J. D. Eggleston.

Religious Education, Aug., 1917, "Organ Recitals for Children" by P. P. Claxton.

Revista de Instruccion Publica (Cuba), Jan., 1926, editorial on Claxton, "The Ideals of Rural Education" by Dr. Ramiro Guerra.

Roanoke *Times*, Sept. 5, 1920 and Mar. 12, 27 and Apr. 15, 1921.

Rochester (New York) *Post Express*, Apr. 7, 1921.

Rochester (New York) *Times-Union*, Apr. 12, 1921.

Rocky Mountain News, Dec. 9, 1920.

Salisbury (North Carolina) *Post*, July 21, 1915.

Salt Lake *Tribune*, July 7, 1920.

San Diego *Union*, July 13, 1915.

San Francisco *Chronicle*, Apr. 16, 1916.

San Francisco *Examiner*, May 3, 1921.

San Jose (California) *Mercury-Herald*, Apr. 4, 1921.

San Pedro *News*, Mar. 28, 1921.

Saturday Evening Post, May 22, 1920, p. 17, photograph of Claxton at Commissioner's desk.

Savannah *News*, Apr. 7, 1921.

School and Society, Jan 9, 1915, "The American Rural School" by Claxton, address to American Association for Advancement of Science at Philadelphia, Dec. 31, 1914.

School Life, April, 1931. Monthly magazine.

School Life, 1918–1920. Bimonthly official organ of the U. S. Bureau of Education.

School Music, Jan.-Feb., 1913, "The Place of Music in Education" by Claxton, address to Illinois State Teachers Association, Dec. 28, 1912.

Scranton Republican, Apr. 11, 1921.

Seattle Times, Mar. 15, 1921.

Shelbyville (Tennessee) *Gazette*, Sept. 29 and Oct. 6, 1938, "Bedford County as I Remember It . . ." by P. P. Claxton; Nov. 23, 1939, "The Summer School of the South" by Claxton; Jan. 19, 1947, "The Ignorance Tax" by Claxton; and Oct. 16, 1947.

Side-Lines, Nov. 18, 1943. Middle Tennessee State College paper.

Sierra Educational News (San Francisco), June, 1919, "The County Library" by Claxton.

Sioux City Journal, Apr. 4, 1914 and Apr. 5, 1921.

Sioux Falls (South Dakota) *Argus-Leader*, Apr. 4, 5, 11, 1921.

Social Service Review, Feb., 1914, "Immigration after the War" by Claxton.

Southern Educational Review (Chattanooga), June, 1905, article by Claxton.

Southern Review (Asheville), June, 1920, "The National Crisis in Education: An Interview with Dr. P. P. Claxton" by David Marboy and "Our U. S. Commissioner of Education" with photograph of Claxton.

Springfield (Illinois) *Journal*, Apr. 10, 1921.

Springfield (Illinois) *Register*, Apr. 10, 1921.

Springfield (Massachusetts) *Daily Republican*, July 15, 1913; May 12, 1920; and Apr. 4, 1921.

Springfield (Massachusetts) *Union*, Apr. 10, 15, 20, 22, 1921.

St. Louis *Globe-Democrat*, Apr. 9, 1921.

St. Louis *Post-Dispatch*, Apr. 9, 10, 1921.

St. Louis *Star*, Apr. 23, 1921.

St. Paul *Daily News*, Nov. 30, 1920.

St. Paul *Dispatch*, Nov. 30, 1920.

St. Paul *Pioneer Press*, July 6, 1914.

Summer School Spectator (Knoxville), 1909, 1910.

Syracuse Post-Standard, Apr. 12, 1921.

Teacher-Education Journal, Dec., 1941, "Summer School of the South" by Claxton.

Tennessee Conservationist, May-June, 1945, "Austin Peay College Conservation Classes Improve Whole District" by F. E. Waukan.

Tennessee Teacher, Apr., 1944, "What the Schools Have Done to Win the War and the Peace" by Claxton.

Terre Haute *Tribune*, Apr. 17, 1921.

Toronto (Canada) *Globe*, Aug. 12, 1927.

Troy (New York) *Record*, Apr. 15, 1921.

Tulsa Spirit, Sept., 1926 and Jan., 1927.

Tulsa *Tribune*, Apr. 7, 1921; July 11, 1923; May 4, 1927; Feb. 26, Mar. 10, 12, May 9, 15, 1928; and May 29, 1929.

Tulsa *World*, July, 1923; Feb. 17, 1926; May 1, 1927; and Apr. 11, 1928.

Tuscaloosa *News and Times-Gazette*, July 22, 1923.

Tuscaloosa *Times-Gazette*, Sept. 18, 1913.

University of Alabama Alumni News, Nov.-Dec., 1921 and Jan.-Feb., 1922.

U. T. Farmer, May, 1919, "Why the Farmer Needs an Education" by Claxton. Publication of Agricultural Club of University of Tennessee, Knoxville.

Utica *Observer*, Apr. 11, 1921.

Venice (California) *Vanguard*, Apr. 20, 1921.

Washington *Post*, Mar. 6, 9, Apr. 10, 19, 27, June 6, 1921, and Nov. 7, 1943.

Washington *Star*, Feb. 15 and Mar. 29, 1914; May 13, 1915; and Apr. 2, 10, 17, 24, 1921.

Washington *Times*, Nov. 9, 1914; Mar. 31, Apr. 21, May 1, 1921; and May 22, 1921, "D. C. Spends More for Face Powder Than on Schools, Says Claxton."

Wheeling *Intelligencer*, July 13, 1920.

Wilmington (Delaware) *Evening Journal*, Feb. 11 and Apr. 11, 1921.

Wilmington (Delaware) *News*, Mar. 29 and Apr. 15, 1921.

Winston-Salem *Journal*, June, 1931, commencement address by Claxton.

Worcester *Gazette*, Apr. 4, 1921.

Worcester *Telegram*, July 25, 1915 and Apr. 6, 1921.

World's Work, Sept., 1912. Photograph of Claxton.

Youngstown (Ohio) *Telegram*, Apr. 9, 1921.

Youngstown (Ohio) *Vindicator*, Feb. 29, 1920.

III. Bulletins, Proceedings, Pamphlets

America's Creed. Music by Edgar Stillman Kelley. Dedicated to Dr. P. P. Claxton. Boston, 1919.

Americanization Bulletin. Bureau of Education. Vol. I, No. 1 (Sept. 15, 1918)—No. 10 (June 1, 1919).

Asheville City Schools: Third Annual Report, 1889–1890.

Austin Peay State College. Bulletin. Nov., 1944 (XIV, No. 2), "What Can We Afford to Pay for Education" by Claxton.

Claxton, Philander Priestley and John Dewey. *Federal Aid to Elementary Education. National Child Labor Committee Pamphlet 280*. New

York, 1917. Reprinted from *Child Labor Bulletin*, VI, No. 1, May, 1917.

Conference for Education in the South. Proceedings. Raleigh, North Carolina, 1898–1914. The first three conferences were held at Capon Springs, West Virginia.

Fifth Conference, Athens, Georgia, Apr. 24–26, 1902, "Report on Work of Bureau of Investigation and Information" by Claxton.

Sixth Conference, Richmond, Virginia, Apr. 22–24, 1903, "A Model School" by Claxton.

Tenth Conference, Pinehurst, N. C., Apr. 9–11, 1907, "Report on Campaign in Tennessee" by Claxton.

Eleventh Conference, Memphis, Tenn., Apr. 22–24, 1908, "Methods of an Educational Campaign" by Claxton.

Twelfth Conference, Atlanta, Georgia, Apr. 14–16, 1909, "A School for Grown-ups" by Claxton.

Sixteenth Conference, Richmond, Virginia, Apr. 15–18, 1913, "The Country Church and Good Literature" by Claxton."

Seventeenth Conference, Louisville, Kentucky, Apr. 7–10, 1914, "The Improvement of the Rural School through Demonstration Schools" by Claxton, and address by Claxton at Robert C. Ogden Memorial Meeting.

Education in the South. Bureau of Education. Bulletin No. 30, Whole Number 540. Washington, 1913. Abstracts of papers read at the Sixteenth Conference.

The Work of the Conference for Education in the South: A Record of Progress through Sixteen Years. Washington, D. C., 1915.

Congressional Record, Apr. 13, 1918 (No. 102).

Cotton Manufacturers Association of North Carolina. Proceedings of 12th Summer Session, July 5, 6, 1918. Charlotte, 1918. Address by Claxton.

Dickerman, G. S. *Conference for Education in the South and the Southern Education Board.* U. S. Bureau of Education Report I, 1907.

East Tennessee Teachers College. Bulletin, XXVI, No. 2, 1936, "Founding and Early Days of the State Normal School," address by Claxton at Silver Anniversary, Oct. 9, 10, 1936.

General Education Board: An Account of Its Activities, 1902–1914. New York, 1915.

Johns Hopkins University Circulars. Baltimore, 1884–1885.

Murphy, E. G. *The Task of the South: An Address on the Subject of Public Education in the Southern States.* n.p., n.d.

Murphy, E. G. *Within the Year: Southern Education,* n.p., 1902.

National Education Association. *Proceedings.* Addresses by Claxton:

Asbury Park, New Jersey, July 10–13, 1894, discussion of paper by James L. Hughes on "Relation of the Kindergarten to Public School System."

Charleston, South Carolina, July 7–13, 1900, "Need of Kindergartens in the South."

Salt Lake City, July 5–11, 1913, "Why Should the Kindergarten Be Incorporated as an Integral Part of the Public School System?"

St. Paul, July 4–11, 1914, "The Readjustment of the Kindergarten and Primary Grades to Conform to the Same General Principles," and a discussion of teaching of science.

Oakland, California, 1915, "The Organization of High Schools into Junior and Senior Sections."
Portland, Oregon, July 7–14, 1917, discussion of "Standards in Teacher Training."

Milwaukee, July 2, 1919, "Education for the Establishment of Democracy in the World." Published as a pamphlet. Government Printing Office, 1919.

Salt Lake City, July 4–10, 1920, "Adequate Pay for Teachers" by Claxton.

Seattle, Washington, July 3–8, 1927, "A New Basis for Delegate Representation" by Claxton.

North Carolina College for Women. *Annual Catalogues, 1892–1902.* Greensboro, North Carolina.

Pan-American Scientific Congress. 2d, Washington, D. C., Dec. 27, 1915–Jan. 8, 1916. *Its Proceedings* . . . Washington, 1917.

Peabody College for Teachers. *Bulletin. The Semicentennial of George Peabody College for Teachers, 1875–1925.* November, 1925.

Southern Education Board:

A *Brief Statement concerning the Origin and Organization of the Southern Education Board.* Anon., n.p., n.d. Pamphlet, 4 pp.

Circulars and Bulletins, Nos. 1–3, May to Dec., 1902. Knoxville, Tenn. No. 3, *Educational Conditions in Tennessee.*

Southern Education Notes, Mar., 1902 to Feb., 1903. Knoxville, Tenn. Biweekly.

Southern Education, Mar. 12, 1903 to Dec. 21, 1903. Knoxville, Tenn.

Southern Education Board . . . Activities and Results, 1904 to 1910. Washington, 1911.

Southern Educational Association: Proceedings. Addresses by Claxton: Richmond, Virginia, Dec. 27, 28, 1900, "Education for Production, with Some Considerations of the Question of Scientific and Technical Education for the South" and "The Function of the Normal School." Columbia, South Carolina, Dec. 26–29, 1901, "Arithmetic and Geometry in the Elementary Schools" and discussion of a paper on "The Pedagogical Treatment of the Bible."

Atlanta, Georgia, Dec. 30, 1903–Jan. 1, 1904, "Local Taxation."

Lexington, Kentucky, Dec. 26–28, 1907, "The Rural High School" and discussion of C. B. Gibson's paper on "Industrial Education."

Atlanta, Georgia, Dec. 29–31, 1908, "A Condition, A Task," his presidential address.

Summer School of the South. University of Tennessee Record. Knoxville, Tenn., 1903–1911.

Announcement and Courses of Study: Summer School of the South. Bulletin. University of Tennessee. 1903–1911.

Tennessee School Report. State of Tennessee, Department of Public Instruction. 1906.

Tennessee. Acts of Tennessee. 1873. Chapter 25.

Message of Governor James B. Frazier to the 53d General Assembly, Jan. 23, 1903.

Public School Officers Association. Proceedings. 1906, 1907.

Report to State Board of Education, Apr. 26, 1946.

[Tulsa, Oklahoma] *Brief Report of Progress of Tulsa Public Schools, District No. 22, for Five Years, 1923–1928.*

[Tulsa] *Report of the Public Schools of Tulsa, 1923–1924.* The Board of Education.

U. S. Bureau of Education.

Report of Commissioner of Education, 1888–1889. Washington, 1891.

Report of Commissioner of Education, 1889–1890. Washington, 1893.

Report of Commissioner of Education, 1894–1895. Washington, 1896.

Report of the Commissioner of Education for the Year Ended June 30, 1911. Subsequent reports to 1921.

Statement of the Commissioner of Education to the Secretary of the

Interior for the Fiscal Year Ended June 30, 1911. Subsequent state-ments to 1920.

U. S. Congress House Committee on Education. The Bureau of Edu-cation. Hearings before the Committee on Education, House of Representatives concerning the Bureau of Education, June 11, 1912. Washington, 1912. Claxton's statement.

U. S. Congress House Committee on Education. Illiteracy among the Adult Population. Hearing before the Committee on Education, House of Representatives, 63d Cong. 2nd Sess. on H.R. 2494, a bill to investigate illiteracy among the adult population of the United States and on H.J. Res. 84 limiting the editions of the publications of the Bureau of Education, Jan. 26, 1914. Washington, 1914. Statement by Claxton.

City School Circular, 1917, No. 4. Foreign Languages in the Ele-mentary Grades.

Suggestions for the Conduct of Educational Institutions during the Continuance of the War. May 22, 1917.

Americanization Bulletin, Nov. 1, 1918.

Home Gardening for Town Children. Washington, 1919. School Garden Army Leaflet No. 1, Nov., 1919.

Circular, "Education for the Establishment of Democracy in the World." Washington, 1919. Address by Claxton at National Educa-tion Association meeting at Milwaukee, July 2, 1919.

Fundamental Educational Needs of Alabama as Indicated by Its Char-acter and Resources. Washington, 1919. Reprint of chapter II of An Educational Study of Alabama, Bulletin No. 41, 1919.

Preliminary Survey of the Schools of the District of Columbia, Made under the Direction of the U. S. Commissioner of Education. Bulletin No. 36. Washington, 1920.

William Terry Harris, the Commemoration of the 100th Anniversary of His Birth. Bulletin No. 17. Washington, 1936.
University of Tennessee.
Catalogues, 1880–1881, 1881–1882, and 1902–1911.

Laws and Regulations . . . , Enacted by the Board of Trustees, Aug. 21, 1879. Knoxville, 1879.

Record. Dedication of New Buildings. Conference on Citizenship. Alumni Home Coming. Commencement. Dec., 1921.

Record. *Commencement Number*, Sept. 1, 1922.

Record. *Commencement Number. Colleges at Knoxville and Memphis.* Sept. 1, 1922.

Sesquicentennial. A Record of 150 Years of Achievement of Public Education on the Higher Level . . . University of Tennessee Press, 1945.

Watkins, Arthur Charles. *The Paris Pact: A Textbook for Teachers and Students in the High School.* Washington, 1931.

Watkins, A. C. *The Paris Pact: A Textbook for Schools and Colleges.* New York and Chicago, 1932.

Watkins, A. C. *The Story of the Paris Pact for Students of the Higher Citizenship.* Washington, 1934.

Watkins, A. C. *America Stands for Pacific Means.* Washington, 1937.

Watkins, A. C. *Prospectus for the Ninth Year* (1937–1938) *for the Study of the Paris Pact and International Relations in American High Schools.* Washington, 1938.

IV. Books

Alderman, Edwin A. and Armistead, C. Gordon. *Life of J. L. M. Curry.* New York, 1911.

Arnold, Matthew. *Higher Schools and Universities in Germany.* London, 1882.

Baker, Ray Stannard. *Woodrow Wilson: Life and Letters: Youth 1850–1890.* New York, 1927.

Barnard, Henry. *German Pedagogy: Education, the School, and the Teacher in German Literature.* Hartford, 1876.

Barnard, Henry. *German Educational Reformers.* Hartford, 1878.

Bolton, F. E. *The Secondary School System of Germany.* New York, 1900.

Bush, G., *Origins of the First German Universities.* Boston, 1884.

Cattell, J. McKeen, editor. *Leaders in Education.* New York, 1932.

Claxton, Philander Priestly. "The American College in the Life of the American People" in *The American College: a Series of Papers Setting Forth the Program, Achievements, Present Status, and Probable Future of the American College,* with introduction by W. H. Crawford, President of Allegheny College. New York, 1915.

Claxton, P. P. and James McGinniss. *Effective English.* Boston and New York, 1917.

Claxton and McGinniss. *Effective English Junior.* Boston and New York, c1925.

Claxton, P. P. *From the Land of Stories: a Supplementary Reader for*

Children of the Second Grade, Mostly from the German of Fraulein M. Meissner, translated, adapted, and arranged by Claxton. Atlanta and Richmond, c1911.

Claxton, P. P. and M. Winifred Haliburton. *Grimm's Fairy Stories, Supplementary to First Reader.* Richmond, 1900.

Claxton, P. P. "Home Gardening Directed by the School" in *Our Public Schools the Nation's Bulwark,* edited by John F. Murray. Berkeley, California, 1916.

Claxton, P. P. Introduction to *The Book of Literature: a Comprehensive Anthology of the Best Literature, Ancient, Mediaeval, and Modern . . .* edited by Richard Garnett and others. New York, The Grolier Society, c1923.

Claxton, P. P. Introduction to *The Colleges in War Time and After . . .* by Parke Rexford Kolbe. New York, 1919.

Claxton, P. P. Introduction to *The Educators* by Eliza Taylor Cherdron.

Claxton, P. P. Introduction to *Humane Education: A Handbook on Kindness to Animals. Their Habits and Usefulness,* edited by Harriet C. Reynolds. Boston, 1919.

Claxton, P. P. Intoduction to *The Little Democracy, a Textbook on Community Organization* by Mrs. Ida Clyde (Gallagher) Clarke. New York, 1918.

Claxton, P. P. Introduction to *Men of the Mountains* by A. W. Spaulding. Nashville, c1915.

Claxton, P. P. Introduction to *Sketches of Froebel's Life and Times.* Springfield (Massachusetts), 1914.

Claxton, P. P. Introduction to *Morrison's System of Natural History Stories* by William James Morrison. Nashville, c1911.

Claxton, P. P. "Supplement: North Carolina" to Alexis Everett Frye's *Complete Geography.* Boston and London, 1896.

Claxton, P. P., member of Editorial Board. *Tennessee's Public Schools.* Tennessee Congress of Parents and Teachers, Inc. Arlington, Tennessee, 1938.

Cole, Percival Richard. *Herbart and Froebel.* Columbia University Doctoral Dissertation, 1895.

Conrad, J. *German Universities of the Last Fifty Years,* translated by J. Hutchison. Glasgow, 1885.

Coon, Charles L. *Facts about Southern Educational Progress: A Study in Public School Maintenance.* Bureau of Investigation and Information of Southern Education Board and the North Carolina Department of Education. Durham, North Carolina, 1905.

Dabney, Charles William. *Universal Education in the South.* University of North Carolina Press, Chapel Hill, 1936. Two volumes.

Daniels, Josephus. *Editor in Politics.* University of North Carolina Press, Chapel Hill, 1941.

Daniels, Josephus. *Tar Heel Editor.* University of North Carolina Press, Chapel Hill, 1939.

Dean, Arthur D. *Our Schools in War Time and After.* New York, 1918. Pages 146–150, quotation from Claxton's circular letter on "Conduct of Educational Institutions during the Continuance of the War," May 22, 1917.

De Garmo, Charles. *Herbart and the Herbartians.* New York, 1895.

Eells, W. C. *Surveys of American Higher Education.* The Carnegie Foundation for the Advancement of Teaching, New York, 1937.

Everett, Carroll and Charles Francis Reed. *When They Were Boys.* Dansville, New York, 1922. Contains a biographical sketch of Claxton.

Finger, S. M. *Biennial Report of the Superintendent of Public Instruction of North Carolina, 1889–1890.* Raleigh, 1893. Institutes.

Fish, Carl Russell. *The Rise of the Common Man.* New York, 1927.

Franklin, Fabian. *The Life of Daniel Coit Gilman.* New York, 1910.

French, John C. *A History of the University Founded by Johns Hopkins.* Baltimore, 1946.

Graves, E. P. *History of Education in Modern Times.* New York, 1913.

Graves, E. P. *Great Educators of Three Centuries.* New York, 1912.

Hale, Will T. and Dixon L. Merritt. *A History of Tennessee and Tennesseans.* Chicago and New York, 1913. Vol. III.

Hall, G. Stanley. *Life and Confessions of a Psychologist.* New York, 1923.

Hall, G. Stanley. *Aspects of German Culture.* Boston, 1881.

Hart, J. M. *German Universities, a Narrative of Personal Experience.* New York, 1897.

Hendrick, Burton J. *Life and Letters of Walter Hines Page.* Garden City, New York, 1921.

Hendrick, B. J. *The Training of an American: the Earlier Life and Letters of W. H. Page.* New York, 1928.

Henry, Robert Selph. *The Story of the Confederacy.* Indianapolis, 1931.

Holt, Andrew David. *The Struggle for a State System of Public Schools in Tennessee, 1903–1936.* New York, 1938.

Hughes, R. E. *Schools at Home and Abroad.* New York, 1902.

Knight, Edgar W. *Education in the United States.* Boston, 1934.

Knight, Edgar W. *Public Education in the South.* Boston and New York, 1922.

Lewis, Charles Lee. *Matthew Fontaine Maury: Pathfinder of the Seas.* Annapolis, 1927.

Malone, Dumas. *Edwin A. Alderman.* New York, 1940.

Merriam, Lucius Salisbury. *Higher Education in Tennessee.* Bureau of Education, Washington, 1893. Chapter on "University of Tennessee" by T. C. Karns.

Monroe, Paul. *Cyclopedia of Education.* New York, 1911.

Noble, M. C. S. *A History of the Public Schools of North Carolina.* University of North Carolina Press, Chapel Hill, 1930.

Odum, H. W., ed. *Southern Pioneers in Social Interpretation,* "Charles Brantley Aycock" by Edwin A. Alderman. University of North Carolina Press, Chapel Hill, 1925.

Page, David Perkins. *Theory and Practice of Teaching or the Motives and Methods of Good School Keeping.* Albany, New York, 1847.

Petersilie, Dr. A. *The Public System of Instruction in the German Empire and Other Civilized States of Europe.* Leipzig, 1897. Two volumes.

Raymont, T. *A History of Education of Young Children.* New York, 1937.

Reisner, E. H. *Evolution of the Common School.* New York, 1930.

Roberts, R. D. *Education in the Nineteenth Century.* Cambridge University Press, 1900.

Rose, Wickliffe. *The Educational Movement in the South.* Washington, 1905. In *Report of the U. S. Commissioner of Education,* 1903, Vol. I.

Rose, Wickliffe. *Southern Education Board: Activities and Results, 1904–1910,* Publication No. 7, Southern Education Board. Washington, 1911.

Rose, Wickliffe. *School Funds in Ten Southern States.* Nashville, 1909.

Sanford, Edward T. *Blount College and the University of Tennessee: An Historical Address.* Knoxville, 1894.

Satterfield, Frances Gibson. *Charles Duncan McIver.* Atlanta, 1942.

Shepherd, Henry E. and other editors. *History of Baltimore, Maryland.* Baltimore, 1898.

Smith, C. Alphonso. *O'Henry.* New York, 1924.

Smith, W. C., editor. *Charles Duncan McIver: Memorial Volume.* Greensboro, 1907.

Snyder, Henry N. *An Educational Odyssey.* Nashville, 1947.

Thorndike, Edward L. *Principles of Teaching: Based on Psychology.* New York, 1906.

White, Moses. *Early History of the University of Tennessee.* Address before the Alumni Association, June 17, 1879.

White, Robert H. *Development of the Tennessee State Educational Organization, 1796–1929.* Nashville, 1929.

Index

burgh and in Toronto, 261, 262, 266, 267.

Travels in Denmark, 1930, 276–279.

Becomes President of Austin Peay Normal School (later Austin Peay State College), Nov., 1930, 279–303.

Tennessee Public School Officers Association gives banquet in his honor, Jan. 13, 1938, 292, 293.

His portrait unveiled in Office of Education, Washington, 263.

Another portrait of him unveiled in Tennessee State Library, 297, 298.

His retirement, July 1, 1946, 302.

President Emeritus of Austin Peay State College, 304–313.

Banquet in his honor on retirement, 305, 306.

Speeches, 146–148, 168, 173, 174, 177–179, 181, 182–184, 188, 189, 200, 201, 209, 210, 221, 222, 224–226, 245, 256, 258, 259, 263, 265–267, 270, 271, 283, 290, 291, 293, 296, 300, 302, 306.

Books and published articles, 74, 87, 174, 184, 202, 203, 210, 211, 228, 247, 285, 299, 313.

Honorary degrees, 144, 184, 238.

Appearance and character, 21, 24, 25, 36, 38, 39, 45, 66, 74–78, 138–140, 160, 199, 222, 273, 274, 282, 292, 293, 297, 298, 306–311.

Claxton, Mrs. Philander Priestley (Varina Staunton Moore), 40, 49, 50, 55, 59, 61, 71.

Claxton, Mrs. Philander Priestley (Anne Elizabeth Porter), 77, 79, 108, 112, 238.

Claxton, Mrs. Philander Priestley (Mary Hannah Johnson), 122, 175, 236, 237, 239, 248, 249, 263, 270, 273, 294, 305, 306, 310.

Claxton, Philander Priestley, Jr., 239, 306.

Claxton, Mrs. Philander Priestley, Jr. (Mary Ann Watkins), 306.

Claxton, Robert Edward, 238.

Clay, Henry, 121.

Columbia, South Carolina, 84, 85, 121.

Columbia University, 103, 142, 146, 165, 227.

Comenius, Johann Amos, 73, 107.

Comfort, Mary Read, 142.

Committee on Public Information, 213, 219.

Compayré, G., 72.

Conference for Education in the South, 113, 116, 118–125, 136, 146.

Conference of Southern Mountain Workers, 189.

Conference on Rural Education, Washington, 300.

Conly, Mrs. Sarah Ward, 263.

Cooke, George, 15.

Coon, Charles L., 108, 118.

Cooper Union, 147, 174.

Cooper, Prentice, 298, 299.

Cooper, William J., 282.

Co-operative Education Association, 118, 161.

Copenhagen, Denmark, 95.

Corcoran Art Gallery, 210.

Corson, Hiram, 46.

Cosmos Club, 205, 238.

Cotton Manufacturers Association, 210.

Crabtree, John G., 120, 221.

Crawford, Samuel B., 20, 21.

Creel, George, 206, 208.

Crockett, David, 16.

Cummings, Robert J., 20.

Curry, J. L. M., 40, 43, 103, 108, 109, 110, 113, 114, 118, 246, 259.

Dabney, Charles W., 108, 110, 112–114, 116, 118, 123, 126, 127, 129, 131, 135, 136, 138, 141, 143, 150, 151, 160, 168–171, 231, 277, 298, 310.

Dabney, Richard H., 118.

Dallas, Texas, 257, 270.

Damrosch, Walter J., 213.

Daniels, Charles, 62.

Daniels, Frank, 36.

Daniels, Josephus, 35, 61, 62, 78, 80, 81, 84, 87, 118, 120, 237, 297, 309.

Davidson College, 49.

Davis, N. K., 73.

De Garmo, Charles, 73, 89.

De Guimps, R., 73.

Deaderick, Thomas O., 20.

Denmark, 94, 95, 107, 123.

Denny, George H., 240, 243, 246, 247, 250, 251, 292.

Dewey, John, 136.

Dickens, Charles, 109.

Dickerman, George S., 113, 114.

Dinwiddie, James, 20.

Divine Comedy, 184.

Hampden-Sidney College, 310.
Hanson-Bellows Company, 201.
Hardee, Amelie, 38.
Harding, Warren G., 227, 229, 231.
Harned, P. L., 157, 159, 163–165, 276, 280, 283.
Harris, William T., 108–110, 127, 133.
Harvard University, 215, 289.
Hebrew University, Mount Scopus, Jerusalem, 259.
Hegel, Georg Wilhelm, 58, 89.
Hempl, George, 43.
Henderson, Archibald, 136.
Henderson, V. M., 206.
Henderson, W. A., 29.
Hendley, John R., 238.
Herbart, Johann Friedrich, 89, 103, 107, 207.
Hickory, North Carolina, 116.
Hobson, Richmond Pearson, 120, 125.
Holt, Andrew David, 157, 283.
Holt, Hamilton, 233.
Hooper, Ben, 166.
Horne, H. H., 174.
Horton, Henry, 159.
Hoskins, James D., 168, 292, 298, 306.
Houston, David F., 118, 123.
Howell, Logan D., 70, 98, 108.
Huff, Annie Laurie, 306.
Hughes, James L., 86, 128.
Hume, Thomas, 108.
Humes, Thomas William, 19, 22, 25, 28, 29.
Hunter, A. B., 113.
Hurley, Patrick J., 259.
Hutchins, William J., 228.

Iliad, 184, 244.
Illinois State Teachers Association, 177.
Indianapolis, Indiana, 148.
Inland Empire Teachers Association, 200.
International Education Conference, 178.
International Educational Congress, 227.
Interstate League for the Betterment of Public Schools, 137.
Iowa State Teachers Association, 169, 181, 271.

Jackson, Andrew, 297.
Jacksonville, Florida, 123.
Jameson, J. Franklin, 43.
Jarvis, Thomas J., 116.
Jefferson, Thomas, 107, 115, 118, 130, 296.
Jena, Germany, 89, 90, 92, 94.
Jenkins, Billy, 15.

Job, 300.
Johns Hopkins University, 40–47, 51, 59, 60.
Johnson, Andrew, 3, 297.
Johnson, Ben H., 250, 272.
Johnson, B. F., 98, 109.
Johnson, D. B., 34.
Johnson, George S., 175.
Johnson, Mrs. George S. (Hannah Iredell Payne), 175.
Johnson, Julia (Mrs. J. D. Eggleston), 66.
Johnson, Lilian Wycoff, 141, 142.
Johnson, Mary Hannah (Mrs. P. P. Claxton), 122, 175, 236, 237, 239, 248, 249, 263, 270, 273, 294, 305, 306, 310.
Jones, Ann Elizabeth (Mrs. Joshua Calvin Claxton), 4, 5, 7, 10, 18, 71.
Jones, Bailey, 9.
Jones, Jenkin Lloyd, 148.
Jones, Robert L., 160–165, 225.
Jones, Wharton, 157.
Jordan, David Starr, 183, 228.
Journal of the National Education Association, 221, 231.
Joyner, J. Y., 70, 108, 116.
Joynes, Edward S., 20, 21, 108.

Kansas State Agricultural College, 200.
Keffer, Charles A., 141.
Kellogg, Spencer, 228.
Kellogg-Briand Pact, 284, 285.
Kent, Charles W., 113, 118, 136.
Kenyon Bill, 222.
Kilby, Thomas E., 244.
Kilgo, John C., 80.
Kindergartens, 67, 86, 103, 137, 177, 180, 182, 183, 232, 247.
Kinston, North Carolina, 36, 37, 39, 40, 41, 62.
Kirkland, James H., 118, 119.
Kirkpatrick, E. A., 73.
Knabe, Gustav Robert, 20.
Knapp, Seaman, 311.
Knoxville, Tennessee, 1, 19, 27, 28, 31, 114, 126, 128, 135, 137, 142–144, 148, 156, 165, 171, 189, 225, 238, 276.
Knoxville Herald, 271.
Knoxville Journal and Tribune, 156.
Knoxville Sentinel, 165, 193, 194, 197.

Lagerstedt, N. C., 94.
Lane, Franklin K., 198, 208, 215, 216, 233, 236.

University of London, 233.
University of Maryland, Medical School, 226.
University of Minnesota, 226, 228.
University of North Carolina, 32, 37, 49, 62, 63, 70, 72, 98, 101, 108, 127, 184, 238, 263.
University of Oklahoma, 251.
University of Oregon, 188.
University of Pennsylvania, 174.
University of Tennessee, 18–32, 37, 39, 47, 60, 108, 110, 111, 126, 137, 141–145, 150, 151, 158, 160, 168, 193, 239–241, 262, 266, 271, 276, 285–287, 290, 292, 298, 300, 306.
University of Texas, 108, 142.
University of Toronto, 266.
University of Tulsa, 251, 253.
University of Utah, 190.
University of Vermont, 143.
University of Virginia, 118, 143, 271.
University of Wisconsin, 234.

Van Dyke, Henry, 40, 270.
Vance, Zebulon B., 107.
Vanderbilt University, 24, 31.
Venice, Italy, 93.
Vocational Education Board, 217.

Wagnerian Opera, 51, 56.
Wake Forest College, 62, 108.
Walker, Claxton, 263.
Walker, John Curtis, 249.
Walker, Mrs. John Curtis (Helen Claxton), 238, 239, 249.
Walters Art Gallery, 45.
Ward, E. J., 234.
Wartburg Castle, 91.
Washington, Booker T., 114, 177, 209, 242.
Washington, D. C., 111, 170, 171, 174, 185, 188, 189, 199, 201, 210, 212, 215–217, 224, 228, 232, 236–238, 240, 243, 246, 283, 294, 300.
Washington, George, 107, 108.
Washington and Lee University, 49, 113, 127.
Washington University, 217.

Washington Woman's Club, 238.
Watauga Hotel, 48, 49.
Waterhouse, Violet, 136.
Watkins, Arthur Charles, 284, 285.
Watkins, Mary Ann (Mrs. P. P. Claxton, Jr.), 306.
Waukan, Fred E., 301.
W. C. T. U., 229.
Webster, Daniel, 16.
Webster's *American Spelling Book*, 8, 9.
Weimar, Germany, 90, 91.
Werrenrath, Reinald, 136.
West Point, 14, 21, 24.
West Tennessee Normal, 291, 302.
Western Reserve University, 238.
White, Emerson E., 127, 134.
Wichita Beacon, 255.
Williams, Albert, 148, 225.
Williams, Charl, 225, 300.
Williams, S. G., 73.
Wilson, North Carolina, 35, 40, 43, 61, 62, 78.
Wilson, James, 84.
Wilson, Margaret, 234, 237.
Wilson, Woodrow, 45, 173, 179, 203, 205, 206, 227, 231–237, 239.
Wilson, Mrs. Woodrow, 237.
Wilson Collegiate Institute, 62.
Winston, George T., 37, 108, 116.
Winston-Salem, North Carolina, 113, 124.
Winston-Salem Teachers College for Negroes, 309.
Wise, Stephen S., 214.
Witherspoon, Henry, 136.
Wood, Henry, 43.
Woodward, Felix G., 306.
Worcester (Mass.) *Gazette*, 195.
Work, Hubert, 263.
World Book Encyclopedia, 201.
World Federation of National Education Associations, 262, 266.

Yale University, 227, 228, 257.
Y. M. C. A., 229.
Young, Lafe, 204.

Zion's Hill Church, 15.